Fʀᴏᴍ the time of Bismarck's great rival Ludwig Windthorst to that of the first post–World War II Chancellor, Konrad Adenauer, the Catholic community in Germany took a distinctive historical path. Although it was by no means free of authoritarian components, it was at times the most democratic pathway taken by organized political Catholicism anywhere in Europe.

Challenging those who seek continuity in German history primarily in terms of its long march toward Nazism, this book crosses all the usual historical turning points from mid-nineteenth- to late-twentieth-century German history in search of the indigenous origins of postwar German democracy. Complementing recent studies of German Social Democracy, it links the postwar party system to the partisan traditions this new system transcended by documenting the attempts by reform-minded members of the old Catholic Center party to break out of the constraints of minority-group politics and form a broader democratic political party. The failure of those efforts before 1933 helped clear the way for Nazism, but their success after 1945 in founding the interdenominational Christian Democratic Union (CDU) helped tame political conservatism and allowed the emergence of the most stable democracy in contemporary Europe. Integrating those who needed to be integrated—the cultural and political conservatives—into a durable liberal order, this conservative yet democratic and interdenominational "catch-all" party broadened democratic sensibilities and softened the effect of religious tensions on the German polity and party system.

By crossing traditional chronological divides and exploring the links between earlier abortive Catholic initiatives and the range of

The Path to Christian Democracy

THE PATH TO CHRISTIAN DEMOCRACY

*German Catholics and the
Party System from
Windthorst to Adenauer*

Noel D. Cary

Harvard University Press
Cambridge, Massachusetts
London, England
1996

Library of Congress Cataloging-in-Publication Data

Cary, Noel D., 1950–
    The path to Christian democracy : German Catholics and the party
system from Windthorst to Adenauer / Noel D. Cary.
        p.   cm.
    Includes bibliographical references and index.
    ISBN 0–674–65783–7 (cloth : alk. paper)
    1. Christian democratic parties—Germany—History. 2. Christian
democracy—Germany—History. 3. Christianity and politics—Catholic
Church—History. 4. Catholics—Germany—History. I. Title.
JN3933.C37 1996
95–40145

In memory of Demetri E. Cary

Contents

Preface

The ghost of the first German republic has persistently haunted the second; it has been anything but exorcised by reunification. But the success of the Bonn Republic in achieving democratization, western integration, and then, in 1990, reunification—in short, virtually everything Konrad Adenauer set out to do forty years earlier—makes timelier than ever the need to explore the indigenous sources of political innovation that led to Bonn's not being Weimar.

Perhaps the most important indigenous innovation was the Christian Democratic Union (CDU). Although Green and neonationalist fringe groups continue to excite more fascination, it is the remarkably centripetal nature of the party system that has consistently distinguished postwar German democracy from the earlier period; and the CDU, the party of Adenauer (and Helmut Kohl), was the essentially new and even paradigmatic feature in the West German party system. The CDU, not the more thoroughly studied Social Democratic Party (SPD), integrated those who needed to be integrated—the cultural and political conservatives—into a durable liberal order. The policies and electoral successes of this interdenominational and socially diverse catch-all party reflected and promoted a transformation in the impact of religious and ideological tension on the western German polity and party system. With the fall of the Berlin Wall, the western CDU became also the paradigm for many easterners, though in a very different context and with consequences that are yet to be seen.

This book investigates the long-term process of democratization in Germany (before its recent reunification) by examining the issue of partisan alignment as played out within the country's largest but politically least researched minority group: the (mostly western) Catholic community. I begin in 1870, with the birth of a specifically Catholic-oriented party, the Center party of Ludwig Windthorst, amidst the religious persecution that accompanied Bismarckian unification. Catholic introspection about the image and function of this party over the next six decades formed the backdrop for recurrent Catholic initiatives to overcome the fragmentation of the party system. Blocked not only by Protestant hostility but also by Catholic trepidations, these initiatives proved premature. But the polemics they engendered provide a lens for viewing the interaction of psychological, cultural, and partisan factors in Germany's tumultuous political development.

The Catholic discussion before World War I about realigning the party system was occasioned by concerns about the continued viability of the solidly Catholic Center party. In an age of industrialization, the Center, as the defender of a religious minority, was unique among German political parties in its social diversity. Able as a result to acquire a pivotal parliamentary role, the onetime pariah of German politics reaped not acceptance and social integration, but resentment and the risk of disunity. As the Center struggled after World War I to maintain its middle role in a polarized parliamentary system, the political basis of what contemporaries called the Catholic "return from exile" remained in question. Each successive answer—partnership with Protestants or with Social Democracy, the Center's submergence into radical nationalism in 1933, and the emergence after 1945 of an interdenominational, moderately conservative, Europeanist CDU— was intensely challenged by advocates of competing alternatives.

In crossing traditional chronological divides and exploring the links between the earlier Catholic discussions and the various competing postwar visions of the new party system, I shift Catholic Germany from the periphery to the heart of the continuity issue in modern German history. This placement is especially valuable as an aid to understanding the origins of the successful Bonn democracy, whose first chancellor, the Christian Democrat and ex-Centrist Adenauer, served longer than the entire Weimar or Nazi era. It is also helpful, in a more complex way, for understanding of the origins of Nazism—a movement whose growth was fueled primarily by Protestants, but whose claim to legal and populist dictatorship, for reasons partly traceable to the Catholic experience of exclusion under Bismarck, was established with the cowed connivance of Catholics.

The contrast between the failure of the mostly Catholic-sponsored interdenominational democratic initiatives before 1933 and the success after 1945 of the CDU lies at the crossroads of two historical pathways: Germany's "peculiar" or "distinctive" path *(Sonderweg)* to acclamatory dictatorship, and Germany's path to stable democracy. While it might have been otherwise, Nazism and Christian Democracy turned out to be the alternative historical agencies of popular political integration in modern Germany. Even the SPD, whose upright democratic record is the longest and most consistent in German history, achieved full civic respectability only after the affirmation of the democratic system by the cultural conservatives. That affirmation, though it required a radical change in the institutional leverage and psychological disposition of churchgoing Protestants, was based on a partisan model of religious and political tolerance whose pioneers, for historical reasons distinctive to Germany, were Catholics.

This book is not a complete history of German Catholic politics; nor is it the full story of the origins of Christian Democracy, the Protestant aspect of which has yet to be studied in comparable detail. It is a historical case study of the political psychology of a minority group that examines how the broad theme of partisan realignment was perceived and discussed within the Catholic milieu. Often that discussion took place with little certainty that Catholics could find an amenable non-Catholic interlocutor, yet with the realization that any genuine realignment had to encompass other portions of the political spectrum. Thus, not just Protestant conservatives but also freethinking liberals, Marxists, and Nazis appear here primarily as elements in the deliberations of the Catholics. For an interdenominational and explicitly Christian party was only one of the alternatives that Catholics discussed. Taken together, as here in this book, these alternatives are like paths in a maze crammed with switchbacks and dead ends. Their context is a series of regimes that began with Bismarck's persecution of Catholics and culminated with Adenauer and his successors' utilization and transcendence of the Catholic political experience in their renewal of German political culture.

Research for this project was funded in part by the Social Science Research Council, the German Academic Exchange Service, and the Woodrow Wilson National Fellowship Competition (Charlotte Newcombe Fellowship). My thanks to these organizations; to Holy Cross College for a one-semester leave; to the Hoffend family, Otto Dann, and the University of Cologne for their hospitality; and to the local, state, federal, and party archivists who aided me in Berlin, Bonn, Cologne, Düsseldorf, Koblenz, Münster, Rhöndorf, and St. Augustin.

I am indebted to two former Bundestag deputies, Joseph Rommerskirchen and Joseph Rösing, for interviews.

Gerald Feldman patiently counseled and encouraged me at Berkeley and beyond; for his wisdom and his many kindnesses I am deeply grateful. Margaret Anderson, who permitted me to try to fill her shoes for a year at Swarthmore College, has continued to offer stimulating comments and steadfast support. Both of these scholars are inspirations to me in my work.

I thank David Large for his timely and substantive display of confidence in me, and Otto Dann, Giuseppe DiPalma, Albert Esser, Elisabeth Friese, Engelbert Hommel, Hans-Peter Mensing, and Anneliese Poppinga for helpful discussions. I also thank my colleagues and students at Montana State University, Swarthmore College, Oakland University, and Holy Cross College.

My father did not live to see this book completed; I can only hope that it does justice to his daily example in combining analytical rigor with genuine interest in human motivation. I thank my mother, Athena Cary, as well as Irene Georgides, George and Christian Cary and their families, my son, Andy, and my daughter, Melina, for all the ways they have unknowingly aided this project. Finally, I want to thank my wife, Irini, who patiently endured learning all she ever didn't want to know about Adam Stegerwald.

[The] Essen [Congress of the Christian trade unions] demanded the formation of a great Christian, German, democratic, and social party of the people and of the state, which was to take over the leadership of the German state and give its stamp to the work of German construction. But Essen failed to find a resonance in German national life. The German people are having to pay the price, and will continue to pay it in the coming years and decades.

—*Adam Stegerwald, December 1924*

Introduction: Another Sonderweg?

West Germany, in its successful transition to democracy, became *"Modell Deutschland"*—a model and a magnet whose economic, social, and constitutional stability excited awe, envy, and emulation. Its transition into a kind of democratic exemplar owed a good deal to the circumstances of 1945: the moral and material traumas spawned by Nazism, the war, and Germany's defeat; the occupation and partition of the country; and Western-sponsored economic and political reconstruction. But the mechanisms of that transition have older origins. The historian's central question—what was decisively different about the German polity after 1945?—has another dimension: what was distinctively enduring in German political culture that facilitated its transition to democracy?

Though not providing a full answer to these questions, the religious or confessional issue, a central component of Germany's distinctive historical path *(Sonderweg)*, is critical to both. (In German, the word "confession" refers both to religious doctrine and to denominational identity: for example, "defending the Catholic confession" might mean defending the faith, defending Catholic people and institutions, or both.) Germany was the land of the Reformation; it was the main battleground of Europe's religious wars. The strong connection between religious tension and dynastic or state politics contributed to the lateness of German national unification, shaped the course of unification and the party system thereafter, complicated parliamentary and electoral politics, and remained a major issue from Bismarck to Hitler. In this context, the dramatic political success of the postwar Christian Democratic Union (CDU) in bringing together large numbers of Catholics and Protestants distinguished that party both from previous Christian parties in Germany and from Christian Democratic parties abroad. This change in the politics of Catholic-Protestant relations must also be seen, however, against the backdrop of earlier efforts to achieve interdenominational

1

political conciliation. And although it takes two to tango, the more serious prospective tangoers in Germany throughout the century had been the Catholics.

Indeed, German Catholics after 1870 had their own "distinctive path," but in a much more ambiguous sense for the future of democracy than is usually implied by the term *Sonderweg*. In heavily Catholic France, the religious question in the late nineteenth century was a left-right affair: "red" versus "black," secularization versus the prerogatives of the Church, freethinking versus the authority of tradition, democratic versus hierarchical organization. In interdenominational Germany, things were more complicated.

By eliminating Austria from German affairs, Bismarck rendered Catholics a minority of one-third of the population whose psychological defeat was the basis for Prusso-German national unification. The combination of nationalism and vigorous anticlericalism helped bond the National Liberals to Bismarck's variety of Prusso-Protestant conservatism, compromising and enervating the nominal liberal movement and spurring the growth of a separate Catholic party. Thus, while practicing Catholics in Germany, like their French counterparts, were branded as hostile toward the state, that state was not secular-liberal, but was founded and guided by a conservative. Persecuted in religious and civil life, locked out of government and administration, and labeled *Reichsfeinde* (enemies of the unified state), Catholics had to rely for domestic political protection on a party (the Center) whose only power was parliamentary. The result was that German Catholics were more protective of parliamentary prerogatives and freedom of conscience than were the National Liberals. Moreover, what Catholics wanted for themselves they also applied to others: the Center party under Ludwig Windthorst opposed both antisemitism and Bismarck's Anti-Socialist Law.

As an enduring (if sometimes reluctant) proparliamentary Catholic force, the Center party was unmatched in either France or Italy.[1] Under the kaisers, the Center generally drew from one-fifth to one-quarter of the vote and was consistently the biggest or second biggest faction in the national parliament, the Reichstag. Despite Germany's loss of Catholic territories in 1919 and the subsequent separation of the Center's Bavarian branch (about one-fifth of its electorate),[2] the party remained strong in Baden, Silesia, Westphalia, and particularly in its Rhenish heartland, with the smallest electoral fluctuations of any German party. The Peace Resolution of 1917, a decisive step toward parliamentary government, was sponsored by a Centrist; the resultant coalition of Catholics, Socialists, and left-liberals went on to write the republican Weimar constitution. The Center was the only party to serve in every Reich (and every Prussian) cabinet from 1919 until 1932; during half this period (nine times), the party provided the Chancellor. Field Marshal Paul von Hindenburg's republican opponent in the presidential election of 1925 was the Center's chairman, Wilhelm Marx. Indeed, unlike the Bonn Republic, the Weimar Republic was dependent upon the willingness of Catholics in interdenominational Germany to do what Austrian and Mediterranean Catholics would not do: seek alliances with democratic socialists.

The fact that imperial Germany's persecuted Catholic minority championed individual, civil, and parliamentary rights, sometimes in alliance with radical democrats, against the attacks of conservative and chauvinistic elites, has prompted Margaret Anderson to declare that Catholics were the era's true liberals.[3] The notion is problematic but suggestive. To be sure, the Center was suspicious of nationalism and was opposed to such standard continental liberal goals as centralized government, laissez-faire economics, and the separation of church and state. Indeed, in church-state affairs *(Kulturpolitik)*, party leaders called for a "Christian state" and demanded denominational schools with clerical supervision. Yet they invoked a liberal vocabulary to justify these policies, citing freedom of religion (the purpose of the Christian state was to resist anticlerical intolerance) and the civil right of parents to direct the education of their children. At the same time, they provided liberal policies with "Christian" rationales: fearing that what was done to one minority could be done to another, Centrists opposed the Anti-Socialist Law by citing the Golden Rule and corporatist arguments for social peace and harmony. By a similar rationale, the Center party, whose socially diverse constituency included workers, advocated the most comprehensive set of social meliorative policies of any non-Socialist party. Spurred on by a young clergyman and Reichstag deputy, Franz Hitze, the Center was instrumental to the passage of social legislation during the 1880s, and despite internal dissension the party supported the establishment of interdenominational Christian trade unions after 1900 (see Chapter 2). Far from being paternalistic, these non-Marxist unions vehemently eschewed clerical supervision and reserved the option to engage in strikes.

These points make the Center party neither liberal nor conservative, but a party compelled by the nature of its constituency to be libertarian, parliamentary, culturally conservative, socially meliorative, and pragmatic. No wonder, then, that its adversaries resentfully characterized it as opportunist—especially after the fall of Bismarck, when the Reichstag's growing influence and the intensification of socioeconomic lobbying rendered this socially diverse minority party the indispensable broker of national politics.

What looked to non-Catholic contemporaries like unprincipled opportunism, however, can be seen rather differently a century later. For the mixture of political, social, and cultural positions just sketched represents a good portion of the domestic political status quo in the postwar Federal Republic. That status quo was fashioned primarily by the CDU—the "conservative" party within the liberal system of government crafted in Bonn. Here, then, is a key aspect of the Catholic Sonderweg in German history. Due to the travails of their minority status, German Catholics built a party—the Center party—that was neither just a Catholic lobby nor just a self-serving political broker, but a model among Catholics for what was fully achieved only after 1945, with the development of the interdenominational CDU: a broad party that could integrate conservatives into a liberal democratic system.

To be sure, the Center party did this only for Catholics, and even then, incompletely. The Center was the Center, not a proto-CDU: while its socioeconomic diversity made it the closest thing to the modern postwar catch-all party until the Nazis, it remained one component of a subculturally splintered party system. Confined demographically to Catholics, it never fully overcame the siege mentality of its early days. A staunchly oppositional party during Bismarck's anti-Catholic *Kulturkampf,* its sometimes sycophantic attitudes under his Wilhelmine successors reflected continued anxiety over Catholic marginality. The same anxiety at least partially motivated the party's early decision to try to stabilize the Weimar Republic by working with the apparently ascendant Social Democratic Party (SPD)—as well as its later misjudgment that its successful cooperation with the Socialists justified a similar attempt to work with the Nazis. The sense of Catholic marginality enabled the Center, alone among non-Marxist parties, to withstand the Nazi electoral wave; it then impelled the party to provide the decisive parliamentary votes, in return for flimsy guarantees about Kulturpolitik, that legalized Hitler's dictatorial power in 1933.

To what extent, then, was the postwar CDU prefigured in the pre-Nazi history of the Center party? To begin with, no interdenominational party was possible until the Protestant majority was willing to shed its powerful anti-Catholic bias. More specifically, a Christian Democratic party could not *replace* the Center party unless Protestants gave convincing guarantees that the self-styled "tower" of Catholic defense was no longer needed; nor could a Christian Democratic party grow out of a reform of the Center party unless Protestants could accept the Catholic lead in making the Center the instrument of reform.

Few Protestants, however, were so willing. To defer to the vision of a supposedly inferior minority seemed an indignity; to do so by entering the very organization of aggrieved minority solidarity was for most Protestants simply unthinkable. Before World War I, Protestants on the whole were proud of the Kaiserreich and politically ascendant; afterward, Protestant liberals simply renamed their old parties, while Protestant conservatives rallied to the regressive German National People's Party (DNVP), which resented the Center for accommodating itself to the Republic and forming coalitions with the SPD. Apart from feelers put out by a few isolated Protestants during the revolution and constitutional transition of 1918–1919 (Chapter 3), only after 1930—when most non-Socialist Protestants were going over to the Nazis—did a smattering of Protestants seriously seek a conservative but democratic political home (Chapter 6). Moreover, such a home seemed less likely to be an interdenominational party than a Protestant twin for the Catholic Center.

Protestant attitudes thus certainly suggest that a CDU was not possible before the so-called "zero hour" *(Stunde Null)* of 1945, when the chastening effect of Germany's collapse, together with the Allies' clear intention not to license the old right-wing parties, changed the situation. Still, Protestant attitudes were not the only factor. A CDU was also more acceptable to Catholics after 1945 than it had been earlier, since they, being less implicated in Nazism, now had the psychological and organizational upper hand. With the dismantling of the Prussian state, the expropriation of the Prussian aristocracy, and the division of Germany into semiautonomous occupation zones (some with Catholic majorities), the nationwide minority status of Catholics became less burdensome. Yet, even in 1945, the CDU was not the only option for the members of either religious group: several other options were pursued (Part IV), including a refounded Center. Thus, the question remains: what is the proper place of the original Center party in the history of Christian Democracy in Germany?

A few particulars will allow a preliminary answer. First, although the Center consistently claimed to be political, not confessional, and thus open to non-Catholics, the inability of serious Centrist reformers to locate a sizable and willing Protestant constituency buttressed skepticism and inhospitality toward those few Protestants who did come forward (Chapters 2, 3, 6). Even Windthorst's early toasts to his party's "future Protestant majority"[4] were as much a reproof as an invitation. For sixty years, such statements stood for most Catholics as an excuse: the persistence of the confessional division in politics, they could say, was not their fault.

Second, the Center, like its rivals, was a Weltanschauung party. German parties traditionally claimed to represent not mundane interests but mutually exclusive world views, or Weltanschauungen, only one aspect of which was political. Catholicism took its place in this framework alongside socialism, communism, elitist and democratic liberalism, and Prusso-Protestant conservatism. To varying degrees, each party was one of a panoply of cultural and economic institutions through which a Weltanschauung received expression. Although allegedly championing a universally valid ideal, each party found its constituency by stressing the solidarity of a distinct region, class, or religious or secular group. By turning sectional interests into nonnegotiable philosophical ideals, the parties made partisan barriers nearly impregnable.[5]

By contrast, although the CDU described itself as the party of the Christian Weltanschauung, it broke with pre-Nazi usage in reaching beyond the exclusivity of a cohesive subcultural milieu. To be sure, it insisted on a fundamental philosophical distinction between itself and the parties whose Weltanschauung it called materialistic—the Nazis, the Communists, and the Socialists. But this very duality changed the function of Weltanschauung. Rejecting subcultural Balkanization, the CDU asserted that an otherwise disparate cross section of the German people, having together been led astray by Hitler, would turn away from all political ideals not informed by the expansive Christian concepts of human dignity and brotherly tolerance. Regardless of group loyalties, this cross section of Germans—potentially a majority— could be brought together in a loosely Christian "Union" whose name reflected its commitment to forge the necessary bonds between groups. In the postwar environment, this integrationist approach preempted support from both the traditional liberals and the recalcitrant right to produce a democratic interdenominational alternative to Social Democracy.[6]

Unlike the Nazi party, whose own (extreme) attempt to fashion a nationally integrative Weltanschauung was at once both participatory and exclusivist,[7] the CDU integrated not by emphasizing its own (and German) distinctiveness but by emphasizing its own (and German) membership in a larger cultural whole (the "Christian West"). Furthermore, as the CDU became a democratic catch-all party,[8] its policies ceased to require the legitimation accorded by a Weltanschauung: their success endowed them with an independent electoral legitimation. Conversely, accepting the policies no longer implied accepting the Weltanschauung (which in any case could have been invoked to justify different policies). As the focus of politics shifted from Weltanschauung to policy, the old subcultural rigidity gave way to a new electoral fluidity that did not spare even the CDU itself. For the longer the party stayed in office, the more its principal achievements became matters of consensus, and the less credible the fear became that those achievements would be overturned by a party with a different Weltanschauung.

By the late 1950s, the CDU's chief remaining rival was itself striving to become a catch-all party. As a holdover from the old system of Weltanschauung parties, however, the SPD had to be more explicit about what it was doing than the CDU had been. With the entry of Gustav Heinemann (former chair of the Protestant synod) and Helene Wessel (former chair of the Center party) into its ranks (see Chapter 12), the SPD documented its new palatability to churchgoers; with its Godesberg program, the party dropped its divisive Marxist Weltanschauung and accepted the CDU-built institutional edifice of Western integration—all without sacrificing its reformist approach, alienating freethinkers, or losing its core constituency of workers. With Godesberg as its foundation, the SPD in the 1960s and 1970s developed new policies that themselves became part of the basic Bonn consensus. Except for consensual democratic anticommunism, Weltanschauung, it seemed, had largely ceased to matter.

The CDU was thus the starting point for a massive transformation of the German party system—a transformation that proved to be a key to stable democratic development. Still, the specific form of this transformation did not come out of nowhere; nor was it due just to Nazi dislocations. Not by accident, many of the founders and early leaders of the CDU were former Centrists who had participated in that party's socioeconomically diverse political culture and who had advocated interdenominational initiatives before 1933. Indeed, although reform-minded Catholics held no monopoly on political and religious tolerance, it was the Center party, unlike its opponents from Bismarck and the National Liberals to Alfred von Hugenberg, that made genuine religious peace an explicit civil ideal. Windthorst's toasts, and the subsequent history of Centrist interdenominational rhetoric, formed a tradition that serious Catholic reformers repeatedly tried to tap.

As early as 1903, a young Franconian cabinetmaker named Adam Stegerwald, who would later cofound the CDU's Bavarian sister party, the Christian Social Union (CSU), had an organizational stake in promoting interdenominational understanding. As the Cologne-based general secretary of the Christian trade unions, Stegerwald was frustrated by the fact that union representatives had to sit apart from each other in parliament, their power diluted by the lack of an interdenominational party. This problem, already important as his fledgling unions attempted to compete with the Socialists before World War I, became downright pressing after the war, when the shift to parliamentary government resulted in some Christian union representatives sitting in opposition while others were in the government. In 1920, capping seventeen years of intermittent effort to reform the party system, Stegerwald tried to cajole the Center to cooperate in its own replacement by proposing a new "Christian National People's Party." What he wanted was a catch-all party, largely led but not dominated by labor, that would be interdenominational, culturally conservative, socially progressive, reliably democratic, and larger than the Socialists. By giving democracy a strong non-Marxist pillar, such a party would alleviate fear, draw votes away from the reactionaries, and stabilize the system on a basis that was, in Stegerwald's words, "Christian, national, social, and democratic" (Chapter 4).

Allied with Stegerwald before World War I was the Center's most important Rhenish bourgeois leader, the Cologne newspaper publisher Julius Bachem. Concerned that Catholic workers, if not given genuine political influence, would drift away to the Socialists, Bachem additionally feared that a parochial backlash against the interdenominational unions was feeding anti-Catholic prejudice across class lines and threatening Catholic progress in attaining civil parity. Twenty years after the Kulturkampf, wrote Bachem in 1906, Catholics could no longer be satisfied just to blame Protestants for denominational alienation in public life but "must come out of the tower" and demonstrate seriousness about ending their own segregation (Chapter 2). Bachem then proposed that Protestants be nominated to fill safe Centrist seats. In so doing, he had his eye on three issues at once: civic reconciliation between Catholics and Protestants, the consequences of the growth of industrial labor (the social question), and the trend toward parliamentarization. This trend made it seem imperative to Bachem not only that the Center retain industrial workers (its fastest-growing constituency) but also that it open new vistas for expansion either by attracting Protestants or by acquiring a Protestant adjunct. Bachem was thus proposing to address the very issues of sociopolitical fragmentation and civil peace that imperial and Weimar Germany never mastered—and that made German society vulnerable, after a lost war and economic calamity, to massive polarization and radicalization.

For reasons examined later in this volume, the efforts of Bachem and Stegerwald were in vain. Like the SPD's revisionism controversy, the Center's quarrel over the desirability of interdenominational integration showed the difficulty of demobilizing from an internal exile that was externally enforced, yet also (if understandably) self-abetted. Still, unlike Protestants, Catholics already had a party that fulfilled at least part of the task of moderate-conservative integration into a pluralistic liberal system. The Center was, socioeconomically, a catch-all party; it accommodated a range of political viewpoints and reconciled them to democracy; after 1918, it provided a governmental check on Socialist proclivities. Limited in its integrative capacity by the primacy it accorded to defensive subcultural solidarity, it needed in the end to be replaced, not reformed. But a part of its own rhetoric, if not always its practice, provided the very basis of its replacement.

On March 6, 1946, the former mayor of Cologne, Konrad Adenauer, stated that the CDU is "a new party, not a continuation of an old party from an era that is dead and gone."[9] Certainly the accents of Chancellor Adenauer's subsequent policies showed that this was true—his *Primat der Aussenpolitik* (primacy of foreign policy), his lack of a *Primat der Kulturpolitik,* his attention to Protestant as well as Catholic sensibilities. But it is not true, as the CDU's principal Rhenish founder, Leo Schwering, once stated, that the CDU was a "party without a history."[10] For the Center party, the civic agent of the German Catholic Sonderweg, was, for better or worse, the closest example in the German past of a political culture that offered an ideal of tolerance. The Center had given a voice and a vocabulary, if not a tail wind, to Christian Democratic aspirations. One component of its tradition now provided postwar non-Marxist Germans, both Catholics and Protestants, with an adaptable pathway toward change. In the new environment after 1945, the road previously not taken became the basis for integrating cultural conservatives into a stable liberal democracy.

PART I

The Center Party and Interdenominationalism in the Kaiserreich, 1870–1917

I see no one inclined to join us, since we are now attacked generally as ultramontanes, and no [Protestant] will want to see himself so designated.

—*Peter Reichensperger (an early Centrist), October 1870*

"Confessionalism and religious politics," Margaret Anderson has written, "are as German as apple *Kuchen*."[1] This was so even after Napoleon's dissolution of the Holy Roman Empire, with its proliferation of small states that were also religious enclaves. The much abused principle of the Peace of Augsburg (1555), which once had given every German state the religion of its prince *(cuius regio, eius religio)*, was still resilient enough in 1870 to guarantee that the Prussian-led unification of Germany would involve a religious dimension.

In Italy, whose recent unification under a liberal regime had shorn the papacy of its territories, the Vatican tried to impose political abstinence on Catholics rather than accept a secular regime it could not countenance. Not content just to nurture a subculture, it aspired to restore the full extent of its cultural and political influence. In the interdenominational German Kaiserreich, however, where even nonbelievers were identified for social purposes according to religious descent, the development of a self-conscious political Catholicism had to proceed with greater finesse. German Catholics would have been quixotic to emulate the stance of socialist polemicists who confidently awaited the day they alone would shape society. The choice was therefore between withdrawing into the purity of subcultural isolation or finding a way to balance conciliation when practicable with defiance when necessary in order to produce a serviceable measure of political and social integration.

1   The Enemy of the State

Though neither church-state clashes nor denominational tensions were new in Germany, the founding of the Center party in 1870 was seen by many non-Catholics as a provocation. What to Catholics seemed an instrument of self-defense and political participation in the new German Reich appeared much more ominous to non-Catholics, who noted both the Vatican's negative attitude toward national unification in Italy and the persistence of Catholic regional loyalties and pro-Austrian sentiment during the Prussian-led unification of Germany in the course of the 1860s. The anti-Catholic animus following German unification would be even greater than the Center's founders had foreseen: alongside economic disadvantage and civil discrimination, Catholics would face the trauma of closed churches and jailed bishops as well as the rankling charge of lack of patriotism. Labeled "the enemy of the unified state" *(Reichsfeind),* the Center was to discover dignity in opposition; yet opposition was a hardship from which the Catholic community would be anxious to escape. The question was whether national respectability in the Kaiserreich could be had without sacrificing self-respect.

Origins of the Center Party

Even before German unification, no state had done more to undermine (or overcome) the Augsburg principle of *cuius regio, eius religio* than had Prussia. Having already acquired Silesian Catholic subjects (both German and Polish) in the eighteenth century, Prussia was awarded the German Catholic Rhineland and Westphalia in the post-Napoleonic settlement of 1815. Afterward, the new Prussian Catholics chafed under the social and governmental predominance of the Protestant East Elbian aristocracy and were angered by a series of confessional incidents that turned into church-state confrontations. In

13

1837, during the so-called Cologne Troubles, the Prussian authorities even arrested the archbishop.[1]

Under the circumstances, German Catholics had an incentive to try to stick together in the revolutionary year of 1848. At the first of what were to become yearly convocations of laity and clergy, a Catholic convention *(Katholikentag)* met in Mainz, and some Catholics formed a Catholic caucus in the Frankfurt National Assembly. Yet, despite their special concerns, German Catholics, like Protestants, were distributed across the political spectrum in 1848. Recalling the anticlericalism of the French Revolution, most German Catholics were horrified when Italian nationalists, angered by the failure of the pope to lead a war of liberation with Austria, drove him to flee Rome in disguise. Still, many of these same Catholics favored German national unification, though they preferred a "large Germany" *(Grossdeutschland)* including the Catholic Austrians to a "small Germany" *(Kleindeutschland)* without them. Some Catholics, like the Rhenish upper bourgeoisie, favored genuine but measured liberal reform; others, particularly the middle peasantry of the southwest, demanded democracy; still others, especially those not ruled by Protestants, supported the predominantly conservative governments.[2]

Though the Frankfurt Assembly was soon dissolved, the suppressed revolution resulted in the spread of constitutional state government. In Prussia, the constitution of 1850 provided for a parliament, or Landtag, that held the power of the purse. The Landtag was elected according to a plutocratic three-class system: those who paid one-third of the taxes got one-third of the votes. Thus, as industrial growth enriched the largely liberal middle classes, the weight assigned to their votes rose along with their taxes, and the Landtag grew increasingly liberal.

Prussian Catholics generally favored the constitution of 1850, not least because it contained written guarantees of freedom of religion. In the new Landtag, some Catholics again formed a moderate Catholic caucus to support the constitutional provisions and to defend Catholic regional interests. After 1858, with the religious situation seemingly stabilized, the caucus renamed itself "Center (Catholic Caucus)." But the determination of King Wilhelm I in the 1860s to institute army reforms despite the refusal of the Landtag's liberal majority to appropriate the funds led voters to choose sides between the government and its chief foe, the Progressive party. Claiming that the

clash between the monarch's power of military command and the
legislature's budgetary rights demonstrated a "gap in the constitution," the King's chief minister, Otto von Bismarck, asserted that the
authority that had granted the constitution (the monarchy) also had
the authority to fill the gap. During this prolonged constitutional
conflict, during which Bismarck operated for four years without a
properly legislated budget, the shrunken and apparently anachronistic
Center caucus disbanded.[3]

Bismarck now used cunning diplomacy and military force to do
what the liberal Frankfurt Assembly of 1848 had failed to do: unify
Germany. After Prussia defeated Denmark (1864), expelled Austria
from "Germany" (1866), and defeated France (1870–1871), Bismarck arranged that King Wilhelm, invited not by a popular assembly
but by his fellow princes, assume the title of German Emperor (Kaiser). Reckoning that peasant voters might prove a conservative counterweight to the liberal middle classes, Bismarck determined that the
new national legislature, or Reichstag, would be elected not by the
plutocratically weighted three-class system employed in the Landtag
but by equal manhood suffrage. Hemming in the power of the new
Reichstag, the individual states retained their own governments and
assemblies, and Prussia was given a plurality in the powerful seat of
collective princely sovereignty, the Bundesrat (Federal Council). The
head of the Reich government, the Chancellor (Bismarck), was responsible not to the Reichstag but to the Kaiser.

Forced to choose between the letter of their liberalism and their nationalism, substantial numbers of Prussian liberals chose nationalism.
Breaking off the constitutional conflict after Bismarck's triumph over
Austria in 1866, this faction of liberals joined with the bulk of the
conservatives to pass an Indemnity Bill, in effect approving Bismarck's
illegal actions retroactively. Together with liberal nationalists from
other regions, these secessionists from the Progressive party formed
the National Liberal party. In their eyes, as Otto Pflanze has noted,
"the exclusion of Catholic Austria from a unified Germany under
Protestant leadership was itself a liberal deed, a victory for modernity
over clerical bigotry."[4] The large new National Liberal party thus was
not just predominantly non-Catholic but outspokenly anti-Catholic.

Embroiled already in church-state clashes with liberal ministries in
the south, Catholics now fearfully anticipated a national ruling alliance of Prusso-Protestant conservatives and anticlerical liberals. After

1866, Catholic populist and particularist (patriotic states' rights) parties sprang up with unexpected strength throughout southern Germany. By the war of 1870, thoughtful Catholics were readying themselves to protect their minority rights in the coming national state. In October, Hermann von Mallinckrodt and other leading Westphalian Catholics met in Soest and wrote a platform for a political party. Two months later, the Prussian Center caucus was reconstituted in the Landtag. When the first German Reichstag met the following spring, southerners formed a Center caucus with the northerners.

The Kulturkampf

From the start, the new Center party insisted that it was opposed not to national (even kleindeutsch) unification but to its perversion by Bismarck's Prussia. It also insisted that it was a political party, not a confessional caucus; it eschewed the old subtitle "Catholic Caucus," and Protestants were told they were free to join. The Center party's political priorities were to integrate the Prussian constitution's religious protections into the new Reich constitution (a point the Center emphasized by calling itself the "constitution party"), and to prevent the overcentralization of the Reich at the expense of the states.

Responding to the latter point, five Lutherans from Hanover, dismayed by Prussian annexation of their state after the war of 1866, became "guests" *(Hospitanten)* of the Center caucus, with voting rights therein. Another guest was the respected Prussian Protestant Ludwig von Gerlach, who denounced Bismarck's "Bonapartist" practices of displacing kings and using elections to seal the results of his actions. But such embodiments of the claim that the Center was political, not confessional only made the party more obnoxious to Bismarck. If it succeeded in being seen as a genuine moderate-conservative opposition, the Chancellor might find himself facing a parliamentary alliance of all the incompletely assimilated forces in the new state. Worse yet, the Center might manage to form a tactical alliance with Bismarck's other enemy, the rump of the Progressives.[5]

Bismarck therefore tried to isolate the Center. Branding it the "enemy of the unified state," he refused to give the desired constitutional guarantees and even dismantled the Catholic Section of the Prussian Ministry of Culture, which had been established to ease tension after the Cologne Troubles. Arguing that Catholics, by subscribing to the recently promulgated doctrine of papal infallibility, ren-

dered themselves obedient to the whims of a foreign power, he put
non-Catholic loyalists of the old order on notice that they would be
tarred as unpatriotic and papist if they associated with the Center.

Pandering to the anticlerical component of liberal thought, Bismarck now joined with the National Liberals in a so-called "struggle
for civilization" *(Kulturkampf)* against Catholic "superstition." The
passage of draconian anti-Catholic legislation, culminating in the May
Laws of 1873 and 1874, resulted in wholesale persecution, overween-
ing state regulation of the education and ordination of priests, and the
arrest and removal of clergy who resisted. The Jesuit order was
banned and its members deported; political agitation from the pulpit
became cause for imprisonment; homes were searched and public
meetings dissolved; Catholic presses were censored and the mail of
Centrist leaders opened. Even the more defensible measure that
opened the floodgates, the abolition in 1871 of church supervision of
schools, became the occasion for a vicious parliamentary debate in
which Bismarck slandered the Center and its Hanoverian Catholic
leader, Ludwig Windthorst, as the fifth column of the French.[6]

Catholics reacted to this onslaught with large-scale passive resistance. When the clergy ignored the new regulations regarding state
examination and registration, the government withdrew state funds,
confiscated clerical property, and arrested priests during services.
Bishops were removed, imprisoned, or exiled, and government commissars administered the dioceses in their place. Even local priests suffered banishment and loss of citizenship. Soon there were one thou-
sand vacant livings and only twenty-four priests willing to fill them;
those twenty-four in turn were snubbed by their congregations. All
over Catholic Prussia, the laity poured its energy and its ingenuity into
acts of civil disobedience.[7]

As a result of the Kulturkampf, there could no longer be any question that the Center—by 1878 the largest party in the Reichstag—was
a party of and for Catholics. Its unofficial logo, the tower, symbolized
the shelter it offered Catholics and its lonely perseverance under siege.
Yet Windthorst's toasts to his party's "future Protestant majority"
only deferred the question of his party's ultimate raison d'être to the
day when the Kulturkampf would end. Windthorst himself once said
that the Center would voluntarily dissolve once the Kulturkampf was
over. A party whose tenacity would compel a Bismarck to sue for
peace, however, was hardly likely after two decades of struggle simply
to dissolve. Once the Kulturkampf was over, Windthorst would use

another religious issue, the legal status of denominational schools, to keep Catholics together.[8] The party's political/confessional ambiguity would thereby be perpetuated rather than resolved.

The Second Founding and the Septennatsstreit

Although the end of the Kulturkampf was a drawn-out process, the first important juncture came in 1878–1879. In those years occurred a set of events sufficiently seminal to lead some historians to assert that Bismarck's so-called "liberal period" had given way to a kind of "second founding" of his Reich.[9] The implied discontinuity is clearer in economic affairs than in politics more generally, given the illiberalism (in the libertarian sense) of the Kulturkampf; Bismarck now merely extended the illiberalism to encompass additional groups. But insofar as Bismarck's earlier triumphs had relied on careful maneuvering and cooptation of some elements of the liberals' agenda, he now sought an opportunity to move the mixed constitutional system closer in practice to his original, more authoritarian instincts and preferences.

Exploiting two attempts on the Kaiser's life, Bismarck proposed his Anti-Socialist Law. The subsequent acquiescence of most liberals (for economic as well as political reasons) in this flagrant violation of liberal principle further demoralized and fragmented the liberal parties. The year 1878 also saw the death of Pope Pius IX, the author of the Syllabus of Errors and the doctrine of papal infallibility. Inheriting Church-state controversies not just in Germany but also in France, Switzerland, Austria, and Italy, the new pope, Leo XIII, was more conciliatory than his predecessor. The Vatican's new position came just as Bismarck was preparing his Dual Alliance (1879) with Catholic Austria. It also coincided with the German Chancellor's turn from free trade to protectionism, a move that aggravated the liberal split but pleased the Center's still largely agrarian constituency.

The breakup of the National Liberals, political Catholicism's greatest parliamentary enemy, compelled Bismarck to alter his tactics toward the Center: although still desiring its destruction, he could no longer refuse to deal with it. The object of Bismarck's "second founding," however, was not to put through a realignment but to weaken every potential source of parliamentary independence. Hence, Bismarck's efforts to wound the National Liberals and smash the Socialists were not accompanied by a fundamental turn toward the Center. Indeed, eight more years were to elapse before the Kulturkampf would end. Even then, Bismarck would nearly manage to plant the kiss of death on German political Catholicism.

The substantive issue in 1887 was Bismarck's demand for a seven-year military budget *(Septennat)*. The Center had opposed the first Septennat (1874) not only out of Catholic antipathy to Prussian militarism but also because Catholics as a group were substantially poorer than Protestants (one-third of Prussia's population, Catholics in 1909 still paid only one-sixth of the state's income taxes) and had traditionally opposed projects that might require new levies or compromise parliament's budgetary prerogatives. When the first Septennat had passed, the Center had derided the National Liberals for selling out on the same issue that had caused the great constitutional conflict of the 1860s (to which the chief National Liberal architect of the measure had replied that it was necessary at a time when the Empire had so many external *and internal* enemies).[10] To renew the Septennat in 1887, however, Bismarck needed the cooperation of the Center.

The pope now played into his hands. Believing his action would win a final religious settlement in Germany and Prussian diplomatic support in Italy, Leo flatly told the Center's leaders in two notes to vote for Bismarck's bill. Hesitating to defy their tradition and their constituents' sentiments, party leaders were unwilling to accept the bill but planned to offer a compromise on the bill's third reading. Learning of the pope's intercession and perceiving the quandary facing Windthorst's party, Bismarck dissolved the Reichstag before the compromise could be advanced.

Publication during the subsequent election campaign of Leo's second note forced the Center to choose between "unmasking" itself as a confessional and foreign tool by bowing to the pope or risking losses among the pious by defying him. Either way, Bismarck could reckon, the Center would suffer the crippling blow he had failed to inflict via the Kulturkampf. The candidacies in some districts of breakaway "Septennat Catholics," some of whom called for a new progovernment Catholic Conservative party, compounded the Center's danger.

In a campaign speech at Gürzenich in Cologne that was to become a staple of Centrist lore, Windthorst deftly saved the situation. According to the papal note, the Center, "considered as a political party . . . is allowed full freedom of action always," but since the prospect of "final revision of the May Laws" made the Septennat a "religious and moral" and not just a political matter, the pope could intervene.

As Windthorst well knew, this position would have turned both the Center and the pope into government hostages: during any future political row, the government could have extracted Centrist obeisance by threatening the Vatican with religious reprisals.

Windthorst therefore shifted the emphasis. The pope, he said, had expressed the "very important principle" that in "secular questions," the Center, "like any Catholic," had *"complete freedom"*; "the Holy Father *does not mix in these secular things.*" This principle, he continued, was "the *basis* of our political *existence,*" for otherwise the Center, just as pro-Kulturkampf forces charged, would not be independent, but would act "solely according to the opinion of the spiritual leaders of our Church." The pope's legislative *request,* said Windthorst, was based not on religious but on "diplomatic considerations"—a distinction that implied the layman's right of refusal. The party could not violate the program on which it had been elected without forsaking its constituents and jeopardizing its existence, which the pope himself cherished (as he had said in the note). Should the Center fall in this struggle, Windthorst grandly concluded, then let its epitaph read:

> By its enemies never vanquished
> But by its friends forsaken.[11]

The speech was a psychological tour de force. Windthorst successfully rallied Catholics to a denominationally based party that had just spurned the wishes of the pope. He cast the pope himself as the authority for this conduct. He justified lay political independence not just as a principle but as a requirement of confessional defense. Above all, he returned again and again to the Catholic identity of the caucus: its independent conduct was that of "any Catholic," and its defeat would be possible only through Catholic disloyalty. Windthorst thereby extricated the Center (for the moment) from its classic dilemma, reconciling its political nature with its Catholic identity and allowing the party to survive the election with only minor losses among Catholics. This success, however, was accompanied by the defeat of seven of the ten Protestant Hospitanten.

Since 1870 the Center's fortunes had depended on the combination of an open appeal to Catholic solidarity and the assertion, mostly for external consumption, that the party was political and not confessional. With the Septennat, the party was compelled to reap the consequences of that combination. Had it submitted to a "patriotic" papal directive, then it could just as easily submit one day to an anti-patriotic directive—or so its enemies would have argued. Windthorst therefore had to give his followers a public object lesson in what the political-not-confessional dichotomy meant in practice for them. Windthorst's interpretation would be disputed: insisting they would have voted for the Septennat from the beginning had the Center leadership informed them promptly of the Holy Father's wishes, some members of the caucus in the new Reichstag defied Windthorst even after he agreed to have the caucus abstain. Yet had Windthorst not publicly refused the pope, it would henceforth have been not just difficult but downright impossible to view the Center as a nonconfessional or potentially interdenominational party. Even at Gürzenich, what Windthorst did was to rescue the *ambiguity* in the party's position: he managed both to defend its political independence and to maintain its Catholic credentials. This combination, so crucial to the party's continued success, was also the reason for its intermittent bouts of soul-searching in the future.

The Return from Exile

The fiasco over the Septennat was the fruit of a papal policy that tried to do through diplomacy what the Center had not yet accomplished through parliamentary politics: favorably regulate the relationship between Church and state in a country with a hostile government. What Leo aimed for was a concordat; what he got was government-sponsored legislation easing the May Laws. Some monastic orders were readmitted, subject to state supervision; selected seminaries were reopened; and the state's right of veto over clerical appointments was made slightly less sweeping. But a return to the constitutional guarantees of 1850 was out of the question. The terms of the Kulturkampf settlement were a far cry from what the Center had been fighting for, but on this obviously ecclesiastical matter, the party dared not buck the pope again. Reluctantly, it approved the bill.[12]

Success, however, inevitably raised the question of the purpose of maintaining—or, as Windthorst had put it, of not "forsaking"—the Catholic party. At one extreme, Catholic "integralists" argued that no decision in life was free of doctrinal implications; the Center's purpose was to see to it that every political decision be taken on the basis of Catholic tenets. How this was to be reconciled with the notion of a political, nonconfessional party was a question that would come back to haunt the party (Chapter 2). From Rome's perspective, however, the purpose of the Center could not be to harass a government with which one now had an accommodation, but to secure the deal by giving Caesar what was Caesar's. This potentially sycophantic outlook made little allowance for the possibility that political considerations not belonging to the realm of Kulturpolitik might, as matters of conscience, prove just as important to an organized party of Catholics. Half a century later, the consequences of this oversight were to be disastrous (Chapter 6). Yet Leo's policy did allow Catholics—not only in Germany but also, eventually, in republican France, and later in the "red Prussia" of the Weimar era—to rally to their respective regimes. In other words, it permitted what one Rhenish Catholic would later call "the return from exile."[13]

Post-Kulturkampf political Catholicism would thus be a mixture of the Windthorstian and the Leonine. From Windthorst came the well-honed parliamentary instrument, the insistence that this instrument was "political, not confessional," and the steadfast determination to maintain it; from Leo came the spirit of *ralliement* and the corresponding tenet, sometimes called "accidentalism," that while some forms of government might be preferable to others, all could be abided if they gave the necessary cultural guarantees. But this was not simply a matter of Leo providing the policy and Windthorst, reluctantly, the tool; for although Catholics, led by Windthorst, had generalized their situation during the Kulturkampf into a paradigm for the shortcomings of the entire domestic order,[14] the Center had always asserted its desire to partake affirmatively in unified Germany's national life. Nor was there necessarily an inconsistency here: if the alternative to Bismarck's "Kulturkampf society" was the parity-state, then Catholics could see post-Kulturkampf society as imperfect, but finally on track. This was even more the case after Bismarck proved unable in 1890 to renew that other affront to civil parity, the Anti-Socialist Law: when he then recommended a coup *(Staatsstreich)* against his own constitution, he was dismissed.[15]

The days of clear-cut opposition thus gave way to a period of reappraisal—and then, under the Nassau politician Ernst Lieber in the later 1890s, to a progovernmental posture. Aiming for the civic and social rehabilitation of the Catholic middle class, Lieber increasingly saw cultivating the authorities as the means to that end. If he went beyond what Windthorst might have countenanced,[16] his object in a sense was not different: both wanted to facilitate the paths of advancement of men like themselves, who came from marginal but ambitious and self-respecting groups (both were Catholic lawyers from states annexed by Prussia), to positions of influence and social dignity. As economic and social issues overtook constitutional and cultural ones, the best means to the goal for Catholics seemed to be to combine a realistic potential for further confrontation with an avowedly conciliatory stance. The fact that the regime now needed the Center—from 1890 to 1932, except for one two-year interval, the party held the pivotal parliamentary position—only further recommended this stance to Lieber.

But Lieber had to take account of the economic concerns of his party's weighty rural and small-town populist wing. In 1894, he tried to compensate the government for the Center's latest rejection of an army bill by supporting the agricultural trade treaties negotiated by Bismarck's successor, General Leo von Caprivi. In reaction, the disgruntled head of the Rhineland Farmers' Association, Felix von Loë, proposed to reconstitute the Center as a collection of autonomous vocationally determined sister organizations with separate electoral slates. This plan would have turned the party into a confessional umbrella organization that voted together only on ecclesiastical matters. Such a plan was anathema to the party's leaders, for it was precisely the weight of the caucus on nonconfessional matters that provided its leverage. Nor were the pious Catholic integralists pleased by the implication that most political issues were independent of religion.[17]

Lieber's reorientation of the party reached its spectacular climax in the decisions to support the government's imperiled Navy Bills just before the turn of the century even without solid ecclesiastical and cultural concessions. These fiscally ruinous decisions were unpopular both within the caucus and among the rank and file. But the bills were more than just a military appropriation: they were a symbol of the power, the vibrancy, and the ambition of the young national state. As such, they provided an opportunity to demonstrate that national feeling and a party of Catholic solidarity were compatible. Moreover, the legislative horse-trading over these bills may have helped lead to the high Bülow tariffs of 1902, which reversed many of the effects of the Caprivi treaties and appeased the party's agrarians.[18]

The legacy of the Kulturkampf thus combined pride in the integrity of the period of resistance with terror and even occasional cravenness before the prospect of renewed isolation. A party that had found unity and self-assurance in the role of opposition was thenceforth to feel insecure unless in a progovernmental role—even though this role, in a time of rapid socioeconomic change, frequently heightened internal tensions. The emergence in the 1890s of the Catholic industrial working class and the explosive growth of the Socialist labor movement exacerbated those tensions. Sooner or later, Centrist leaders would have to confront the question: How long could the party live off the Kulturkampf? And what was the alternative?

2 Labor, Party, and Zentrumsstreit

The debate within German political Catholicism about an interdenominational realignment of the party system took its cue in the early twentieth century from the organizational initiatives of Catholic labor. In 1899, largely at the instigation of Catholic social reformers, a national association of Christian trade unions was established to compete with the so-called free Socialist unions. Though preponderantly Catholic, the Christian unions were lay-run and interdenominational, for the founders were convinced that only unions potentially large enough to stage strikes, not tame, clerically tutored workers' clubs, could draw the workers. Almost immediately, however, Catholic integralists and other critics attacked the new unions both for being interdenominational and for condoning strikes. What had begun as a matter of economic practicality quickly became a question of theological principle: could economic concerns be separated from confessional doctrine? And what were the implications for other interdenominational organizations?

The dispute over interdenominational unions soon touched off a corresponding dispute over the nominally interdenominational Center party. Pro-interdenominational politicians such as Julius Bachem, publisher of Germany's leading Catholic newspaper, the *Kölnische Volkszeitung (KV)*, discerned in the Catholic integralist challenge to the unions a threat to their own freedom from clerical authority in nondoctrinal affairs. Moreover, they felt that tactless references to dangerous Protestant influences in the unions would undermine two decades of effort to assure that Catholics would never again be as isolated as they had been in the Kulturkampf. And, in the industrial Rhine-Ruhr region especially, they feared the loss of the Center's labor wing, without which, in an industrial age, the cause of Catholic defense would surely be hopeless.

In a reversal of what was to become the standard order of argument, the *KV* noted in 1905 that since the Center was an "inter-confessional political party," the unions too "should not be damned because of [their] interconfessional character."[1] Yet union proponents also argued that the interconfessional character of the unions "automatically" required their "neutrality in party politics."[2] This position begged the question: if the Center was interconfessional, why couldn't interconfessional unions officially affiliate with it?

The reason, of course, was that the Center party of 1905 was not interconfessional. As the Trier cleric and integralist Jakob Treitz put it, the Center was "a—or rather, we say, *the*—Catholic party. The few Protestant *guests* of the party do not change this at all."[3] The *KV*'s contrary claim was a way to defend lay political independence and to repel charges that the party was ultramontane and antinational. To turn the claim into a reality would require a positive initiative, not a defensive assertion. But even if a denominationally better balanced Center were to prove viable (Treitz thought not), it clearly would not be the same entity as the Center party of 1905.

The Dilemma of Christian Labor

No one more than Christian labor wished that the Center's claim to interdenominationalism could be taken seriously, for the numerical strength of the unions could then be concentrated at one political locus. The Center was a natural such locus, for despite the official nonpartisanship of the unions, they owed a good deal to the social Catholic movement of the late nineteenth century.

Starting with Adolf Kolping's midcentury network of journeymen's leagues, hostels, and adult education classes and sustained by support from the revered bishop of Mainz, Wilhelm Emanuel von Ketteler, organized social Catholicism gained new impetus after the expiration in 1890 of the Anti-Socialist Law. Realizing that the future strength of the Center would depend on its ability to head off Social Democratic incursions, clerical and lay activists built up two fledgling organizations: the People's League for Catholic Germany (Volksverein), with its headquarters in the Rhenish city of Mönchengladbach, and the Catholic Labor Leagues (Katholische Arbeitervereine, or KAV), with regional seats in Mönchengladbach, Munich, and Berlin. Pope Leo XIII's landmark social encyclical *Rerum Novarum* (1891) further encouraged the activists. At the Volksverein, a young priest from Cologne, Heinrich Brauns, developed a pragmatic course of study for workers on sociopolitical, economic, and organizational matters. Through this so-called "Gladbach course" passed many soon to be prominent Catholic men of affairs who came from modest origins, among them a young Alsatian worker who was to become a leader of the western Arbeitervereine, Joseph Joos.[4]

The Arbeitervereine were not unions but local Church-sponsored workers' associations whose mission was economic and cultural self-help. Each was chaired by a clergyman who worked closely with a leader from the rank and file. In 1899, the western association in Mönchengladbach began publishing a weekly newspaper, the *Westdeutsche Arbeiter-Zeitung (WAZ)*. The editor, Johannes Giesberts, was a former boiler-room employee of Bachem's *Kölnische Volkszeitung*. Soon to become only the second worker to attain a seat in the Center's Reichstag and Landtag caucuses, the busy Giesberts gradually gave way at the *WAZ* to Joos.

The first successful Christian trade union was founded in Dortmund in 1894. Five years later, a national federation of Christian unions was proclaimed at a congress in Mainz. Immediately a dispute known as the neutrality controversy *(Neutralismusstreit)* broke out over the unions' nonpartisanship. Fearing a Protestant exodus, Catholics such as Giesberts, Brauns, and the young prolabor journalist Matthias Erzberger overruled those who argued that the unions' legislative demands required a partisan affiliation (which could only have been with the Center). Although Giesberts hoped the unions would gain influence across the non-Socialist political spectrum,[5] the non-Centrist membership (about one-fifth) was too dispersed to give the unions weight within any other party, yet just large enough to cause partisan dissension within the unions. Politically minded union leaders longed to bring the party system into congruence with the structure of their own organization.

The task was complicated by both denominational and class considerations. Seeking a populist farmer-labor coalition as a non-Socialist alternative to the "iron-rye" coalition of big business and agriculture, Christian trade unionists decided not to oppose the agricultural tariff of 1902. Consequently, the SPD scored significant electoral gains in Catholic urban strongholds the next year. Yet union leaders persisted in hoping that the idea of a non-Socialist reform bloc would attract enough governmental and multipartisan support to produce prolabor legislation that would convince workers of the advantages of the Christian unions' approach. But after muckraking revelations in

1905–06 by Erzberger, now a Centrist Reichstag deputy, and Hermann Roeren, integralist deputy for Trier, about corruption and cruelty in the colonies, Chancellor Bernhard von Bülow turned the election campaign of early 1907 (the "Hottentot elections") into a stridently nationalistic and anticlerical display reminiscent of the Kulturkampf. The subsequent formation of the Bülow bloc, in which Conservatives, National Liberals, and Progressives aligned themselves with the government in an attempt to break the Center's parliamentary hold, marked the calamitous defeat of this round of interdenominational bloc-building by the unions.[6]

The alternative to bloc-building involving the established parties was to reshape the party system. Three options were discussed, with inconclusive results. The first idea, to create a separate Christian labor party, had originally been floated by union dissidents during the tariff controversy of 1902–1903. When the idea resurfaced in July 1906, Giesberts warned that such a party would isolate Christian labor and allow the old parties to turn their backs on social reform. The second solution was to concentrate Christian labor's strength behind two parties, one for Catholics, one for Protestants. For a time, Protestant hopes rested on the small Christian Social party of former Imperial pastor Adolf Stöcker, a reform-minded conservative and antisemite (a quality his proponents now downplayed). As early as 1903, trade unionists had begun pressing for electoral pacts between the Center and the Christian Social party. The third solution, the most radical and the most inchoate, was to seek an overarching partisan realignment that would make a commitment to interdenominational understanding the unifying principle for one very large and socially diverse party.[7]

Whereas the neutrality dispute involved the crucial matter of the unions' political alignment, the so-called trade union controversy, or *Gewerkschaftsstreit,* involved their very right to exist. This controversy began just before the Mainz congress with a series of articles by Franz von Savigny, a nephew of the Center's co-founder who had connections with the Berlin seat *(Sitz Berlin)* of the eastern Arbeitervereine. Savigny insisted that only clerically led confessional associations could insure the proper application of religious principles to labor's economic affairs. His concern seemed borne out for some when the pro-union *WAZ* published a pamphlet characterizing Christian unions as a temporary response to the revolutionary and anticlerical stance of the Socialist unions and depicting unified "neutral" unions free of Weltanschauung as the ultimate goal. Cardinal Georg Kopp of Breslau, a foe of the Volksverein, thereupon induced the annual bishops' conference in Fulda to call for purely confessional organizations. In May 1902, Sitz Berlin launched clerically led "craft associations" *(Fachabteilungen)* to free Catholic workers of the allegedly corrupting influence of materialistic Protestant workers. The Catholic craft associations renounced strikes and advocated legislation to institute compulsory arbitration boards. Soon afterward, the bishop of Trier led the Arbeitervereine of his area out of the western (pro-union) regional organization and over to Sitz Berlin.[8]

Although economic self-interest and fear of labor inspired some opponents of interdenominational unions, a genuine element of religious and subcultural concern was also involved. One school of thought, known as the "Berlin-Trier" or (more simply) "Berlin orientation" *(Berliner Richtung)*, stood for the integralist principle that no element of human endeavor could be separated from confessional strictures. Jakob Treitz insisted that this did not preclude Catholic-Protestant collaboration on some economic questions; he objected only to "the union of different confessions and outlooks in one and the same organization." Heinrich Pesch, a Jesuit, added that a Catholic vocational organization "need in no way 'lock' itself up" against Protestants: "whoever from the other side avows the same program is welcome," perhaps through a federative relationship between autonomous organizations.[9]

The opposing school of thought, known as the "Cologne-Gladbach" or "Cologne orientation" *(Kölner Richtung)*, was led by Giesberts, Brauns, and (after 1903) the twenty-nine-year-old Cologne-based general secretary of the Christian unions, Adam Stegerwald. Far from excluding religion from economic life, the Christian unions, wrote Brauns, had made it "possible" for Christian workers to "be active in trade unions without violating or endangering their religious convictions." Moreover, noted the *KV*, the Septennatsstreit had shown and the pope had recently repeated that some areas of decision-making "do not concern religion." Denying that they were promoting a nonexistent "neutral Christianity," union spokesmen pointed out that other vocational organizations were not confessional and concluded that separate Catholic and Protestant organizations would be unnatural without separate factories. According to the Gladbachers, the Berliners were the ones hurting religion; by identifying the Church with opposition to collective bargaining, they were compromising the Church in workers' eyes. Had it not been for the interdenominational miners' union in the Ruhr, wrote Brauns, the growth of the Social Democratic union could not have been stemmed. He predicted huge Social Democratic windfalls if Christian unions were stopped.[10]

After a decade of frequently intense polemics, Pope Pius X, in the encyclical *Singulari quadam* (1912), manifested a decided preference for the craft associations. Denying that the "social question" was purely economic, the pope, citing "dangers for the purity" of the workingman's belief, wrote that organizations that "touch directly or indirectly" on religion and morality should not be denominationally mixed. Yet, under pressure from the anti–Social Democratic governments of Prussia and Bavaria, the pope stopped short of banning the unions outright. As long as their Catholic members also joined the local Arbeitervereine, the unions were to be tolerated where they already existed.[11]

The initial reaction of union circles was gloom and outrage: Stegerwald wrote Joos that the unions had to choose among slow death, passive resistance, and open defiance. Convoking a special congress of the unions, Stegerwald drafted an address in which he vehemently lashed out at "the machinations of Sitz Berlin." Cartels, trusts, and property owners' associations, he said, pursued practices far more deserving of churchly reprobation than did the unions; and Catholic workers in England and America belonged to catch-all unions with "far more radical policies." Yet Stegerwald's intention was not to reject the encyclical (a course that could well have been suicidal), but to exploit its loopholes. In this course he now found a partner among the bishops. Fearing that the steady exodus of Catholic workers from the Church might turn into a stampede, the Bishop of Paderborn, Karl Josef Schulte, prevailed upon the bishops to issue a statement interpreting the encyclical in the most favorable possible light. The statement was distributed at the special union congress and was interpreted as a signal to continue as before. When the pontiff declined to intercede again, each side claimed that the encyclical supported its position. The quarrel remained unresolved until the exigencies of war production decided the question in favor of the much larger unions.[12]

The trade union controversy was a trial by fire that established the self-image of the Christian trade unions. Whereas the Center's heroic period, the Kulturkampf, had profiled the party as the Catholic community's defender under siege, the unions' heroic period came in fighting not employers or Social Democrats but a portion of the Catholic hierarchy. This experience left Stegerwald lastingly suspicious of those Centrists whose priorities remained ecclesiastical and cultural, including labor colleagues like Joos, whose prime activity was in the cultural-confessional Arbeitervereine (albeit not Sitz Berlin).[13]

The trade union controversy did one more thing: it opened up a parallel controversy in the Center. For many of the questions it raised—Were there areas of secular life not concerned with religion? Were Catholics better served by isolation or by integration?—applied also to the party.[14] Moreover, like the unions, the party viewed itself as an exemplary German resource serving national integration. Internally, the unions claimed to model the overcoming of denominational conflict; externally, rather than reveling in class conflict like the Social Democrats, they aspired to make the working class a respected part of civil *(bürgerlich)* society. The Center too saw its internal diversity, in this case socioeconomic, as a model; it too saw its sectional role, in this case denominational, as essentially affirmative and constructively engaged. This self-understanding seemed confirmed by the Center's passage from scorned pariah to indispensable conduit of parliamentary mediation. But while the mediating function of the unions was limited by their essence as an interest group, that of the party was limited because only Catholics belonged. By nature, a trade union is a working-class organization; a party, however, need not be a confessional organization—and the Center claimed it was not. It was natural, then, that the discussion of interdenominationalism would extend to the party. It was natural, too, that the impact of this issue would be strongest in the party's Rhenish heartland, where labor's share of the Center's constituency was greatest.

"Out of the Tower!"

Even before the so-called Hottentot elections and Bülow bloc of 1907, the Catholic "return from exile" was reaping a Protestant backlash. The appointment in 1902 of Martin Spahn, son of Centrist leader Peter Spahn, to a chair in history at the University of Strassburg unleashed a vehement academic attack on the Catholic capacity for intellectual integrity. Catholic-baiting by the Evangelical League and attacks on Catholic student organizations in 1904–1905 underscored the persistence of confessional tension in civil life. Erzberger and

Roeren's subsequent colonial investigation was opposed by Centrist leaders precisely because it threatened the party's relations with the government. In January 1906, hints of an impending anti-Catholic bloc accompanied the Reichstag's latest rejection of a Centrist bill of religious toleration.[15]

Trusting in the long-term feasibility of interdenominational cooperation, men such as Julius Bachem were both distressed by the wave of confessional incidents and embarrassed by the recently provocative rhetoric of the integralists. On March 1, 1906, Bachem published his soon-to-be-famous article, "We Must Get Out of the Tower!" Bachem's dramatic summons was intended to reduce the "prejudice" that the Center worked exclusively for Catholic interests and to instill "a better recognition in the non-Catholic provinces" of "the whole range" of its activity. The confessional division in politics, he told Catholics, was a historical circumstance, not a principle; it had never been the Center's ideological underpinning. Well-meaning men of both denominations had a "duty" to work at overcoming confessional prejudice; "one cannot evade this duty even by referring to [the fact] that a prejudice is also active on the other side." Accordingly,

> we must work unconditionally for the election of such non-Catholic deputies who are willing . . . to support good contact with the Center. Indeed, it would . . . be good politics to support such deputies not only in overwhelmingly Protestant election districts, but also in a number of districts where the Center alone could perhaps obtain the majority . . . From such candidates, on church issues, one may demand nothing other than that they . . . [defend] religious freedom and . . . the civil equality of . . . the Catholic people; for the rest, their viewpoint on social issues must be decisive!

This passage crystallized the ensuing controversy. Bachem seemed to be advocating that safe seats be reserved for Protestants who need not necessarily be party members, but who might be sympathetic outsiders. He went on to suggest the Christian Social party as a source of likely candidates.[16]

Bachem's so-called tower article *(Turmartikel)* cast a glaring light on the contradictions that beset the Center's position in German politics: the anomaly of a political, nonconfessional party with almost no Protestant members; the irony of the onetime "enemy of the state" *(Reichsfeind)* now cast as the centerpiece of a progovernmental parliamentary bloc; the complementary irony that this party, born in suspicion of kleindeutsch nationalism, had been clamoring since the navy bills to assert its claim to this nationalism—not, as before, in a manner self-righteously disdainful of the nationalist excesses of its rivals, but in the eager, overstated way of a convert.[17] Finally, there was the emphasis on social policy as the "decisive" criterion for partisan attachment, when the Center was the one German party whose adherents did not join for socioeconomic reasons. Behind these matters lurked the question of how long a party based upon Catholic solidarity could continue to be a major force in an age of socioeconomic interest-oriented politics. Bachem's opponents turned the question around, asking what would hold the socially heterogeneous party together in such an age if it did not assert the primacy of the religious bond.[18]

Bachem's tower article triggered a full-scale internal debate—the "Center controversy" *(Zentrumsstreit)*—about the historical character of the party. Bachem's seemingly heretical strategy had, in his view, the sanction of party tradition; to him, the strategy was as much a return to the party's original intentions as it was a new initiative. But Bachem's opponents immediately challenged his "Colognist" assertion that the party's Weltanschauung was simply Christian rather than Catholic. Led by Roeren, they conceded that the party was political, not confessional, and that Protestants therefore could join—but only if "the political activity the Center practiced in accordance with the Catholic Weltanschauung corresponds to the principles [those Protestants] consider . . . salutary for [a] political . . . party."[19] In other words, Protestants who based their politics on Catholic principles were welcome.

Quite apart from such logic, what mattered to the average Catholic was that the Center was a political home for Catholics. Anything that threatened that notion could seem disconcerting and even dangerous. Still, influential Centrists much preferred acceptance and respectability to self-righteous isolation. According to one Reichstag deputy, Protestants in the caucus, by "bearing witness" to the sincerity of Catholic and Centrist patriotism, would abet Catholic rights and influence. There could be no greater disservice to Catholicism, wrote the *KV*, than to declare the Center a Catholic party.[20]

What Bachem had intended as a drive to bolster the Center's ties to Protestants thus turned into a debate over the character of the Center itself: was it or was it not in principle a Catholic party? On this point, after eight years of polemics, Bachem's Christian Weltanschauung prevailed. In March of 1912, Roeren, feeling pressured and isolated, resigned from the Reichstag caucus. Two years later, after the greatest flurry of pamphleteering in the long debate, the party expelled the remaining intransigents.[21]

On the question Bachem had originally been raising, however, he fared much worse. For his purpose was not just to assert the principle that interdenominational organizations were allowed, but to persuade some Protestants actually to bind themselves to Catholics in the party system. A breakthrough to Protestants, though, could not be achieved by resignations and expulsions. In the end, things were to get no further than a second-ballot election accord with the Conservative party in 1912—something that neither side in the Zentrumsstreit publicly faulted and that each would use to justify its own position.

The War of the Quotations

As the polemics in the Zentrumsstreit illustrated, Bachem's original proposal was ambiguous. Was he calling (like Martin Spahn) for an interdenominational Reichspartei, or party of government, united not by Weltanschauung but by its outlook on social policy?[22] Or did he want the Center to extend the "guest" arrangement to groups beyond the Hanoverians (a view encouraged by Bachem's frequent recourse to Windthorst's precedent)? Were safe Centrist seats to go to Protestants who belonged to a different caucus? Or was the aim just the more energetic pursuit of election accords with appropriate Protestant partners? Each interpretation carried different implications about the degree to which the Center and the party system needed to be transformed. Accordingly, the issue soon shifted to defining the nature of the party. Instead of focusing on possibilities for the future, the disputants became more and more preoccupied with interpreting the party's past.

The two boldest departures in the debate ultimately suffered the same fate: the other side gained the initiative, and the inciting faction, denying it was advocating change, defensively rehearsed the historical pedigree of its position. This is what happened to Bachem in 1906. Three years later, his adversaries extricated him from his defensive posture with a bold departure of their own.

On April 13, 1909 (Easter Tuesday), a conference of Bachem's leading opponents defined the Center as "a political party" that represented the public interest "in harmony with the principles of the Catholic Weltanschauung." In a letter to the bishops on May 12, two of the conferees, Reichstag deputies Roeren and Franz Bitter, decried "systematic efforts to spread the view . . . that economic, social, and political questions are separable from" that Weltanschauung. Roeren and Bitter rejected "a so-called interconfessional cultural community" that would "reconcile the confessions on a patriotic footing" by "limiting religion to the inside of church buildings."[23]

The Cologne group now seized the opportunity to deride this "private and confidential group" for attempting to define a party whose forty years of existence spoke for itself. Instead of claiming they were "returning to Windthorst," wrote the *KV*, "Bitter and his friends should state openly that they now want to make the Center something other than what Windthorst and the founders made it, what it is today, and what it always has been." Calling the Easter Tuesday line "something completely new," the *KV* concluded: "We need no new definition, no new course; we need only go forth . . . in the old spirit and in the old concord!" Predictably, Roeren responded that he had not proffered a new definition but had "merely [made] explicit . . . how in [our] view the old character of the Center . . . is to be interpreted."[24]

Holding most of the party's leadership posts, Bachem's faction extracted a statement from Roeren on November 28 affirming that Catholics and non-Catholics could work together politically within the Center party. One year later (October 24, 1910), after additional pressure, Roeren promised to forsake "all further direct or indirect representations of another formulation." Specifically, he agreed not to promote the views of Edmund Schopen, the host on Easter Tuesday, who had alleged in a pamphlet that Cologne's attempt to "resolve the national problem" through "confessional mixing" and "the mutual lessening of orthodoxy" was an "inner danger" to the Catholic religion in Germany.[25]

Yet, despite the pressures on Roeren, the polemics continued. Indeed, the debate had become what one participant called the "war of the quotations"[26] as each side scoured the utterances of Windthorst, Mallinckrodt, and Ketteler for any favorable passage. The Cologne group even referred to a final prewar purge as the *"Abwehraktion"* (defensive action), a slogan reminiscent of the tower image. "Out of the tower" fell into disuse almost immediately after 1906. Instead, Cologne's favorite slogan, culled from a passage in a speech by Windthorst, became: The Center is what it was, and will remain what it is.[27] This phrase without content—unlike "out of the tower," either

side could have claimed it—was imagerially value-laden, exalting sto-
lidity, resoluteness, and continuity over daring, resourcefulness, and
dynamism. The Bachemites' task became to fill the slogan of immuta-
bility with what remained of the tower article's message of bold renewal.

The shift in emphasis from renewal to continuity changed the nature of the debate. However seriously Bachem might at first have
meant to call for steps toward a truly interdenominational party, he
had quickly given way to defending against its preclusion—not because any Protestants might really be enticed to join, but because
withdrawing the possibility would reinforce the resentful Protestant
tendency to isolate a party whose claim to moral ascendancy was
based on its Catholicism. In effect, the tower article challenged the
party to find another basis for its moral claim.

To Roeren, however, such a step would mean compromising the
moral primacy of confessional creed. A good Catholic had to base his
partisan morality, like all other morality, upon the Catholic Weltanschauung. The "Christian Weltanschauung," said Roeren, was a theological absurdity; hence, "the possibility is excluded that the founders
of the party established it on such a basis." Weltanschauungen were
mutually exclusive, and consisted only of the following: Catholic,
"positive-believing Protestant," "free Protestant," and "materialistic-
atheistic." Every individual held one or another of these, and so must
parties, for party platforms were otherwise ambiguous. Like the integralists in the trade union controversy, Roeren denied that this viewpoint must lead to isolation: when two Weltanschauungen mandated
the same policy, he said, the correct formula was "march separately,
strike together."[28]

Julius Bachem's younger cousin, the Reichstag deputy Carl Bachem,
answered that the phrase "Christian Weltanschauung" was intended
only as "a political formula," not a theological amalgamation. On
most questions, he insisted, there is no Catholic Weltanschauung
"that I can 'represent' . . . it is one thing to do nothing that contradicts
Catholic beliefs and moral teachings and something else to demand
that in all matters of state these teachings . . . are to be 'represented.'"[29] Julius Bachem added that the Center had always based its
moral claim on its commitment to the Christian principles of conciliation and moderation, or the golden mean. Conciliation was the essence of Christianity; and each member was free to identify his own
creed, be it Catholic or Protestant, with the party's Christian Weltan-

schauung. If this part of Centrist tradition had been neglected in the past, the reason, said Bachem, was that it was easier to base an electoral appeal on Catholicism than on a mediative program. That program, and the Christian principle of social justice on which it was based, were the keys both to the party's internal unity and to its outstretched hand to Protestants; they made the party a moral example of responsibility and sacrifice for all of Germany. Moreover, the party was mediative in the Catholic interest, for only such a party could evade the liberals' attempts to "defame" it as confessional. The party, stated the *KV*, "would not have to change its program, statutes, practical policies or inner direction in the least" to tap the Protestant resource.[30]

Yet, beyond these assertions, no steps were taken to recruit Protestants or to carry out the original "safe seats" plan, even after Cologne emerged triumphant. Accordingly, whereas some observers have implied that Julius Bachem's goal was something like a CDU, others have seen just a public relations strategem to shore up the Center's sagging relations with governmental Conservatives. A third view holds that while Bachem was not so unrealistic as to envision the interdenominational transformation of the Center, he was serious about launching numerous Center-backed Protestant labor candidacies in largely Catholic urban districts. According to this view, the Zentrumsstreit was just a deeper phase of the trade union controversy, not a parallel or related dispute. Indeed, the argument goes, Bachem probably wrote the tower article at Stegerwald's request.[31]

While the trade union question certainly was critical to Bachem's initiative, the Zentrumsstreit was more than just a phase of that controversy. Bachem, a veteran of the Kulturkampf, was the party's leading figure in a Catholic region ruled by Protestant Prussia. He wanted full civil and social parity for educated Catholics. These factors mattered to him as much as did his interest in the trade unions.[32] Hence, when Bachem's nightmare of a new anti-Catholic bloc (the Bülow bloc) came true just months after the tower article, Bachem shocked Stegerwald, who was too young to have experienced the Kulturkampf, by refusing an election accord with a pocket of willing National Liberals in Westphalia. To Stegerwald, such an accord offered the only hope of preventing a Social Democratic sweep in the western industrial districts. But to Bachem, the main fear was that the National Liberal party, the archenemy during the Kulturkampf, might replace the Center as the pivotal party in the Reichstag.[33]

Indeed, the lines of division in the Zentrumsstreit and the trade union controversy were not fully coincident. At the Easter Tuesday conference, disagreement over the trade unions forced the conferees to drop all specific reference to the labor question from their program. Shortly thereafter, a leading spokesman stated that the choice between the unions and the craft associations had "nothing to do" with the Easter Tuesday conference and was "expressly excluded from its deliberations." Later, Carl Bachem exempted Roeren from his criticism of the Berlin side in the trade union controversy: though the Trier deputy was the most distinguished opponent of the tower article, he had "never participated in the uproar" against the unions and had "always acknowledged that he considered them reliable."[34]

At issue in the Zentrumsstreit was not just how to improve conditions for Catholics and Catholicism, but what constituted improvement. Whereas Bachem deemed interdenominational cooperation in a mixed society to be morally and practically desirable, Roeren saw denominational separatism in politics as both the guarantor of Catholic solidarity and the shield of Catholic purity. To be sure, the socioeconomic and political concerns of the unions help explain why the party's crisis of conscience could be held off no longer. Both sides were striving to come to terms with them—Cologne by giving sociopolitical satisfaction to those in the party whose Catholic loyalty seemed most endangered; Berlin by attempting to blur socioeconomic opposition through an emphasis on the religious bond. Both sides claimed to be acting practically. But while the Roerenites' priority was to preserve subcultural purity, the Bachemites' was to infuse Catholic values into the mainstream of German society, to the benefit of both Church and nation. They held up this ideal of infusion as proof that good Catholic motives underlay their pro-Christian stance.[35]

Protestants into the Center?

How serious, then, was Bachem about recruiting Protestants when he wrote the tower article? The answer seems to be that Bachem, as befit a good politician, was willing to take whatever arrangement with Protestants he could get. In a sequel article, he asserted in April 1906 that the "external form" of the tie between Protestants and the Center was of minor importance. Bachem thereby left all doors open, seemingly unconcerned whether Protestant candidates ran as full-fledged Centrists or as members of other parties. Even the comment by a

Christian Social organ that its members could never consent to be "guests" of the Center did not faze him: he replied that his concern was not with parties but with individuals.[36]

The sequel article is the key to understanding Bachem's plural strategy. He had in essence a maximal goal and a developing series of fallback options. The party, he believed, had to prepare itself in the long run for a truly interdenominational constituency while it contained the recent short-term damage to Catholic-Protestant relations. The first fallback option—to Bachem, the only realistic place to start—was to offer to back nonaligned or minor-party Protestant candidates, knowing full well that few Protestants would accept. If the offer were accepted, so much the better: but even if it were not, Bachem himself pointed out, "the attempt in itself would be a gain" because its public relations effect would "contribute . . . to decreasing the Protestant prejudice vis-a-vis the Center party." This was Bachem's minimal position, and it is only as a last fallback that Bachem's aim was just public relations.

At no time did Bachem intend, nor could he have expected, that more than a trickle of Protestants would soon attach themselves to the party. Had he emulated Windthorst with a toast, it would have been "To the party's future Protestant *minority*." No other aim would have indicated serious Catholic interest in an interdenominational party, since no other aim would have been consistent with the realistic requirements of Catholic self-defense, which Bachem insisted he did not wish to subvert. Indeed, even a Protestant minority within the Center, though Bachem might dream of it, was more than he had originally proposed. For the emphasis in the first article was on asserting that Protestant candidates need not belong to the party. Only in his sequel did Bachem turn his attention to the more ambitious aspiration of placing the Center "upon a broader basis" through "the wished-for entry of more Protestant members."[37]

It was, in fact, Catholic criticism that forced this change. The critics wanted to know why the party should voluntarily weaken its parliamentary delegation by transferring safe seats to Protestants who could remain outside the caucus. The Center's Berlin newspaper, *Germania,* questioned whether Bachem's initiative could bear fruit, but even if it could, Centrists themselves ought to reject it. *Germania* claimed to have no objection to electing a Protestant Centrist, "but where is he to be found? . . . There are no Protestant adherents of the Center party." In their absence, one must not turn over the party's seats to Protestants who at best would "stand with only one foot on the basis of its program while the other stands in another camp!" Instead, Protestants ought to accept election accords in which they voted for a Center candidate in one district if they expected Catholic help for a Protestant candidate in another district.[38]

Avoiding Roeren's theoretical considerations, *Germania* argued exclusively on practical grounds. The paper conceded that the party's almost entirely Catholic composition had "happened very much against the desire" of Windthorst. But thirty-five years of history showed that the current controversy was "academic. The Center does not come 'out of the tower' because Protestants do not want to accept any mandates from Catholics and do not want to elect any Center candidates." Moreover, Bachem's spectre of a party condemned to "splendid isolation" was a myth: over the years, the government and the other parties had accustomed themselves to working with the Center. The best way to soften confessional animosities, said *Germania*, was not to propose unrealistic initiatives, but to continue as before.[39]

Germania's claim that it "urgently" wanted to elect Protestant Centrists was thus a way of rejecting the initiative Bachem was proposing. Because he was in earnest, Bachem was less demanding in what he asked of Protestant candidates and voters, but also less far-reaching than to insist on a complete transformation of the Center itself. In the end, as we have seen, he was to settle for something less far-reaching still: a second-ballot election accord with the Conservative party in 1912.

This does not mean, however, that this election accord was all that Bachem ever wanted.[40] Indeed, *Germania* sensibly depicted such an accord as the alternative to Bachem's initiative, not as its realization. Roeren too supported the accord of 1912.[41] Moreover, that accord was not with the Christian Socials, but with the quintessential government party, the Conservatives. In 1906, Bachem had not even mentioned the Conservatives as the object of his initiative—as indeed they could not have been, if his intent was to attach Protestants to the Center either as members or as looser affiliates. The *KV* had even contrasted the political *un*suitability of the Conservatives as lasting partners to the far greater suitability of the socially conscious Christian Socials, whose differences with the Center were "considerably less."[42]

Besides principle, of course, a question of power was involved. A deal with the Christian Socials would have brought into greater parliamentary prominence an otherwise prospectless Protestant force and obliged it to loyalty toward its Centrist mentor. For Stegerwald, such an arrangement would have been doubly advantageous: it would have pushed the Center toward a more urban-oriented social policy, and it would have concentrated the Christian unions' political influence behind two allied parties. By contrast, in any deal with the governmental Conservatives, the Center, though twice as large, was, in imperial Germany, the junior partner. Moreover, the accord of 1912 resulted from a Center-Conservative, or "black-blue" (clerical black, Prusso-conservative blue), bloc that had come into being in 1909 at Christian labor's expense. This bloc had been based on the Center's decision to join the Conservatives in voting against Bülow's proposed inheritance taxes. The concession on this issue by Christian labor deputies, made for the sake of breaking up the anti-Centrist Bülow bloc, had been vigorously opposed by Stegerwald, who was never to be more discouraged about finding his unions a political base. The unions were left reeling—their rate of growth dropped, and they organized barely a third as many Catholic workers as the Socialists by the eve of World War I—and the Center in 1912 suffered the biggest electoral losses it had yet endured, with Social Democrats the prime beneficiaries.[43]

The moves of 1906 and 1912 did have one aim in common: both were intended to promote the "return from exile" by giving Catholics a reliable Protestant political partner. Thus, whether or not the 1912 accord was his original aim, Bachem could only welcome it, especially after the Bülow bloc. Yet, what was for Bachem an acceptable though not ideal outcome proved far less satisfying for Stegerwald. Instead of achieving labor legislation that would convince workers that moderation paid, his unions now were stamped as unreliable. They still played no significant role in any party other than the Center, where they were impeded by the trade union controversy.[44]

World War I gave Stegerwald a second chance. The need for massive arms production increased the power of all trade unions, and Stegerwald became a major figure in the Center party in his own right. In this capacity, he pressed for democratic reform of Prussia's plutocratic suffrage and greater attention to labor's other interests. Egged on by Martin Spahn, whose extreme anticonfessional position during the Zentrumsstreit had caused the Bachemites to disavow him,[45] Stegerwald warned Karl Trimborn, the Center's Rhenish chairman and expert on urban affairs, that the Center could not continue to "sound the Kulturkampf bell" in order to overcome the clash of interests within the party; the Catholic bond would "certainly no longer suffice after the war." If the Center wanted to retain its urban districts, it would have to cease viewing its labor policy "only from the standpoint of party tactics" and foster a deeper "social consciousness" among its middle-class constituents.[46]

Stegerwald thus was demanding the fulfillment of the line in Bachem's tower article that "social politics must be decisive." How little inclined the Center was to heed this counsel, however, was soon demonstrated by Julius Bachem's successor (in 1915) as publisher of the *KV*, Carl Bachem. More conservative, less visionary, and less adventurous than his cousin (who died in 1918), the younger Bachem was annoyed by Stegerwald's talk of a "new orientation" for the Center. Fearing that a democratic suffrage in Prussia would result in the demise of the denominational public schools, Carl Bachem considered labor's demands both arrogant and a threat to party unity. He thus was in no mood to see the debate over interdenominationalism in the party revived.[47]

In January 1917, Carl Bachem received a letter from an official for the general staff in the military press agency, Dr. Ferdinand Runkel—a Protestant. Runkel introduced himself as the author of a manuscript entitled "Protestants into the Center." Believing that the war had rendered past confessional battles obsolete, Runkel stated that a Protestant printer was prepared to publish his pamphlet if Bachem was willing to edit it. Runkel offered to launch a speaking campaign to urge Protestants to join the Center, and referred to a "circle of Protestant theologians" who "share my conviction."[48]

Bachem's response was cautious to a fault. Though he noted to an associate that Runkel's was "a very serious" initiative, he waited eleven weeks before replying. Elaborately excusing the delay, he said that although the *KV* "sympathize[s] from the heart" with Runkel's convictions, "it is another question" whether the issue of Protestants in the Center "ought to be reopened": "the efforts of the *KV* . . . in this direction before the war led to long discussions within the Catholic community that to some extent took a very difficult form. These discussions subsided because of the onset of the war and we do not hope that they revive . . . after the war." Bachem insisted that the Center was serious about wanting Protestants, yet rebuffed what he himself described as a serious opportunity to bid for them. The reasons he offered were the scarcity of willing Protestants and concern that a Centrist initiative "in the present period of the [four hundredth] anniversary of the Reformation" would be taken as a provocation.[49]

Eleven years earlier, his cousin had said that it was the lack of a Centrist intiative that was a provocation for Protestants, and that the fewer interested Protestants there were, the more important it was to recruit them.

Apart from these ironies, it is clear from Carl Bachem's letter that what he really feared was not the Protestant reaction but the aggravation of old wounds among Catholics. What Bachem wanted to do now was to bury "Out of the Tower"—to retain the assertion of openness to Protestants as quietly as possible while concentrating on conserving Catholic solidarity. His position, and that of most of his party, was no longer very far from that of *Germania* a decade earlier.

If the Center could soften confessional animosities by continuing unchanged, if election accords were all that it meant when it said it was interdenominational, then the rhetoric of reform and that of conservation could be fused in the service of the existing all-Catholic party. In such a context, those who took reform seriously, be they Protestants like Runkel or Catholics like Stegerwald, would change from being the old guard's allies into being its adversaries. A new division would thus be established, and would become decisive in the years to come. It pitted not integralists against ecumenicists, nor left versus right, but conservers versus reformers—those such as Carl Bachem (the keeper of the party's history)[50] and even Joseph Joos (more and more the keeper of its soul), both of whom still asserted the primacy of Kulturpolitik, against those such as Adam Stegerwald and his early postwar rival, Erzberger's protégé Joseph Wirth, both of whom gave primacy to other issues of state over confessional consciousness and who would find themselves allies in spite of themselves in the waning years of the Weimar Republic. And both groups, the conservers as well as the reformers, would hearken back to the rhetorical tradition of Cologne.

PART II

Initiatives and Inertia, 1917–1922

The Center as bequeathed to us, just as it is, has the right to offer itself as the political point of crystallization for a great constitutional party [*Verfassungspartei*] and to send out invitations to the Protestant part of the population . . . [its] political course, in all particulars and at any time, could be adhered to by devout Protestants without moral difficulty.

—*Joseph Joos, August 1922*

The [interdenominational reform] attempts made from within the Center have up to now only increased the danger of confusing and losing what one has, with no prospect whatsoever of something else and something better. We say: An end to reforming the party.

—*Joseph Joos, October 1922*

Joseph Joos was no integralist. A protégé of Johannes Giesberts and Heinrich Brauns, he was theoretically as receptive to interdenominational parties as to interdenominational trade unions. But as *Germania* had once shown, interdenominational rhetoric could sometimes be used to preclude interdenominational practice. Though such dissimulation was not, perhaps, Joos's original postwar intention, his avowed willingness to accept Protestants into a party that would nonetheless remain "just as it is" was only a step removed from outright hostility to any change. That step was shortened by the fact that war, revolution, and a new parliamentary order had altered the implications of interdenominationalism in ways not earlier foreseen.

At the root of those altered implications were two developments: the wartime split among the Social Democrats, and the shift of governmental responsibility to the parliamentary parties. By freeing the so-called Majority Socialists (MSPD) of their former radical wing (the Independent Socialists, or USPD), the Socialist split made a Center-left alignment a viable option for the first time since the days when Windthorst could form alliances with the Progressives. Increasingly, an alignment with the MSPD appeared to be the only way to keep the growing sentiment for peace and domestic reform from costing the Center the support of Catholic labor. But if the motive for aligning with the Majority Socialists was to prevent an exodus to them, then the Center presumably would have to reemphasize its confessional bond. This seemed even more the case after the revolution of November 1918, when the Center, to prevent anticlerical and other revolutionary "excesses" by governmental Socialists, felt obligated to help stabilize a new republican order that most Protestants regarded with reserve or outright hostility.

Fearing that a political overture to Protestants would move the party to the right, prolabor figures such as Joos, Matthias Erzberger, and the emerging Badenese politician Joseph Wirth now subtly adapted the *Germania* arguments of 1906. Noting the futility of earlier attempts to woo Protestants, they argued that the party ought to concentrate instead on recouping its leftward losses among working-class Catholics. But since the Christian trade unions were interdenominational, union leaders like Stegerwald were in a quandary. Many of their Protestant members belonged to parties that opposed the new Weimar Republic. Union leaders feared both for the unity of their organization and for the viability of the new parliamentary order unless those Protestants were successfully courted.

Beyond these considerations, Centrists were concerned that the dichotomy of government and opposition in a parliamentary system might split their middle party. To the opponents of interdenominationalism, it was precisely this risk that necessitated greater emphasis on the time-tested confessional bond. But proponents of interdenominationalism argued that a seemingly sectarian party would now appear anachronistic. Only an interdenominational party, they believed, could provide a democratic and social alternative to the SPD and challenge its claim to lead the new state while protecting religion and assuring social harmony. By combining a social conscience with a national outlook, an interdenominational and democratic party would take support away from both the left and the right. Such a party would head off the further radicalization of German politics—a fear made concrete by the presence of worker-soldier councils in emulation of revolutionary Russia—and would facilitate the formation of stable parliamentary majorities.

The issue of reforming the party, and with it the party system, thus cut across the old lines of division within both the Center party and its labor wing. It involved not only differing visions of the future of political Catholicism but also differing estimates of the relative importance and cooperative potential of other political groups. Even more fundamentally, the priority of the reform issue had to be assessed in the context of a postwar world troubled by seemingly more urgent and more readily addressable problems.

3   Defeat, Revolution, Reorientation

In July 1917, Matthias Erzberger, shocked by the results of his wartime investigation of Germany's military situation, convinced a Reichstag majority composed of Socialists, Catholics, and some liberals to endorse a formula for peace laid out earlier by the SPD: no annexations or indemnities. This Peace Resolution, a breakthrough in the alignment of the parties, was a warning that government could no longer be conducted in Germany without the full involvement of Parliament. Yet, despite his own such warnings, Adam Stegerwald did not welcome the Peace Resolution. To protect the pronational reputation that distinguished his unions from their Marxist rivals, he continued to try to combine traditional patriotism with loud demands for social and political reform. In effect, he sought a third position in a party divided both by the Peace Resolution and by the drive for democratic reform. On one side of him, favoring both these initiatives, stood Erzberger and Joos; on the other side, opposing both, stood Carl Bachem and his *Kölnische Volkszeitung*.

Stegerwald's Wartime Reform Agenda

The reformist banner that Stegerwald preferred was that of equal suffrage in Prussia. Here was an issue with direct ramifications for workers, for only an end to the plutocratic three-class suffrage system would give workers influence in a state that embodied two-thirds of the Reich. Thus, when Centrists in the Prussian Landtag helped defeat equal suffrage in the spring of 1918, Catholic labor functionaries lashed out at their party. Warning that Catholic workers were "no longer in a position to give their votes" to those who had "failed" and "insulted" them, protesters at a rally on June 23 threatened joint action with the Social Democrats. With food prices rising because of the British blockade, the workers complained that the Center, as usual,

was favoring its agrarian wing. Only if compelled by democratic reform, they implied, would the party pay greater heed to its working-
class constituency.[1]

To appease the workers, the party's Reich Committee issued a set
of guidelines on the "Present and Future Tasks of the German Center
Party." Drafted with some union input in the editorial offices of the
KV, the guidelines were not a comprehensive policy statement but a
series of ambiguities designed to cover up the widening divisions in
the party. Their formulation, the *KV* explained, was buoyed by the
conviction that the party's internal differences had "nothing to do
with [its] principles" and would "settle themselves" once peace was
concluded. The guidelines were said to show that "the doubts held by
people in other camps as to whether the old party framework would
continue to hold together can find no abode in the Center party."[2]

That such doubts were by no means limited to "people in other
camps" was shown by Stegerwald's speech in Cologne on July 27.
Immediately issued as a pamphlet, the speech was an open call for
party reform. Labor's dissatisfaction, said Stegerwald, was due not
only to the suffrage question but also to "the entire position of the
Center party" in political life. Religious sentiment could no longer
substitute for a "uniform civic outlook" to bond a diverse electorate.
A good Catholic, said Stegerwald, could be either conservative or
democratic, monarchist or republican, nationalist or particularist: Catholicism provided "no sufficient universally valid" political orientation, and neither did the Center. Only by developing "an autonomous
political Weltanschauung" could the party maintain its unity; only by
addressing the political and social concerns of urban voters could it
restore their morale and commitment. For "in view of the momentous
world events of the present" (by this time including the Bolshevik revolution), "no party that looks to the future can live off its services that
lie in the past."[3]

Equal suffrage in Prussia, said Stegerwald reassuringly, need not result in purely parliamentary government: workers were not motivated
by "abstract democratic allures," nor did they idealize the "French"
system of shadow rule by bankers, lawyers, and journalists. "A wide
middle road" lay between the western and Prussian systems. Finding
that road, however, required facing up to political exigencies like suffrage reform even at the cost of confessional unity. What mattered,
argued Stegerwald, was not "unity at any price," but "how the goals
. . . by means of which [the Center] . . . is able to justify . . . its contin-

ued existence alongside the other parties . . . can be most surely achieved." This begged the question raised by the Zentrumsstreit: could the party's aims be distinguished from its Catholicism? Stegerwald answered as Julius Bachem once had: he defined his desired "autonomous political Weltanschauung" as Christian and social. Having argued that Catholic tenets could not provide a clear political orientation, he now asserted that "Christian ideals," by all rights a less specific concept, could.[4]

This sleight of hand served a purpose. Denying that he was "purely a man of economics" with "no understanding of the [place of] high moral and cultural values in the life of the people," Stegerwald bestowed a Christian moral aura upon the substantive social and political positions he wanted the party to adopt. In this way, he bolstered his claim that those positions or policies ought to constitute the party's missing "point of orientation." At the same time, he warned that if the Center did not proceed with "the political emancipation of Catholic labor," he would try to replace the Arbeitervereine with "worker voters' leagues" or to "form a special Christian Social Labor Party within" the existing party. These words could only have had a chilling effect on party veterans such as Carl Bachem who had been principals in the dispute with Felix von Loë about a similar arrangement for the agrarians in the 1890s (Chapter 1). The effect could hardly have been lessened by Stegerwald's almost defiant assurance that workers striving for their proper place in the party "were not willing to throw in the towel and simply to carry out an exodus *en masse.*"[5]

Stegerwald warned both the Center and the Conservatives that neither party had a future in the "new" Germany unless excessive agrarian demands were curbed. Half the Center's voters, he claimed, were now workers; to get along with them, Centrist farmers had to distance themselves from the aggressive agrarian pressure group, the Bund der Landwirte (BdL), just as Centrist workers had from Social Democracy. "Under no circumstances" would workers go along "a second time" with policies like those of the regressive black-blue era. "Ruined by the BdL," a "popular" and "ethical" conservative movement would reemerge in Germany only after the existing Conservative party had "suffered a catastrophic political defeat in Prussia."[6]

Stegerwald's speech was a dramatic demonstration of Christian labor's intention to play an assertive postwar role not just in traditional trade union matters but in all areas of intraparty politics.

Whereas Stegerwald during the Zentrumsstreit had let his bourgeois mentors take the lead, he now staked the claim that a politically astute man of working-class origins had a right to be taken just as seriously as they on general partisan affairs. Having failed to heed the lesson of the election defeats of 1912, the Center was put on notice that its behavior on the Prussian suffrage question was forcing workers to conclude that the party was beyond redemption. Party reform, Stegerwald was saying, was no longer a request or even a demand, but a necessity.[7]

Yet, except for his comments on the Arbeitervereine, Stegerwald declined to outline what would emerge if a Centrist reform failed to materialize. To be sure, he thought that the conservative portion of the political spectrum also needed a makeover; there too, there was a need to combine tradition with populism, a modern mass base, and a Christian "ethical outlook"—in short, a need to emulate his own movement. But Stegerwald expected no reform here until after the "catastrophic political defeat" that he hoped to spare the Center. For the present, his task was to light a fire under the Center, not to blaze a clearing alongside it. Only a still greater crisis would prompt him to think again.

Party Reform and the November Revolution

In the third week of November 1918, amidst military collapse and revolutionary chaos, Heinrich Brauns journeyed from Cologne to Berlin to meet Matthias Erzberger. Brauns shared Stegerwald's suspicion of the man whose colonial revelations had once contributed to the destruction of the trade unionists' hopes for an interdenominational political reform bloc. But Erzberger was a member of Germany's first parliamentary government, the short-lived autumn cabinet of Prince Max of Baden. Though even this government, the first to include the Majority Socialists, had just been swept away by the revolution, Erzberger was keeping the Center afloat in Berlin. Whereas old-guard Centrists such as Reichstag President Konstantin Fehrenbach and Cabinet Secretaries Karl Trimborn and Adolf Gröber had fled the capital, Erzberger, after negotiating an armistice for the defeated German army, had hurried back to Berlin—too late, he regretted, to prevent the formation of a shaky all-Socialist government, the Council of People's Commissars (three Majority Socialists and three Independent Socialists).[8]

Brauns had hitherto played little public role in politics beyond his tracts during the trade union controversy. To survive the revolutionary wave, however, the Center would need to secure its ties to labor and to develop a competitive democratic organization. On both counts, Brauns and his Volksverein were the party's best hope. During the war, the "social priest" had backed Stegerwald's warnings that the Center, by failing to overcome sectarianism and to tackle social issues and the suffrage question, was courting disaster. Now it was Brauns's initiative in quickly drafting a new program and offering to carry it to Berlin that spurred the party's Rhenish and Westphalian leaders to shake off their paralysis. Erzberger and Brauns were brought together by the fact that their characteristic displays of resolve during the first difficult days of revolution made them the temporary keepers of their party's destiny.

Different assumptions nonetheless underlay their common understanding that some reform must take place. Whereas Erzberger's goal was to rescue the existing party, Brauns wanted to go further. As he had just written the vice-chairman of the Rhenish Center, Cologne jurist Wilhelm Marx,

> We need *a new party* whose program is such that the *socially* and *democratically minded elements* of the old Center party from all strata can willingly take part. The new founding must proceed in such a way, however, *that other non-Socialist [bürgerlichen] circles* who now are seeking a new political orientation can *also* take part . . . [Therefore,] *the name "Center" must be dropped,* and the first proclamations must not come from the old party as such, nor even merely from Centrists . . . The matter is urgent, so the masses do not . . . swing over to Social Democracy . . . Everything now depends upon acting resolutely and decisively. Only whole measures can help; away with all half-measures!

Just as with the trade unions, so too with the party system: only a large interdenominational and socially minded party, Brauns believed, could compete with the Socialists.[9]

By contrast, Erzberger shared neither Brauns's faith in the possibility of a more broadly based party nor his view that only structural reform could secure programmatic reform. To Erzberger, augmenting the Center's social platform was a way to reinforce its subcultural and psychological bonds; saving the party and endowing it with a new program were complementary goals. Not only were these goals detachable from the idea of wooing Protestants; they were also, he believed, more realistic and important.[10]

Brauns's letter to Marx was part of a trend: every non-Socialist party witnessed individual calls for not just a programmatic facelift but a wholesale political realignment in order to prevent a Marxist victory. The breadth of such sentiment gave reformers grounds for hope, but also raised the fear that the realignment might not be in the Cologne-Gladbach tradition. This danger was already manifest in the efforts of Georg Heim, an agrarian Centrist, to launch not a national multiclass party but a regional, agrarian, and (despite interdenominational rhetoric) still all-Catholic Bavarian People's Party (BVP). The *KV* now moved to reinforce the unity of the tower. Most Centrists, the paper wrote, "by no means shared" the Bavarian view that "the old parties have been done in by the political collapse"; while the rest of the party system might undergo "a complete transformation," "*a fusion with other parties does not come into consideration* for the Center." This viewpoint prevailed at a meeting in Duisburg of western workers and party notables on November 17. Brauns's ideas on programmatic reform were favorably received, and his preferred name, "Christian People's Party," was appended to the name "Center." But "the main thing," Marx later wrote, was that Marx managed "to save the old name," in effect killing Brauns's plan to found a new party.[11]

It was in the wake of this Duisburg meeting that Brauns went to Berlin. Led by Erzberger and Johannes Giesberts, the few party deputies still in the capital were also drafting a new program and trying to organize a party secretariat under Max Pfeiffer. Stegerwald, however, had other plans. On the same day as the Duisburg meeting, a diverse group of politicians and academic figures met in Berlin and formed a Democratic People's League. Their avowed purpose was to "gather all who acknowledge the changed times, who want to collaborate in a new order on a democratic foundation, and who demand the immediate convening of a [constitution-writing] National Assembly." Among the reported signers of this proclamation were Stegerwald, liberals Friedrich Naumann and Alfred Weber, moderate Social Democrat Konrad Haenisch, celebrated historian Friedrich Meinecke, Jewish industrialist and social planner Walther Rathenau, and Ernst Tröltsch, one of the socially minded, pietistic professors known as the "academic socialists" *(Kathedersozialisten)*.[12]

Fearful of civil and social breakdown, the members of this diverse assemblage were sufficiently independent-minded to seek solutions across traditional political lines. But whereas Stegerwald wanted to prevent an all-Socialist majority in the coming National Assembly by winning converts from the right wing of the SPD, Haenisch could have sought no more than a safety valve to check the power of the Independent Socialists, with one of whose members, the vehemently anticlerical Adolf Hoffmann, he shared the Prussian Ministry of Culture. Indeed, despite earlier speculation in the press that some sort of non-Socialist melting pot *(bürgerlicher Sammelbecher)* might be in the offing,[13] the League's predominantly liberal founders proved more interested in addressing the historical split in the liberal movement than in realigning the entire non-Socialist spectrum. On November 20, the liberals founded the German Democratic Party (DDP).[14] Pending the revival of conservatism, the DDP would indeed be a temporary way station for many non-Catholics who despaired of otherwise preventing an all-Socialist majority. Yet, with its only mild departures from traditional liberal positions on church-state issues and the economy, it was far from the type of party Stegerwald had in mind.

No Centrist leader in Cologne, however, had any way of knowing whether Stegerwald's involvement in the new league was an exploratory mission or a defection. The uncertainty was heightened by Trimborn's and Bachem's knowledge of an earlier effort to recruit Stegerwald for a very different group, a collection of very conservative Catholics that included Martin Spahn's former student Eduard Stadtler.[15] The report of Stegerwald's involvement in the Democratic League therefore set off confusion and alarm in Cologne. At a hurried conference on the evening of November 18 in the editorial offices of the *KV*, a Reichstag deputy and trade unionist, Johannes Becker, was commissioned to nudge the general secretary into line with the Duisburg course.[16]

Becker immediately wired Stegerwald "to practice restraint for the time being regarding the formation of a [new] party." In an express letter the next day, he added that even a name change for the Center was inadvisable. If the old name were dropped, it would "doubtless" be appropriated by the integralists, who would claim to be "raising the old banner . . . that had been laid down by former elements" of the party. Especially with women voting, a name change would cause "great losses" at a time when it was "not yet certain" that sufficient numbers of Protestants could be won over. Accordingly, Becker appealed to Stegerwald not to undertake a private initiative but to consider himself a Centrist envoy to "devout but progressive Protestant circles": "You know these gentlemen . . . We here were of the opinion that you might be willing to get in touch with [them] so that they participate . . . in the final drafting of the program for the Center. You would be able to explain to them . . . why it would not be good to drop the name Center just yet . . . but that we would give the party a subtitle that could indeed become the only title at a later time." Participation in drafting the program, wrote Becker, would convince Protestants that they were "dealing with an absolutely transformed Center" with an "unmistakably progressive and interconfessional character." Any further steps would have to await "the corresponding education of our [Catholic] voters."[17]

Stegerwald was now trying to bring the Christian unions together with the much smaller liberal Hirsch-Duncker unions under a new (and ultimately short-lived) umbrella organization, the German Democratic Labor Federation (DDGB). Such an organization was the ideal complement to a unification effort on the political front. Indeed, Stegerwald's later remark that he would not have sought political office had he not been left in the lurch by his own trade union constituency in November 1918 suggests that he intended the merged unions to provide the mass base for a new party, with himself as extra-parliamentary power broker.[18] This remark also suggests why he did not further pursue the possibility of a new party. His leading colleague in Berlin, Giesberts, was collaborating with Erzberger in rescuing the Center, while Becker and others in Cologne were collaborating with the *KV* in the same cause. Meanwhile, Brauns and the Volksverein had acceded to the cooptation of their own reform effort. With his rear guard unsecured, Stegerwald's interparty initiative got nowhere.

Announcing the Duisburg draft program on November 20, the *KV* cautiously repeated Becker's reasons for lengthening rather than changing the party's name. The next morning, however, the paper again emphasized not a "transformed" or "remodeled" party, but the continuing relevance of the party as it was. The Center was "not an empty name," but "a symbol" and "a source of spiritual energy." It represented "history and tradition," "the political experiences . . . of half a century." Its great leaders had given its name, "and with it, German Catholicism, an honored reputation." It was the heroic party of the Kulturkampf, and Culture Minister Hoffmann's plans to end church subsidies and religion in the schools signaled "a new Kulturkampf . . . much more radical than the first." As a Christian middle party, the Center was the conscientious overseer of parliamentary understanding; no "Catholic caucus," class party, or "particular-istic" party like the BVP could take its place. Nor could fifty years of loyalty be transferred to a "new party": once uprooted, Centrist vot-ers would disperse to other parties and be "lost forever."[19]

Within two weeks of the revolution, then, the Center's Rhenish leaders had made it plain that the party would not risk its identity to facilitate the anticipated realignment of the party system. Their atti-tude stemmed less from concern that Protestants might not be recep-tive than from fear that Catholics were not ready for a Christian catch-all party. Like the prewar SPD, the postwar Center had to cope not only with the growing power of trade unionists but also with a hard-line faction left over from a revisionism controversy (the in-tegralists); in addition, the party faced agrarian and regional insur-gencies. The Center had been a viable exception in an age of socioeconomically homogeneous parties because everyone knew why the exception existed. But why would a Catholic not join the appro-priate class-based party (which would thereby become interdenomi-national) if the party of Catholic solidarity were to give way to an interdenominational party? In particular, what would keep Catholic farmers from going over to a party sponsored by the BdL? This risk seemed especially great since the demand for a new "Christian" and "social" party was coming from that segment of the existing party, organized labor, whose interests were most at loggerheads with those of the farmers. The agrarian-led Bavarian secession only deepened Rhenish leaders' fears that political Catholicism was in danger of hav-ing its agrarian backbone shattered.[20]

To the *KV*, reform had become just a rhetorical display: useful if it helped keep Catholics united, it was not to be bought through pro-grammatic points or a name change that might threaten rather than secure Catholic unity. Under these circumstances, a bid for Protestants was desirable only if it did not change the Center at all—on the basis of traditional Kulturpolitik, not progressive Sozialpolitik. Thus, when Brauns, rejecting "half-measures," moved to implement Stegerwald's warning that confessional unity could no longer be a reason to post-pone reforms, the traditional Cologne leaders quickly stepped in to make sure that half-measures would be all Brauns would get. Whereas Brauns wanted bold steps to seize the fleeting moment, Marx and the *KV* wanted to buy time. The message from Cologne was that gestures, not genuine initiatives, must again suffice.

The Cologne leadership's position reveals the extent to which loyalty to the Center in its own right had entrenched itself alongside loyalty to the Church. Even the fear that integralists using the old party name could destroy the party under a new name was based on the cover provided by the name, with the habit of attachment it invoked. Abandoning the name, Cologne feared, would destroy its claim to be conserving the party "as it had always been." No longer could it charge that the integralists were the radicals who were departing from party tradition.

Lacking access to the party name, breakaway integralist groups were to fare poorly in the years to come. More interesting, however, is the stock Centrist leaders put in identifying themselves as the true conservers. Coexisting within the Cologne orientation alongside the reform impulse, this tradition-mindedness had increasingly separated Trimborn, Marx, and Carl Bachem from Stegerwald and Brauns. Little wonder, then, that the reform opportunity of 1918, such as it was, fell victim not just to Protestant apathy, but to the purposeful reinforcement of Catholic *immobilisme*.

Interdenominationalism, Kulturpolitik, and the National Assembly Elections

Brauns's consultations in Berlin during the last week of November produced a working draft of the Center's new program. After further revision, the program was approved in Frankfurt by the reconstituted Reich Committee of the Center on December 30. By this time, fears of a mass defection had given way to gratification over the buoyant popular groundswell against Hoffmann's anticlerical offensive. As a result, the so-called Frankfurt Guidelines were little more than a traditional recital of Centrist calls for national unity, states' rights, denominational schools, and civil-religious parity. Anticapitalist references in the Berlin draft, and the Cologne draft's call for land reform, were significantly toned down.[21]

The party's name, however, remained undecided. The *KV* reported with satisfaction on January 2, 1919, that "the Reich Committee unanimously resolved to leave the name Center unchanged and even to desist from any supplementary name." Yet, in the elections on January 19 to the constitution-writing Weimar National Assembly, the party appeared on most ballots as "Christian People's Party (Center)." This name was especially prominent in overwhelmingly Protestant Berlin, where the introduction of proportional representation held out the prospect that the Center, for the first time in its history, might win a seat. Even here, however, a small group of Protestants who briefly sought to affiliate themselves with the party called themselves the "League of Christian Democrats, Protestant Branch of the Center."[22] Campaign speakers referred to the party as the Center, and even as a supplementary name, the designation "Christian People's Party" soon fell out of use entirely.

While the *KV* saw no need to alter the character of the Center, it did see Hoffmann's attacks on the temporal role of the churches as a chance to bid for Protestant support. The liberal successor parties, it asserted, were even less inclined than their predecessors to heed Protestant cultural demands. When Protestant counterparts of the Catholic Labor Leagues advised voters to reject parties that opposed denominational schools, the *KV* assured those voters that "the Christian democratic party of the Center" would "decisively" defend the schools and "the rights of all religious communities." Lest the party's local branches again (as in the Zentrumsstreit) indulge in rhetoric that nullified this opening, the paper pointedly reminded them "to allow the Center to appear everywhere as what it really is: a nonconfessional, political, and democratic party on a positive Christian basis."[23]

Meanwhile Haenisch, the Majority Socialist co-Minister of Culture, was becoming concerned that Hoffmann's activities were feeding Rhenish separatism. On December 18, he privately warned the Prussian Ministry of State that attempts to decree the separation of church and state would have "the gravest political consequences." Ten days later, he managed to suspend Hoffmann's month-old decree removing religious instruction from the schools. Building on this success, the Center held a large demonstration in Berlin on New Year's Day. The speakers included two Protestant leaders of the League of Christian Democrats: Johannes Haecker, a minister; and Karl Dunkmann, a theologian. Dunkmann subsequently wrote an article urging Protestants to vote on the national level (but not on the state level) for the Center.[24]

The *KV*'s Berlin bureau now exulted that the demonstration "throws overboard . . . the house of cards of artificial theories that maintained the impossibility of Catholics and Protestants getting together in the Center party." With "uncivilized defenders of civilization" *(kulturloser Kulturkämpfer)* on the loose and "fundamental questions touching on Weltanschauung" at stake, "old . . . prejudices . . . no longer have their former significance." The Cologne school of thought perceived herein its own vindication: "For decades, the constant emphasis upon the fundamentally nonconfessional standpoint of the Center party has served more to prevent harm than to produce positive benefit. But perhaps the time is coming now when one will recognize how uncommonly important it was that one did not burn one's bridges to future developments and opportunities by confessionalizing the Center." A new sympathy for the Center was said to be abroad among voters who had "hitherto stood far removed" from it; they "yearned" for a "strong party" that would defend the ideals of those who "place religion at the focal point of life." Now as before, the Center was that party.[25]

Two days after the Berlin demonstration, Hoffmann and his Independent Socialist colleagues withdrew in disgust from the Prussian government. But the *KV* was not satisfied: Haenisch, it told its readers, was no better; as long as Socialism stayed in power, a "new Kulturkampf" would follow at the first propitious moment. Further attacks over the next two weeks stridently impugned the patriotism of both Socialist parties and lumped them together as the common enemy of the "bourgeois" parties in a clearly two-sided election campaign.[26]

Meanwhile, the paper continued to profile the Center as the most viable Christian obstacle to anticlerical Socialist rule. The Cologne librarian Leo Schwering, who a quarter century later would be instrumental in founding the new CDU in preference to reviving the Center (Chapter 7), now warned against the other non-Socialist parties because they were "new" and their potential was uncertain. In an "irony of history," said Schwering, only Bismarck's old antagonist, the Center, could save his Reich from "sinking . . . irretrievably" into Marxist socialism. The League of Christian Democrats added that now that the Center was a "new Christian People's Party," "politically homeless" Protestants who did not wish their church blamed for "reactionary, pan-German, feudalistic endeavors" should join. The more Protestants joined, the stronger their position in the party would be.[27]

But few Protestants joined. While the Center and BVP, with 19.7 percent of the vote on January 19, improved on the Center's weak showing of 1912 (16.4 percent), the rise was due not to Protestants but to female suffrage. Among men, the Center and BVP drew 16.8 percent. The two parties drew five out of every eight Catholics who voted, but most churchgoing Protestants voted for either the Democrats (DDP 18.5 percent, a success never repeated) or the newly launched instrument of monarcho-conservative intransigence, the German National People's Party (DNVP 10.3 percent).[28]

Centrist leaders nonetheless had reason to feel gratified. The tower of Catholic solidarity had weathered the revolutionary storm intact, with even the Bavarians provisionally joining the Centrist caucus in the National Assembly. As in 1912, the 91-member caucus (including 3 Protestants) was the chamber's second largest. The party had won a seat in Berlin for the first time, and local leaders depicted this success as a turning point in religious politics[29]—though the seat went to a Catholic, Pfeiffer, rather than to the Protestant Haecker. Furthermore, the mutually suspicious Socialist parties had failed to win a majority. The Center thus held a key position in the 421-member chamber. To its right sat 44 German Nationalists (DNVP), 19 former National Liberals in the tardily organized German People's Party (DVP), and 5 others; to its left sat 163 Majority Socialists, 22 Independent Socialists, 75 Democrats, and 2 others. Since the Democrats were unwilling to form a government with the Majority Socialists alone, the parliamentary arithmetic pointed to a revival of the "peace coalition" of 1917 (MSPD, DDP, Center). This, however, left the Center in a quandary: how was one to explain to an electorate imbued with alarm about the perils of socialism that one now contemplated a pact with the devil?

Weltanschauung and the Weimar Coalition

Though governing coalitions between recent campaign rivals are not unusual in multiparty systems, they seemed so to an electorate that had never experienced the transition from election campaign to parliamentary ministry. Indeed, in many parts of Germany, the campaign had seemed bipolar rather than multilateral: due to regional and subcultural differentiation, only one of the non-Socialist parties had really been acceptable to the local non-Socialist voters. Among Catholics in the Rhineland, that party had been the Center, and it had accused the Socialists not just of misguided policies but of treason. The intensity of regional bipolar electioneering made it difficult to sell public opinion on the need to bring rival parties together in parliamentary governments. That task was still more difficult when the parties depicted themselves as bastions of uncompromisable philosophical systems (Weltanschauungen).

As a party of the Christian Weltanschauung, the Center faced two soul-searching issues. Having derived its self-styled status as a "constitution party" *(Verfassungspartei)* from Catholic doctrines of natural law, the party felt morally obligated to facilitate a speedy end to the current extralegal situation. For most Centrist leaders, that meant writing a new republican constitution in collaboration with the Majority Socialists. On the same constitution party basis, however, many Centrists felt profoundly disturbed about forsaking the old order in favor of a regime born of a revolutionary discontinuity in the rule of law. Besides, how could a party dedicated to Christian vigilance collaborate with godless socialists?

To navigate these shoals, the *KV* christened a new variant of the old German dictum of the primacy of foreign policy. Since the Entente would insist on a republican constitution, said the *KV,* law-abiding German citizens were exonerated from moral culpability for accepting the formally illegal regime. Despite its revolutionary origins, therefore, a good Catholic had to accept the Republic and work in the National Assembly in Weimar to render it legal, for this was the only way to restore the condition of legality itself. By contrast, German National calls for a monarchical restoration could be fulfilled only through a new act of moral irresponsibility—a new revolution—culpability for which could not so easily be evaded. Thus, as long as the National Assembly was not "tainted" by "revolutionary ties and obligations" (that is, as long as it was not overseen by the revolutionary worker-soldier councils), the correct moral course was to codify the legal status of the Republic. From the standpoint of Christian vigilance, any other course would yield the field to the Social Democrats. While the *KV* professed the "gravest of reservations" about joining the government, they were not enough to follow the DNVP into "a policy of abstinence and opposition" when the ship of state was in danger of sinking.[30]

The official formation on February 13 of a Socialist-led "Weimar coalition" (MSPD, DDP, Center) spurred further justifications in the Centrist press. According to Cologne trade unionist Johannes Bergmann, the Center, with its large labor contingent, was a better match for the SPD in economic policy than was the DDP, the "party of big capitalism and the stock exchange." Yet Bergmann concentrated not on why the Center should choose to join the coalition, but on why it could not allow the Socialists to bar it from joining: with the Center safely out of the way, all issues, particularly "cultural" ones, could be decided against it. Though this was the most traditional of Centrist concerns, Bergmann insisted that the party was making "a great sacrifice," for its posture would be easier in opposition.[31]

To defend the coalition, Bergmann and others had to credit the SPD with a sacrifice of its own: it had abandoned its longtime "all-or-nothing policy" and agreed to work with bourgeois parties. The *KV* insisted that the SPD, not the Center, had made the programmatic concessions; nothing in the government program, not even cultural policy, violated the Center's principles. The Center's "sacrifice" consisted only in that the coalition obscured the unbridgeable "chasm that separates us fundamentally from Social Democracy." This sacrifice had to be made, for the Center would "contradict all [its] traditions" if it stood idly by while another party ruined the nation. But since this "political marriage of convenience" *(Vernunftehe)* was only a "working partnership [*Arbeitsgemeinschaft*] with limited goals," the "sharply drawn boundary lines" between the parties remained intact.[32]

The *KV*'s sudden effort to downplay policy differences with the SPD left the rank and file to choose between two conclusions: either the Center had indeed made concessions of principle, or the SPD was more flexible than heretofore depicted. Attempts by party leaders to redirect their constituents toward the second conclusion met with only mixed success.[33] These efforts were complicated by three additional developments. In late June, the party decided to remain in the coalition with the Social Democrats after the harsh terms of the Treaty of Versailles caused the DDP temporarily to withdraw. Then came a series of compromises on cultural policy involving all three parties and culminating in the school provisions of the new constitutions in Prussia and the Reich.[34] Dissatisfaction over such issues was a serious matter for a coalition that had been justified to Centrist voters on the bases of foreign and cultural policy. Nor was the task eased when Erzberger, the first Finance Minister to come from the traditional party of federalism, implemented centralistic reforms in the Reich's financial system.

Regarding Versailles, party leaders explained that without a functioning government recognized by the Allies, Germany would have been invaded, divided, and saddled with separate peace treaties. They poignantly added that a party accused throughout its history of opposing a unified national state could not now withdraw from the government and risk the charge that Catholics were responsible for breaking up the Reich. Nor had the party abandoned federalism: Erzberger's reforms, said Trimborn, were simply a financial necessity. He admonished Catholics to stop blaming the coalition for things whose real cause was the lost war.[35]

As for cultural policy, though the DDP (not the SPD) successfully pressed some last-minute demands, the final compromise produced more than anyone could realistically have expected: religious freedom, tolerance of the Jesuits, new provisions for civil parity, continued taxes for funding the churches, church-supervised religious instruction, and legal recognition for denominational schools alongside the state-favored interdenominational schools. At the Rhenish party convention in September 1919, Wilhelm Marx, the head of the Catholic School Organization, noted that "we have now achieved with Democrats and Social Democrats what we never managed to bring about . . . with the Conservatives."[36] Yet the DNVP continued to agitate on the basis of guilt by association that the cultural compromises were a sellout.

Concerned about German National inroads among Catholics, party chairman Trimborn, at the Center's first-ever national convention in January 1920, again addressed the issue that had given the DNVP its opening: the Center's decision to accommodate itself to the demise of the monarchy. Here was where the Center's claim not to have betrayed its principles seemed hardest to maintain. This decision, explained Trimborn, had been taken not because the party suddenly preferred a republic, but because the alternative was civil war. Though monarchism may once have been a "basic [party] plank," patriotism and defense of the Church were higher principles. For that reason, "today we allow declared republicans too in our ranks." Another delegate added that "there exists no ideal" form of government; each party member could decide his preference for himself. Interestingly, no delegate—not even Joseph Wirth, who was later far more militant—thought it necessary to insist that party members ought to be republicans.[37]

Arguments such as these show how traumatic for Centrists the republican transition was, even with the best of will. Yet the fundamental dilemma posed by the coalition arose neither from Kulturpolitik per se nor from the issue of monarchy versus republic—nor indeed from any concrete matter of policy. Rather, it arose from the notion that a shared philosophical starting point (Weltanschauung), not a similar set of policies, was the true standard of political compatibility. This notion had posed few problems as long as the parties had remained in effect political lobbies. Once they became co-responsible partners in governing coalitions, however, they found it much more difficult to maintain that they were being true, as Weltanschauung parties, to their own standards of purity. For Catholics, a constitutional pact with avowed revolutionary atheists and advocates of class struggle did not qualify as the kind of philosophical starting point implied by the word "Weltanschauung." Thus, despite the happy denouement to their cultural fears of the previous fall, Centrists found it difficult to admit that the political values of the coalition partners were convergent.

But convergent they were. On matters as basic as securing minority rights, protecting parliamentary prerogatives, recognizing the international order, and affirming constitutional legality, even conservative Centrists were closer in their views to the revisionist Social Democrats than to the unreconstructed German Nationals. Thus, after a failed right-wing coup—the so-called Kapp Putsch—in March 1920, Carl Bachem, whose family's newspaper had recently complained that the collaboration with left-wing parties had gone too far,[38] produced a coldly reasoned memorandum on why a coalition with the left remained (unfortunately) a necessity.[39] The *Katastrophenpolitik* of the DNVP could hardly appeal to this cautious man whose prime formative experience had been the Kulturkampf. As his friend Trimborn had said earlier, the Center could not "speculate on complete ruin in order to erect the monarchy upon the ruins and then say, 'We always foresaw ruin.'"[40] Yet even at this juncture, Bachem and most Centrists persisted in denying that the coalition partners shared anything more abiding than an accidentally coincident interest in constitutional normalization.

To uphold this denial, old-guard Centrists portrayed the political need for a majority coalition as a consequence of a moral imperative, the need for order, which they derived not from the constitutional principles of a parliamentary state but from the Christian Weltanschauung. Since this moral imperative was said to have no status as a value apart from the Weltanschauung, it was not a value shared by those (the Socialists) whose Weltanschauung was different. Rather, the Christian Weltanschauung led to a practical course that momentarily coincided with what the left, for reasons of its own, was also doing. Since neither that coincidence nor the DNVP's mistaken course derived from the true relationship of values among the parties, the current political alignments reflected an anomalous situation. As the *KV* later put it, the Center's differences with the DNVP were transitory *(zeitbedingt)*, whereas its differences with the Socialists were irreconcilable *(unbedingt)*.[41] By implication, then, even the status of the republican constitution was in the long run just one of several important issues, on most of which the Center was closer to the DNVP. Once the need passed to prioritize that issue, or once the DNVP understood that its course was detrimental to principles it held in common with the Center, the anomalous situation would end and a more natural political alignment would follow.

This method of reasoning was evident in the frequent statements of Centrist spokesmen that the coalition was an *Arbeitsgemeinschaft,* or working relationship, as opposed to a *Gesinnungsgemeinschaft,* or relationship based upon shared conviction. Of course, every political coalition is really a working arrangement; rarely is it constructive to analyze the ultimate metaphysical compatibility of the partners. But the need to make this distinction explicit revealed not a healthy understanding of this point but embarrassment over a coalition that so obviously did not fulfill the desired metaphysical standard. Hence, party leaders routinely stated their unhappiness with the coalition they were defending. Hence too, they based their justifications on Kulturpolitik, depicting the coalition as the best arena for defending the faith against attacks from their own coalition partners. The more committed many Catholics were to the coalition, the more important they deemed it to profile not common ground but differences with the Socialists. These Catholics were particularly sensitive to complaints by Centrist renegades that the coalition was indeed a Gesinnungsgemeinschaft.[42]

The distinction between Arbeitsgemeinschaft and Gesinnungsgemeinschaft purportedly educated voters about the parliamentary ground rules; in reality, it reassured them, in contradiction to those ground rules, that greater gulfs of conviction separated the Center from its coalition partners than from the opposition. But defending the constitution by denying that the form of government was a matter of high principle surely reinforced the perception that both the status of the regime and the party's commitment to it were tentative. Similarly, defending the coalition by denying that its democratic, social, libertarian, and constitutional goals represented shared convictions only reinforced the suspicion that the party's actions were unprincipled. For no matter how the alleged disparity between the Center's conviction and its choice of political associates was justified, what was critical was the appearance of disparity. This argument asserted that the appearance corresponded to reality.[43]

Whereas the arguments of Trimborn and Bachem were indicative of the usual solution to the Center's dilemma about the coalition, at least

one member of the party did defend the coalition as a logical arrangement between historically compatible partners. He was Heinrich
Teipel, a young journalist from Opladen who was soon to make his
name as a protégé of Wirth's and a political editor for *Germania*.
Writing in the wake of the Kapp Putsch, Teipel, though he too used
the term *Arbeitsgemeinschaft*, did precisely what other Centrists did
not: he rejected the notion that discrepant starting points precluded a
confluence in political values.

In Teipel's view, the moral basis for the coalition was not just the
need to maintain order through a parliamentary majority but the common interest of Socialists and Catholics in opposing the militaristic
evolution of Prusso-German Protestantism. Teipel depicted German
Socialism as a natural, though extreme, historical reaction to that evolution, and defended the Peace Resolution as a manifestation of the
Catholic conscience and the peace plans of the pope. Majority Socialists and Catholics shared a belief in human morality; the Socialists'
starting point, dialectical materialism, was irrelevant. (As for Bolshevism, it was but a "Jewish-Asiatic import.") For Teipel, the salient
thing about German Socialism was not its theoretical materialism, but
its practical, value-driven opposition to the materialistic transformation of the social fabric since Bismarckian unification. When one understood socialism in this way and also recalled the social character of
Christian teachings about property, the fears of Centrists who opposed the coalition seemed unfounded.[44]

Like Trimborn and Bachem, Teipel defended the coalition as a consequence of the existing constitution; unlike them, he considered the
content of the constitution, not just the fact of constitutionalism, to be
the issue of principle. Either way, one was defending the status quo.
But the two positions could have very different ramifications.

The same was true of two positions opposing the status quo. The
first was that of the principled monarchists; the second was that of
Stegerwald. The monarchists had two choices: either to join the newly
launched Catholic Committee of the DNVP or, like the now fully autonomous BVP, to secede from the Center while continuing to claim
its heritage. In the Rhineland, a motley collection of integralists,
agrarians, and separatists did the latter. By forming a new party that
claimed to be "return[ing] to the old Center of Mallinckrodt and
Windthorst" and by concluding an alliance with the BVP, the secessionists raised the spectre of a nationwide competition between Catholic parties.[45] If, however, one accepted the Center party line that the

constitution did not represent an abandonment of principle, then the way to alter the status quo was to create the kind of large pro-constitutional alternative to the SPD that the DNVP could never be. In that way, if a coalition still proved necessary, Christian forces might at least outnumber Socialists within it. This was the direction of Stegerwald's thinking.

Interdenominationalism and the Weimar Coalition

In his post-Kapp memorandum of March 1920, Carl Bachem justified the Weimar coalition through a process of elimination: the Center having proven unable to expand, a majority could be formed only through a coalition; a coalition with the right having proven impossible, the coalition had to be with the left.[46] He might just as well have completed the circle: due to the left coalition, the party, in Bachem's view, had little further prospect of interdenominational expansion. Indeed, while interdenominationalism during the trade union controversy had been a Centrist weapon against Social Democratic incursions, interdenominationalism under the Weimar coalition could be a German National weapon against the Center, as the launching of the DNVP's Catholic Committee showed. Moreover, Bachem feared that a Centrist interdenominational initiative now would be little more than a ploy by labor in the ruinous power-jockeying among the party's constituent groups. He likened such a ploy to recent secessionist threats by farmers, academics, and merchants.[47]

The response of old-guard Centrists to the formation of the Catholic Committee was thus to gather the wagons around the tower: they reasserted their party's claim to be the only genuine representative of Catholic interests. Indeed, ever since the last-minute wrangle with the DDP over Kulturpolitik at Weimar and the general display of hostility there by the DNVP, the old guard's Hoffmann-era optimism about appealing to Protestants had completely disappeared. As a result, even sympathetic Protestants had backed away from the party.

Already by May of 1919, the Protestant head of the League of Christian Democrats in Berlin had had enough. Asked to write a pro-paganda leaflet for the Center, Haecker declined to issue further public endorsements until the Center was genuinely transformed. Lacking "every possibility of influence" in the party, he concluded that Protestant distrust of the Center was "not entirely unfounded." Even in overwhelmingly Protestant Berlin, all the top electoral candidacies had gone to Catholics, such as general secretary Max Pfeiffer; apparently, said Haecker, the Center viewed its Protestants only as propaganda tools. An aide to Pfeiffer retorted that the first Berlin mandate in the party's history could not go to a Protestant newcomer and would not have been won had Haecker headed the list.[48] This was tantamount to admitting that neither Protestants nor Catholics would vote for Protestant Centrists.

As usual, Heinrich Brauns disagreed. His speeches at the Rhenish and national conventions of September 1919 and January 1920 showed no trace of the defensive undertone that marked the speeches of his colleagues. Nor did he see any conflict between maintaining the Weimar coalition and recruiting Protestants to the Center. Only an interdenominational, "national, social, and democratic" party, Brauns argued, could complete the work of the Weimar coalition by paralyzing left-wing radicalism and right-wing reaction and giving "flesh and blood" to the new constitution. To prevent "a further skid to radicalism," he said, "the great dividing line" had to be drawn not to the right but to the left of the Majority Socialists. Although the Center therefore had to make concessions, one must "not forget" that the Majority Socialists too had "had to make really colossal sacrifices." Still, "the domestic political chaos" would not end until churchgoing Protestants could join a middle party unified not only by religion but also by "political ideals" and by an economic program that stressed not class conflict but class interdependency. Far from curing "the rising clashes of interest" within the Center, making it "confessional in principle," in defiance of "Windthorstian tradition" and the "warning signals" of the Zentrumsstreit, would lead to breakaways and render the party obsolete. Without a labor branch, said Brauns, no party could lead Germany in the parliamentary age; conversely, no labor movement could prosper with its membership split between government and opposition. The DNVP was no alternative: its "disastrous" obstructionism risked civil war, and its attempts to discredit the Center for participating in the coalition were hurting a party that was preventing a more radical swing to the left.[49]

Of all the parties, said Brauns, only the Center was capable of becoming the Christian, national, social, and democratic party he desired. The transition would require a far more vigorous social policy, "sure mandates" for Protestants, appropriate Protestant representation in the party organization, and an end to the practice of treating Catholic organizations, including the Arbeitervereine and Brauns's own Volksverein, as if they were party organizations. Even the press association, the Augustinusverein, had to choose between being a Catholic organization or a party organization: "The two concepts are not identical. Things are not so clear-cut as they offhandedly are made to appear."[50]

Few other Centrists agreed, however, that a reform agenda was still so urgently necessary. In one sign of party sentiment, Peter Schaeven of Cologne, speaking also for Stegerwald's young protégé Jakob Kaiser, was shouted down at the national convention when he again urged that the party change its name in order to attract Protestants. Indeed, on the same day as Brauns's speech, the *KV* lashed out at non-Catholics almost across the board. Reeling from the BVP's withdrawal from the joint parliamentary caucus and the DNVP's formation of its Catholic Committee, the paper commented that the "malicious rejoicing . . . on all sides" over the Center's misfortunes ought to convince Catholics "that German Catholicism cannot count on real understanding . . . outside the old Center tower. Since August 1914 and especially since November 9, 1918, none of this has changed in the least."[51]

Yet, in continuing to pursue reforms, Brauns was obviously not alone: he was speaking and acting in conjunction with Stegerwald. In his own convention speeches, the union leader attributed Germany's wartime political crisis to the failure of the old regime to understand that social policy was not a political football but a matter of Christian morality and the key to patriotism. No less than the "class struggle from below," the "caste spirit from above," embodied by the landed East Elbians, had to end. The industrialists too had to "silence" those who showed "no understanding for the tasks of the new age" or they risked "the same fate as the officer corps," with "catastrophic effect" for the nation.[52]

In viewing social policy as the key to national integration, Stegerwald aimed not only to raise the standing of social-mindedness in polite society but also to show that Socialists held no monopoly on social conscience. The connection between nationalism and social policy was a continuing theme with him: one was proof of his commitment to the other, since a nation without social justice would perish. Kaiser, a close colleague himself known for his nationalism, amplified the point: the revolution "confirm[ed]" how far Germany still stood from the ideal of an integrated, socially minded national state; "the dissatisfaction of the masses" was "loud and clear" not only "in Social Democratic circles" but among "Christian labor as well." The previous relationship of capital to labor could "no longer be in the new Germany"; "moral ideas" would have to take hold in the economy. The Center was especially obligated to promote a "Christian social policy"; no longer would Christian workers accept being "tolerated merely as a brake against Social Democracy."[53]

Stegerwald too called for an "economy . . . made moral." Although this did not mean Marxist socialization, the twelvefold wartime increase in the public debt (which now almost equaled the gross national product) meant that "our fields, forests, houses, furnishings . . . have been mortgaged to the Reich, that is, virtually socialized." Thus, "the quarrel over socialism" was "no longer a question of principle, but a question of form and expediency." Germany had the world's strongest socialist movement; it would not go away; it therefore had to be accepted.[54]

For this reason, Stegerwald brusquely rejected Joos's complaint at the Rhenish convention that the Center had shown insufficient energy in pursuing its differences over cultural policy with the SPD. "Energy alone," retorted the union leader, "does not produce good politics." Further pressure on the Majority Socialists would only result in an electoral exodus to the Independents, which was "of no advantage to us." There could be "no politics without Social Democracy" in the coming years; reconstruction was otherwise impossible. The Center's only choice was therefore between "a politics-of-show like the German Nationals," or "a working relationship [*Arbeitsgemeinschaft*] with the Majority Social Democrats. That is the only clear lie of things; one must look it squarely in the face."[55]

Though Stegerwald did not want the Center to ignore its differences of Weltanschauung with the SPD, the purpose of Weltanschauung in politics was not to dwell on narrowly defined matters of cultural policy when a tolerable modus vivendi was in place on these issues and fundamental questions awaited on other fronts,[56] but to demarcate the large parties without which there could be no functional political system. For only "strong parties and Weltanschauung parties" would prevail in the real task at hand: rebuilding the state and the economy "according to a uniform plan." The final shape of this plan, Stegerwald implied, would depend on the balance of strength *within* the coalition, and a changing national mood could shift this balance— but only to a socially progressive party with a sufficiently broad base. "The hour has come," he told the national convention, to form groups again around great ideas . . . Even Social Democratic leaders hold that . . . a religious wave will arise out of the misery of our time. Let us take advantage of this hour, let us take part energetically in the spiritual struggles of our age, let us create a good program for ourselves, a true Christian Social popular mood, let us pursue politics according to guiding ideas and along great lines; then the Christian People's Party will become the true founding party of the Reich, the party of the future![57]

Stegerwald's ringing appeal to the image of a "Christian People's Party"—an appeal that was prophetic in envisioning a "founding party" for a German state, though it was twenty-nine years too soon—was applauded by the convention as an affirmation of the Center's Christian and social self-image. But whereas Brauns had stated that only the Center could become the desired Christian social party, Stegerwald gave clear priority to the goal, a larger such political grouping, over the specific instrument of its attainment. If the Center for a third time (after July and November 1918) failed to take up his agenda, then he tacitly reserved the option of promoting a new party. He was not yet ready to go that far—Brauns's vision of transforming the Center constituted the intermediate step—but he could soon get there; and, with the aid of events, he soon would.

4   The Essen Program and Its Aftermath

The pivotal event in the months following the Center's national convention was the Kapp Putsch. Sparked in March 1920 by paramilitary freebooters, the Putsch was aided by the complicity of part of the army (Reichswehr) and by the refusal of the chief of the General Staff to protect the legal government. Thanks to a general strike by the free trade unions, the Republic survived. In the Ruhr, however, radicalized workers persisted in armed disorders, and the government, fearing another revolution, wound up depending on freebooters and on units of the recently so compromised Reichswehr to restore order.

The Kapp fiasco seemed to leave the country with no alternative but to live with the existing political system—though only grudgingly, as the June elections to the first republican Reichstag soon confirmed. Together, the Independent Socialists and German Nationals more than doubled their representation, their combined total surpassing that of the Majority Socialists and Democrats. The DVP, whose behavior during the Putsch had been far from irreproachable, tripled its vote, primarily at the expense of the staunchly republican Democrats. And while the BVP's new allied party in the Rhineland failed to have an impact, the challenge from the German National Catholic Committee made the Center inclined to emphasize Catholic solidarity and to avoid interdenominational rhetoric. Shorn of the BVP, the Center retained only sixty-four seats, none of them held by a Protestant. The Weimar parties, with 78 percent of the seats in the National Assembly, were reduced to 45 percent in the first Reichstag.[1] Never again would they hold a majority.

Yet, for the Centrist old guard, the storm clouds unleashed by Kapp had a silver lining. The new Reich government, a Center-led minority coalition under Konstantin Fehrenbach, included the DVP, the Democrats, and a moderate military man (General Wilhelm Groener). Tolerated by the Majority Socialists, the government could function as if it had a majority without the embarrassment of an explicit association with Social Democracy. Barely three months after Carl Bachem had written that the failure of Centrist interdenominational expansion made a left coalition imperative, his party discovered that even without pursuing Protestants, it need not renew the left coalition. For the first time in the Weimar era, the Center seemed restored to itself, to its own image of its integrity.

No such consolation was given to the Christian trade unions. Having again parted company with the Hirsch-Duncker unions in November 1919, the Christian unions' umbrella organization, the German Labor Federation (DGB), now included only the blue-collar League of Christian Unions, a white-collar federation led by the DNVP-affiliated German National Association of Commercial Employees (DHV), and a public employees' union. With its Protestant membership belonging almost exclusively to the DNVP and the DVP, the DGB, having always held that a general strike would endanger its vision of interclass understanding, refused to sanction a nationwide strike during the Kapp Putsch (though it did sanction some pivotal regional strikes).[2] The strike's success in saving the Republic thus seemed to demonstrate that the free trade unions were more effective than their Christian counterparts not only in the economy but also in politics. Christian union leaders again began to seek a way to end the dissipation of their energy behind feuding parties. Whereas interdenominational partisan reform had become a dangerous proposition to party men like Bachem, union leaders now deemed it an immediate imperative.

"Bring on the Christian National People's Party!"

It was Lorenz Sedlmayr, an official in the Bavarian business office of the unions, who first articulated the renewed sense of urgency about reform. This was fitting: cut off from their working-class brethren in the west and consigned to the agrarian-dominated BVP, Bavarian workers required no act of renunciation to seek a new political home; the Center for them was no more. Psychologically and politically, they were the group most free to pursue an innovative alternative.

In April 1920, writing in a journal edited by Professor Theodor Brauer of the University of Cologne (the Christian unions' leading theoretician), Sedlmayr called for concentrating "all Christian and national-feeling Germans" in a new "Christian" and "democratic" party. "The danger of a dictatorship of the socialist proletariat," he wrote, "will best be overcome . . . if the majority of the German people is reasonable enough not to throw itself into the arms of the real political and social reactionaries out of a feeling of disappointment over bitter isolated experiences with democracy." If capitalistic materialism were "repressed," he claimed, then the theory of class struggle would also lose its appeal. The best way to fight socialism was to infuse the Christian spirit into politics through a democratic party large enough to challenge Socialist governmental preeminence. Neither scruples over the form of government (not a "fundamental question" from a "Christian standpoint") nor confessional disputes (not a matter for parliaments) ought to stand in the way.[3]

Unlike his Bachemite forebears, Sedlmayr left no doubt that he was calling not for the expansion of the Center (he did not even mention it in his article) but for a whole new "Christian National People's Party" (CNVP). Nor did he conceal the fact that his call was inspired by the situation of the unions: "outmaneuvered and set at odds" by the "senseless partisan splintering," their two million voters were, he said, a squandered Christian resource. Reading the spring events as an object lesson in the power of labor, Sedlmayr suggested that the DGB invite politicians from the existing parties to a meeting to launch the new party. Yet Sedlmayer ruled out a party "based one-sidedly upon class." Though inspired by the "Christian solidarism" *(Solidarismus)* of the unions, the CNVP was to be not a new labor party but a catchall party.

Though Stegerwald must surely have had a hand in Sedlmayr's initiative, he knew better than to be seen during a difficult election campaign driving nails into the Center's coffin. As a trade union boss, he was less interested in radical gestures than in pragmatic results. These he would not win by relentlessly defying the powers that be, but by establishing himself as their bargaining partner while keeping the threat of bolder action in reserve. True to this pattern, he had dropped plans in 1918 to found a new party when so requested by Cologne. Finding now that even some labor circles were dubious of Sedlmayr's initiative (on April 10, Joos's *WAZ* called it "unthinkable"),[4] Stegerwald simply let the trial balloon float. On the campaign trail, he blasted the reactionary Putsch, called for a Christian "middle way between socialization and high capitalistic industry," and, like

Sedlmayr, denied that he was "foolish enough" to seek a "third labor party." Unlike Sedlmayr, however, he did not go beyond his earlier call for strengthening the Center into a "Christian bloc party" that could lead the nation from "formal" democracy to "true Christian Democracy."[5]

Although the formation in June of the minority government eased Stegerwald's fear that prolonged cooperation between the Center and the SPD might undermine the Christian labor movement, the middle coalition was a weak substitute for the large Christian party Stegerwald wanted. Encompassing barely a third of the chamber, the coalition seemed hardly more than a stopgap. Moreover, since the DGB's largest Protestant contingent (the German Nationals) remained outside the government, the unions' fundamental problem still remained. Besides, the coalition consisted of three distinct parties, two of which came from strong anticlerical traditions. Since each of the three had to service a different balance of internal forces than would have been the case for one large party, individual constituencies of special significance to one of the three had disproportionate influence within the whole coalition.

This last point was particularly true of the powerful industrialists in the DVP. Although Stegerwald was anxious to implicate them in republican governmental responsibility, he was well aware that they would try to exploit the governmental absence of the Social Democrats to curb organized labor. During the coalitional negotiations, industrial circles in the DVP infuriated Brauns and Stegerwald by attempting to remove the prolabor ministers Joseph Wirth and Johannes Giesberts.[6] Soon thereafter, Protestant union leaders stepped up their own complaints that the DVP was abetting the management-inspired, malleable "yellow unions." In October, several DGB leaders left the DVP in protest.[7]

Anticipating the last development, Stegerwald's staff produced an analysis in September of the political situation of the Christian unions. This eight-page memorandum was soon to be the starting point for the draft of Stegerwald's November address to the congress of the unions in Essen. With Germany ravaged by "plutocra[tic]" elements and passing slowly through a "valley of misery," the memorandum asserted, working-class interests were no longer separable from general national ones. Accordingly, the task of the union movement was not just to improve working conditions but to lead German reconstruction. Social Democracy had shown itself to be inadequate to this task: after fifty years of rejecting the old state, the SPD had now declined to accept governmental responsibility. Hence, leadership must pass to Christian labor.[8]

But Christian labor, the memorandum continued, lacked an appropriate political vehicle. Forced by the outmoded party system to sit divided in parliament, yet together with "yellows" and other reactionaries, Christian labor representatives were forfeiting the opportunity to convert Socialists. Although "no law of nature" required workers to be Marxist and anti-Christian, only an interdenominational and socially minded "people's party" *("not a purely labor party")* could supersede the SPD as the leading party of government. By exorcising "the poison of materialism," such a party would restore the spirit of sacrifice needed for recovery. The time was said to be ripe, for the republican system was ending the popular tendency to identify the churches with reaction and injustice.

Although the Center "in its present form" was judged "out of the question" for attracting Protestants, its social diversity rendered it the natural "point of departure" for the new party, just as it had been for the new coalition. This meant expanding and democratizing its organization: workers should get full representation, and "a Protestant Centrist press" should be created "alongside the Catholic." Under Christian labor "leadership," the party should be molded such that "all truly German, Christian, democratic and socially minded elements can be active and can feel at home in it."

The September memorandum called not for a new founding, but for seizing and transforming the apparatus of the existing party. To be sure, interdenominationalism would no longer mean, as it had meant to Julius Bachem, that the Center would "remain" what it always "was and is"; instead, as the leading Bachemites had always denied, the Center was to be put on "an entirely new road."[9] Apparently, there was to be a massive power play within the Center. This power play, which was to succeed in some unspecified way, was supposed to attract Christian and social elements from all the other parties, including the SPD—all without tearing apart the Center's existing constituency.

Anxious to avoid the lack of coordination among Christian labor that had hindered his initiatives in November 1918, Stegerwald now briefed Giesberts and other leading trade unionists and KAV secretaries.[10] Then, at a meeting on October 19 to constitute the party caucus for the fall session of the Reichstag, Stegerwald moved to cajole Center party leaders before going public.

From "Erzberger Problem" to "Stegerwald-Brauns Problem"

Stegerwald's remarks to the party caucus came during its discussion of an embarrassing affair involving Matthias Erzberger. The previous winter, a German National deputy, Karl Helfferich, had goaded Erzberger into filing a libel suit by accusing him (apparently unjustly) of massive personal financial wrongdoing. When the court failed to clear Erzberger of some of Helfferich's accusations, Erzberger had to resign as Finance Minister.[11] Though Erzberger's appeal was still pending in October, some party leaders wanted him to give up his mandate and his seat on the party's Executive Board. Revered by Catholic democrats in the southwest but loathed by conservatives and Bavarian federalists, Erzberger personified the tensions among Catholics that had led to the BVP and the German National Catholic Committee; as the main figure in the Hottentot and July (1917) crises and as the signer of the armistice, he was, for many Protestants, the embodiment of the Catholic Reichsfeind. Thus, when Erzberger's defenders argued that he was being smeared and that dropping him would drive the SPD into opposition without leading either to Centrist-Bavarian reunification or to German National support for the government, Stegerwald coldly retorted: "We need a great political transformation . . . a new party of reconstruction . . . on the broadest foundation. The Christian-national labor movement is inclined to take part . . . the moment is favorable. [But] Herr Erzberger makes Protestants see red. Pitted against the person of Erzberger, therefore, stands a patriotic necessity; Herr Erzberger must make allowance for this." That Socialist parties should "lastingly" lead the country when they had only two-fifths of the vote was, said Stegerwald, "an impossible state of affairs." Furthermore, since socialization would jeopardize production and prevent reconstruction, Catholics and Protestants had to form a party with a broad enough base to deny the Socialists that leadership role. Only if Erzberger were out of the way could such a party be established.[12]

Stegerwald opposed Erzberger because the embattled deputy was an obstacle not to cooperation with the DNVP but to splitting it. Giesberts immediately complained, however, that the trade unionists and KAV secretaries "would not have gone along" with Stegerwald's plans had they known that dropping Erzberger was the prerequisite. Erzberger himself warned of a Centrist split should the party act "too sharply" against him. He scolded the deputies that the Center would never have buckled before such an obviously partisan verdict during the Kulturkampf. Standing up for Erzberger, he was saying, was equivalent to standing up for the most cherished traditions of the Center itself.[13]

Finessing Stegerwald's invocation against him of a larger cause, Erzberger said that the way to produce a larger party was not to bid for Protestant workers but "to win back . . . the 4 million . . . Catholic workers" whose exodus to left-wing parties Stegerwald's movement had failed to prevent. Since the Center had garnered 3.8 million votes in the last election, Erzberger was contending that the party could double its vote. The key was to orient the party more to the left, and the man most identified with this course was Erzberger himself.

In reply, Brauns, now Labor Minister, asserted that Erzberger stood in the way of a relationship not only with the Protestant right but *"both toward the right and toward the left."* For a transformation of the Center would result in an "influx . . . from the Social Democratic camp as well." As Stegerwald put it, the road to winning back Catholic workers did not run only through the existing party; indeed, success was possible only if the goal were pursued in "not too narrowly confessional" a way. "Many groups" outside the Center, said Brauns, including even in the SPD, would welcome its interdenominational expansion; "constructive elements are not found only in the Catholic camp." "Only a large new movement" could be effective; "personal interests" would have to stand aside "until the great transformation has been completed."[14]

The next day, following his usual maxim that "counter-attack is the best defense,"[15] Erzberger developed his alternative to the plans of Brauns and Stegerwald. Saying that "Christian solidarism"—the same phrase Sedlmayr had invoked—had "hitherto been a phrase without content," he proposed that it should mean "an organized economy" based upon cooperatives involving producers, consumers, employers, and employees. Rejecting traditional socialism, Erzberger nonetheless insisted that the age of laissez faire was over; only an "organized economy" could raise production high enough for Germany "to live and to avoid [Allied] financial control." As part of his program, Erzberger called for an obligatory "year of national economic service," complete with barracks living, to replace the universal military service banned by the Treaty of Versailles. Only such service, he said, could increase production and save the economy; it would also have moral value as civic education for youth. Such a plan, however, could only be carried out "in socialized factories."[16]

Erzberger's plan, which he was not to flesh out until the following spring,[17] owed its origins to two streams of political thinking. One was that of the Jesuit and self-styled Christian socialist Heinrich Pesch, a onetime student of the academic socialist Gustav Schmoller. Pesch had soiled his name in union circles by opposing interdenominationalism during the trade union controversy. The other stream was that of the maverick Social Democrat and former Minister of Economics, Rudolf Wissell. At a Social Democratic party congress just days before the Center's caucus, Wissell attempted to revive a plan by his associate, Wichard von Moellendorff, to organize the economy as a corporatist collaboration of producers, consumers, workers, and the state. Erzberger's proposals thus did not come out of nowhere. Still, it was characteristic of him to respond to attacks by launching into sensational disquisitions on policies he might not have fully thought out.[18]

Like Brauns earlier (Chapter 3), Erzberger asserted that only "a clear economic program" (not Kulturpolitik) could create "a broad basis for the Center party"; the party that boldly mastered the country's economic difficulties would be the party of the future.[19] But Erzberger feared that an interdenominational initiative, far from drawing Protestants into a state-supportive role, would only alienate more Catholic workers by increasing the pressure on the party to adopt positions that Catholic workers opposed. What was needed was not an *organizational* initiative directed toward right-leaning Protestants who had never shown sympathy for the Center party, but a *policy* initiative directed unambiguously toward the departing left-wing Catholics. Protestants, in the old language of the Zentrumsstreit, were welcome; but recruiting them could not be a priority or even a desideratum, especially on the basis of an anti-Socialist gesture. Thus, whereas the arguments of Stegerwald and Brauns displayed a certain continuity with the prewar Bachemite argument, Erzberger's contrary stance, while it owed something to Pesch, owed nothing to Savigny. What Erzberger wanted the Center to do was to win back Catholic workers by aligning itself with that same Social Democratic party from which the workers were being wooed and that the original opponents of interdenominational unions had considered an enemy.

Indeed, for all their differences, Erzberger and Brauns—the prime movers of the Center's regeneration in the dark days of November 1918—remained in one respect birds of a feather. Keenly aware of the need to win back Catholic workers, both invoked the vocabulary of social Catholicism, corporatism, and the primacy of economic policy to advocate soaring measures with major implications for the entire political system. Though their conceptions of how to revitalize the party were different, they shared a similar understanding of the scale of the problem. Much like Wissell, whose views were stormily attacked in the SPD, Erzberger and Brauns—and Stegerwald—were problematic figures because they were prophets of innovation among a group of party leaders with an instinctive aversion to boldness.

Thus, in addition to the "Erzberger problem," the caucus now had what the venerable Franz Hitze, esteemed by Stegerwald as the godfather of the social legislation of the 1880s, quickly dubbed the "Stegerwald-Brauns problem." Ten days later, on the eve of the meeting of the party's Reich Committee, a compromise was reached on the original "problem": Erzberger agreed to refrain indefinitely, perhaps as long as a year, from parliamentary activity. A move to expel him thus was headed off. Still fearing a split, party chairman Trimborn then ruthlessly squelched an attempt within the Reich Committee to organize a gathering of those who wanted to hear the proposals Erzberger had unveiled before the caucus. This left the Committee free to return to the party's second "problem." On October 31, the Committee gave center stage to the proposal of Brauns and Stegerwald.[20]

"We Have to Be Ready"

It was Brauns who introduced the subject. Concerned that the SPD was about to establish political hegemony by reuniting with the right wing of the Independents, Brauns worried that a Centrist coalition with an expanded SPD would put the party at risk. (By comparison, a coalition with the DNVP was simply out of the question.) The Center, he said, must "change in form" into a strong "new party of the middle" alongside of which would remain "but one right and one left opposition." To be an effective "counterweight against Socialism," this "new" party would need clear social, economic, and cultural programs; it would have to take a clear stand in support of the Republic; and it would have to be interdenominational.[21]

Since only the Center was in a position to transform itself into the desired new party, it alone, Brauns implied, would retain its entire constituency therein, thus assuring the place of Catholic interests among the new party's concerns. Yet, although it was not to be a labor party, "the impulse" for the new party had to come from the "employees and workers who already possess interconfessional organizations." If the DGB were to "come to us with new suggestions," Brauns hinted, "we have to be ready."

With the tie broken between the Brauns-Stegerwald initiative and Erzberger's fate, Giesberts declared that he "agreed completely" with Brauns. Impelling Giesberts, however, was the prospect not so much of a Socialist fusion as of a liberal one (DDP plus DVP). In the face of these blocks and a "very strong" DNVP, "the Center party must watch out that it is not ground up between right and left."[22]

Believing that political and economic unrest had peaked, Giesberts saw Brauns's proposal as one element in "a new foundation for practical politics." In contrast, Stegerwald, echoing the September memorandum, argued for "a party transformation" not because things were looking up, but because only such a step could ease Germany's passage through the coming "valley of misery." (Indeed, "with the impending misery in store for us, even the Social Democratic masses will learn to pray.") According to Stegerwald, only serendipity and Adolf Hoffmann had saved the Center and prevented a Socialist absolute majority in 1918–1919; since then, the non-Socialist parties had remained "too weak" to lead a parliamentary government. That there still existed four such parties was "an absurdity"; only by tapping the full potential of the Christian labor movement could Socialist preeminence be ended.[23]

Vouching for the willingness of the Protestant members of his movement to join a "recast . . . Christian middle party" upon which "a government could lastingly rely," Stegerwald announced that "all the preparations have already been made" to unveil such a program at the trade union congress in Essen. In effect, he was telling his party that it could either back his call for a "recast" party or it could stand aside as he proclaimed his program anyway.

Joseph Wirth, Erzberger's forty-year-old heir apparent as leader of the Center's left wing, was the first to react when Stegerwald had finished. As different as the passionate, rhetorically gifted mathematics instructor from Baden was from the self-made, streetwise trade union boss, both were mercurial figures whose insecurity about being accepted by their political peers coexisted with a supreme confidence in their own soaring visions and a tendency to deride those of others. Thus, Wirth was as sure that Stegerwald's plan would spell ruin as Stegerwald was that it was the only proper course.

At a moment when the Center possessed "authoritative influence" in the government (it held the chancellorship and four ministries) and was serving as "savior of the Reich," Wirth deemed the thought of "a new party" to be "downright grotesque." New parties, he scoffed, had never been spawned by mere reflection. Moreover, "the confessional fissure is not yet to be bridged": far from showing the idealism needed to found a new party, many Protestants were in a materialistic and reactionary mood. While Wirth agreed that Germany faced "unimaginable difficulties" in the coming months, he concluded not that one must reform the party system while there was still time but that one must buy time for later action. In the short run, social conflict would only increase, even within the Catholic camp: the proletarianization of the middle classes due to hyperinflation was "worse than socialism." "All our effort," therefore, should be directed toward "salvaging" the Center party "as it is" until 1921, by which point things might perhaps have improved.[24]

What Wirth rejected as "grotesque" was not an eventual reform of the party system but the nature and the timing of this particular reform.[25] This view, however, momentarily aligned his left-oriented faction with old guard elements whose priority was Kulturpolitik and to whom all talk of reform was anathema. To their warnings that expansion would complicate the schools question, breathe life into the integralists, and disorient the clergy, the clergyman Brauns retorted that failure to take the initiative would result in others doing so, to the detriment of Catholic interests. "The confessional fissure is not yet bridged, that is true, but something must be done," he asserted; "Catholicism ought to be the leaven and must not withdraw into its shell." The gap between Catholics and others, said Brauns, had narrowed; the liberalism of the DVP was not the liberalism of the Kulturkampf. Brauns asserted that he was not asking the Center to give itself up; he even added, in true Bachemite fashion, that "nothing new" was being created. Yet he insisted that "the party is not an unchangeable construct." "It is the tragedy of the situation that one must govern with the Socialists"; it was therefore necessary to find a way "that we maintain the absolute upper hand."[26]

Trimborn then summarized what he deemed to be the results of the discussion: to "expand [its] base" and attract a following "from other circles," the party would adopt a "new program" based on the old, but with a clear economic conception and a strong social component. "On no account," however, could the trade unions be "put in the foreground. Things must not result in a labor party." Moreover, "The name Center must . . . be retained," lest the integralists "seize it and . . . carry on as the old, genuine Center."[27]

While both Brauns and Stegerwald had indeed eschewed a labor party, they had hardly eschewed a new name, or a role "in the foreground" for the unions. Trimborn's remarks thus came close to being a rebuff by the chairman of the party. Where Brauns and Stegerwald had been disconcertingly ambiguous as to whether they were calling for a whole new party, Trimborn imposed precision. A commission was formed to outline a new program specifically for the Center; Stegerwald was made a member of the commission.

The program commission offered the appearance of reform where little or none was intended—a standard defensive ploy. Nevertheless, its formation did not derail Stegerwald's plans.[28] His aim, after all, was not so much to convince party leaders to go along with him as to incite a popular groundswell that would force them to go along. Were such a groundswell to materialize, a program commission on which he sat might prove useful to him in negotiating with others interested in a reform project. Indeed, it was a tool in line with the organizational recommendations of the September memorandum. Stegerwald's next task, then, was to raise the necessary groundswell.

The Essen Speech

Stegerwald's speech to the trade union delegates who assembled in Essen on November 21 was the culmination of all the themes he had been developing since the spring. Germany's crisis, he said, was part of a broader crisis of capitalism. Because mankind's moral development had lagged behind the development of science and technology, a century of economic change had led not to social progress but to social dislocation, exploitation, the breakdown of religious and community ties, war, and materialistic "false prophets" (the Marxists) promising instantaneous relief. The only way to something better was to transplant the Christian spirit to public life. Contrary to the teachings of the French Enlightenment, a state was not a mere aggregate of individuals, but a "community with a common destiny" and a common cultural heritage. Defying Germany's Christian cultural heritage, the

Kaiserreich had failed to respond to the legitimate aspirations of the socially disadvantaged. Nor was Weimar's "formal democracy" the final answer, for its "French centralism" was insufficiently grounded in Germany's native democratic tradition. A truly "Christian state" would check both the hegemony of regressive agrarian elites and the tyranny of materialistic demagogues, be they "plutocrats" or radical socialists. Only then would social harmony and progress be assured.[29]

In a parliamentary age, said Stegerwald, the only way to achieve the social Christian state was through a new democratic party. The function of the party would be twofold: to rally conservatives to the idea of a reformed, socially progressive, corporatist democracy; and to rally workers to the idea of socially minded class collaboration based on the notion of national community. "The national idea," said Stegerwald, "must not be the monopoly of certain groups"; only if "borne by the workers" could it thrive.[30]

Condemning the antidemocratic right's attacks on the "party state" allegedly imported from the West, Stegerwald asserted that the problem was not parties per se, but the anachronistic structure of the German party system. Designed under "entirely different circumstances" from the present situation, this party system was inappropriate to parliamentary government. With so many small parties, petty disputes became grounds to sever coalitional alignments; the "shifting sand" of weak and rapidly fluctuating coalitions then made a steady course impossible. The problem had only worsened when the Social Democrats left the government: "at any moment a parliamentary situation can now arise that puts into question everything accomplished thus far [and] that forces us to start over again from the bottom with a new plan." One could not make policy when the larger parties left the government whenever difficulties loomed so that they could avoid blame as a prelude to reentering the government. Nor was the solution an "English two-party system," which did not match German political realities.[31]

To achieve stable parliamentary government in a multiparty setting, Stegerwald called for a "large" and "moderate party" with sufficient coherence and numerical strength to be the long-term anchor of government. Whereas the requisite cohesiveness was impossible for collections of economic interest–oriented parties, it was fully possible for a party with "a deep and broad basis in the [Christian] conviction of the voters." None of the existing parties fit the bill: the non-Socialist ones were "agglomeration[s] of the most varied outlooks, especially regarding social issues"; the "class parties of the left" were mired in their own "perpetual battle" over "who represents the gospel of the only true Marxist socialism." Although the prewar policy of pushing the SPD into "fundamental opposition to the state" had been "completely devoid of statesmanship," German reconstruction could not be led by a party still struggling to overcome its "antistate" attitude. The internal victory of the "positive forces inside Majority Social Democracy" was "still far off; we cannot wait that long. In the meantime Germany would long since have been finished."[32]

By "pool[ing] the patriotic, Christian, popular, and truly social-thinking circles from all strata of the population," said Stegerwald, a "large moderate party" with "an outspokenly democratic and social stamp" would win converts from the SPD, with Christianity providing the moral counter to the lure of socialism. Since conservatives would have to recognize that without the workers they were lost, socially-minded conservatives would also join. The Christian unions proved that Protestants and Catholics could cooperate within one socially-minded organization. Broadening this cooperation was now a political necessity, for it would be highly "dangerous . . . if the dividing line between government and opposition constantly lies between" the confessions.[33]

Thus did Stegerwald outline his vision of a Christian and democratic party. Yet, aside from calling for the founding of a daily newspaper, a labor bank, and a "parliamentary action committee," he was silent as to how his vision ought to be realized. Like Sedlmayr the previous April, but unlike the September memorandum, Stegerwald did not mention the Center; yet neither did he actually proclaim a new party. For as the October meetings had made clear, his strategy was not to challenge the Center directly, but to cajole it. It would take an irresistible ground swell to extract the Center's sanction for his enterprise. It remained to be seen whether such a ground swell would be forthcoming.

The Response of the Centrist Old Guard

How the *KV* would comment on Stegerwald's speech was crucial to the fate of his initiative. After all, many Catholics took their political cues from the *KV,* which had initiated the original discussion about getting out of the tower. The *KV,* however, was the voice of the western party hierarchy: although the Bachem family had recently sold the paper, the new owners were a consortium under Hugo Mönnig, Trimborn's aide and eventual successor as Rhenish party chairman. The Cologne leaders were motivated by one supreme concern: maintaining the unity of the existing party under their authority. Justly fearing that the result of Stegerwald's initiative might be not a larger political union but further splintering, Cologne hoped to head off Stegerwald's desired ground swell and yet forestall any Christian labor backlash.

Under Karl Hoeber's tried and steady editorial hand, the *KV* therefore distinguished painstakingly between ends and means. It seized upon Stegerwald's statement that the desired Christian gathering point *(Sammlung)* could not be achieved overnight, but would require "gradual preparation"—a statement that seemed to preclude an imminent founding of a new party. While a strong Christian-national counterweight to socialism was "certain of our complete approval and support," this goal was but the long-standing ideal of the existing Center party; it could not be achieved without or against the existing party. The Center was based on "the same Christian, national, democratic, and social convictions" that Stegerwald had invoked. Indeed, the aspirations voiced at Essen were "nothing new"; since they had "never yet led to the goal" because the confessional chasm had always proved "unbridgeable," one "understandabl[y] . . . doubts" whether a new effort could succeed this time, "even with the help of such a strong spearheading group as the Christian labor movement." The *KV* insisted that it was a longtime friend of Christian labor and that its fidelity had been proven "in hard struggles" (the old trade union controversy). No one could take it as a sign of ill will, therefore, if those who wished to plot a new course were first expected to prove that it was navigable and would lead to the desired goal.[34]

In subsequent issues, the *KV* cited the reservations of other papers to drive home its own skepticism. Reporting that the organs of other parties were suspicious, the *KV* seemed less distressed by their lack of trust than by their behaving as though they were about to be "merry onlooker[s] at a new dispute *(Streit)* within the Center."[35] Meanwhile, with even Cologne now repeating *Germania's* prewar claim that Protestant refusal to join the Center was alone responsible for the confessional partisan division, Julius Bachem's dictum that it was not enough to reproach others for this division was a dead letter.

With some justification (as shown by the September memorandum), many Centrists suspected that Stegerwald's aim was political aggrandizement at the expense of the authority structure of the existing party. This suspicion was hardly lessened by the parallel uncertainty over whether Stegerwald was advocating the transferral of loyalties from other parties to the Center, or dissolution in favor of a whole new party. Rejecting what it saw as a bid for worker control of the Center, the respected *Dortmunder Tremonia* lectured the unions that "it would be their sure death" if they were to leave. "That, in a few words, is our standpoint towards the speech of Herr Stegerwald, toward which we stand essentially in sympathy." Other Catholic papers noted that since Stegerwald's desired party already existed and needed only to be expanded, he surely was not thinking of creating a new one. Perhaps, as in 1918, he just wanted to add "Christian People's Party" to the name; anything further would tear the party apart. The principal Catholic paper in Wirth's home region (Baden) stated that leaders could not simply ordain new parties from above, but "must bring together what naturally belongs together"; whether that was what was happening remained to be seen.[36]

As for the non-Catholic press, its reaction was often not nearly as negative as the *KV* depicted it. If the *KV* was not pleased by other papers' reactions, it was because those papers were cool not to the idea of a large new party but to the idea of expanding the Center. To be sure, right-wing presses interpreted the speech in ways favorable to them before claiming to agree with it, but then so did the Center. Predictably, each side's claim increased the other's distrust.

Some rightist papers did use the speech to taunt the Center: the *Kreuzzeitung* claimed that the speech constituted Stegerwald's recognition that Catholic protection no longer required such a party. But while liberal organs naturally wanted to know the concrete implications of Stegerwald's Christian emphasis, at least two were mildly intrigued. The right-liberal *Kölnische Zeitung (KZ)* mentioned the suspicion that Stegerwald was only promoting the expansion of his own party, but added that he would probably indignantly deny this, and asked for further clarification. The more left-leaning *Frankfurter Zeitung (FZ)* was convinced that other papers had misunderstood the speech: the aim was neither to seize nor to expand the Center but to create "a new party." (In Stegerwald's papers, the phrase "new party" is underlined in pencil.) Neither a labor party nor the expansion of the Center, the *FZ* stated, would redress the lack of steadiness in German politics that was the main theme of the speech; any claim to the contrary, the paper shrewdly noted, was an attempt by Centrist circles who "knew about Stegerwald's idea [in advance] . . . to turn it around." The right's portrayal of the idea as a right-wing concentration *(Sammlung)* against Social Democracy was also a distortion. The *FZ* concluded that it was not yet so jaded by partisanship as to turn away in fright from proposals like Stegerwald's. His attempt to create something new, though as yet just an idea, answered a great need and was of historic significance.[37]

Speaking officially for the Center, *Germania* disclosed the content of the meeting of October 31 and insisted that no dissolution or new founding was intended by anybody. But Giesberts soon seemed to belie these words. The onetime champion of having Christian union representatives in several parties now told an audience of Christian workers that "the luxury" of a splintered party system was no longer permissible. If cooperation among diverse elements was possible inside the DGB, it must also be possible in partisan politics. The goal would be achieved with the existing parties rather than against them; workers did not want to found their own party. But if too many difficulties were put in their way, they must not shrink even from this. "You are the pioneers of a new age. Go forth and spread the word to the masses. Each individual must accomplish a bit of missionary work."[38]

In the face of such messianic remarks from the workers' representative in whom it long had had the most trust, the Centrist old guard was relieved to discover a potent ally elsewhere in the ranks of labor. Catholic workers, stated Joos's *Westdeutsche Arbeiter-Zeitung,* do not forget "what the Center was for them and today still is"; without it, the Christian labor movement would never have flowered. The *WAZ* praised Stegerwald, then called for clarity on one thing: the union leader did not want to found a new labor party, nor indeed "any new party at all," but "to gather together, to combine." Whether this could be done was questionable, for a growing antilabor mood had become visible among the other classes, without whom the result would be a purely labor party. Joos's paper agreed with the *KV:* Stegerwald's goal "finds unanimous applause," but the means to the goal would remain a "subject for discussion," not "action," "for a long time to come."[39]

Annoyed that other parties welcomed Stegerwald's idea only in order to speculate on the disintegration of the Center, the *KV* asserted that "construction plans" ought "not to begin with wishes for destruction." This position was symptomatic of the major obstacle to

Stegerwald's plan: the party system, though not conducive to stable parliamentary relations, was itself stable. Apart from name changes and regional idiosyncrasies, it had survived both the revolution and the Kapp Putsch. Under the circumstances, the *KV* was correct to think that the most likely effect of proclaiming a new party would be "to increase the number of parties by one." Concluding on December 7 that it preferred "less radical methods" even if they greatly slowed progress toward the goal,[40] the *KV* returned the ball to Stegerwald's court. It would be up to him now to force the issue.

Action or Discussion?

Like the party press, Stegerwald had been proceeding with striking circumspection. The man who had been careful enough to inform his party colleagues of his plans in advance now again hedged his bet: by letting the ambiguity linger over whether he was calling for expansion or for an entirely new party, he avoided a flood of outright condemnation from his former allies in the western press. He thus allowed time for a popular ground swell to develop without opening himself to the charge of being a renegade.

But a ground swell did not develop. Thus, when Stegerwald appeared in mid-December before the convention of the Prussian Center party, he did so without benefit of a backdrop of popular agitation for his initiative. Moreover, the occasion was the party's fiftieth anniversary, spawning a celebratory atmosphere highly inauspicious for a reformer. Opening the convention, Prussian party chairman Felix Porsch employed exactly the sort of double-talk that Stegerwald could no longer abide: he characterized the Center as the "political representation" of "the loyal Catholic people," yet still claimed that it did "not want to limit itself to Catholic deputies." Attributing the uncomfortable Weimar coalition in Prussia to a party system ill suited to parliamentary government, he concluded not that the party system had to be reformed, but instead, invoking Windthorst, asked everyone to understand the situation and "never forsake" the Center.[41]

As the *Frankfurter Zeitung* had made clear, the acid test of Stegerwald's seriousness would be his willingness to state that what he wanted was not expansion of the Center but a whole new party. He did not pass the test. To be sure, he denied that any existing party matched his formula of "German, Christian, democratic, and social." Also wrong were those who claimed he wanted "nothing new, but only what Julius Bachem had striven for earlier."[42] If every party stuck obstinately to its old name and tradition, Stegerwald clairvoyantly warned, then the party system, rather than being overhauled responsibly from within, would be overturned from without. While he agreed that Protestant Prussia had been historically heavy-handed in assimilating its Catholic acquisitions, he "left the question open" as to whether Catholics had always employed the appropriate political response. He thus put into question the entire development of a separate Catholic "political representation." Moreover, the "new . . . state cannot succeed . . . with the party system of today"; "the Fatherland must be saved, even if the party should go to ruins." Yet he added that Essen did not mean that the Center should simply dissolve and its members join parties of the left or right; indeed, he declared it a matter of equanimity whether the goal were pursued through expansion or through a new party.[43]

Two weeks later, in preparation for elections the following February in Prussia, Stegerwald agreed to endorse the electoral appeal of the Centrist workers' political committee if it contained a passage favoring the Essen program. The appeal was published on December 30 and signed by both Stegerwald and Joos: "We stand for our Center party, from which we confidently expect that it . . . will unselfishly help with the great reform of the entire political party system."[44] In effect, Stegerwald won the rhetorical battle here while Joos won the substantive one. In deciding that it was unrealistic to launch a new party before the elections, Stegerwald conceded Joos's earlier assertion that Essen was as yet but a subject for discussion rather than action.

The discussion, however, continued, even during the campaign. On January 2, Trimborn declined to commit his party to the Essen agenda until Stegerwald clarified whether he wanted dissolution of the existing parties or "merely . . . a working association" *(Arbeitsgemeinschaft)*. A well-planned, long-term association of the current partners in the Reich (DDP, Center, DVP) would be welcome, but the Center would certainly not dissolve: "We do not contemplate celebrating our jubilee by committing suicide!" Rather, "we want to remain what we were: a Christian-national people's party encompassing all classes." Conceding that some criticism of the party system was "all too justified," Trimborn counseled the restless to "wait quietly for further developments."[45]

Unwilling to "wait quietly," Stegerwald's colleague Jakob Kaiser told the Rhenish party convention ten days later that the Center, whatever its past services, now had to show the maturity to "grow beyond itself." Parties, he reminded his listeners, "are means to an end . . . and must never be ends in themselves." Kaiser called on Trimborn to state unequivocally whether the German bourgeoisie was prepared to align itself politically with workers who rejected class struggle.[46] Kaiser thus linked the continuation of Christian labor's class collaboration with the Center's position on interdenominational reform.

But Trimborn smoothly brushed aside Kaiser's challenge. The party, he stated, would "certainly make no difficulties about cooperating in the reform of the German party system." Indeed, the executive boards or caucuses of the three governmental parties could begin by meeting regularly together. What absolutely must not happen, however, is that the Center dissolve while the other parties remain. As to whether the bourgeoisie wanted to work with labor, Trimborn was unconditionally affirmative, for "we remain the old Center party, which encompasses all strata."[47]

Trimborn's position was a prudent and realistic one. It was also the kiss of death for Stegerwald's reform plans. Whereas Kaiser had stated that Christian labor could no longer be satisfied with just "the old party," Trimborn used the alleged constancy of its "Christian-national" past as a recommendation. The function of such rhetoric was immediately clear in the *KV*'s coverage: "Kaiser . . . demanded an all-embracing transformation of partisan political life to the right of Social Democracy and asked the leadership of the party in a very concrete form whether it was prepared to cooperate in this transformation. Snappily, clearly, and decisively came the answer from Trimborn, which culminated in a crisp and pointed 'Yes,' with the explicit comment that the Center party already in times past had been prepared to cooperate in this."[48] In other words, Trimborn, according to the *KV*, was saying that Essen had changed nothing, one way or the other. Again reformist rhetoric was being used to justify the status quo.

What this showed was that Essen had failed. In the absence of a new founding or a mass rush to embrace the idea of a new party, neither Centrist nor rightist leaders felt obliged to take any action. Long the black sheep of the labor movement, Stegerwald's supporters had been excited to be depicted at Essen as the leaders of a renewal of German politics. But his was not the only voice to which Catholic workers listened: Erzberger, Joos, and Wirth enjoyed not just the sometimes grudging respect accorded Stegerwald, but genuine affection; all three opposed his initiative. Even party leader Trimborn, known to the workers as their best friend in the party's upper echelons for over a generation, was a man whose word was not easily doubted, and when Kaiser had pressed him in public, he had deftly given his word. What this meant for the party system was not clear; what was clear was the impression Trimborn gave of a renewed commitment to workers' interests. The hope of creating a new and better party soon paled in comparison to the reality of promoting workers' issues in the existing party. Rather than producing a spontaneous transformation of the party system (as Brauns had once expected),[49] the election campaign put pressure on each existing party to close ranks, as Stegerwald's signature on the statement of December 30 had shown.

To be sure, Stegerwald did not cease to speak of reform, and soon launched *Der Deutsche*, the "socially minded" daily newspaper that he had called for at Essen. In the following months, he claimed that his Essen program was going "full throttle": the main point, he wrote in September 1921, had been the call for a steadier politics; transforming the party system was just one way to achieve this aim. In Essen, however, he had depicted the transformation as essential to the aim; from that perspective, the game was up. Henceforth, he would have to settle for half-measures—perhaps, as he himself now noted, a "league of Christian parties" *(christliche Parteiverband),*[50] or the three-party working partnership suggested by Trimborn—rather than the full realignment he had desired.

From Party-System Reform to Coalitional Initiative

The energy and fanfare with which Stegerwald launched his Essen initiative is in striking contrast to the equivocation and ambiguity that marked his long retreat. Despite the pleasure this self-educated political thinker took in grandiose political tinkering, Stegerwald proved too much of a politician to risk everything—or, indeed, much of anything—for the sake of a venture with little prospect of success. Though he had reminded his old party, which had recently been preoccupied with agrarian complaints, that his constituency too was still demanding satisfaction, this modest warning was a far cry from the complete transformation of German politics toward which he had aimed. Indeed, his failure to ignite a brushfire at the grassroots had brought him to that critical juncture where continued action might have become a demonstration not of power, but of impotence. Yet, as if to demonstrate that he had not yet crossed that threshold, an opportunity opened that he quickly seized. In April 1921, Stegerwald was commissioned by the Landtag to form a new Prussian government.

Concerned as always with asserting working-class respectability, Stegerwald must have felt gratified to attain the position once held by Bismarck, along with trepidation as to whether he would be accepted in the role. Nor would Stegerwald have granted that his Social Democratic predecessor had made the issue a moot one: the whole point of the Christian trade unions was that these workers were not enemies of "bourgeois" or "civil" society *(bürgerlichen Gesellschaft),* but staked their claim to be a part of it. Moreover, Stegerwald's new post offered a chance to restore some of the credibility that his unions had lost at the time of the Kapp Putsch.

Stegerwald now tried to do through the dynamic of coalitions what he had failed to do through party-system reform. By bringing the DVP and SPD together in a "Grand Coalition" (MSPD, DDP, Center, DVP), he could partially reproduce the balance of forces he had hoped to create through a Christian-led coalition of CNVP and MSPD. The coalition would fall short of Essen in three respects: it would be harder to coordinate than a government dominated by two large parties; the SPD would still be the largest party; and the DNVP would remain intact—whereas the Essen idea, as DGB secretary Heinrich Brüning reiterated, involved splitting it.[51] Still, the Grand Coalition would achieve something Stegerwald considered essential: it would force the Social Democrats and the economically powerful industrialists to share responsibility for the republican government's policies. Accordingly, when the Center, hoping to commit Stegerwald to itself and thereby to put Essen behind it, made him its candidate to head the Prussian government, he tried assiduously to form such a Grand Coalition. But the SPD, despite the approval of its emerging leader in Prussia, Otto Braun, refused to take part. To teach the Social Democrats that "one can also govern without them," Stegerwald wound up leading a minority government (Center and DDP) tolerated by the parties to its right. By September, the SPD was ready to consider a Grand Coalition; by November, it managed to secure that such a coalition would be led not by Stegerwald but by Braun. Stegerwald nonetheless claimed credit for having made the Grand Coalition possible.[52]

Meanwhile, the DVP's refusal in the spring of 1921 to accept an

Allied ultimatum on reparations caused a governmental crisis in the Reich. Stegerwald pushed hard for a Grand Coalition on this level too, and promoted the Mayor of Cologne, Konrad Adenauer, as his candidate to lead it. But negotiations soon collapsed, and a minority coalition of the Weimar parties, led by Wirth, was formed as a last resort.[53]

With Wirth heading the Reich government and Stegerwald, briefly, the Prussian one, a fundamental Centrist dilemma became crystallized. Instead of the comfortable Fehrenbach coalition, the party was now engaged in two uncomfortable arrangements at once. Convinced that only a firm partnership of reliably democratic parties could uphold the Republic, Wirth now spoke of republicanism not as an expediency but as a conviction and advocated ever closer ties with the MSPD and DDP. Warning that another break with the Majority Socialists "would only accelerate" their potentially "dangerous" drift toward reunification with the USPD, he nonetheless "welcomed" the latter's "break with Putschism" and did not rule out working with moderate Independent Socialist elements.[54] But Stegerwald remained convinced that no form of government could last without the cooperation of "both labor and the leading intellectual and economic forces of the country"; the formalities of democracy by themselves would be helpless if the influential were not won over.[55] Accordingly, whereas Wirth insisted that the Weimar parties be vigilant and take a hard line toward the parties to their right, Stegerwald so desired their cooperation that he led a minority government tolerated by them rather than maintain a Weimar coalition in Prussia that actually had a majority.

The tragedy of Weimar is that both men were correct: while democracy could not be built by antidemocrats, neither could it be built by pasting a veneer of democratic process on an edifice of obstructionism by the economically powerful.[56] Indeed, what distinguished Wirth and Stegerwald from others in their party—even Erzberger[57]—was that in surveying the task of democratic construction, neither man was preoccupied with Kulturpolitik or with loyalty to the Center for its own sake. Though other prominent Centrists were equally committed to democracy, few were willing to stipulate that its needs might be separable from the need to preserve the existing party. This unwillingness was not unreasonable: in a polity deeply divided by sectarian suspicions, realism seemed to favor caution. Such caution, however, assured that democracy would be held hostage to sectarianism.[58] Both Wirth and Stegerwald doubted that the hostage under such conditions could survive.

Sequel to Essen: "Partnership of the Middle"

On August 26, 1921, Matthias Erzberger was assassinated by right-wing extremists. Ten months later, on June 23, 1922, Erzberger's longtime tormentor, the DNVP's Karl Helfferich, delivered a vitriolic speech attacking Wirth's Foreign Minister and Stegerwald's onetime colleague in the Democratic People's League, the Jewish industrialist and DDP politician Walther Rathenau. The next day, Rathenau too was assassinated.

Erzberger's murder caused a storm of indignation among Catholic workers against Helfferich's party and severely tried relations between Catholics and Protestants in the DGB. Stegerwald's former ally, Martin Spahn, poured salt into the wound when he announced just six days after the murder that he was going over to the DNVP. In the weeks that followed, Spahn's diatribes against the fallen Erzberger and public exhortations to Stegerwald to join the German Nationals badly discredited the Essen initiative. When Stegerwald declined to follow him, Spahn scolded the union leader that an interdenominational party was not possible on a "western-constitutional" or "middle" basis but only on a "right" basis. Stegerwald broke with Spahn and repudiated his version of interdenominationalism. But he never escaped the stigma of their old association.[59]

Rathenau's assassination confirmed Wirth in his conviction, as he famously put it shortly afterwards, that "the enemy stands on the right!" Wirth later stated that Rathenau's death had cut short the two men's plans for an overarching republican movement or party. The assassination did spur the Majority Socialists and the moderate wing of the Independents to complete their own reunification, but since the new Communist Party (KPD) lived on alongside the reunified SPD, the reunification had less effect than expected on the party system. Nevertheless, the very prospect of Social Democratic reunification did help prompt one further attempt to consolidate the non-Socialist portion of the party spectrum.

On March 6, 1922, Stegerwald had tried to revive interest in such an initiative. If the country could not have one large interdenominational party, he said, then Protestants should at least form a socially minded party that could form an enduring cartel with the Center. On the basis of its Christian Weltanschauung, the Center should focus on the larger questions of state and the economy; treating the status of denominational schools as the cornerstone of politics was a "very narrow view." The "deeper sense" of Essen lay in facilitating a broader and more "political way of thinking for the German people"; once this way of thinking was in place, the parties would outgrow their old narrowness.[60]

Stegerwald thus had come to the point of broaching a "two Center" solution—one for Catholics, one for Protestants. Unlike Roeren's during the Zentrumsstreit, however, Stegerwald's purpose in proposing a "two Center" solution was not to affirm but to transcend the notion that all political decisions had to be based on a confessional Weltanschauung (or even on the primacy of Kulturpolitik). Whereas Stegerwald at Essen had proposed to tear through the old subcultural divides and complete the national integration of Germany in one step, he now effectively conceded that the structure of the party system was not just a source but a symptom of the problem. In a sense, he was trying to meet the argument of Joos and others that the party system was a historic construct and could not be arbitrarily transformed. Given the apparent unreadiness of Catholic and Protestant Germans to trust each other, the solution would have to come in two steps, with each confessional milieu teaching itself to think nationally and politically even while it joined with the other to carry on the nation's business.

For the moment, the idea produced little resonance: on June 20, a discouraged Stegerwald stated publicly that a transformation of the party system was "scarcely to be expected in the next period; the time for that was after the revolution."[61] But Rathenau's assassination opened another round of activity. Outraged by the new disruption from the right, few Centrists demurred when Wirth proposed a tough "Law for the Protection of the Republic." But concern about the right soon gave way to fear that massive demonstrations by the left presaged a new radical wave. In a step reminiscent of the recently deceased Trimborn's alternative interpretation of the Essen program as a permanent association of DVP, DDP, and Center, the three parties agreed late in July that only together should they make themselves available for coalitions. By thus pressuring the Social Democrats to accept a Grand Coalition, they could counter the effect of the impending Social Democratic merger on the balance of power within the government.

A prime mover behind this proposal for a formal "partnership of the middle" *(Arbeitsgemeinschaft der Mitte)* was Heinrich Brauns. But Brauns wanted more than just a tactical counter to the Socialist merger. In contrast to the *KV*'s claim that the intent was not fewer parties but weaker cleavages,[62] Brauns insisted that his aim remained a coalition of just two strong parties, one Socialist, one non-Socialist, that would distance themselves from the extreme right, commit themselves to the constitution, and govern together. Because the Center wanted to be the "core" of this sort of non-Socialist party, Brauns announced, it had resolved to give a significant number of Protestants secure places on its list in the next election campaign.[63]

Brauns's announcement seemed intended to force a confirmation from party leaders. Just as at the end of the war, however, the leaders, fearing an imminent upheaval, toyed with the idea of an initiative only to decide not to pursue it. This time, the resolution dated from Rathenau's assassination, yet was not published until July 23, after Brauns had forced the issue.[64] A brief public discussion ensued, during which Adenauer, presiding over the annual convocation of German Catholics (Katholikentag), urged a genuine initiative.[65] But once again, boldness soon gave way to backtracking: the Center, wrote a "guest commentator" (Brauns?) in the *KV*, had "never acknowledged" confession as the "boundary of its effectiveness"; nominating non-Catholic candidates would be "nothing new"; "one would do well," therefore, not to overestimate "the immediate practical significance of the entire discussion."[66]

For Stegerwald, the idea of a partnership of the middle complemented the talk of a new interdenominational initiative.[67] For the traditionalists, however, the partnership was not meant to prepare a party-system reform but to avoid it. This became clear when the new chairman of the party, Wilhelm Marx, who had signed the announcement of the interdenominational resolution on July 23, stripped it of all significance three weeks later. Dismissing the resolution as a result of the post-Rathenau panic and insisting that it changed "nothing" about the Center "in any way," Marx nonetheless reasserted his support for a partnership. Joos then made the point explicit: Centrist initiatives for party-system reform were counterproductive because other parties viewed them as a threat; rather than pursuing the resolution, the party should pursue the partnership, since it would require no change in the existing party.[68]

In the end, Joos got his way. When the SPD again refused a Reich-level Grand Coalition in November 1922, the Center allowed Wirth to fall rather than give up the idea of a partnership of the middle. Shortly before, the party had issued a statement reinterpreting the interdenominational resolution in a way befitting the heirs of the Zentrumsstreit: instead of speaking of more Protestant candidacies, the statement spoke only of not precluding them. The action came just as Joos was publicly demanding that the entire counterproductive discussion of party-system reform now come to an end.[69]

PART III

From Weimar to Hitler, 1923–1933

The Center is a confessional political party of Catholic Germany with a scarcely used rear staircase for non-Catholics.

—*Eduard Stadtler (former student of Martin Spahn),*
December 1928

From 1917 to 1922, the unrealized visions of party reformers formed the basis of much discussion within the Center party. With both the party and the nation in flux, this discussion appeared unavoidable, for the survival and unity of organized political Catholicism seemed to hang in the balance. But late in 1922 came a new national catastrophe: postwar inflation, already a serious problem, accelerated into the worst hyperinflation of modern times. When the French, their patience over war reparations exhausted, occupied the industrial Ruhr in January 1923 and sought to take reparations in kind, the Germans responded with factory slowdowns that cut production and further exacerbated the hyperinflationary spiral. By November 1923, four trillion marks were worth one dollar. In such a crisis, with even more of Catholic Germany's heartland now under foreign occupation, a discussion about party reform no longer seemed appropriate.

The Center played a key role in the resolution of the crisis. With resistance via factory slowdowns having backfired, a new government under Gustav Stresemann (DVP) reached an interim understanding with the French. This government, the first-ever Grand Coalition on the national level, was very much an emergency government, and the uneasy SPD soon withdrew. At the end of the year, Centrist chairman Wilhelm Marx resurrected the post-Kapp stratagem of 1920: a minority coalition of the middle with Social Democratic toleration. Like

101

Stresemann, Marx was aided by parliamentary passage of an enabling act giving the government temporary power to legislate by decree. During 1924, Marx's government successfully negotiated a new reparations payment scheme (the Dawes Plan) with the Allies and launched a currency reform that brought inflation under control.

Though the mid-Weimar years were hardly a period of political quiescence (there were six governments in four years), a more subtle transformation did take place. The paradigm of minority government tolerated by the left was extended to encompass minority government tolerated by the right. In two cases (1925 and 1927), the DNVP even entered the government. On the surface, the country seemed headed toward greater stability.

Caught up in governing (four of the six cabinets were headed by Marx), Center party leaders did not want to dally in a debate over party-system reform that had brought nothing but difficulties in the past. Besides, government by middle coalition did not seem far from what the functional role of a reformed Center party might be. Marx could therefore hope that the partnership of the middle to which the DVP, DDP, and Center adhered tacitly (but not formally) for most of this period had ended any need to tamper with the Center's internal religious bond.

Nevertheless, minority government remained unstable government, and the Center, as a middle party, remained peculiarly vulnerable to the political crosscurrents. Buffeted first one way and then the other, the party seemed constantly on the verge of being shorn in two. From some perspectives, an even worse result was conceivable: that the Center might become the captive of whichever party was currently buoying up the minority coalition (DNVP or SPD). Moreover, neither Brauns nor Stegerwald had imagined that the expanded middle party or cartel they desired would rule indefinitely without a majority.

In the Republic's middle years, then, the soul-searching continued over the Center's dual function as the party of Catholics and the party of national mediation *(Ausgleich)*. With the subsequent onset of the worldwide economic crisis (1928–1929), the German party system began its gradual collapse, which would lead by 1933 to the one-party regime of Adolf Hitler. The magnitude of this calamity went far beyond the particular concerns of Catholics. But the Center, standing as always in the pivotal position, bore a large share of the burden of coping with the crisis. To this task, it could not but bring the special concerns of its minority constituency. Thus was the stage set for the greatest crisis yet in the history of the party.

5 Political Mavericks and Catholic Consciousness

During 1924 and 1925, over Joseph Wirth's strident objections, Adam Stegerwald and other Centrists tried to encourage what they thought were signs of a more constructive German National attitude by drawing the DNVP into governmental responsibility. But after the failure of the Center-right coalition of 1927–1928 to pass a school bill, Centrist electoral losses would lead the party to reemphasize its distinctive Catholic consciousness *(Besinnung)*. Whatever their differences over the initial opening to the right, neither Wirth nor Stegerwald could sanction the notion that a "political, not confessional" entity would give primacy to confessional consciousness over state and social politics. The Center's two political mavericks were thus to find themselves working in tandem as the mid-Weimar period came to an end.

The Center Party Crisis of 1925

The new wave of controversies within the Center first began to crest after the balloting in the Reichstag on the Dawes Plan in the late summer of 1924. This vote came just three months after parliamentary elections (May 4) in which the KPD, the DNVP, and the just-emerging Nazis posted big gains (the KPD won 12.6 percent of the vote, up from 2.1; the DNVP won 19.5 percent, up from 15.1; and the Nazis won 6.5 percent). By forming a joint caucus with the small agrarian Landbund (2.0 percent of the vote), the DNVP (105 seats) surpassed the reunified SPD (100 seats, down from 171) to become the largest parliamentary delegation. But in the Dawes balloting, the German National delegation split: while some members argued that any favorable vote on reparations was precluded as a matter of principle, others approved the plan because it offered them economic relief. Encouraged by the split, the chairman of the DVP, Gustav Stresemann, who

103

had watched his own party decline at the polls by one-third (to 9.2 percent), now concluded that the DNVP had to be tamed by being brought into the government.[1]

Chancellor Wilhelm Marx's failed bid to get both the SPD and the DNVP to join a government of "national community" (Volksgemeinschaft) led to new elections in December 1924. By this time, the Dawes Plan and currency reform seemed to be curbing the hyperinflation. Though the DNVP held on to its earlier gains, the Social Democratic vote rebounded to 26 percent (131 seats). The other moderate parties recorded smaller gains, while the Communists (9 percent) and Nazis (3 percent) fell.

Relaxing its intransigent position, the DNVP now moved to penetrate and transform the Republic from above. Even before the death of President Friedrich Ebert (SPD) on February 28, 1925, one segment of the party was developing a strategy for winning and using the henceforth popularly elected presidency to launch massive administrative and constitutional reform.[2] On a second front, the DNVP in January eagerly joined a government under the independent reform-conservative Hans Luther. Dubbed by opponents the Bürgerblock, this government was a coalition of DNVP, DVP, BVP, and "contact men" from the Center (Brauns) and DDP.

Both the presidential election and the new coalition exposed tensions within the Center. Groups to the right of the Center wanted a presidential candidate with the political skill to carry out conservative reform, the partisan connections to gain endorsements from all the non-Socialist parties, and the populist credentials to win. A worker and a Centrist, Stegerwald seemed to some on the right to satisfy all three criteria. But when his name was floated in the right-wing press in March 1925, the KV was notably reticent, while the pro-Wirth, Frankfurt-based Rhein-Mainische Volkszeitung (RMV) was openly opposed. Centrists suspected that right-wing groups aimed to capture Stegerwald, his union, and his party while preventing the Weimar parties from uniting behind the likely candidacy of Marx. Stegerwald bowed readily to these concerns, but the incident further fueled left-Centrist distrust of him.[3]

That distrust had grown as Stegerwald had come to advocate the inclusion of the DNVP in the government. He had two reasons. First, only if the Social Democrats learned that governing could proceed without them would the SPD finally outgrow the annoying habit of refusing to share in the governance of the republic it had largely created.[4] Second, having failed thus far to split the DNVP, Stegerwald feared that it would continue to grow if it stayed in antirepublican opposition. Without a Center-right coalition, he argued, the rightist parties would soon have an absolute majority; indeed, their gains since 1920 exceeded the number of seats they still needed. Better to rein them in now, when they could not form a majority without the Center, than to wait for the day when they could. Short of Swiss or American-style federal or presidential government (an allusion to constitutional reform that may have piqued right-wing interest in Stegerwald for President), the only solution to the perennial coalitional crises was for the Center to train both the left and the right in parliamentary responsibility by alternating its governmental alliances.[5]

Justifying the opening to the DNVP, the Centrist deputy and clergyman Georg Schreiber wrote that the German Nationals, by entering the government, were compelled to accept policies they had heretofore fought; the Center could "quietly" but "vigilantly" wait for the DNVP to experience "revisionism."[6] But others proved unwilling to draw the Social Democratic analogy. Both Wirth and the head of the Christian miners' union, Heinrich Imbusch, refused to give the new government their vote of confidence in the Reichstag, and seventeen other Centrists, including twelve from the DGB or Arbeitervereine, either abstained or absented themselves from the proceedings.[7]

Ever since the Dawes vote in 1924, Wirth had been campaigning to prevent the coming Bürgerblock. Such a government, he said, would polarize German politics along class lines: the bloc would eventually "have to resort to ... fascist terror" to keep power or it would "quickly be supplanted" by a "strong socialist-labor government." The Center, said Wirth, had historically had the political task of heading off such polarization; the high expression of this role was the Weimar constitution itself. For Wirth, the Center's middle role was possible only through a liaison with the left.[8]

On August 24, 1925, Wirth went one step further. When the government approved a protective tariff for the agrarians, Wirth, espousing solidarity with urban workers, dramatically withdrew from the Center's Reichstag caucus. Privately, he told Marx that it would be better if the Center were to split into the two "pure" parties it already contained.[9]

This remark, which was bound to touch a raw nerve in any case, was especially painful at that point. As Prussian Minister-President-designate, Marx had spent most of the previous winter trying to form a Weimar-style or SPD-tolerated cabinet, only to be undermined by a small group of Westphalian agrarian Centrists led by Franz von Papen. Afterwards, the Center's Landtag caucus had briefly demanded that Papen and his friends lay down their mandates, but had backed off for fear the Papen group might try to organize a Westphalian offshoot of the BVP. When Otto Braun (SPD) subsequently became Minister-President in Prussia and Marx became the runoff presidential candidate of the three Weimar parties (the Volksblock), both Papen and the BVP joined the right-wing Reichsblock behind the hastily improvised countercandidacy of Field Marshal Paul von Hindenburg. On April 26, Hindenburg was elected. The Center, and Marx in particular, thus stood in the confounding position of supporting the Weimar coalition in Prussia and in the presidential election but the right-oriented coalition in the Reich.[10]

To justify opposite coalitions in Prussia and the Reich, the *KV* equated the arrangement with Marx's earlier bid for a government of national community. This did not stop the liberal and conservative press from speculating that the apparent drive toward a two-bloc system would soon destroy the Center. Thus, when Wirth withdrew from the caucus in August, his musing about the utility of a split played into an atmosphere of crisis that was already well advanced. Nor did it help that a conservative Catholic, Hermann Port, had chosen the previous month's issue of the Catholic magazine *Hochland* to raise the issue of "Center and two-party system."[11]

Parliamentary government, argued Port, depended on a bipolar system of government and opposition; yet the Center, as a middle party, was "the enemy of a two-party system." Avoiding the obvious conclusion, Port assigned the Center essentially a nonpartisan role. With its religious concepts of harmony and hierarchy, the Center, wrote Port, ought to fill the vacuum left by the fallen monarchy and serve in "splendid isolation" as the "regulator" of German politics.

Port's article opened the floodgates for a new wave of discussion on the character of the Center. The debate took place mostly in the columns of *Germania*. The paper had become a battleground between Papen, who was busily buying up its shares, and the left-Centrist editors whose presence was a legacy of the Erzberger era: Heinrich Teipel, Eduard Hemmerle, and Marx's former chief of staff, Karl Spiecker. According to Papen, what Port had proved was that neither a middle party nor a government of national community was possible in a parliamentary system and that the Center must therefore align itself with the right. Three days before Wirth's withdrawal from the caucus, his ally Adam Röder (the Center's only Protestant deputy) replied that Papen had insulted Christians on the left. The Center's true task, wrote Röder, was to win the left to Christianity.[12]

At this point, Teipel jumped in with the most spectacular suggestion yet: "We Must Get Out of the Tower!" Unlike Bachem's original, Teipel's tower article was not an appeal for interdenominational cooperation in a Christian party. Rather, Teipel answered Port's glorification of "splendid isolation" by calling for the most radical form of Catholic integration: the Center must dissolve. For Port was correct that parliamentary democracy required two clear sides, but the sides had to be delineated along truly political lines. "It is not at all necessary," wrote Teipel, "that those who think differently about confession or Weltanschauung be divided politically. From different motives, one can come to [favor] exactly the same political endeavors."[13]

Teipel's polemic was an attack not on the Center but on the whole party system as presently constituted. This system, he argued, prevented political thinking because it was dominated by the self-preserving instinct and "fanatical traditionalism" of the parties. Though no more at fault than any other party, the Center was further compromised by its middle position. Parties had to adjust to the form of government, not the other way around; this meant a bipolar alignment— ideally, a two-party system. To Teipel, the lesson of the presidential campaign was that such an alignment produced not latent civil war but caution and moderation. The two blocs of that election were not quite the correct blocs, since the individual parties within the blocs were themselves organized according to Weltanschauung rather than politics. Nevertheless, the election had been a "significant pedagogical event"; by teaching people to think in a more genuinely political manner, it had shown the way toward greater moderation and had demonstrated the desirability of a two-party system.[14]

The correct alignment, said Teipel, would pit a "national-conservative" party against a "progressive-Europeanist" one. The two parties already existed in latent form. Neither party could be class-based. Moreover, given the present state of the world's economic development, both would have to be capitalist. This, however, would not pose a genuine political problem (as opposed to the sectarian and artificial problem of Weltanschauung), for the presence of workers in both large camps, as well as the structural impetus in a two-party system toward moderation, would result in a powerful social-meliorative impulse. While a third force, Bolshevism, would probably continue to exist, its role would be far less significant than in the current splintered party system.[15]

To facilitate the emergence of the two latent parties, Teipel advocated immediate electoral reform. A switch from proportional representation to British-style small districts and single-round, first-past-the-post elections, he wrote, would place all the parties into a Center-like crisis. As candidates looked for advantages, they would seek new combinations. Only in this way, not through the unrealistic expectation that the existing parties would cooperate in their own demise, could a new party system be achieved.[16]

Denying that the Center was still needed as an instrument of subcultural defense, Teipel noted that fewer Catholics were now within the Center party than outside it (correctly reckoning the BVP, as well as most nonchurchgoers, to be outside). The Center was neither sacrosanct nor a value unto itself; and the Catholic ethic, rather than being isolated in one small party, would find a significant place in both the coming political streams. Besides, wrote Teipel, "I have given up hope" that Catholics could stay together in one party, for they differed not over nuances but over political fundamentals. The Center was exhausting itself in its effort to claim a monopoly over the Catholic electorate, a claim that also forced its Catholic opponents to do battle on false ground. What storehouses of political energy would be released, he mused, if political Catholicism were not confined to the unproductive task of nervously maintaining the Center![17]

Teipel added one more point: the Center must give up the illusion that it could bridge the confessional gap. In reality, it was one of the obstacles to a bridge, for it translated confessional tension into political tension, albeit unintentionally. Were the Center to disappear, concluded Teipel, national unity would be enhanced; this was tragic for the Center, but not for German Catholicism.[18]

Teipel's pamphlet was remarkable in many ways. For perhaps the first time, a Centrist pulled no punches about what parliamentary government might finally mean for the party of the middle. But Teipel was even more comprehensive: he called not just for a "political, nonconfessional" party, but for a political, nonsectarian—that is, non-Weltanschauung-oriented—overhaul of the whole party system. Moreover, he pronounced the Center's mission accomplished even in respect to Kulturpolitik. He thus broke nearly every taboo in the Center's rhetorical storehouse.

Teipel's startling article both heightened the pressure to mollify Wirth and offered an ersatz target for Wirth's opponents. Papen now had little trouble removing his troublesome editor. As for Wirth, the party loyalists who knew him best urged Marx to negotiate with him.[19] At the party convention in Cassel in November, Wirth warned that if his "movement of Christian republicans" became a splinter party, it would cost the Center many seats; yet he added that he preferred to struggle within the Center.[20] For the moment, then, he did not openly take the leap being advocated by Teipel. Apparently, he again thought that by keeping his Centrist bridges open, he might be able to take the bulk of the existing party into an explicitly republican unity bloc. Indeed, by this time, the first experiment with German National governmental participation was over. Protesting Stresemann's negotiation of the Locarno treaty, which fixed the German border in the west and renounced force in the east, the DNVP withdrew from the government. The original cause of the year-long Centrist crisis was thus removed.

At Cassel, both Stegerwald and Marx tried to play down their differences with Wirth, but Wirth was having none of it. Scoffing at those who had expected the coalition to tame the right (Brauns and Stegerwald retorted that such hindsight also applied to coalitions with the left), Wirth rejected what he labeled the Marx-Stegerwald "pendulum politics" and insisted that the right was the "destroyer of the German nation." Capitalizing on disillusionment with the rightist coalition, Spiecker then pushed through a resolution affirming not only that the Center was a "constitution party" but that it was explicitly committed to the Republic.[21]

Despite this success, Wirth waited nearly eight more months before reentering the caucus. By then, he had a further reason to feel satisfied: on the same day as Wirth's reentry, Stegerwald proposed another swing of the pendulum. On July 4, 1926, he called once again for a Grand Coalition.[22]

The Republican Union

Stegerwald was deeply chagrined by German National intransigence over Locarno. Just as the SPD in his view had placed doctrine over domestic responsibility by withdrawing from the governments of 1920, 1922, and 1923, the DNVP now had acted with similar irresponsibility in foreign affairs. At least, thought Stegerwald, the DNVP could no longer reap votes by claiming to be untainted by the Republic. But with Hindenburg instead of Ebert as President, only a Grand Coalition would now secure Stegerwald's dictum that all reasonable groups had to feel implicated in republican stability.[23]

Now came the next step in Wirth's drive to bolster the position of the "Christian republicans." The context was a series of interparty organizational initiatives. After the DNVP's governmental withdrawal, regular meetings of the old partnership of the middle, suspended in 1924, were resumed. In addition, a Liberal Union was founded to cultivate ties between the DVP and DDP. In response, Baron Wilhelm von Gayl (DNVP) and the Reichsblock's pre-Hindenburg presidential candidate, Karl Jarres (DVP), in July 1926 called for expanded formal links between their two parties.[24]

Writing in the left-liberal *Berliner Tageblatt,* Wirth now summoned "all resolute republicans" to form "a firm Republican Union." Lest partisan misunderstandings harm the Republic, this interparty organization was to "provide direction" and a "common operational basis" for the Weimar parties. Like Stegerwald earlier, Wirth was exasperated with the SPD, whose support for a radical referendum on princely expropriation (out of fear of being outflanked by the KPD) was damaging its relations with its former Weimar partners. Committed republicans, wrote Wirth, had gotten the Center at Cassel to take a firm stand for the Republic; their next task was to convince the SPD to prioritize progressive republican consolidation over socialism. If the SPD did not learn to value governmental participation, the republican movement would lose ground among the middle parties and sentiment for a Bürgerblock would revive.[25]

The response to Wirth's call was decidedly negative. Democrats and Centrists worried that a "union" of the Weimar parties would abort the right-wing trend toward accepting the Republic and shove Catholic conservatives and the DVP into the arms of the recalcitrant right. A pro-Centrist Protestant, Friedrich Thimme, warned that a two-party system with a single "Weimar party" might well mean civil war. But Wirth denied that the Republican Union would "mix the colors" into one Weimar party. Indeed, unlike Teipel, Friedrich Dessauer, owner of the pro-Wirth *RMV,* stated that the Center must remain the "political" party of the "Christian Weltanschauung." To the *RMV,* the Center's mission was to see that shortsighted Christian aloofness did not cause the consolidating Republic to follow the French anticlerical example. A corollary was that the Center's aims in Kulturpolitik ought to be carried out with the left rather than the right.[26]

If the Union was not exactly what Teipel had in mind, it was the closest thing to it. In essence, it was an attempt to turn at least the Volksblock of 1925 into a permanent arrangement. Wirth now formed his new organization, together with Ludwig Haas of the DDP and Reichstag President Paul Löbe of the SPD, under the name Republikanische Arbeitsgemeinschaft (RA). The RA, however, had no official standing with the three Weimar parties; it was the private organization of its founders. Its main activity was to publish a weekly journal of opinion, *Die Deutsche Republik (DR),* to which only Wirth and his circle of left-wing Centrists proved reliable contributors. Teipel soon came on board as editor, and Dessauer joined Wirth as copublisher.

The thesis of *Deutsche Republik* was that the Republic had to be defended not just as a form of government but in its specific content, as codified in a constitution produced by like-minded partners. Accordingly, loyalty to the Weimar coalition took precedence over loyalty to one's own party. "More than only a formality," the Weimar constitution created a balance in Kulturpolitik and embodied the "common political formulations" of those parties that historically had paid the greatest attention to "the social problem." For this reason, the right's new strategy of trying to penetrate the Republic and "reform" its constitution was just as dangerous as its previous hard line.[27]

The new publication's immediate task in the fall of 1926 was to press the SPD to enter a Grand Coalition. Since most Centrists at this juncture agreed, they could only have felt relieved to see the project of a Republican Union result in nothing more threatening than a journal. Wirth's reassurance at a party congress in Erfurt in November that no new party was intended seemed to suggest that a more peaceful period in the party's affairs was at hand.[28]

Indeed, even the old feud between Stegerwald and Wirth seemed patched up. By December, Teipel, who had once worked at *Der Deutsche,* was bidding openly for Stegerwald's support. Essen, wrote Teipel, had been a laudable attempt at party-system reform. Since then, Stegerwald had tried to cooperate with bourgeois partners, but they had abandoned him on social policy, so he had swung to the left. Having lost hope of realizing the Essen program, Stegerwald ought to be recruited to support the RA.[29]

The SPD now put on a spectacular demonstration of its ability to frustrate all efforts to include it in the government. Adding to Wirth's distress, the issue that destroyed the nascent alliance came out of his own tenure as Chancellor of a Weimar coalition. Early in December, the *Manchester Guardian* exposed the German practice, begun under Wirth, of evading the Versailles restrictions on armed forces through a clandestine arrangement with the Soviets. Two weeks later, former Chancellor Philipp Scheidemann (SPD) delivered a scathing attack on the army in the Reichstag, which outraged not only the government parties (with Wirth in the lead) but also both the KPD and DNVP, who for once were genuinely on the same side of an issue. Of course, Wirth was hardly a disinterested observer in this affair, and the SPD's position had merit. But the KPD and DNVP were still disingenuous enough to vote for the Social Democratic motion of no confidence that followed, thereby destroying the prospects not only of a Grand Coalition but also of a reconstituted minority government. A chagrined Wirth wrote that one was forced to reevaluate the political maturity of a party (the SPD) that would force a government out of office without first examining what its successor was likely to be.[30]

The DNVP now quickly insisted on its own governmental participation, and Wirth again led those Centrists, this time including Stegerwald, who were opposed. To mollify Wirth and reassure themselves, Centrist leaders put him in charge of drawing up a manifesto, to be signed by the German National leaders, backing strong social legislation and recognizing the Republic. The DNVP swallowed its scruples and signed. Marx thereupon formed his fourth government, his first with the DNVP. Citing public statements by DNVP chairman Count Kuno von Westarp and others that contradicted his manifesto, Wirth then refused to give the new government his vote. In contrast to 1925, however, a Centrist headed the Bürgerblock, and Wirth was the only Centrist to vote no.[31]

Wirth now went on the attack. In the spring of 1927, he toured the country, appearing at rallies of the republican paramilitary association, the Reichsbanner. Although its membership came mostly from the SPD, the Reichsbanner also included rank and file Centrists and Democrats, as well as Wirth, Marx, Spiecker, and Joos. On May 15, Wirth said that the monarchist DNVP's vote to renew the Law for the Protection of the Republic was only to be expected from a party that had "raise[d] a shoddy lack of conviction to the status of a principle." Wirth seemed to be trying deliberately to discredit accommodative elements in the DNVP in order to protect the ascendancy of the Weimar parties. He proclaimed the Reichsbanner to be "a higher unity" that stood above any partisan consideration—as well he might, for the Reichsbanner was the only thriving organization whose composition mirrored his party ideal.[32]

When Marx took exception to Wirth's remarks about his coalition partner, Wirth, defiantly insisting that he would continue his rallies, publicly dared the Chancellor and party chairman to throw him out of the party. One week later, Wirth threatened to walk out and take many voters with him. He also rebuked Joos and Dessauer for continuing to tolerate the coalition. Meanwhile, Teipel blasted Marx for betraying the supporters of his 1925 presidential campaign.[33] Citing diplomatic grounds, Marx quit the Reichsbanner on July 23 after it supported demonstrations by its exclusively Social Democratic Austrian counterpart, the Schutzbund, against the Catholic-led government. These demonstrations had resulted in ugly confrontations with the right-wing paramilitary organization, the Heimwehr. The intraparty controversy over Marx's action was cooled with some difficulty by Joos, who retained his Reichsbanner membership.[34]

Even before the conclusion of this controversy, another had begun. From a clerical perspective, the schools question had been rather favorably settled at Weimar: even though the constitution in theory gave preference to interdenominational schools, it retained existing arrangements in each state pending a national school law that had never come to pass. In most states, this had meant the retention of public denominational schools. In Baden and Hesse, however, the established schools were formally interdenominational. As a result, Catholics continued to call for a national school law that would give equal status to denominational schools wherever interdenominational schools were the norm. In late 1926, the DNVP had used the promise of a school law to ingratiate itself with the Center and thus to reenter the government.[35]

Sponsored by Chancellor Marx and by the devout Protestant Walter von Keudell (DNVP), the draft school bill permitted the establishment by parental petition of local alternatives to the existing schools. But the DVP insisted that since interdenominational schools were constitutionally preferred, no petition ought to be necessary in cases (the majority) where the existing school was denominational. Viewing interdenominational schools as the key to an integrated national school system, liberals and others could see little justice and much clerical arrogance in Catholic complaints about schools. Even in interdenominational schools, after all, religion was a regular subject of instruction, and the constitution mandated that it be taught as desired by the churches. In Baden and Hesse, residential demographics usually resulted in denominational segregation anyway.

Wirth now chastized his party for allowing the schools question to override everything else. By reopening a delicate matter that had been adequately settled at Weimar, he said, the Center put the whole constitution at risk. Liberal opposition within the government, he warned, would kill the Marx-Keudell bill in any case. The only result would be to tie the Center to the DNVP in the next campaign, thereby freezing the SPD out of the republican state and repeating the error of the Kaiserreich. These considerations, he announced in early August 1927, made it impossible for him to support the school bill.[36]

Wirth was immediately attacked for "putting politics above Weltanschauung."[37] And indeed, his priorities here were the reverse of Centrist tradition. As early as May 12, Heinrich Scharp, editor of the *RMV*, had shown the way toward Wirth's developing position: the schools issue, he had written, must not be allowed to divide the true republicans; Weltanschauung was a matter of individual conscience, not of parliamentary majorities. By the eve of the annual Catholic convocation (Katholikentag) in September, Teipel was attacking the school bill both as a right-wing trap and as an extension of a ghetto mentality. It was "disastrous," he wrote, that cultural divisions coincided with partisan ones.[38]

The Catholic convocation now became the occasion for a wave of speeches asserting the primacy of the schools issue—alongside of which Father Ludwig Kaas, the Center's chief spokesman on foreign affairs, added the issue of a concordat. Kaas said that the demand for denonominational schools was "unrenounceable" for all Catholics, for it "belongs to the holy sphere of that duty" that lay outside the realm of the individual's "arbitrary interpretation." When Teipel then wrote in the left-liberal *Frankfurter Zeitung* that the school bill was both "integralist" and a tool of the reactionaries, the Center's Executive Board expelled him from the party. Going further, it censured and threatened to expel *any* Centrist who attacked the school bill or who openly favored interdenominational schools. When Wirth in turn censured those who would use the schools issue to undermine the Republic, he vividly demonstrated the reversal of priorities between him and his party.[39]

For Wirth, the squabble over schools was a case study in the larger

German problem identified by Teipel: people were being divided politically for reasons not of politics but of Weltanschauung. The SPD's
behavior regarding the army's actions seemed to him to demonstrate
the same point: ideological dogma had led the party, which had been
a member, after all, of the offending Wirth government, into a political cul-de-sac. Thus, Teipel noted that Weltanschauung parties were
agents of isolation rather than integration and ridiculed the argument
of Joos and others that such parties had to be retained due to their
organic place in the nation's history.[40] Wirth added that Catholic political solidarity was overestimated anyway, since so many Catholics
were now in the SPD or DNVP. Although a separate Catholic party
during the Kulturkampf had been a "democratic necessity," both democracy and religious tolerance had now been realized in the Weimar
constitution. Wirth thus came very close to saying that thanks to the
Republic, a party of Catholic unity was both no longer viable and no
longer needed.[41]

Like Teipel two years earlier, Wirth now openly questioned the utility of all Weltanschauung parties in a democratic state. Thus, a unified
party of the anticlerical "liberal Weltanschauung," he said, would be
no more viable than a reunified Catholic party. Teipel was more explicit: not only did the presidential election demonstrate that people
could form political groupings and still retain their Weltanschauungen, it also showed why one had to oppose a reconciliation of the
Center and the BVP. He called for parties whose purpose was to
pursue common goals, not to provide subcultural direction for
every aspect of their members' lives *(Zweckgemeinschaften,* not
Lebensgemeinschaften). Besides, since almost as many Bavarian Catholics voted for the left as for the BVP, Catholic political unity would
be no better advanced by merging the Center with the BVP than by
merging it with the parties of the left—proof that Catholic political
unity was "impossible."[42]

Though Wirth became more cautious after the Catholic convocation, he continued to complain about the "misuse of Weltanschauung
for political purposes." In an article entitled "Zentrumsstreit," he lamented that those who wanted to emphasize "politics" instead of the
alleged "Centrist conviction" *(Zentrumsgesinnung)* were barely tolerated "guests" in the Center. The DNVP, he wrote elsewhere, was trying to break the "Weimar front" on Kulturpolitik in order to unravel
the whole constitution. In light of this political aim, "it would not do
to argue that 'working partnerships [*Arbeitsgemeinschaften*] are not

partnerships of shared conviction [*Gesinnungsgemeinschaften*].'" As Teipel earlier put it, whether or not a common "Christian" basis existed between the Center and the DNVP, no common "political" basis existed between them, whereas such a basis did exist between the Center and the SPD.[43]

In February 1928, the coalition collapsed, largely due to liberal resistance to the Marx-Keudell school bill. Wirth promptly drew up a reckoning: at a time when the schools were not even in danger, the Center had exacerbated subcultural tensions in an already deeply divided nation; it had diverted the nation's energy from higher priorities; it had endangered the development of the cooperative instinct in the DVP; and it had failed to secure the bill's passage. For months, said Wirth, a position he had taken on political grounds had been used to impugn his loyalty to a Weltanschauung. But what he had opposed was not the defense of religious values, but the endangerment of the state due to an "untimely overemphasis" on Weltanschauung in the party system. Although the Center had gathered strength in the early postwar years from its Christian sense of duty, it could never have achieved so much, said Wirth, had it let battles over Weltanschauung rob it of its partners.[44] This, he might have added, was why he had tried to create a Republican Union. But while the rightist coalition was over, Wirth had come no closer to achieving his party ideal.

The Congress of Consciousness and the Second Essen Speech

Besides schools, another issue raised tensions in the Center in the last months of the coalition: pay raises for civil servants *(Beamter)*. Centrist Finance Minister Heinrich Köhler championed the raises, while Stegerwald and Imbusch opposed them unless something was also done for union labor. So heated did this controversy become that Imbusch dressed down Marx over it; Stegerwald even resigned as deputy party chairman, though he was soon persuaded to return.[45]

In December 1927, the government's bill favoring the pay raises passed by a vote of 333 to 53, with the SPD voting in favor, Imbusch joining the Communists in voting against, and the other Christian trade unionists pointedly abstaining. Stegerwald reacted by vociferously demanding "a complete transformation of the entire party apparatus." Serving notice that "the battle within the Center has only just begun," he vowed to "disturb the peace in the party . . . until [its] structure . . . corresponds to the structure of its constituency." Chid-

ing the SPD for speculating on winning over the civil servants by raid-
ing the pocketbooks of workers, he nonetheless "emphatically demand[ed]" that the Center get the SPD into the government, for it was
intolerable "in the tenth year of the Republic" that the old authorities
were again in power while all of labor was either formally (the SPD)
or factually (the Christians) in opposition, "exactly as in the time of
the old regime."[46]

Stegerwald soon got more than he bargained for. In national elections on May 20, the SPD, after five years in opposition, was the big
winner (30 percent). To its right, every major party lost seats, mostly
to middle-class special-interest parties; the DNVP was rewarded for
its recent relative moderation and governmental participation by losing the most seats of all (from 103 to 73). The Center, the DVP, and
the DDP together now held only 132 seats, 21 fewer than the SPD
alone. Not quite as Stegerwald had hoped, a Grand Coalition was
indeed formed—but under Social Democratic leadership.

While the Center's decline from 13.6 percent to 12.1 percent would
have been only a mild setback for any other party, it sent the occu-
pants of the tower of stability into a panic. Not only was this the
party's worst showing ever, but many Catholic workers had moved
leftward—some to radical Christian and even philo-Communist splinter groups such as Vitus Heller's Christian Social Reich Party, but far
more to the SPD.[47] Party leaders weighed two potential responses to
this calamity. The first was to implement a major restructuring that
would demonstrate a commitment to social policy and thus bring
back the workers. The second was to do what the party always did
when times were tough: to revive "Zentrumsgesinnung," that is, to
reemphasize the confessional bond. In contrast to 1920, Wirth by
now was no more willing than Stegerwald to grant that one could
genuinely do both. When party regulars predictably rallied to the traditional cure, the stage was set for the party's two leading mavericks
to conclude an alliance.

Hints of the impending alliance had been present at the Catholic
convocation the previous September, when Stegerwald, its president,
had made only pro forma statements supporting denominational
schools. Praising a Republic that had brought Catholics parity, he had
echoed Teipel's warning against a ghetto mentality. While the choice
for Stegerwald was not between a political and a Weltanschauung
party (the Center, he said, was a "political" party of the "Christian
Weltanschauung"), he had now experienced for himself how a rightist

coalition could shift Centrist politics away from the issues of social
equity and republican stabilization that he believed would determine
Germany's future. To Stegerwald, Christian politics had always
meant "more than putting through parity and protecting the denominational school"; during the DNVP's initial overtures toward a coalition in November 1926, Stegerwald had ridiculed Martin Spahn for
suggesting the "impossible" idea that the Center, a "political" party,
"should make the school question the cornerstone of its entire policy." Wirth too had now experienced the "irresponsibility" of the SPD
and had chafed at the narrowness of the Center. Thus, when the
Badenese party refused to list Wirth among its candidates for the May
elections because of his stand on schools, Stegerwald secured his old
adversary the second spot (otherwise his own spot) on the Center's
national list.[48]

The high point of the Wirth-Stegerwald alliance was the Fifth Party
Congress, held in Cologne in December. This congress took place
against the backdrop not only of the recent electoral trauma but also
of the Vatican's extension of its Catholic Action movement into Germany. The purpose of the movement, as described officially by a clerical leader of the Arbeitervereine, was to combat lay autonomy in society and public life. The well-tuned ears of the veteran social
Catholics in Mönchengladbach were quick to sense what this might
mean, both for the Christian trade unions and for the now financially
troubled Volksverein, and Brauns privately feared a new confrontation with integralism. But Joos seemed not to share this fear. To him,
the electoral losses proved again that the only way to keep workers
from going over to the SPD was to revitalize the party's Catholic
bond.[49]

In the months before the party congress, the advocates of Zentrumsgesinnung and the advocates of significant reform each insisted that theirs was the only way to renew loyalty to the party.
Stegerwald, who had announced before the election that he now believed the Center could be turned into a great "Christian democratic"
party without a new founding, stated on July 2 that the transformation would begin at the Cologne congress. In September, he told party
leaders that the election was final proof of the inadequacy of Catholic
defense as a motive for party unity. Since the Center's ailment was
that it lacked a coherent set of policies, the cure required a civic, not a
Catholic, emphasis. Moreover, like Teipel and then Wirth, Stegerwald
now stated that the party had to stop claiming that its coalitional

alignments were simply working partnerships not based on shared conviction—a claim that trivialized the party's political orientation, reduced the party to the status of an interest lobby for the Church instead of a party of the commonweal, and rendered it no different from the economic special-interest parties.[50]

Wirth agreed that the party's Catholic bond was not enough to save it. Yet he declined invitations from the left-liberal press to join the DDP by saying that this was impossible as long as a change of parties continued to mean a change of *Weltanschauung*. For him as for Stegerwald, reform for the time being had to come through the Center—but it did have to come. His stated aim was a party system that facilitated the parliamentary consolidation of the representatives of the populist majority.[51]

As usual, Teipel went a step farther than Wirth: since it was impossible in a country so divided in its beliefs to run politics on the basis of *Weltanschauung*, the SPD must change, renouncing not socialism, but a party of socialism. The parallel with the Center was obvious. To facilitate formation of a socially minded parliamentary majority, Teipel called for a large nonideological Labour party, as in England.[52]

Opposing all such schemes, Joos insisted that the parliamentary ideal, a two-sided alignment of government and opposition, was "simply not possible for us."[53] Since parties were historical constructs, one had to adjust the parliamentary system to conform to the existing parties rather than proceeding the other way around. Admitting that loyalty to the Center was indeed a matter more of Catholicism than of politics, Joos wrote that those who wanted to emphasize some other bond were only causing further attrition. Defections based on economics must stop: "It must again become an uncontested opinion in Catholic Germany that we as Catholics ... belong politically together." To this end, Joos called on the clergy to take a more active political role. The lay "propagandists of a split," he wrote, must cease and desist.[54]

These were the issues as the party congress approached. In October, further drama was added when Marx, distressed and exhausted by his string of confrontations with Wirth, Imbusch, and Stegerwald, announced that he was stepping down as party chair. Vice-chairman Stegerwald quickly let it be known that he expected to be Marx's successor. Not since the days of Ernst Lieber had the Center had an openly contested battle for the chairmanship. But neither had it ever had such a controversial heir apparent. Soundings by Hugo Mönnig confirmed that local party leaders, as well as many in the rank and file (especially the many civil servants), were suspicious of having as chairman a man so identified with one economic interest group. Stegerwald, however, was sure that no such objections would have been raised had he been anything other than a worker.[55]

To avoid alienating the workers, old-line leaders contemplated elevating another worker, Joos, to the chairmanship. In Mönnig's words, Joos had "grown a great deal of late."[56] Mönnig, of course, meant that the conciliatory pro-Catholic Joos was no longer the working-class tribune who had locked horns with Carl Bachem over the Prussian suffrage issue during the war. The only other alternative seemed to be a clergyman such as Kaas, since this would avoid giving the post to any interest group and would reassert the confessional bond. No priest had ever served as chairman before, though some currently headed state organizations.

The atmosphere as the congress convened clearly favored those who wanted a greater Catholic emphasis. This was evident in its designation as the "Congress of Consciousness" *(Parteitag der Besinnung),* by which was meant the recovery of a meditative and self-aware political Catholicism. Prominently trumpeted by Joos, the phrase was eagerly disseminated by *Germania* and the *KV,* which showed none of its old compunction about referring to the party's Weltanschauung as "Catholic."[57]

The speeches at the gathering (except Stegerwald's) were similarly tinged: instead of a "political, nonconfessional party," the word now was that the party was "political . . . but . . . Catholic." Speaker after speaker used the words "Catholic" and "Center" interchangeably; Marx added that one of the party's main purposes was to demonstrate the political virtue residing in Catholicism. To shouts of "Bravo!", a guest from Austria's Catholic party even asserted "how much more important Weltanschauung is than the political questions of daily life." The leader of one of the largest groups in attendance, the anti-Stegerwald civil servants, shrewdly joined this chorus: Joseph Baumhoff said that the declining emphasis on Weltanschauung in recent years had been a sign of the general materialization of the age. The party, cried Baumhoff, must continue to be the "home of all strata," who must not become "captive to prima donna attitudes."[58]

As for the chairmanship, the party's Executive Board, in keeping with tradition, decided before the congress to nominate the vice-chairman. When Stegerwald said that he could not give up his union posts unless he became chairman of both the party and the caucus, the Board agreed. But when the full Reich Committee met on December 7, the leading KAV prelate, Otto Müller (a Joos supporter), moved to separate the two chairmanships. The Committee, half of whose members were civil servants, seized this opening to derail the nomination. The Executive Board then tried to nominate Joos, whereupon Johannes Giesberts led an angry group of trade unionists out of the meeting. Embarrassed by this fiasco, Joos was relieved when Heinrich Brüning suggested a triumvirate consisting of Joos, Stegerwald, and Kaas. But when this idea reached the floor of the congress on December 8, it suffered a stunning rejection. Topping a day of surprises, the congress elected Kaas to the chairmanship by secret ballot, with 184 votes to 92 for Joos and 42 for Stegerwald.[59]

Dissenting from those who hailed this unprecedented election as a victory for democracy, Stegerwald pointed out on December 16 that only 44 of the 488 officially sanctioned delegates were workers; since one-third of those could not afford to attend, 40 percent of the Centrist electorate had been represented by 5 percent of the delegates.[60] The fact remained, however, that a priest had won in a landslide; the Center thus further documented its drift into an openly confessional party. As the *KV* put it, Centrists would no longer tolerate their Catholicism being used as a reproach against the party; if this made the Center a confessional party, so be it.[61]

Struck by the new rhetoric since May, a group of integralists had announced before the congress that the party had learned its lesson and they could now rejoin.[62] Indeed, although Kaas now claimed that he wanted to see some 3 million Protestants join the Center's 3.75 million Catholics (numbers well chosen to preserve a Catholic plurality),[63] the fact was that the party, though it had not turned to integralism, had taken a fundamental decision regarding its future—a decision that, while made especially manifest by the election of Monsignor Kaas, would not have differed in substance had the victor been Joos.

For all of Wirth's friendship with Joos and problems over the years with Stegerwald, the Badener's insistence that the Center emphasize issues of state politics over religion was closer to Stegerwald's conception than to Joos's. Thus, Wirth prominently supported Stegerwald during this drama—and prominently absented himself (forcing the gallant Joos to deliver a speech in his stead) when Stegerwald lost. Afterward, Wirth explained that he sided with Stegerwald because he favored reform, and lamented that a labor leader could spend his whole career working for class collaboration and then be treated the way Stegerwald had been. Teipel added that the choice in Cologne had not been between two political directions, but between a political and an unpolitical one. Moreover, Stegerwald as party leader would have resigned his trade union posts, thus ending his need to put the solidarity of his unions ahead of properly "political" factors. Teipel seemed sympathetic to renewed hints from Stegerwald, stated in a so-called "second Essen speech" at a protest rally in that city on December 16, of a new "Christian Social People's Party."[64]

Joos and the Arbeitervereine refused to endorse the proceedings in Essen. Indeed, Joos sided with Carl Bachem and the *KV* against the complaints of Stegerwald, Kaiser, and Giesberts that the workers had been unfairly treated. For a worker could well have been elected, and that worker was Joos. The *KV* now told Stegerwald something akin to what *Germania* had once told Julius Bachem: if he tried to found an interdenominational party, "not a single 'active Protestant'" would join. The *WAZ* added: "The Weltanschauung foundation of a Center party appears to us incomparably more firm and strong than the altogether insecure basis of a Christian Social People's Party."[65]

In fact, there was just enough dissatisfaction among Protestant workers in other parties to make a new party conceivable. Anton Erkelenz of the Hirsch-Duncker unions, who had expressed sympathy for the Essen program eight years earlier (Chapter 4), was enmeshed in new feuds in the DDP, and some Democrats talked of combining the DDP, the paramilitary Young German Order (JDO), and the Center in a larger, more "socially minded" entity. More promising, the labor contingent in the DNVP had reached the end of its rope after the intransigent industrialist Alfred Hugenberg took over as party leader following the May electoral debacle.[66] The most likely way to harness these tensions, however, was for Protestants to organize their own alternative. Not only would they be unlikely to join a Christian Social People's Party at Stegerwald's command and over his problems rather than their own, but such a party now would involve no nonlabor Catholics and would split the labor wing. It would be seen by most Catholics as a sulking manifestation of personal impetuosity, not as an idealistic step toward a better functioning party system.

In the aftermath of the "second Essen speech," then, Stegerwald did as he usually did: he calmed down, adapted to the limits on his power, and settled for a consolation prize. This time, the prize was the caucus chairmanship. With it came a promise from KAV leader Joos that

Catholic Action would not be allowed to compromise the "autonomy of the labor movement" and a confidential assurance that Kaas would "strive earnestly" to make Stegerwald his successor once unity was restored.[67] Deciding to turn full-time to politics, Stegerwald now resigned his union posts in favor of Bernhard Otte and Heinrich Imbusch.

As for Wirth, his stock in the party, already lowered by the schools controversy and by his quixotic insistence during the coalitional negotiations of 1928 on being Vice Chancellor,[68] was further hurt by his cantankerousness at the party congress. Wirth's apparent instability, perhaps exacerbated by drinking (he had bouts with alcoholism during his later Swiss exile), would make him less and less capable of the kind of sustained effort that had marked his earlier challenges to the party. In light of his weakened state and the Center's renewed religious consciousness, his party was unlikely to put up with much more from him. On December 23, the *KV* stated that the Center would not tolerate any further deliberately provoked crises. According to Kaas, the era of crises was over.[69]

Like the Essen program, Wirth's Republican Union was an attempt to work with the party system not as it was, but as the necessities of state ought to have compelled it to be. But as Wirth had once warned and as Joos had now reiterated, a reform of the party system could not simply be decreed, for the existing party system reflected ongoing subcultural and historical realities. The fact that most of the parties had developed under the Kaiserreich not as agents of responsible government but as lobbies or as agents of political defiance shaped their outlook, limited their constituencies, and constrained their room for maneuvering. These realities were as much in evidence during relatively good times (as in the provocative behavior of the SPD over military issues[70] or the stubbornness of the Center over schools) as in more trying times. Yet, though they may not have been entirely realistic, Stegerwald and now Wirth were not wrong to think that the health of the political system depended on a timely adjustment of the party system to fit the form of government. For by impeding rather than facilitating effective republican government, the party system continually reinforced those who called not for republican realignment but for the Republic's destruction.

On January 20, 1929, the Center party's Executive Board formally resolved not to issue any new interdenominational statements or to offer financial aid or mandates to Protestants until they showed suc-

cess in recruitment.[71] Since Adam Röder's candidacy had not been renewed the previous spring (he had opposed the school bill), there were
now no Protestants in the Center caucus. More than ever, if Protestants were to have a moderate-conservative and socially minded
party, they were going to have to form it themselves.

6 The Fall of the Tower

The notion of a Protestant twin for the Center—a second "political, not confessional" party that would join it in a cartel—was neither a new nor an exclusively Catholic invention. Tentatively broached by the Protestant Adam Röder during the Zentrumsstreit,[1] it intrigued enough people in the mid-Weimar years to generate a flurry of discussion. No formal cartel was ever created. After 1928, however, when the Center sealed off its "rear staircase for non-Catholics"[2] but left open the possibility of an informal arrangement with a Protestant party, the idea did produce notable, if never substantial, results.

Whereas the Center could be minimally interdenominational even with just a handful of Protestants, launching a twin party was impractical without substantial splinters from the existing Protestant parties. Alfred Hugenberg's takeover of the DNVP in October 1928 finally produced the splinters. In late 1929 a new party, the Christian Social People's Service (CSVD), was born, and in 1930, when difficulties between the SPD and DVP brought down the Grand Coalition, the CSVD enthusiastically supported the innovation of a "presidential cabinet" under Stegerwald's former protégé, Heinrich Brüning. But the CSVD failed to unite the German National renegades, and Brüning, who ever since Essen had seen a clean split in the DNVP as the key to producing a large new party, now faced a party system more Balkanized than ever. Moreover, Hugenberg's victory in the DNVP was a reaction to electoral losses stemming from its governmental participation; those losses were a sign that the weakening of the DNVP, instead of enhancing the prospects for a more moderate party, might feed a radicalism even greater than Hugenberg's. The subsequent economic crisis turned this possibility into a reality. Thus, when Brüning's long-anticipated party-system "reform" finally came, it produced not a dominant Christian cartel, but the National Socialist German Workers' Party (NSDAP) of Adolf Hitler.

The Twin-Party Movement

The idea of a Protestant party had three main sources in the mid-Weimar period. Two were exclusively Protestant: the Evangelische Volksgemeinschaft (EV), a small Hessian party; and the Christlich-Soziale Gesinnungsgemeinschaft, later Christlicher Volksdienst (Christian People's Service or CVD), an agent of organized political Protestantism that drew from pietistic clubs and the Christian trade unions. Both the EV and the CVD dated from 1924–1925.[3] The third source was an interdenominational group of publicists led by the Protestant Friedrich Thimme and including *Germania*'s Eduard Hemmerle. In May 1926, this group launched a monthly journal, *Der Zusammenschluss* (ZS—"the joining of forces"), whose mission was greater political cooperation between moderate Catholics and Protestants. Between 1926 and the summer of 1928, frequent articles by Thimme and by two Protestant members of the Center, Alfred von Martin and Richard Bornemann (a member of the JDO), pondered whether to aim for a truly interdenominational Center party or a two-party cartel. In February 1927, Heinrich Brauns contributed an article conceding the greater practicality of a cartel.

Although a cartel would be easier to accept both for Catholics (who would not have to give up their protective tower) and for Protestants (who would not have to face the jeering of their co-religionists for joining an ultramontane party), a cartel also had a significant disadvantage: any party explicitly for Protestants risked becoming a vehicle for anti-Catholic sentiment. Centrist participation in the plans could ease but not preclude this danger.

Indeed, to be viable, a self-consciously Protestant party needed to provide good reasons why Protestants should leave their current parties. For the small Protestant parties of the mid-Weimar period, there were two such reasons: Kulturpolitik, and frustration that German National intransigence had weakened the traditional role of organized Protestantism in government. From the Center's standpoint, both these factors were two-edged swords. Thimme, for example, eventually opposed the school bill as a threat to interdenominational cooperation, and Röder was to lose his Centrist seat over the issue. Moreover, a party committed to the promotion of Protestant Kulturpolitik might interpret its mission as the blockage of Catholic cultural hegemony, as the rampantly anti-ultramontane Evangelical League tried to get the EV to do. If the Protestant desire for a greater say in government were to be motivated not by the wish to cooperate in a stabilized Republic but by the wish to block ultramontane or black-red political hegemony, then governmental Protestantism might threaten the civil gains achieved by Catholics since the end of the Prussian state's preferential relationship with the Protestant Church.

Such considerations led not only Catholics but even some Protestants in Thimme's *Zusammenschluss* circle to hesitate to endorse the possibility he favored: a union of the Protestant groups in preparation for a cartel with the Catholics. Bornemann warned that the EV might actually increase confessional tension and questioned whether its aim was to combat or to collaborate with the Center. While he was willing to promote twin "political, nonconfessional" parties, he clearly would have preferred to strengthen the "Protestant wing of the Center party." Meanwhile Röder, like Heinrich Teipel, now criticized the two-Center plan for increasing the primacy of confession and Weltanschauung in party politics. What Röder wanted was a large, outspokenly republican, conservative-democratic party that would protect the Christian cultural legacy but would transcend Weltanschauung. He advocated expanding the Center via the accretion of the BVP, the Hanoverians, the small-business Economic Party, the Christian Social Protestants, and a culturally tolerant DDP. (Apparently he thought the monarchist elements on this list would soon accept the Republic.) To Thimme, however, republican conservatism seemed an insufficient basis for a party unless buttressed by Weltanschauung.[4]

On January 6, 1927, with the knowledge of Marx, Stegerwald, and Brauns, Bornemann and Thimme approached the EV and the Hanoverians about forming a "Protestant People's Party" that would have a vote-pooling arrangement with the Center. The EV's leaders assured the *Zusammenschluss* group that their "Protestant-Christian Weltanschauung party" shunned the Evangelical League, rejected antisemitism ("the seeds of death of the Stöcker movement"), and considered the Republic "the only possible form of government for the foreseeable future." They would cooperate with the Center, they said, if their organizational autonomy were guaranteed, religious differences were left to the churches, and political differences were settled by a joint committee with parity. The Center commissioned Brauns, Joos, and Heinrich Krone to pursue the matter. But a conference of EV leaders with Joos, Krone, and Centrist General Secretary Heinrich Vockel in Cassel on March 10 went poorly. Thimme suspected that those in the EV who opposed any accommodation with

Catholicism had determined from the start to wreck the conference, a suspicion reinforced by the EV newspaper's simultaneous attack on "atheism, . . . materialism, and . . . ultramontanism." Thimme now transferred his hopes to the CVD.[5]

The latter group was slow to decide its own direction. Many members envisioned not an electioneering party, but a public interest lobby or Protestant national political conscience. Moreover, some branches were anticlerical while others favored interdenominational cooperation. These matters were still being debated during the 1928 election campaign, in which some regional branches did not participate. Holding the group together was a commitment to a positive Protestant role in strengthening republican government through constitutional reform.[6]

Leery of pursuing another initiative after their experience with the EV, Centrist leaders were by now preoccupied with raises for civil servants, the schools issue, and the controversy over the rightist coalition (Chapter 5). Thus, when the Center dropped Röder's candidacy for the May 1928 elections, Thimme and Bornemann felt they had been left high and dry. In vain, Bornemann again appealed privately to the Center to put Protestants on its lists in all denominationally mixed districts, even if they were placed too low to be elected. In this way, he suggested, the current elections could set the foundation for progress in the next. Warning that Protestant members were tired of being shunted aside as if they were an embarrassment, he asked that twenty-five prominent Protestants be recruited to launch a sustained campaign to attract Protestants. Meanwhile, a disappointed Thimme toyed with the idea of an alliance of the CVD and the radical Catholic splinter party of Vitus Heller.[7]

After renewed talks on June 22 and new assurances from Brauns, the mercurial Thimme was sufficiently encouraged to predict in the final edition of *Zusammenschluss* that a Christian unity party was on its way. On August 18, Vockel even sent around a circular asking which Protestants to approach.[8] But once again the Protestants were to be disappointed. Both the May electoral shock and the arrival of Catholic Action in September made a new interdenominational initiative difficult. Nor did it help that Thimme and Bornemann had been talking to the wrong man—for Brauns, the Centrist who sympathized most, was on the way out. Blamed by some for bringing together the rightist government of 1927–1928, by others for giving primacy to social issues over the confessional bond, Brauns was losing his influence in the party. Forced by the SPD to vacate the Labor Ministry, he returned full-time to the financially troubled Volksverein and became less and less influential in senior Center party councils.

The Protestants now were told that the Center could not give further consideration to their demands until Catholic affairs were brought into order. Thimme accepted Vockel's assurance that the Center's imminent campaign to demonstrate a "strengthened Catholic outlook" would avoid adopting an aggressive stance toward Protestants. Bornemann, however, was less easily put off. "Beyond general promises for the future," he wrote Vockel bitterly on October 18, "the Catholic side apparently intends not the slightest trace of the genuine accommodativeness" needed to "continue the common work." The Center, he concluded, was not to be weaned from basing all its deeds on a single motive: "strengthening . . . the Catholic confessional party." Having "paralyzed" all initiatives to promote the growth of a Protestant wing, it had destroyed the patriotic prospect of a "great Christian party of the middle."[9]

Bornemann thus had come to the point reached by Runkel, Haecker, and Röder before him. Time and again, the party's old guard had confronted the problem of how to rid itself of pesky individual Protestants who took its interdenominational rhetoric seriously. For by calling its bluff, these Protestants forced the party to show that what it wanted was not to *be* interdenominational, but to be able to *say* that it was. On January 20, 1929, party leaders decided that there would be no new public statement about the party's character, nor would funds be allotted for attracting Protestants either to the Center or to a Protestant twin. So informed by Kaas on February 8, Bornemann was told that this was the end of the matter. Luckily for the Center, he chose not to make further trouble.[10]

Reform and the Brüning Era

Essentially a Grand Coalition, the government formed in 1928 by Hermann Müller (SPD) was a "cabinet of personalities" without official party ties. The DVP at first would go no further unless the Weimar coalition in Prussia became a Grand Coalition too. But Social Democratic support for a Prusso-Vatican concordat (without school provisions) drew the Center away from the DVP's position. In April 1929, a true Grand Coalition took shape in the Reich, with the DVP getting budgetary concessions and the Center getting additional ministries.

Those ministries, Occupied Territories and Transportation, went to Wirth and Stegerwald.[11]

Stegerwald's new post allowed the elevation to the caucus chairmanship of his 44-year-old former protégé, Heinrich Brüning. After entering the Reichstag in 1924, Brüning had risen rapidly due to his reputation as the party's financial expert. The new caucus chairman was soon involved in the stormy domestic debate over the Young Plan, an internationally approved restructuring of Germany's reparations payments. The Young Plan was a step forward for Germany, and President Hindenburg intended to sign it. In December 1929, however, an extraparliamentary committee set up by Hugenberg and including Adolf Hitler sponsored a referendum that would have made liable for treason anyone who signed any treaty that implied recognition of war-guilt obligations. Although this so-called Freedom Law did not pass, it got nearly six million votes and made Hitler's name a household word. Brüning then persuaded his party to link its acceptance of the Young Plan to a reform of the Reich's finances. He had become convinced, in light of the rapidly worsening depression, that the country could not simultaneously pay reparations, pay the higher civil service salaries mandated by the measure of 1927–1928, and fund unemployment insurance.

The Young campaign was a significant event in the history of the Republic. Even before the "Nazi breakthrough" Reichstag election of September 1930, it helped produce mini-breakthroughs in state elections in December 1929 (11.3 percent in one state) and June 1930 (14.4 percent).[12] Brüning's attention, however, apparently was elsewhere. In February 1929, the EV had been absorbed by the CVD. Now the Freedom Law provoked wholesale secessions from the DNVP. A sizable contingent from the Christian Social wing joined the CVD, making it the CSVD. Another secession produced the agrarian Landvolkpartei, and still another, under Brüning's friend Gottfried von Treviranus, produced the People's Conservatives (Volkskonservativen). Belying the earlier hopes of Brauns and Thimme, the secessionists were neither united nor inspired by the Center. Still, Brüning, who had hoped for a German National split almost longer than anyone,[13] now savored the prospect that a compatible Protestant partner was on the way.

Brüning's concerns over the fiscal situation played into the tug-of-war within the coalition over how to fund payments to the unemployed. In March 1930 the issue came to a head, and the Müller government resigned. The "political general" in Hindenburg's entourage, Kurt von Schleicher, had in the meantime discussed with Brüning an alternative to party-system reform as a way to free governmental authority from the unpredictable DNVP and SPD. According to Article 48 of the Weimar constitution, a chancellor had the power in an emergency to govern by decrees cosigned by the president, though the Reichstag could subsequently revoke the decrees. Brüning now agreed to head such a "presidential government."

By repeatedly resorting to Article 48, Brüning hoped to keep financial reforms from being held hostage by any party. This course, however, made Brüning hostage to President Hindenburg's rather dubious circle of advisors without freeing him of the need for later parliamentary ratification of the decrees. In the last analysis, then, Article 48 was not enough: Brüning still needed a genuine constitutional reform and/or a genuine realignment of the party system.

To Brüning, the purpose of constitutional reform was not just to close the structural weaknesses of the Weimar state but also to commit rightists to a constitutional consensus they would have helped to shape. If party-system reform had heretofore not succeeded, it must be helped along by transforming the state into a form closer to that desired by its opponents. Brüning apparently contemplated everything from a corporatist assembly that would balance the power of the Reichstag to a limited monarchy under the Kaiser's grandson with Hindenburg as regent. These plans were neither made public nor generally confided to Brüning's party colleagues. Rather, the Chancellor gave repeated assurances that his purpose was to reinforce parliamentary democracy by turning it into "authoritarian democracy."[14]

The first time the Reichstag overrode a decree, Brüning dissolved the house and called new elections, hoping that the moderate splinter parties would profit. Instead came the spectacular Nazi breakthrough. With 18.3 percent in the September elections (up from 2.6 percent two years earlier), the Nazis supplanted the DNVP (7.0 percent), which lost half its voters, as the second largest party. The CSVD got only 2.5 percent, and Treviranus's group, on which Brüning had placed his greatest hopes, got 0.8 percent and only four seats. On the left, the SPD lost ground (to 24.5 percent), while the KPD's substantial gains (to 13.1 percent) moved it past the Center (11.8 percent) as the third largest party. Among the biggest losers were the Center's former partners in the middle. The DDP, which had merged with the JDO and renamed itself the State Party, mustered only 3.8 percent, while the

DVP fell by nearly half, to 4.5 percent. Far from strengthening the Protestant middle, the elections robbed the Center of all significant parliamentary allies. Intending to free government from dependence on the SPD, Brüning now could not govern even by decree without that party's tolerance.

Thus was partisan realignment finally realized in the Weimar Republic: instead of producing a large state-supporting partner for the Center, it produced a radical opponent of the Center and the state. Aided by the depression, the NSDAP did among Protestants what only the Center, among Catholics, had previously done: it garnered significant, if not uniform, support from virtually every vocational stratum. In 1932, with the nation constantly at the polls (due to state and local elections, two presidential rounds, and two Reichstag dissolutions), the Nazi wave crested at 37 percent in the Reichstag election of July 31. Thanks to denominational solidarity and Führer-like rallies for Brüning, the tower withstood the rising tide. But the Nazis, in the reverse of their pattern among Protestants, did better among urban than among rural Catholics. Disgruntled city-dwellers whose Weltanschauung would not allow them to go over to Marxist parties had found another outlet.[15]

Brüning had come to power in 1930 with one idea: to "save democracy" by overriding its most fundamental ground rules. He had shown respect neither for the cultivation of public opinion nor for the power of numbers. In essence, he had hoped that the objective correctness (as he saw it) of his political and economic prescriptions would carry him to success before the democratic process had time to catch up with him. However, his twin measures for structural political change—constitutional and party-system reform—actually had contradictory prerequisites. If Brüning wanted party-system reform, he had to give the new moderate-conservative parties time to attract support and to organize for elections. But since he was determined that the institutional power of "the parties"—a generic condemnation that distinguished him from his Labor Minister, Stegerwald—be broken, he resorted early to Article 48, ran afoul of the existing parties, and had to call early elections. The result was the debacle of September 1930.[16]

Despite Stegerwald's opposition, Brüning now tried to buy time by promising an eventual share of power to Hugenberg and Hitler. In late 1930, he privately told Hitler that he would be willing to form trial Nazi-Centrist state governments; the next year, he advised both Hugenberg and Hitler that he would hand power over to them once his program was complete. In 1932, he envisioned serving as Foreign Minister in a rightist government with Nazi participation under the conservative mayor of Leipzig, Carl Goerdeler. This plan even included replacing the Prussian government with a Reich commissar. According to Brüning's memoirs, he withheld these plans from the members of his party, except for Kaas (but surely also Joos and Stegerwald). His concept now was to dissipate Nazi strength through governmental participation, heretofore the surefire way to cure the arrogance and cool the growth of any party under the Republic. Once the flood of radicalism had receded, thought Brüning, a Protestant-conservative party that could work with the Center would finally emerge.[17]

These plans had two hitches. First, they depended on the false proposition that the NSDAP, like the other parties, preferred being in opposition rather than governing, and would not know how to use power once it had it. Second, having destroyed any hope for a genuine parliamentary base, Brüning was at the mercy of the President, and the President could not be trusted. Indeed, his camarilla's aversion to the SPD extended also to the DGB. Insisting on the integrity of collective bargaining, Labor Minister Stegerwald was a thorn in the side of industrialists who wanted to use the depression to break the trade unions. Stegerwald's proposals for easing unemployment via land resettlement east of the Elbe made the President's agrarian friends see bright Red.[18]

These two factors combined in the spring of 1932 to bring Brüning down. When Hitler, defying Brüning's efforts to gain an uncontested second term for Hindenburg, announced his own presidential candidacy, Brüning had no choice but to base Hindenburg's reelection, like his own government, on support from the SPD. Although he was successful, his reward was not gratitude but resentment. When Brüning subsequently faced facts about the source of domestic disorder and tried to ban the brownshirted Nazi storm troopers, he was deserted by Schleicher. Although the intrigue-minded general seems to have led Brüning into a trap, it is difficult to deny from Schleicher's perspective that the Chancellor's action was a change of course. Labeling Brüning and especially the land-resettlement advocate Stegerwald "agrarian Bolsheviks," the camarilla determined to break the government's dependence on labor and to win the tolerance of Hitler by fashioning an uncamouflaged authoritarian government.

By elevating Franz von Papen, still nominally a Centrist, to the chancellorship in May 1932, Schleicher may have hoped to win the Center for an open break with the constitution. If so, he badly miscalculated. Having believed that Hindenburg's reelection would force the Nazis to participate in the government on his terms rather than theirs, Brüning felt stabbed in the back "just one hundred meters from the goal." Branding Papen a renegade, the Centrist press reacted furiously to what it saw as a ploy to split the party and announced that the Center would neither participate in nor tolerate this government. Kaas himself suffered a nervous breakdown when he heard of Papen's appointment.[19]

The Center's reaction to Brüning's fall was not mere partisanship: foreseeing that Hitler would not be satisfied, party leaders questioned how Papen proposed to govern with no mass support. Thus, the *KV* asserted that it would have preferred having Nazis in the government, and Joos, acting chairman during Kaas's illness, stated that Nazi participation had been Brüning's aim all along. Whereas Papen claimed to be advancing "Christian solidarity" and "national concentration," Joos warned that the new government was a devastatingly divisive step. In mid-July, Papen dissolved the Prussian government (still led by Otto Braun) and installed himself as Reich Commissar. Joos branded the action unconstitutional and compared this Prussian coup to the Kapp Putsch and to Bismarck's Anti-Socialist Law. Party leaders despaired that Social Democratic workers who had voted for Hindenburg, concluding they had been betrayed, would go over to the Communists. Lurking just under the surface was the fear of civil war.[20]

Still, there was partisanship as well as statesmanship behind the Center's reaction. In 1931 Kaas, proclaiming that the Center had become a constitutional "function" rather than a party, referred to Brüning in a way the "above-party" Chancellor himself avoided: as the Center's own agent of constitutional reform.[21] The Center's strength, however, had always been parliamentary; and Brüning, who had never been a party man like Trimborn or Marx, seems never to have asked himself where a presidential government in less benign hands might leave the Center. With Brüning's fall, the Center was just another party; indeed, since it alone had served in every Weimar government, it was particularly vulnerable to the new cabinet's blanket condemnation of the "party state" and the "Weimar system." It now seemed to dawn on party leaders that Brüning's government had been an improvisation dependent on the tenure of trustworthy personalities and utterly lacking in institutional safeguards. As they watched the authoritarian state pass into the hands of people whose purpose was not to save democracy but to dismantle it, Centrists reacted angrily not only to their party's first exclusion from power since 1918 but also to the end of its privileged role under Brüning as the antiparty middle party.

Selbstbesinnung

The shocking end of "authoritarian democracy" led some Centrists to conclude that the only alternative was a return to parliamentary government. Yet the mere threat of a Reichstag vote of no confidence was sure to lead to a dissolution and new elections. Whereas Brüning had counted on avoiding elections until the "fever curve" of radicalism was broken, the Centrist press now demanded that they take place immediately.[22]

There followed the campaign of July 1932, in which the Center, borrowing a page from the Nazis, glorified Brüning as "our Führer" (but with overtones of martyrdom) and depicted Papen as a front man for the Kulturkampf-minded Hugenberg. With the Nazis polling 37.4 percent, the non-Catholic middle was decimated. The liberal parties, the special-interest splinter parties, and the German National renegades put together received less than 5 percent of the vote, including 1 percent for the CSVD. The Center's "twin" in any case had not supported Brüning's ban on the Nazi storm troopers and increasingly wallowed in anticlerical rhetoric. The Center itself showed a small gain (from 11.8 to 12.5 percent), due mostly to Catholic excitement over Brüning's fate, but also to a smattering of Protestants who felt they now had no other way to register anti-Nazi sentiments. Such voters truly were clutching at straws, for Joos had publicly rejected emergency proposals from the State Party that the Center transform itself into a large non-Catholic middle party. To Joos, "homeless" voters could not cause the Center to alter its "own political home" for the sake of risky "experiments."[23]

Determined to show that a parliamentary alternative to Papen did exist, Joos now opened negotiations for a Nazi-Center coalition. Such a coalition would have commanded 305 of 608 seats (327 with the BVP). The negotiations took place despite two years of Centrist claims that the Nazis were not only irresponsible and uncommitted to the path of legality but also virulently anticlerical, heathenistic, and pagan in their Weltanschauung. The Center's flirtation with this manner of returning to parliamentary government was a demonstration of the cul-de-sac into which Brüning had led it. Stegerwald too dropped his scruples against dealing with the Nazis, for the talks now seemed the only way to prevent the hegemony of the reactionary anti-unionists who had brought Brüning down.[24]

Party leaders comforted themselves about the talks in two ways. First was the fear that failure to tame the Nazis might lead to further growth of the godless Communists. So great was this fear that at the end of 1931, with the Nazi tide cresting and Hitler and Hugenberg briefly pooling their forces in the so-called Harzburg Front, the monthly magazine *Das Zentrum* had devoted an entire triple issue— nearly half its total pages for the year—to a tirade against Marxism and Communism.[25] Second was the false analogy with the "working partnership, not shared conviction" idea regarding the coalition of 1919. Whereas the SPD's revisionism had been the prerequisite to the black-red cooperation of 1919, black-brown cooperation now was supposed to educate the Nazis in revisionism. With astounding gull- ibility, Joos claimed that his aim was a parliamentary majority gov- ernment that would guarantee the constitution.[26]

The Center was spared the historical ignominy of a coalition with the Nazis only because Hitler, holding out for the power of decree that went with presidential government, refused the offer. With the failure as well of Papen's efforts to win Nazi cooperation, the Reichstag was again dissolved. New elections on November 6 produced the first Nazi decline (to 33.1 percent), but in what was now essentially a five- party system, the SPD (20.4 percent) also declined, while the DNVP (8.9 percent, up from 5.9 percent) and KPD (16.9 percent, up from 14.5 percent, with 100 deputies to the SPD's 121) posted big gains. The Nazis' sudden metamorphosis from dangerous adversary to po- tential partner helped cost the Center its July bonus, and it slipped back to the level of 1930 (11.9 percent; BVP 3.1 percent).

Harder to measure is the effect of the coalitional flirtation on the morale of the rank and file. Whereas the July campaign had evoked some of the heroic feeling of bygone times, the events thereafter had again belied the party's desired image as a tower of steadfast principle. The tower was still standing, but it had hidden cracks. Having de- stroyed their own recent efforts to give the Center a clearer political identity, party leaders had cause to wonder how vigilantly their voters would still defend the tower.

As for the government, two dissolutions in four months had shown the futility of trying to govern without a mass base. Just as Brüning had once hoped to split the DNVP, Schleicher now hoped to split the Nazis. Bypassing the parties, he intended to use the rank and file of the Nazis' left wing and of the free and Christian unions as a popular base for a socially minded military government. Assuming the chancellorship himself, he held talks with Gregor Strasser (NSDAP), Heinrich Imbusch, and the leaders of the free unions. Having lost members to the Nazis, Imbusch and Jakob Kaiser expressed interest in the plan, since there seemed to be no other. Even the Centrist press seemed intrigued. But when Strasser could not interest Hitler, he resigned his party offices in isolation. Schleicher then asked Kaas whether the self-styled "constitution party" would tolerate constitutional violations to steady his government. With Kaas's negative reply, Schleicher had come to the end of his rope.[27]

On January 30, 1933, Hindenburg named Hitler to head a presidential government of the Harzburg parties, with Papen as Vice Chancellor. The new minority government contained three Nazis and nine conservatives, including Hugenberg. The Center reacted by condemning this latest Papen intrigue—not because it opposed making Hitler Chancellor, but because it distrusted the anticlerical Hugenberg, had not been brought into the negotiations, and feared the implications for Kulturpolitik. Yet, in contrast to its intransigent stance of the previous May, the Center seemed to be angling to be included. The government in turn seemed to be hinting at the prospect, for one ministerial post was left unoccupied. But when Kaas presented Hitler with a list of policy questions and asked for tangible assurances that the Chancellor would act constitutionally, Hitler refused to answer and dissolved the Reichstag. As the country entered its third campaign in eight months, the ever forthcoming Joos was still stating that the Center would have tolerated the new government had it been properly asked.[28]

The subsequent campaign was marked by rampant Nazi terror, backed now by the authority of the government. Many Centrist civil servants were summarily dismissed, and Stegerwald was attacked and beaten as he tried to deliver a speech.[29] With deputized storm troopers standing at the polls, the Nazis received 43.9 percent of the vote on March 5, including an influx of Catholics. The Center recorded the lowest figure in its history, 11.2 percent. Buttressed by the DNVP's 8.0 percent, Hitler had an absolute majority. Nevertheless, he now asked the Reichstag for an Enabling Act that would let him rule with-

out the legislature for four years. This constitutional "revision" required a two-thirds majority, and with the Communist deputies arrested or in hiding, the Center had the power to produce it.

Confronted with its last chance to play a role, the party caucus
stood utterly demoralized. The last thing it wanted was a return to the
ghetto. Members who had spent their lives denying that Catholics
were less patriotic than other Germans agonized over resisting the
tide, while those such as Carl Bachem who remembered the
Kulturkampf feared precipitating a purge of all remaining Centrist
civil servants—a purge that would cause further economic hardship
during a depression, reverse decades of progress on bureaucratic parity, and remove a safeguard against religious persecution. Even
priestly stipends seemed at risk. A vote against the Enabling Act, the
thoroughly intimidated Bachem later claimed, would have caused
the deputies to be physically attacked and expelled from the chamber;
the party organization would then have been forcibly dismantled, like the
SPD's or the Catholic party's in Italy. The caucus would have made a
"heroic exit, without being of any use to the cause of Catholicism or
the Center."[30]

In this atmosphere, the caucus groped for a way to protect its own
concerns while giving Hitler what he wanted. The solution was a list
of conditions that Hitler incorporated into his speech (but not into
the Act) on the day of the vote (March 23). Hitler pledged not to end
the existence of the states or houses of parliament, not to disturb the
rights of the President, not to purge the bureaucracy or judiciary, and
not to launch one-sided measures against any segment of the population (such as Catholics) that loyally supported his government. He
would respect the role of the churches in the schools, honor the Bavarian, Prussian, and Badenese concordats, and not use the state to repress the churches (no Kulturkampf). He agreed to form a liaison
committee between the government and the Center. (The committee
met twice.)[31]

By failing to mention the civil rights of others, the Center silently
abandoned its venerable claim to be defending not just Catholic rights
but the general principle of minority rights. Instead, it prioritized the
status quo in Kulturpolitik, civil parity for Catholics, and a facade of
constitutional compliance to appease its conscience.

The Center and BVP now voted unanimously for the Act. In doing
so, they signed their own death warrants. For they put their trust in
Hitler's word while removing the institutional and compromising the

moral bases of their power to hold him to it. Few besides Brüning and Wirth seemed to understand this; together with Imbusch, Kaiser, Dessauer, and the sometimes overly conciliatory but always upstanding Joos, they voted in the preliminary party caucus to oppose the Act.[32] Stegerwald's stance is unknown, but as has been seen, his history was always to accommodate himself to circumstances.

Opposition to the Enabling Act would seem, prima facie, to have been the only position in accordance with the Center's self-image as a "constitution party," for it would have forced the Nazis to reveal the illegal nature of their dictatorship. But this is to ignore the facile adaptability of Leonine accidentalism. To ex-Chancellor Marx, Pope Leo's admonition to Catholics to cooperate after a political upheaval in promptly restoring order applied in 1933 as in 1919: "The Hitler government officially calls itself the 'government of national revolution.' The Center has never participated in revolutions. But since the Hitler government, through the Reichstag election, found . . . the acknowledgment of the great majority of the German people, . . . the Center was simply duty-bound not to go into opposition, which doubtless would have been tactically more successful." One year later, after the Center had dissolved, the former Chancellor recalled how he had "enraged republicans, . . . especially Dr. Wirth," by saying in 1927 that "the Center is not a monarchistic, but also not a republican party; it is a constitution party!" Now, however, Germany had neither a monarchy nor a republic nor even a dictatorship (according to Marx), but a "Führer":

> If the Center were really a republican or a monarchistic party, then those who call the Center a party of "enmity against nation and state" would be correct. [But] the Center will never be able to grant that this is correct . . . [for] according to its—the Catholic—principles, [the Center] recognizes the Hitler government as the legitimate government and will not refuse it obedience in all things that are in agreement with the Catholic conscience. Now as before, it will stay and remain a party loyal to the state. But it can only recognize the new governmental form as legitimate if it is a constitution party or better still a legality party *(Rechtspartei)!*

The statement would seem almost cynical if it were not so pathetically naive.[33]

During the Center's controversies with Wirth, the liberal Lujo Brentano had noted: "The Center . . . clings unrelentingly to the denominational school and would form an alliance with the Devil in order to bring the children of its constituents to heaven."[34] Although this was an exaggeration, there can be no gainsaying the negative impact of the primacy of Kulturpolitik on Centrist behavior during Weimar's great crisis. The Devil and his Judas (Papen) tried to flush Catholics "out of the tower" via Kulturpolitik. Their task was eased after the Enabling Act by the cooperation of the bishops, who rescinded their anti-Nazi prohibitions and urged Catholics to support the state.

For the time being, therefore, the government could use the carrot more than the stick. On April 10, Papen turned up at the Vatican to negotiate a Reich concordat. On his way, he met Kaas, and the two pooled their efforts. Rumors soon spread in Germany that Kaas was gone for good. Joos tried to quiet the rumors, but it was becoming increasingly evident that the Center, like the other parties, was on the road to dissolution. The partially tamed Catholic press spent most of the month insisting that the Center still had an independent role to play in the new state: instead of being "coordinated" *(gleichgeschaltet)* like other organizations, it would mediate in bringing Catholics into constructive "collaboration" *(Mitarbeit)*. On April 29, however, the *KV* published an article under the headline *"Selbstbesinnung"* ("reflection" or "introspection") that hinted at dissolution.[35]

On May 6, party leaders tried one final ploy to revive flagging morale: they replaced the departed Kaas with Brüning and gave this reluctant Führer dictatorial powers to revamp and purge the party. Brüning, the *KV* commented, was not a party man, but the embodiment of the overcoming of the old party system; he was just the one to integrate the old party into the new state. Bachem, meanwhile, was toying with an idea raised by Kaas on the day before passage of the Enabling Act: preserving the Center as a purely religious lobby. On May 19, the *KV* floated a trial balloon:

the Center of the future will be . . . the Center of Windthorst and Baron von Mallinckrodt. Such a Center will be worthy of the love of all German Catholics, wherever they might stand politically. For it will be Catholic to the core . . . This Center will undertake nothing other than the transmission of Catholic values to the new state. It is simply a Catholic movement on a political basis. It is the necessary attempt of a minority to secure the Catholic legacy in public life . . . more than a party, it is a lay movement in the framework of the state.

Thus did the *KV* take final leave of the tradition of the tower article. Brüning, meanwhile, lapsed into inactivity, for he was convinced after the Enabling Act that the Center in any form was finished.[36]

As the concordat negotiations continued in Rome, further "Selbstbesinnung" articles relayed a purported readers' debate as to whether the Center ought simply to dissolve. In late June, the party joined the Nazi-dominated government of Danzig. The *KV* then virtually begged the Nazis to let the party live on as an appendage of the NSDAP, somewhat like the East German non-Communist parties later. But Goebbels demanded that the Center dissolve. By this time, it was the only non-Nazi party organization still openly operating. The Center, stated Goebbels pointedly, had become superfluous; its dissolution would be a service to the Church. The *KV* responded that "honest collaboration" *(Mitarbeit)* should not mean dissolution. But it added that the Center had never been a goal in itself, and angled for appropriate face-saving measures.[37]

What sort of face-saving was easily discerned, for two sets of negotiations were nearing their completion. In Berlin, Albert Hackelsberger, a pro-Nazi Centrist industrialist, was trying to get as many Centrist deputies as possible accepted as "guests" *(Hospitanten)* of the Nazi caucus, with very limited success. Of higher priority by then, however, were the negotiations in Rome. On July 2, Kaas telephoned from the Vatican to ask Joos why the party had not yet dissolved. Three days later, with the concordat essentially complete, the party took Kaas's advice. On July 10, the *KV* rejoiced over the concordat and explicitly noted the coincidence with the Center's dissolution. On July 19, the paper denied that the Vatican had ordered the dissolution, yet also stated that the concordat was a Centrist triumph and the culmination of its work. Among the terms of the treaty, which was signed the next day, were guarantees for denominational schools, continued governmental subsidies to the Church, the banning of priests from politics, and the dissolution of all the political and many of the social and vocational organizations that made up the German Catholic subcultural infrastructure.[38]

Freed from the oversight of a vigilant Catholic party, the Third Reich, through its concordat with the Vatican, was henceforth to be the guarantor of the civic and religious interests of German Catholics. The flimsiness of the guarantees was to be abundantly proven over the next twelve years, when the Nazis, first through civil "coordination" *(Gleichschaltung)*, then through the *Kirchenkampf* (church struggle), broke virtually every one of the promises Hitler had given on March 23 and July 20.[39] But the die had long since been cast. What Bismarck and Leo XIII, in the face of Windthorst's resistance, could not arrange, Hitler and Pius XI, with Kaas's eager collaboration, did. In what was for Centrists the ultimate party-system "reform," the Center, confounding Windthorst's words of half a century earlier, was both "vanquished by its enemies" and "forsaken by its friends."

The Center Party of Kaas and Brüning

For six decades, Ludwig Windthorst's Center had insisted that it was not a one-sided defender of Catholicism but a medium for bridging religious and socioeconomic gaps. Its success in the second area had been far greater than in the first. Although the Center had frequently spoken of welcoming Protestants, it had consistently drawn back, not only because of Protestants' aversion, but also because of its own insecurity and defensiveness.[40]

This problem had been compounded after 1918 by the introduction of parliamentary government. A middle party because of its socially mixed constituency, the Center was now a necessary component of all coalitions. The party of Catholic defense was thus thrust into the role of providing governmental continuity with a wide variety of partners. These partners included conservative Protestants, whose goodwill the Center had long desired and who now opposed the state whose constitution the Center had helped write. They also included Social Democrats, whose professed ideology was anathema to Catholics and whose clumsy statecraft led to dismay even among sympathetic Centrists such as Joos and Wirth.[41]

The Center spent the Weimar years sorting through the resultant dilemmas—socioeconomic, religious, ideological, constitutional, and psychological. Its solution, neatly summarized in the ambiguities and ambivalences of the phrases "constitution party," "working partnership," and "Christian Weltanschauung," was so complicated that the party, despite its relative stability at the polls, reeled from one crisis of conscience to another and seemed constantly on the verge of a split. By 1928, what for another party would have been a minor electoral dip plunged the leaders of the Center into despair. There seemed to be nothing left to do but to appeal for a recovery of "Catholic consciousness" *(Besinnung)*—a euphemism for reinvigorating the Catholic bond. The new course was symbolized by the election, amidst unprecedented fanfare, of Kaas to the party chairmanship; it was gradually supplied with an elaborated political rationale by Joos.

In effect, the new explicitness about Catholicism meant subordinating external mediation to internal unity. Ultimately, this became a formula for an authoritarian solution: the Center was to follow its leaders lockstep into any and all arrangements with outsiders that they, in their conscientiously Catholic judgment, chose to make. The morality of those arrangements was indivisible: it applied only to their totality, not to individual components. Thus, moral reservations about one particular arrangement—say, the Prussian coalition with the left, or the Reich-level talks with the Nazis—were brushed aside by referring to the higher moral claim of the complex of arrangements of which they were a part. That higher claim, which derived from "Catholic consciousness," was the domain of the leaders, by virtue of their superior vantage point. For the rank and file, Catholic consciousness expressed itself in the necessity to maintain unity by enthusiastically following.

What applied to the rank and file, however, soon applied also to the leaders. For when Catholic consciousness proved an insufficient basis for political effectiveness in the face of the deteriorating economic situation, the Center overlaid a new political style. In essence, the party abdicated in favor of its rising star and economics expert, Heinrich Brüning. In much the same way, Brüning's government asked the Reichstag to abdicate in favor of his government-by-decree. The Chancellor summarized his program in a typically ambivalent Centrist formulation: "authoritarian democracy."

The superposition of this program upon the results of the Congress of Consciousness created the alliance of Kaas and Brüning—the Catholic priest whose presence documented the party's return to consciousness and conviction (*Besinnung* and *Gesinnung*), and the one-time Stegerwald protégé who was thought to personify single-minded political leadership. The bond between them, and the bridge to the party's left, was Joos, the man of "mediation" and "balance" *(Ausgleich)* and the working-class champion of Kulturpolitik. This triumvirate tensely pursued its plans behind the scenes, with Joos, via frequent signed columns in the party press, as spokesman. Largely unbeknownst to the party, those plans included broad constitutional reforms and far-reaching political arrangements that would eventually have resulted in a radically different political system led by a right-wing government with prominent Nazi participation.

The pairing of Brüning and Kaas was an unlikely one but, for a time, it worked. By governing essentially above his party, Brüning freed it from the micromanagement of politics—for Kaas was far less engaged in daily politics than Marx had been. Moreover, by trying to develop a separate Protestant partner, Brüning allowed the Center to be what it was, and what Kaas was elected to symbolize: a Catholic party. The issue of interdenominationalism thus was taken off the agenda. What Brauns had always insisted must not happen—the reason he had opposed the idea of twin parties in the prewar years—now emerged as the logical outcome of the situation: if the Center wanted a Protestant twin, then it followed that the Center was the Catholic twin. On these grounds, the Center of Kaas and the Center of Brüning could be made to match.

Brüning's fall drastically changed the situation. Every one of his successive plans—twin parties, "authoritarian democracy," constitutional monarchy, a Goerdeler-led rightist government—had failed. Despite the showy Centrist rallies for Brüning ("our Führer"), the former Chancellor, who had never been inclined to the give and take of partisan politics, now virtually abdicated from further leadership, preferring to sulk in martyrdom. With Brüning reduced to a symbolic figure, Kaas, as head of what was still the pivotal party in Germany, could no longer serve just as a Catholic symbol, but had to be a genuine political leader. This, by judgment and by temperament, he was not.

Thus, when Hindenburg withdrew his support, the whole house of cards came tumbling down. As if to complete a parable, the "betrayal" of Papen left the party desperately trying to reassert the parliamentary rights it had recently tried to curtail. But the solution could hardly be a coalition with those (the Nazis) who were the real source of the problem. Yet, even after Hitler became Chancellor, Kaas continued to cast the Nazis, like the Socialists before them, as radical talkers with whom one could do business once they provided assurances on religious affairs. In the end, he struck a deal through which the "political, nonconfessional party" was sacrificed on the altar of Kulturpolitik. That it was the statesman Brüning who pleaded with his party not to yield its *political* morality for such a price was perhaps fitting; that it was the layman Brüning who had to plead that Kaas's course ran counter to *weltanschaulichen* morality was more ironic. Compounding the irony, Brüning's plea was directed against a party (the Nazi party) that his teacher and early mentor, Martin Spahn, now proclaimed to be the realization of the dream he and Brüning had once shared: a national, social, and interdenominational catch-all party.

In a sense, Spahn was not wrong. The logic of integration through a cultural-political settlement seemed to fit the logic of "coordination." In this scenario, the Center, instead of guaranteeing the defense of Catholicism, seemed to endanger that defense. For it was no longer clear why one needed the party if the Church was contracting directly and comprehensively with the Nazi state. A separate Catholic party could only raise the suspicion that Catholics still saw themselves as apart from other Germans. This, many Catholics increasingly felt, could only make them once again a target.

Nevertheless, far from representing the Essen vision of national and social integration, Nazism represented an alternative. The NSDAP was indeed a large and integrative anti-Marxist catch-all party such as Germany had heretofore lacked; but it was anything but moderate, Christian, and democratic. Whereas Spahn saw it as the *realization* of the interdenominational national party he had been urging, Stegerwald quickly labeled it a consequence of the *failure* to implement Essen.[42] It stood to reason, then, that when the Nazi state finally collapsed, former Centrists and Christian trade unionists would be at the vanguard of an effort to make good on Brüning's wistful prophecy of July 3, 1932: "when the waters recede and the disillusionment of the voters with radicalism sets in . . . a great insight will dawn on [the people of] Germany, and the positive believers of both confessions will be able to reach out a hand to each other in politics . . ."[43]

PART IV

Reshaping Party Politics, 1945–1957

An old world has sunk and we want to build a new one . . . by returning to the cultivation of those moral principles and spiritual values that constituted . . . the honorable tradition of our land.

—Andreas Hermes (CDU), July 1945

A new page of history has turned, whose first lines speak of the necessity of union of the two Christian confessions in politics.

—Karl Zimmermann (CDU), November 1945

Europe is depending on the workers and the Christians.

—Walter Dirks (CDU), March 1947

Amidst the administrative problems and political chaos in Germany at the end of World War I, the swift recovery of the party system had seemed an element of stability. As a result, the impulse to change the structure of the party system had quickly given way to other priorities, and later attempts to achieve a democratic restructuring had been frustrated. After World War II, the situation was fundamentally different. This time, the setting of administrative priorities was in the hands of four occupying powers: Great Britain, France, the United States, and the Soviet Union. Exhausted, disillusioned, hungry, dispirited, and afraid, the German population was generally inclined to stay out of politics. As early as June 1945, however, the occupying powers began to license political parties. The reshaping of the party system was thus among the first areas where a few Germans could directly influence future institutions.

This time, no preexisting party system had to be displaced: Hitler had seen to that. Indeed, only the Socialists and the Communists had an émigré organization, and even they lacked much of an underground. Organizations that once had linked the parties to specific subcultures had vanished, had been "coordinated" *(gleichgeschaltet)*, or, like the Catholic Church, had severed their party ties in order to make their peace with the Nazis. The result was a breakdown in the rigid system of regional, denominational, ideological, and class cleavages that had characterized German society and the old party system. Although the extent of this breakdown during the Nazi period is disputed,[1] the process unquestionably was accelerated by the collapse of the regime. Nearly universal poverty, the shared onus of collective guilt, and religious integration due to the influx of twelve million German expellees from eastern Europe all were factors in this process.[2]

With the breakdown in both the subcultural rigidity of the electorate and the partisan manifestations of that rigidity, building new parties no longer seemed necessarily more difficult than refounding old ones. In one key sense, the innovators were helped by the occupying powers, who were clearly not going to license parties that were too far to the right or that involved known servants of the Nazi regime. The foreign presence, however, cannot by itself explain the form taken by the party system's transformation after 1945.[3] As that form was to show, the moment belonged neither to radical experimenters nor to restorers, but to those who best diverted alternate pathways first blazed in the past. In this specific and limited sense, the party-system renewal was a creative exercise in historical continuity, inaugurated with the aid of the same generation of German political leaders who had seen out the first republic.

With most of the country's communications network destroyed, local proclivities would be crucial in forming parties. Haphazard coordination existed among some local centers thanks to wartime resistance circles.[4] Party organizers also included former inmates of concentration camps, returning émigrés, and people who had withdrawn from public view during the Hitler years, preferring what some called "internal emigration."

The impact of Nazism on traditional notions of political alignment in these groups was quite varied. Believing that the Nazis would never have come to power but for the political disunity of labor, some leftist émigrés and former camp inmates talked of merging the old Marxist parties. Others, such as the Social Democrat Kurt Schumacher, wanted nothing to do with the Communists, whose parliamentary obstructionism had contributed to the Weimar Republic's collapse.[5] In the non-Communist resistance, meanwhile, Catholics had worked with Protestants, and aristocrats had worked with Social Democrats. Many non-Socialist "internal émigrés" concluded that the events of 1933 had discredited their old parties. They were aware that a generation had grown up for whom an appeal to party tradition would conjure up no memory and would seem anachronistic. With the political scales seemingly tipping toward the left, they believed they had to form larger combinations if they were not to be overwhelmed.

Nowhere was this last concern more apposite than among Protestant conservatives. Implicated more than Catholics in the coming of Nazism, some had tried to resurrect their group's collective honor by playing major roles in the resistance. But many of those leaders, such as the former Mayor of Leipzig, Carl Goerdeler, had been executed in the wake of a failed plot to kill Hitler in July 1944. Their postwar plans, in any case, had hardly been realistic, involving a separate peace with the western powers and the rejection of a liberal "party state."[6] The old conservative elite, having both collaborated in Nazism and been subjugated by it, was now in shambles. Moreover, the old German National partisan rump was discredited and hardly likely to be licensed.

Although Protestant elitist conservatism had shown its resilience after the setbacks of 1918–1919, the conditions of 1945 were less propitious. The Prussian army was destroyed, the Prussian state was dissolved, and Germany was divided into semiautonomous occupation zones, some with Catholic majorities. Furthermore, the eastern heartland of Prussian conservatism lay under the Soviets' thumb. East Prussia was lost to Soviet-Polish annexation, and in the Soviet-occupied portion of the remainder of Germany, the east Elbian aristocracy was soon to be expropriated. To be sure, some north German Protestants later did procure a license (1947) for a conservative Protestant party known as the German Party (DP), but this party's roots lay somewhat less in the DNVP than in the former regional Hanoverian party, with its ties to the Center. The new party nevertheless served as a warning to those who wished to overcome subcultural partisan splintering that success was by no means inevitable.

Somewhat better placed than the mainstream Protestant conservatives were the Protestant or freethinking liberals. Historically disunited before 1930 and decimated in the last few elections of the Weimar Republic, they were neither unstained by Nazism nor assured of a renaissance in a war-shattered society that sought solace, absolution, or evasion in religion. Though less ravaged in their potential for autonomy than German conservatism, the traditional varieties of secular German liberalism faced partisan prospects that were at best uncertain.

Since Germany still contained large numbers of culturally conservative Protestants, much depended upon their willingness to join hands either with Catholics or with freethinking liberals whose historical ties to democracy were stronger than their own. Important in this connection was the emergence during the Nazi era of the breakaway Confessing Church in response to Nazi coordination of the official Protestant church. Nazi attacks on both the Catholic and the Confessing Church during the Kirchenkampf of the 1930s had produced the biggest popular protests of the Nazi era. Isolated and uncoordinated responses to particular provocations, these protests and the subsequent wartime religious revival were a shared fund of grass-roots experience.[7] To the advocates of interdenominational democratic cooperation, this shared experience of religious persecution seemed to enhance their own political prospects while reducing those of both the religious separatists and the anticlerical liberals.

Less tainted by Nazism and less weakened than the Protestants, Catholics nevertheless were not unburdened by the past. A twelve-year cataclysm separated them from the party that had withstood the Nazi electoral tide only to acquiesce in the Enabling Act. Among the major Weimar Centrists, only Konrad Adenauer (sixty-nine years old in 1945), Adam Stegerwald (seventy-one), and former Finance Minister and Rhenish agrarian leader Andreas Hermes (sixty-seven) were to play significant postwar roles—though Joseph Joos (sixty-seven and a concentration camp victim), Wilhelm Marx (eighty-two), Hugo Mönnig (eighty-two), and even Carl Bachem (eighty-seven) lived to see the end of the war. Although the reclusive Heinrich Brüning (sixty, living in Vermont) and Joseph Wirth (sixty-six, in Switzerland until 1948) also occasionally influenced postwar events, the former second-tier leaders Jakob Kaiser (fifty-seven), Leo Schwering (fifty-seven), Johannes Albers (fifty-five), and Heinrich Krone (fifty) now came into their own. With the brief and idiosyncratic exception of Wirth, none of these men favored a Centrist revival.

For former Centrists, the bridging of rivalries that had once debilitated the defense of democracy was part of their heritage. Four old domestic projects now vied for primacy: the bridge between Catholics and Protestants, the bridge between labor and the middle classes, the bridge within the labor camp (between Christians and Socialists), and bridges within the splintered non-Socialist, or so-called *bürgerlichen*, camp. Prospects for a fifth project, the bridge to other countries in Europe's Christian West, seemed likely to be enhanced by the emergence of democratic Catholic parties in Italy and France; a sixth, the bridge between the Soviet-occupied eastern zone of Germany and the three western zones, had no precedent in the Weimar era. By ranking their bridge-building priorities, ex-Centrists helped produce a matrix of possibilities for a reformed party system.

The first possibility grew out of the experience of Catholics who had worked with Socialists in the resistance. In his own version of the theory that greater labor unity might have stopped the Nazis, Stegerwald's onetime protégé, Jakob Kaiser, led a move to supplant the SPD with a British-style Labour party (Partei der Arbeit) that would be religiously tolerant and freed of Marxist ideology. Perhaps the most active Centrist in the anti-Nazi resistance, Kaiser had had close wartime relations with Max Habermann, the Protestant head of the old DNVP-affiliated retail workers' union (DHV), and Wilhelm Leuschner of the old Socialist unions. Both Habermann and Leuschner had been executed after the failed plot to kill Hitler in July 1944; Kaiser had spent the rest of the war hidden in a cellar in Berlin.

Alongside the Partei der Arbeit, Kaiser envisioned a unified trade union organization that would be strictly neutral on issues of Weltanschauung. In this way, his first priority, labor unity, would be reinforced by both partisan and union bonds, while his second, interdenominational cooperation, would be extended into the party system. Part of Stegerwald's Essen program would thus be fulfilled. Unlike Stegerwald, however, Kaiser did not shrink from the concept of an explicitly labor-oriented party. Believing that the war had revolutionized social relations and impoverished the middle classes, he expected their cooperation in pursuit of "Christian socialism." In his view, the "bourgeois age" was over, and it was up to the burghers to adjust.[8]

Kaiser's plans had three problems. First, the traditional Social Democrats were unlikely to be persuaded not to revive the SPD. Second, while a Labour party would seem to presuppose the existence of rival parties to its right, Kaiser advanced no clear conception of those parties. Third, some of Kaiser's associates seemed to think of a non-Marxist Labour party not as neutral in regard to Weltanschauung, but as Christian. This view was especially evident in western resistance circles, where the phrase "Christian socialism" was originally most prevalent.

These points helped bring to the fore the idea of forming a Christian Democratic Party (CDP) alongside the SPD. Like the Center, such a party was to have a socioeconomically diverse constituency; unlike the Center, the political reconciliation of Catholics and Protestants would be the CDP's most fundamental premise. Opinions differed, however, as to whether such a party could or should be progressive enough to keep the SPD out of the embrace of the KPD. In the British zone, the veteran Cologne trade unionist Johannes Albers and his forty-four-year-old Düsseldorf colleague Karl Arnold envisioned a Christian socialist CDP in coalition with the SPD. But Andreas Hermes, Kaiser's colleague in the Berlin resistance, deemed a democratic interdenominational party an alternative to, not a derivative from, the idea of a Labour or socialist Christian party. To document the fact that the new party was to be a political union of Catholics and Protestants, Hermes insisted on calling the Berlin party the Christian Democratic Union (CDU), an idea western groups accepted at the end of 1945. The party's posture toward the SPD remained, however, unsettled.

A variation on the Christian and Labour ideas came from Stegerwald himself. The former trade union leader, who had run for his life and spent three months in exile following the purge of June 1934, had lived relatively quietly thereafter in Berlin. Bombed out of his home in 1944, he had relocated to his native south, where he had briefly been arrested following the failure of the plot to kill Hitler, though he was not involved. From Würzburg in the American zone, he now advanced the idea of an interdenominational farmer-labor party. Lacking Kaiser's experience of collaboration with Social Democrats in the resistance, Stegerwald explicitly put interclass conciliation ahead (but not in place) of interdenominational and intralabor bridging.

Alongside these reformist visions, a refounded Center nevertheless remained a possibility. Advanced in part by traditionalists like Wilhelm Hamacher, the sixty-two-year-old former history teacher and General Secretary of the Rhenish party, the idea really took hold only in response to the early initiatives to found the CDP/CDU. It was promoted by ex-Landtag deputies Helene Wessel (a social worker) and Johannes Brockmann (a schoolteacher), who had worked with the Social Democrats on the Prussian cultural legislation of the Weimar era and who feared, as Wirth had once feared, that an interdenominational party would be dominated by Protestant reactionaries who had no place else to turn.

With the revival of the SPD in the late spring of 1945, the ground was cut out from under the advocates of a Labour party. Some, like Kaiser, now joined Albers, Arnold, and Stegerwald in falling back on the idea of a nationwide Christian party with no specific class-based designation. By integrating the new party into a democratic popular front and unifying the trade unions, Kaiser hoped to bridge all four traditional gaps (denominational, class, intralabor, intra-*bürgerlich*) that had once destabilized domestic German politics. On another score, Kaiser made a virtue of necessity: since the "democratic" front in the Soviet zone would have to include the KPD, it might also bridge the gap between East and West.

The East-West problem was the wild card in the deck. Few foresaw in 1945 that the country would be lastingly partitioned or understood the implications for the party system. One who did was the former Mayor of Cologne, Konrad Adenauer. In a rump Germany, he believed, a Christian Democratic party with ties to comparable parties in western Europe would have an advantage if it maintained a clearly anti-Marxist, including anti-SPD, profile. For non-Marxist politicians in the Soviet zone, however, the task could not be how to gain advantage in a rump Germany, but how to prevent partition. Thus, Kaiser tried to profile the CDU itself as a bridge between East and West, even though this meant cooperating with the Communists. By contrast, many progressive leaders outside the Soviet zone, such as the former Landtag deputy Leo Schwering (founder of the CDP in Cologne), held instinctively to the expectation that there would be a nationwide political competition between the Christians and the Communists.

Not all who were intrigued by the concept of a Labour party joined Kaiser in embracing the notion of an interdenominational Christian party. Among those who did not was Karl Spiecker. Formerly the head of the Berlin Center Party and press secretary to Chancellor Marx, the fifty-seven-year-old Spiecker had a long pedigree as a follower of Wirth: he had served with Heinrich Teipel on the editorial staff of *Germania*, had made his name at the Cassel party congress of 1925 through his strong advocacy of the Center's republican character, and had been special plenipotentiary for dealing with Nazi violence during Wirth's tenure at the Ministry of the Interior under

Brüning. With a record like that, Spiecker (like Wirth and Brüning) had done well to flee Nazi Germany early. He had spent the war years in Britain and North America, where he had been impressed by the absence of the controversies over Weltanschauung that had bedeviled relations among the German parties. In particular, he had noted the tolerance for religion displayed by the British Labour party and the coexistence of Weltanschauungen within it.

Spiecker's early return to his native Westphalia (in the British zone) in the fall of 1945 was rumored to have been facilitated by the British Labour government in order to establish a Labour party in Germany.[9] With the SPD already reestablished, however, Spiecker argued that the only way to avoid a devastating struggle between the SPD and a rightist Christian party under the guise of defending Christianity from Marxism was to put a large centrist party in between. Like his friend Teipel in the mid-Weimar years, Spiecker wanted to get Weltanschauung out of politics; unlike Teipel, his instrument would be the Center. Thus, in contrast to Hamacher, Spiecker wanted the new Center to declare its freedom from Weltanschauung in favor of a tolerant and progressive program open to all. Together, SPD and Center could function like an ersatz Labour party; a future realignment might then produce a two-party system as in Britain or America, in which the competition would be amicable because it would not be based on Weltanschauung.

By the fall of 1945, the place of political Catholicism in the party system had come down to two choices: the interdenominational Christian "Union parties," loosely organized for the time being as local foundings; and the revived Center, or Bavarian regional party. Each of these options housed two or more different conceptions. But as the former resisters, émigrés, and frustrated Weimar innovators grasped the opportunity to make a fresh start, idealism and the difficulties of communication among local centers prevented a fuller understanding of the differences. In a Germany historically troubled by a splintered party system, it was not a moment in any case to sort out differences, but to gather people together. On this point, at least in the Union parties, all the Catholic founders were agreed.

7 Catholics at the Zero Hour

However widespread the inclination was in 1945 to recast the party system, success was by no means assured. After all, the only political leaders with established democratic credentials came from a generation reared on the old partisan rivalries. Even early electoral success for some new, more broadly conceived party was no guarantee of staying power, as the fate of the DDP had once shown. Nor was the possibility excluded that Catholics might react to the Kirchenkampf of the Nazi period by seeking to restore their defensive tower. From the very beginning, therefore, Catholic political reformers had to define their relationship to tradition. Was Catholic defense still a properly partisan matter? Was Centrist partisan loyalty transferrable? Did middleness remain the political and moral goal? Were they the Center's true redeemers or revolutionaries bent on eradicating the past?

As in 1918–1920, trade unionists frequently took a bolder position than did middle-class reformers. Whereas Adam Stegerwald rejected even a retrospective honoring of the Center's legacy, such a rejection was difficult for many middle-class Catholics. While some believed that only a clear disavowal of a Centrist connection would win Protestants, others tried to wean their Catholic peers (and reassure themselves) by portraying the CDU as the realization of the Center's own agenda.

At least one trade unionist got an early taste of the problems in store for reformers. On June 8, 1944, Johannes Albers met with former party secretary Wilhelm Hamacher to discuss what was to happen on "Day X," the day of Hitler's removal. Hamacher had already told Josef Hofmann, longtime political editor of the old *KV*, that "there was nothing at all to consider, the Center would come again." The gap between Albers and Hamacher was not closed on June 8. Approached again by Hofmann one year later (June 6, 1945), Hamacher rebuffed him with a quintessentially Centrist argument: since the Center had never been a confessional party, there was no need for something new. If the old name were dropped, he flatly stated, he would not join the movement.[1]

Despite the perception that the demise of the Nazi state had brought German history to a "zero hour" (Stunde Null), a familiar set of issues had indeed survived the Third Reich. The old Center tower had collapsed, but the ruins had yet to be cleared. The shape of the new construction would depend on the place of the old tradition, as well as the new vision, in the thinking of the architects of change.

First Founding Initiative in the East:
Andreas Hermes and the CDU

On June 10, 1945, one month after Germany's unconditional surrender, the Soviet Union became the first occupying power to allow political parties and trade unions to form in its zone. Within a week, a unified trade union was founded (with Communist participation), and the Socialists and Communists reconstituted their parties. On June 19, the Marxist parties formed a joint working committee.

With Berlin under Soviet occupation (the western powers were not to occupy their sectors until July), it seemed imperative for non-Marxist groups to establish themselves quickly in the capital. As late as mid-May, Jakob Kaiser had talked with Socialist leaders about a Labour party. But in traditionally "red Berlin," there was little chance of heading off the reconstitution of the SPD.

On May 19 and 25, Kaiser participated in discussions of Andreas Hermes' idea of a party of Christian union. Several Protestants attended the second meeting, including Emil Dovifat (formerly editor of *Der Deutsche*), Ernst Lemmer of the old Hirsch-Duncker trade unions, and Prussia's ex-Minister of Trade, Walther Schreiber (formerly DDP). On June 16, Hermes' group founded the Christian Democratic Union. The same day, other former Democrats met to discuss refounding the DDP. Alarmed, Kaiser mobilized Lemmer to try to prevent a renewed splintering of the party system, which he feared would play into the Communists' hands. But on July 1, at a Soviet-sponsored meeting attended by Walter Ulbricht of the KPD, the other former Democrats founded the Liberal Democratic Party (LDP). As one of the founders later wrote, they had to reject the CDU—the "camouflaged Center with a Democratic appendage."[2]

In the overwhelmingly Protestant Soviet zone of Germany, the CDU was at pains to combat the "frequent misunderstanding" and "false claims" that it was a cover for a revived Center—"the cloak" that concealed "the Center's cowl." Branding such claims a speculation on the residual effect of "Goebbels propaganda," the Berlin CDU asserted that the word "Union" in its name proved that the concern about "confessionalizing" politics was unfounded. While "party" meant "a part" and implied boundary and division, "union" meant "gathering together" *(Sammlung)*. The Union was "the gathering together of all those anti-fascist democratic forces" who "do not find their political home in . . . the KPD and SPD."[3]

This "gathering together," the Berliners announced, was neither a random coalitional expedient nor a formal merger of old parties but "a new political movement from the ground up." Cautioning local operatives against simply disavowing the old Center, the Berliners nonetheless asserted that politics in the wake of Hitler's criminality required a broader foundation than a party whose origins lay in the Prussian state's battle with the Catholic Church. While the Church had to fight for its members' spiritual rights, the beacon to God must not again become dimmed in profane partisan struggles. The CDU, said the Berliners, neither challenged nor concealed religious differences; but confessional tensions had to be kept out of public affairs.[4]

Knowing that the Soviets would not license a traditional conservative party, many religious Protestants felt they had to make their mark within the CDU. The politics of land reform seemed to confirm the point. To be licensed, the CDU had to enter into the mandatory solidarity of an all-party "antifascist bloc." In this system, known as *Blockpolitik,* decisions were made at meetings attended not only by the four parties (KPD, SPD, LDP, CDU) but also by the unified trade unions and other mass organizations. The Soviets allowed the Communists to stack the coordinating bodies of these organizations, turning the unions into a mockery of what Kaiser and the deceased Wilhelm Leuschner (SPD) had had in mind. In September 1945, when the Soviets sponsored a land reform that expropriated not only the Prussian aristocracy but also the intermediate holders (mostly Protestants), Hermes (himself a farmer) and his party withheld their blessing in the bloc. In the ensuing crisis, the Soviets forced Hermes in December to relinquish the party chairmanship to Kaiser.[5]

Caught up in this problem and residing in a region containing few Catholics, Hermes was inclined to downplay the Centrist connection. But as a westerner who aspired to lead a national party, he had to deal with pro-Centrist sentiment in western regions. During a trip to the Rhineland in November, Hermes told Hamacher, who had meanwhile proclaimed the Center's revival, that anyone who splintered the common Christian front at a time of impending Marxist partisan dictatorship in the eastern zone was assuming a grave responsibility before history. Though Hamacher was shaken, a pep talk from his Westphalian counterpart, Johannes Brockmann, soon steeled his resolve. Hermes then grandly announced that the Center and CDU were at war.[6]

The next month, because of the crisis over land reform, the Soviet military government forbade Hermes from attending the first nationwide gathering of Christian Democrats in Bad Godesberg. In his speech, which was read out in his absence, Hermes denied that the party was either a "continuation of the old Center" or a party of Protestant reaction in which "a conscientious Catholic could never find his home." The Nazi years, he stated, were only a temporary interruption in the long history of the KPD and the SPD, but Christian Democracy was "an entirely new phenomenon" and a "call to gather together" issued to those who were uncomfortable in Marxist parties but who had not "made themselves guilty" while following Hitler and Hugenberg. The only precursor Hermes recognized was Adam Stegerwald—not as a man of the Center, but as a man who had tried to outgrow it. Due to their shared experience with Nazism, wrote Hermes, the two churches had overcome their historical political antagonism. Christian Democratic unity was no longer a dream, but "a reality of pivotal weightiness."[7]

After Hermes' removal, the Berlin CDU continued to claim "recourse to no partisan tradition of any kind."[8] Its new leader, Kaiser, was among the least troubled by the decision to "sacrifice" the Center, for he had never believed that the old parties could still command respect, and nothing in the overwhelmingly Protestant Soviet zone convinced him otherwise. By contrast, in the British-occupied heartland of political Catholicism, the Rhineland and Westphalia, the Center had largely held its own during the last election campaigns of the Weimar era. Meanwhile, in American-occupied Bavaria, Adam Stegerwald was moving to fulfill his vision of a quarter century earlier.

First Founding Initiative in the South: Adam Stegerwald and the CSU

One day after the establishment of the joint working committee of the Marxist parties in Berlin (June 20, 1945), the American authorities in Würzburg asked their new district governor in Franconia, Adam

Stegerwald, to outline his vision of the future party system. He replied that a realistic goal would be a four-party system with large Social Democratic and Christian Social parties and smaller Communist and rightist parties. The SPD, said Stegerwald, would have to head off the extreme left, while "the Center party and BVP would have to give up their confessional character and, perhaps under the name Christian Democracy, should take in worthwhile forces from the right."[9]

Early in July, Stegerwald met with Josef Müller, a Bavarian Catholic who had been the conduit between resistance circles and the Vatican, and found that Müller shared his vision of an interdenominational rallying movement. Preparations nonetheless proceeded slowly. Not only was the American military government reluctant to allow the resumption of political activity, but the working-class impetus was weaker in the American zone. Moreover, even the federalist BVP, despite its strong regional profile, had faced competition during the Weimar period from harder-line Bavarian particularists; now, disillusionment with German nationalism was bound to make particularism stronger.[10]

Opposing any sort of regional exceptionalism (even an autonomous sister party to the CDU), Stegerwald wanted the entire national party, not just its Bavarian branch, to commit itself to social policies by calling itself the Christian Social Farmer-Labor Party, a name his Bavarian colleagues shortened in August to Christian Social Union (CSU). The CSU, Stegerwald said, was the realization of his old Essen idea. Had it been founded in 1920, it would have formed a Grand Coalition (CSU plus SPD) and blocked the landowning and industrial elites who had delivered Germany to Hitler. By freeing farmers from the east Elbian reactionaries who had prevented farmer-labor understanding in the past, the CSU would be the "bridge of understanding" between city and country as well as between denominations.[11]

Gone was the ambiguity of 1920 as to whether Stegerwald wanted a transformed Center or a whole new party. Whereas many western Christian Democrats spoke of the Center with an air of respect for the dead, Stegerwald attacked it as "a confessional party." Scoffing at its claim to having been the party of national mediation, he characterized its slogans about Catholic solidarity and "live and let live" as covers to "plunder" the workers. "A democratic state and a confessional minority party are mutually exclusive concepts." Thus, "the Center cannot be transformed. Rather, a new party must be created upon a much wider basis, in which there cannot be a [Protestant] appendage, but only people with equal political rights." With the birth of the CSU, a historical development was "radically finalized"; "the question of who is to have the political leadership of Germany, Protestantism or Catholicism, is eliminated once and for all."[12]

In October, while touring the Rhineland and Westphalia with Albers, Stegerwald met with his old political friend and foe, the Social Democrat Carl Severing. True to form, Stegerwald was not satisfied just to build a party, but was thinking about the coalitional implications of the whole party system. Yet, as he had already shown during the summer, he viewed a Grand Coalition with the SPD as just a stopgap. Whereas he had doubted in 1920 that a system of two alternating parties could survive even in Britain, he now called for British-style, single-member, single-ballot districts that would "force" such a party system on the Germans: "One party heads the state, the other keeps tabs on the government and prepares itself to head the future government. Everything else is democratic dilettantism." In deriding the Center as a born minority party, he stressed that a democracy needed parties that could individually attain a majority. If this was not yet possible in the four-party system he expected, it was no longer out of the question for the future.[13]

But Stegerwald was not to pursue any more coalitional visions. On December 3, 1945, he died suddenly of pneumonia. He was seventy-one years old.

In a wartime letter to Adolf Hitler, Adam Stegerwald reputedly told the Führer that Hitler, with his "social and national community" *(Volksgemeinschaft),* had accomplished what Stegerwald had always wanted to do.[14] If true, does this not confirm the worst historical judgments about Stegerwald, lending credence to one historian's claim that his attitude during the Weimar period was "near-fascist"?[15]

Stegerwald never converted to Nazism, but he did think that Hitler's draconian attempt to impose a "national community" was the natural outgrowth of German society's long failure to nurture a healthier version of that concept—a failure that Stegerwald believed he had tried to redeem through his Essen program and that ultimately had led to the collapse of German democracy. In this sense (and in this sense alone), Stegerwald saw the Nazi revolution, as he had stated in March 1933, as a kind of alternate, if unfortunate, implementation of the vision of Essen: "In the domestic and foreign policy confusion after the Essen congress, the Christian trade union movement lacked the strength necessary to accomplish the goals that had been laid out. Thus did it come to pass that the ideas expressed in Essen have, in the meantime, been seized and pushed forward from another quarter." He added that "the Christian trade unions stand apart from the revolution" and warned that dictatorship in a "modern civilized nation" was in the long run impossible. But he also urged his followers "to collaborate most vigorously in the shaping of a better economic and social order."[16]

Though this call for autonomous collaboration was morally and politically flawed, the alternative was to recommend to an impoverished constituency that it risk both political repression and socioeconomic ruin. To Stegerwald, such a course seemed both irresponsible and suicidal. One month later, on the eve of Hitler's repression of the unions, Kaiser too publicly recommended "responsible collaboration." The key issue, he said, was whether trade unionists, the best elements of the working classes, would be given time freely to develop confidence in the new state.[17] It soon became apparent, however, that Hitler was interested not in collaboration but in coordination (*Gleichschaltung*).

Stegerwald's subsequent record was not particularly good. The sorry cravenness of his wartime letter to Hitler was probably part of an effort to get his full pension reinstated; it was not augmented, so far as is known, by any actions that served the Nazis.[18] But Stegerwald displayed neither Adenauer's aloof correctness nor Kaiser's discreet but passionate aversion toward the regime. He apparently was deeply affected by the physical attack on him in the 1933 campaign, and once he understood that what was happening was a revolution, he made no further effort (as Adenauer briefly did)[19] to stand in its way. Broken in spirit, he was guided in his later attitude toward the Nazis neither by enthusiasm nor by abhorrence, but by utter demoralization.

Stegerwald seemed less distressed by the wanton excesses of the regime than by its failure to live up to its own rhetoric regarding a "national community"—a failure demonstrated by the regime's reversion to the pre-Weimar pattern of branding Catholics anti-"national" and treating them as second-class citizens. As early as March 1933, he noted with dismay that "the old struggle between Protestantism and Catholicism is going on again all along the line." Four months later, he told Albert Hackelsberger, who was negotiating to have the ex-Centrists in the Reichstag become Nazi "guests," that if the Nazis persisted in demanding the exclusion of Joseph Wirth and the trade unionists, then former Centrists should resign their mandates en masse, thereby disgracing any deputy who did not go along and preserving the good name of political Catholicism for the future.[20]

This last recommendation is an indication that Stegerwald initially expected the dictatorship to be of short duration. But as the years wore on and the regime did not collapse, his view of its viability went to the other extreme. Impressed first by Hitler's diplomatic triumphs and then by the success of his war machine, he became convinced that the Nazis would win. Holding this belief, he could have no interest in plans for a post-Hitler order. Hence, though his name appeared on at least one prospective cabinet list, he did not participate in the resistance, nor did his friend Kaiser bring him into his confidence. Rather, Stegerwald became preoccupied with preventing the isolation and heightened persecution of Catholics that were bound to follow a German victory. Even here, his once fertile imagination deserted him. Despite the Nazis' failure to adhere to the concordat, Stegerwald's only recommendation, in gross incomprehension of the full nature of the regime, was that the Church seek a postwar guarantee of free rein in an "unpolitical" sphere of activity.[21] This was little more than a variation on the attempted arrangements of 1933.

Having first expected that the dictatorship would not last and then that it would rule indefinitely, Stegerwald in 1945 retroactively recovered his prophetic powers. "Even a blind man could foresee," he now stated with perfect hindsight, "that the German world program of 1938–1939 would and must end with catastrophe." As in 1933, he argued that the fault lay in the failure to integrate the nation on a Christian and social basis. Confessional hostility, he said, had diverted attention from the truly decisive issue: liberation of the masses from the control of narrow castes. As in 1920, he asserted that industrialization had alienated people from God and nature while producing not steady growth but boom and bust. For this spiritual and material malaise, Nazism had falsely presented itself as the cure: "Here, National Socialism stepped in. It promised lasting employment to the masses, security for the individual and his family, a generous provision of good housing for families with many children, and equally generous pensions for old age. It dusted off the old formula, 'Public interest before selfish interest,' and made it come alive. But its own leaders didn't do business that way!" In short, Nazism had posed as the solution to problems whose true solution was Christian Democracy.[22]

The same notion of Nazism and Christian Democracy as alternatives pervaded Stegerwald's specific remarks about reforming the party system. Some such reform, he said, had been inevitable in 1918; but when he had attempted a democratic realignment, he had found that any bid to pull the old parties apart also endangered "the unity of my own life's work, the Christian-national labor movement." Free of "considerations of this kind regarding other parties," Hitler had been able to "storm away uninhibited," while Stegerwald had "had to drag a china-shop along behind me." As a result, Hitler had been able "in his way" to accomplish what Stegerwald had not: the dissolution of the old parties, the true prerequisite to realignment. Now, with the collapse of Nazism and the formation of the CSU, "the reshaping of the party system" was being carried out "exactly as I called for twenty-five years ago."[23]

It is instructive to compare Stegerwald's position with Martin Spahn's. Whereas Nazism for Stegerwald was the consequence of the failure to implement the Essen program, it was for Spahn the realization of his own interdenominational vision. Whereas Stegerwald and Heinrich Brüning had worked, albeit ineffectually, to prevent a Nazi dictatorship, Spahn had actively sought a Nazi state and had joined the Nazi delegation in the Reichstag. Whereas Stegerwald had intermittently sought an understanding with the Socialists (including a coalition with his desired Essen party), Spahn had seen the Socialists as the ultimate enemy and had made the rejection of a coalition with them his chief political commandment. As a result, he had first tried to identify the party envisaged at Essen with the existing DNVP, a position Stegerwald had repudiated, and had later polemicized against Stegerwald for talking like a Socialist and defending the Republic.[24] In short, whereas the kind of party urged by Stegerwald would have moderated the far right and taken votes from the DNVP or NSDAP, the kind of party urged by Spahn *was* first the DNVP, then the NSDAP.

As in his speeches about "Christian Weltanschauung" and "formal democracy" at the end of World War I, Stegerwald now defined Christian Democracy to entail not just democratic institutions but "community consciousness" and "brotherly dealing" according to "the old Christian doctrine of 'Do unto others.'" Without social consciousness, democracy to him was meaningless.[25] His focus, however, was predictably less nationalistic than before. Saying that the Depression and the war had everywhere exacerbated the anomie of modern industrial society, Stegerwald highlighted parallels between Christian

Democracy in Germany and socially conscious pro-Christian movements in other countries. He included not just Christian Democratic parties—above all the new Popular Republican Movement (MRP) in France—but also the Roosevelt coalition in America and even the British Labour party, whose leaders, he said, had triumphed at the polls after solemnly affirming their own Christian inspiration.[26]

In the 1920s, Stegerwald had favored the inclusion of industrial interests in governing coalitions, arguing that a democracy in which the economically powerful lacked a stake would be doomed. Now his only mention of industrialists and other conservative elites was to condemn them. They were the ones who had compelled Brüning to resign and who had then put Hitler in the saddle to carry out their reactionary program, including the emasculation of the trade unions. After what the right had done with its power, Stegerwald believed that German and European politics would necessarily swing to the left.[27]

Ironically, it was here that Stegerwald would be proved wrong. For the CDU/CSU would be what he had once called for but now seemed to reject: the democratic alliance of popular and elite constituencies, achieved if possible without the SPD. Had Stegerwald lived, the important thing for him, as for Kaiser, would surely have been not a Grand Coalition (CDU/CSU plus SPD), but the fight to assure the predominance in his own party of social Christian ideas. Indeed, one of the chief agencies of that fight, the influential Social Committees of the CDU, grew out of Stegerwald's suggestion that Albers form a caucus of the party's trade unionists.[28]

After Stegerwald's final trip west, four tasks still remained: to form a unified transregional party; to develop the new party in a "social" direction; to insure that old party loyalties were truly left behind; and to eliminate competitors or prepare for coalitions. The first of these goals was never to be reached: the CSU, contrary to Stegerwald's vision, remains an autonomous sister party of the CDU.[29] How the other three matters developed, in Berlin and above all in the Center's old western heartland, is examined below.

First Founding Initiative in the West: Leo Schwering and the CDP

Critical for any new Christian party was the capital of political Catholicism, Cologne. The city's relatively vibrant resistance circle, headquartered in the Ketteler Haus offices of the Arbeitervereine, included Bernhard Letterhaus and Nikolaus Gross, both hanged by the Nazis, as well as Johannes Albers. Cologne's onetime Landtag deputy, the former Volksverein official Leo Schwering, provided a link to middle-class opinion. Through Letterhaus, Hermes, and Kaiser, the group had ties to the conspirators in Berlin; through the Christian trade unionists Wilhelm Elfes (Mönchengladbach) and Karl Arnold (Düsseldorf), it had ties to groups in neighboring cities on the Rhine and the Ruhr.[30]

Best positioned to take the initiative in Cologne was Schwering. Imprisoned after the attempted assassination of Hitler on July 20, 1944, Schwering was taken ill and, unlike Albers and Hermes, was spared the rigors of a concentration camp. In April 1945, at a hospital in Königswinter, he and the former Mayor of Krefeld, Wilhelm Warsch, reluctantly embraced the "downright sacrilegious notion" that the Center "would have to be sacrificed to a greater idea." Arriving in Cologne on May 9, Schwering found that the former general secretary of the city party, Peter Schaeven, and the former head of the Center's youth clubs (Windthorst Leagues), Theodor Scharmitzel, also favored a new party. A colleague, Hans Schaeffer, had even drafted a program.[31]

Since decisions made here were bound to be emulated elsewhere, it was important to win the cooperation of the former Lord Mayor. Though Konrad Adenauer had not participated in the resistance, he had been harassed during the first five years of the regime, had hidden in a convent during 1933–1934, and had been arrested after July 20, 1944, a circumstance that led to the illness and later the death of his wife. In April 1945, Schwering contacted Adenauer about a new party. But the cautious ex-Mayor, who would soon be returned to his post by the occupation regime, would not commit himself until he could take political soundings among northern Protestants in July.[32]

On Sunday, June 17, unaware that an interdenominational Christian Democratic Union had been founded in Berlin the day before, eighteen ex-Centrists met in Cologne to chart their course. In contrast to the Berliners, Schwering, in his keynote address, described the Cologne initiative not as a radically new venture but as a name change to realize an old Centrist ideal. It was an "altogether difficult sacrifice to let the old renowned name fall," for no party had such a long and rich history of service to the Reich—including, he said, as the "single truly tenable dam against Hitler." Even so, a new name was now necessary; that name was "Christian Democratic Party" (CDP).[33]

Schwering placed his initiative in a direct line of descent from those of 1906, 1918–1919, and 1920. The moment was "favorable for a new 'Out of the Tower!'"; it must not be said later that "we" did not try. Though the Center "truly was" a political, not confessional, party open to all, "it remained, according to its historical mission, a Catholic party." Its old name "now represents a historical burden"; to retain it would be to "hold [the party] to . . . its old mission." Schwering thus squared the circle. By linking his initiative to Bachemite reform and yet insisting (contrary to Julius Bachem) that the old party's mission had indeed been purely Catholic, he moved to prevent a Carl Bachem–like return under cover of reformist rhetoric to business as usual in the old party.[34]

Stressing (like the Bachems) that the interdenominational basis of the party referred not to religious dogma but to political tasks, Schwering nonetheless insisted that the real differences in Weltanschauung were no longer between denominations but between Christianity and "the new heathenism" of both left and right. With Nazism discredited, the chief opponent would be Communism. The old liberalism was dead, and even a refurbished and less anticlerical SPD faced a difficult future. With the old right tainted by its association with Hitler, said Schwering, the Center (as if it still existed!) was the only remaining representative of conservative ideals. Only it could form the core of an antiheathenistic party. The lesson of Weimar was that "democracy without a Christian Weltanschauung at its head" was "not viable . . . and never will be, at least with us here in Germany."

Over the next two weekends, Father Laurentius Siemer of the Cologne resistance hosted a fourteen-member program commission in his Dominican cloister at nearby Walberberg. Besides Schwering, Schaeven, Scharmitzel, and Albers, the deliberants included two Protestants (one a minister) and another notable Walberberg Dominican, Eberhard Welty. The leading theoretician of Christian socialism, Welty had written a pamphlet late in the war whose German title, "Was nun?" (What Now?), resembled that of Lenin's 1902 pamphlet, "Was tun?" (What Is to Be Done?). In the pamphlet, Welty asserted that the failure of the "so-called free market" to cover people's basic material needs "truly screams to high heaven." This failure compelled state intervention, even if some private property became public. Those hurt by such measures "should stop and think what would happen to them and their property" if forces should come to power who had

elsewhere used "the most brutal violent means" of confiscatory na-
tionalization.[35]

Working from a draft by Schwering that contained ideas from
Welty's pamphlet, the commission hammered out what became
known as the Cologne Guidelines. The guidelines linked three areas:
moral values, democracy, and a just socioeconomic order. To restore
"Christian and western values," education would take place in denominational schools or in mixed schools with regular but segregated
religious instruction. To bolster democracy, both the civil service and
the private sector would be purged ("cleansed"). Land reform, fair
wages, and a balanced distribution of goods would give those without
property a chance to acquire it. Monopolies would be broken, coal
mining and energy production would become public enterprises, and
banks would be subject to state control. In place of the "avaricious
materialism" that had led Germany into the abyss, a "new national
community" *(Volksgemeinschaft)* based on "social justice and social
love" would "combine the God-given freedom of the individual" with
"the rights of the community . . . In this way we represent a true
Christian socialism, which has nothing in common with false collec-
tivistic goals that contradict the nature of man from the ground up."[36]

On the topic of Christian socialism, the Walberberg Dominicans
were more radical than their lay colleagues. The categorical language
and scare argument used by Welty in his pamphlet were absent from
the guidelines. The sentence about Christian socialism was adopted
late in the sessions under pressure from Siemer, who tried to get the
party to name itself the "Christian-Socialistic Community"—whereupon Schwering declared that his own, milder program was "already
socialistic enough." According to Schwering, Siemer's attempt "to
force through his 'socialistic party'" prompted a heated exchange between Siemer and Scharmitzel, a Weimar-era conservative. The majority supported Scharmitzel.[37]

Although Schwering's differences with the monks were partly tactical, they reflected different substantive priorities. For Welty, the chief
goal was moral and economic justice; the Communist threat was a
weapon to secure the cooperation of the unwilling. For Schwering,
fear of Communism was the prime consideration. Unlike Kaiser and
others who thought that "bourgeois society" was dead, Schwering,
seeing "the bourgeoisie in danger," was concerned to defend it. In this
"life and death struggle" against "collectivism," he wanted not to

blackmail the middle class but to court it. If the party was serious about winning Protestants, there could be no other way.[38]

Indeed, the same was true if the party was serious about winning Catholics. Through the first weeks of July, the CDP's uncertain prospects and leftist-sounding idealism caused many leading Catholics to hesitate. It was Adenauer, in a note to Schwering and Scharmitzel in mid-July, who (in Schwering's words) "broke the ice." The Mayor's lead was immediately followed by Josef Ruffini, Hamacher's former deputy in the Rhenish Center party organization, and by Schwering's brother Ernst, himself later Mayor of Cologne.[39]

In making his decision, Adenauer went one step beyond Leo Schwering in his pragmatism. Rather than presenting his Protestant counterparts with a Centrist-inspired fait accompli, he visited them in their own northern heartland and asked them directly what their inclinations were. Even while taking the initiative, Adenauer thus treated leading Protestants as equals. Furthermore, he did not confine himself to the tiny bands of Protestants Schwering knew from the resistance— the People's Conservatives and former members of the CSVD who had once supported Brüning—but set out to determine the prospective strength of the CDP's most likely Protestant competitor, a traditional liberal party. For this purpose he augmented his own soundings by gathering exact figures from earlier elections in each locale on his northern itinerary and passing the figures on to Schwering.[40]

With British permission, the Cologne CDP officially established itself on August 19. Schwering now redefined the events of June 17 not as a "change of name" but as the dissolution of the old party. The Center, he said, had not died with the brutal repression of 1934—he thus passed over in silence the disgrace and dissolution of 1933—but had "lived on internally in the hearts of millions." Now, however, it was time not to pour old wine into new barrels but to build "a new construct from the ground up." The meeting of June 17 had shown the "firm and unmistakably clear, if also bitter and difficult, decision to dissolve the party from within." Only in 1945, then, and "in all honor!" had the Center ceased to exist. In the "completely new political situation," this "sacrifice of the party" was the only possible choice.[41]

This striking passage is even more remarkable in the context of drafted portions that were later deleted. What Schwering originally wrote was, "Only now—'by its enemies never vanquished but by its friends forsaken,' to employ a saying of Windthorst's—did the colors come down in all honor! . . . Now this movement had found its voluntary end."[42] Invoking Windthorst in this way was particularly dangerous, for Windthorst had intended his aphorism of 1887 as a reproach to those who would desert the Center in its hour of need, not as a formula for taking honorable leave of it. The aphorism was actually of greater use to advocates of a restoration than to those who wanted a new party (which is perhaps why it was deleted). Yet Schwering continued to cite it later as if it were an argument in favor of the founding of the CDP.[43]

Other Christian Democrats more appropriately cited another remark attributed to Windthorst: that the Center's mission would end when civic reconciliation between Catholics and Protestants in Germany was a reality. Yet, when a liberal paper had suggested in 1907 that granting parity to Catholics would cause the Center to dissolve, the *KV* had answered that a party does not dissolve at a moment of triumph, but experiences a new upswing and new tasks. To the *KV*, rapprochement between the denominations would have constituted not the transcendence of the Center's mission (as Schwering now argued), but an opening for realizing Centrist demands.[44]

Indeed, Schwering's use of Windthorst's aphorism was the opposite of the Bachemites' old argument that it was not they but the integralists who were forsaking the party. Moreover, even without the aphorism, Schwering was explicit enough: it had taken the removal of the Center (in June 1945) to open the way for a broader party. Schwering's assertion that the Center had continued to exist throughout the Nazi period left the door open to those who asked on what authority Schwering's little band presumed to dissolve a national party with a seventy-five year history, and (echoing the old *KV*) why a party that had "survived" the brutal repression of the Nazi era to "live on" in people's hearts should dissolve itself "voluntarily" at the very moment the repression was over. Stalwarts of the old party were repeatedly to pose both these questions in the months that followed.

CDP versus Center in the West: The Travails of Wilhelm Hamacher

Elsewhere in the Rhineland and Westphalia, other Christian Democratic groups were also coming together. As early as April 30, 1945, Karl Arnold's Düsseldorf circle tried in vain to get permission from occupying forces for a "Christian People's Party." One month later, the British did grant an ambiguous request by the all-Catholic Wattenscheid circle in the Ruhr, led by former *Tremonia* publisher Lambert Lensing, Jr., and former trade unionist Anton Gilsing, to begin preparations for a "Christian" and "democratic" "Center." On June 3, Father Caspar Schulte of Paderborn hosted a gathering in Essen of KAV members and clergymen. Here, Gilsing pleaded unambiguously for an alternative to both an ideologically neutral Labour Party and a restored Center: an interdenominational party on the model of Stegerwald's Essen speech.[45]

Westphalian sentiment in favor of restoring the Center surfaced at a mid-July meeting in Lippstadt. Present were leading ex-Centrists from the Münster area, a Catholic stronghold whose archbishop, Clemens Graf von Galen, had bravely protested Nazi crimes. Among those in attendance at Lippstadt were the former Landtag deputy, Johannes Brockmann; the former editor of the Center party newspaper, Fritz Stricker; the influential lawyer, Bernhard Reismann; and the former provincial governor (removed by Papen), Rudolf Amelunxen. Unaware of developments elsewhere, this group had resolved to relaunch the old party when Lensing and former Landtag deputy Helene Wessel suddenly arrived and informed them of the Wattenscheid initiative. Joint meetings were then scheduled; the one in Dortmund on August 6 was attended by Schwering, Scharmitzel, and Schaeven. Their report on the reasons for the "change of name" (Schwering) led to a lively discussion, with opponents arguing that the old party would have to pass an official resolution before a CDP could be proclaimed or Protestants approached.[46]

Christian Democrats now began to organize regionally. In the Rhineland, a large meeting of former Centrists on August 20 produced the decision, over Hamacher's vehement dissent, to found a regionwide CDP. A similar decision was made in Westphalia, where pro-Centrist forces led by Brockmann and Wessel declined to attend further meetings.

On September 2, interdenominational assemblies in Bochum and in the Kolpinghaus in Cologne officially founded the regional parties. In Bochum, Lensing said that the aim of the new party was to continue and expand upon the work of the old: "*We* open to *you*," he told the Protestants, "not our old house, the Center tower; rather, we want to build a new political home together with you."[47] In Cologne, Scharmitzel was less presumptuous: the purpose was simply to "found a new political democratic party." Since only a Christian Democratic alliance, he said, could viably defend against a leftist bloc, he, Schwering, and Schaeven had concluded in May that the Center would have to be "sacrifice[d]." Baron Max von Gumppenberg of Düsseldorf added that the Christian Democratic group in Berlin must not stand alone in its struggle against "historical-economic materialism," which was "a very close relative of Hitler's biological materialism." In Gumppenberg's view, liberal doctrines separating religion and politics had contributed to the moral catastrophe; hence the decision "to try a completely new way."[48]

The new party's roots, said Gumppenberg, lay not just in the Center but also among liberal democrats and in the Confessing Church. When he specified what each group had sacrificed to join the others, however, his old loyalties became visible. Secular liberals, he said, had accepted the place of Christianity in party politics; the Confessing Church had set aside the suspicion that the CDP was the Center under a new name; and Centrists had sacrificed an organization that had allowed them to resist Nazi blandishments longer than any non-Marxist group. According to Gumppenberg, then, liberals and Protestants had each given up a cherished but mistaken viewpoint, but Centrists had given up a noble organization that had just proven its value under the most stringent of tests.

Speaking next was Otto Schmidt of the Wuppertal circle, the first Christian Democratic Protestant group in the Rhineland. In the barracks and bomb shelters, said Schmidt, Protestants and Catholics had prayed together and groped to understand the degeneration and destruction all around them. Now, believers from both denominations had to act together to assert the voice of Christian conscience in public life. Confessional solidarity was no longer enough, and "Christianity can no longer be a private matter."

In the meeting of August 20, in a letter to Adenauer six days later, and now at the Cologne assembly, former general secretary Hamacher developed his reasons for opposing a new party. That Germany could suddenly end its centuries-old confessional schism struck Hamacher as sheer fantasy. Instead of chasing a chimera, he said, the traumatized nation ought to hold fast to the Center, one of the few surviving (!) institutions of proven reliability and political sobriety. The crucial middle role in German politics could hardly be filled by a diverse amalgam or "gathering party" *(Sammelpartei)* that harbored Nazis and reactionaries. Besides, Catholic confessional defense remained a necessity; a "mishmash" party was incapable of filling this need.[49]

Hamacher thus placed greater emphasis on the elements of continuity in the situation of 1945 than on the elements of discontinuity. Still, he did believe that something had changed. No longer could Protestants capitalize on the institutional or bureaucratic favoritism of a Prussian state. Furthermore, British Field Marshal Montgomery had once stated that the Center would be the only non-Socialist party to be licensed; hence, Protestants would have to accept the Catholic lead. Far from making demeaning overtures to others, said Hamacher, Catholics ought to seize the opportunity to make their ideas the guiding principles of German public life. With an international network and a coherent world view, Catholics could "make the end of the war a turning point . . . in shaping the western world."[50]

If Protestants still felt they could not join the Center, said Hamacher, then Centrists should do what Brüning had done with the CSVD: help Protestants launch their own party, which could form a cartel with the Center. In this way, "lack of clarity would be avoided; we then march as the old Center with the old colors into the new age, or we even form entirely clear fronts, following the example of Holland: a Roman Catholic State-party . . . and, [for] the Protestants, a Christian party or however they want to call themselves." This essentially Roerenesque conception—"march separately, strike together"—Hamacher thus tried to sanctify by invoking the authority of Brüning. What for Brauns and Brüning had been a last attempt at interdenominational cooperation after the failure to launch a unified party was to Hamacher a way to block the emergence of just such a party.[51]

While Hamacher was occupied outside the room, the assembly voted unanimously to found the new CDP. Afterwards, Schaeven answered him in the clearest possible terms: "Does [Hamacher] want to continue the old party in spite of the resolution? . . . With the resolution just now, we have taken our leave from a respectable past and switched over to a new party." On September 9, he added that since the CDP was a completely new entity, the modes of close cooperation between the denominations still had to be learned.[52]

By this time, then, claims of continuity with Centrist tradition were occasionally giving way to statements that a sincere and sustained effort at interdenominational cooperation was in fact unprecedented. This rhetorical shift became more difficult, however, once it became clear that an attempt might indeed be made to "continue the old party." Thus, Father Schulte on October 6 again cited Centrist tradition—this time, the briefly used "Christian People's Party" subtitle of 1919—as precedent for the current "process of self-opening." Were a return to the old Centrist boundaries nonetheless to prove necessary, said Schulte, the party should be able to say it had dutifully tried to break the confessional barrier in politics. This argument only further angered Hamacher, who cited it repeatedly thereafter as proof of the need for a Center to which "experimenting" Catholics could return.[53]

The Cologne assembly of September 2 was the last at which Christian Democrats and Centrist stalwarts sat together. Learning of his potential ally in the Rhineland, Brockmann now wrote to Hamacher (their first postwar contact) and pressed his better known colleague to lead a Centrist restoration. Stating that groups all over Westphalia were committed never to "forsake the Center," Brockmann referred to the Christian Democrats as the "Cologne orientation" *(Kölner Richtung)* and disparaged the slogan "Out of the Tower." He mused that earlier historical "efforts to strip the Center of its name" in favor of a Christian "gathering party" as a "counterweight to the Socialist left" had repeatedly failed. Besides, "the Center was and remains the true gathering party," for "no party in German history" had been so socioeconomically diverse. There had never been any reason why Protestants could not join, and "many Protestants" had been Centrist deputies. If the Center had shown special concern for the interests of the Catholic Church, it was because those interests had been especially endangered. In any case, "reconciliation of the Christian confessions is a matter for the theologians [and] churches, not political parties!"[54]

Brockmann argued that the Center's dissolution of 1933, having been extracted through "brute force," was just as null and void as every other Nazi action. The Center was "a political actuality that has existed for seventy-five years"; it did not need to be created. Never did its policy appear so vindicated as at the present moment: "A party does not voluntarily give itself up at the very moment that the unprecedented breakdown of the policy of its opponent proves the correctness of its own policy and the necessity of its existence! . . . The hour must never come when it would be said of the Center, as Windthorst prophetically warned: 'By its enemies never vanquished, but by its friends forsaken!'"

Brockmann's effort to embolden Hamacher fell on fertile ground. Reluctant to part ways with his co-religionists and political colleagues who were founding the CDP (his first impulse after September 2 was to retire from politics), Hamacher needed to be assured that he was not alone. Hence, he wrote again to the man he revered from their days together in the pre-Nazi Prussian State Council, Konrad Adenauer. Hamacher told Adenauer that he was Hamacher's "last hope" of stopping the "nightmare." First, he complained, the Cologne circle had presented a fait accompli; then, it had undemocratically railroaded its plans through the assembly of September 2. Hamacher likened the presence and (in his view) aggressiveness of Protestants at the Kolpinghaus to an invasion; it was as if the Reformation had walked in the door and loudly proclaimed its presence ("Das Thema der Reformation meldete sich an"). Approvingly quoting a Centrist stalwart—"The entire misfortune in which we now stand comes from Cologne"—he was outraged that "the center of Catholic thought . . . and . . . political education" could have been the source of such an "experiment." He added: "Is Cologne really an inner danger for German Catholicism?" Hamacher thus revived the notorious phrase coined by Edmund Schopen in the title of his anti-Bachemite pamphlet of 1910, a pamphlet so extreme that even Roeren had disowned it.[55]

Hamacher was living proof that not only ecumenism but also a new parochialism was a logical consequence of Nazi devastation and the resultant religious revival. For Hamacher, Prussian Protestants were responsible for the events that had brought Hitler to power and the Christian West to ruin. Only Catholics had the moral fiber to show the way out of this calamity; the institutional destruction of Protestant Germany provided them with just the opportunity to do so. That they would then squander this chance in favor of associating with those he deemed responsible for the calamity dumbfounded him. Even his cartel solution for the party system, a solution that involved two frankly confessional parties, was based on his notion of "political education": Catholic Germany needed to take Protestant Germany in tow.

Alongside the religious component, Hamacher's motive was loyalty to the Center in its own right. A former Rhenish party secretary, Hamacher was an organization man with organizational loyalties. Even the later hints of Catholic bishops could not induce him to abandon the Center. Still, this loyalty was, for him, the political extension of his Catholic identity. Parliamentary considerations did not much influence him: his cartel idea was motivated not by a drive to establish an effective party system but by the need to parry the CDP's cultural argument for interdenominational solidarity. Even his argument that a party of the middle was a necessity for a people inclined to ideological extremes was a matter of religion: he linked middleness organically to Catholicism, the religion that was based on finding the golden mean in all things.

By contrast, Brockmann, a former parliamentarian, based his loyalty to the Center explicitly on his vision of its parliamentary function. "A party," he stated, "can never be a goal in itself! Its task lies in parliament!" For the Center, this task was twofold. First, by foiling a division into hostile Christian and Socialist camps, the Center would spare moderate Social Democrats an alliance with Communist radicals. (That a traditional liberal grouping such as the future Free Democratic Party, or FDP, might play such a role seemed at this point unlikely, since the liberals were reckoned to be socially to the right.) Second, by not giving sanctuary (as the Christian Democrats allegedly did) to the "antisocial" and "reactionary" elements that had "brought Hitler to power," a restored Center would weaken the right. For Brockmann, this argument was primarily antirightist and secondarily anti-Protestant; Hamacher's priorities were the other way around.[56]

On October 14, Centrist stalwarts gathered to refound (or, as they preferred to put it, to "rebuild") the party in the tradition-laden Westphalian town of Soest, the birthplace of the party in 1870. In his keynote speech, party chairman Hamacher compared the CDP's interdenominational politics with Hitler's allegedly similar pretensions. "We Germans of the present," he asserted, "must reckon with the historical fact that we have lived for four centuries in two separate confessions." The Center was neither to blame for the failure of the interconfessional impulse, nor could it be sacrificed for the sake of that impulse. However small at first, a Protestant party in a Brüning-style cartel was preferable to a single "gathering party" that included the Hugenberg-style reactionaries who had sabotaged Brüning's policies because he was Catholic.[57]

Hamacher believed he was advocating but the merest extension of what Brüning had done. Backed by a smattering of social Protestants and abetted by Social Democratic toleration, the Center would govern; the only change was that it would now be more frankly Catholic. Though the facilitation of this or any coalition was not why Hamacher wanted to restore the Center, he clearly preferred this arrangement to the Weimar coalition.[58] That the effacement of the Protestant right might make not the Center but the SPD ascendant seems not to have occurred to him: since Brüning's demise "just one hundred meters from the goal" had been the source of the entire catastrophe, all that was required was to pick up where Brüning had left off.

Important ex-Centrists now bombarded Hamacher with private attempts at persuasion. According to Gilsing, Windthorst's old warning against forsaking the Center meant that Christians must not choose the "hour of greatest danger" to break the "common phalanx of the Christian people." Essen trade unionist Heinrich Strunk added that the forsaking of the Center, as well as the political "suicide" that Brockmann wanted to prevent, had happened long ago—in 1933. The question now was whether the Christian Democrats or the Communists would be the largest party; Hamacher's separatism would hand victory to the Communists. In the British system of single-member single-ballot districts, a cartel with a Protestant party would be of no avail. Not the Center but the CDP, wrote Thomas Esser, represented Brüning's ideal of 1930 (from America, Brüning himself agreed); the CDP would carry out Centrist policies under a new name. How, asked Esser, could the Center survive without the trade unionists, without youth (which knew nothing of the old party), and without the clergy?[59]

Hamacher was a pious, dutiful man of deep personal integrity but sharply limited political vision. Well suited to be an organizational functionary, he was ill equipped to deal with party politics from a position on the firing line. More and more, he would come to be a figurehead in a party managed by Brockmann and steered toward its own brand of innovation by Helene Wessel and Karl Spiecker. Yet Hamacher is significant because he embodied the subcultural, religious, and organizational loyalties that accounted for most of the refounded party's constituency. His papers are full of letters from the rank and file, pleading with him to reassert the traditional Centrist outlook in the face of Spiecker's innovations (Chapter 10). A history teacher by profession, Hamacher considered it presumptuous to believe that Germany could be set aright by discounting four hundred years of confessional division and seventy-five years of party tradition; running roughshod over Germany's heritage was, he thought, precisely the Nazis' mistake. Yet, except for what he deemed the accessory role of Protestantism in the catastrophe, he himself froze history at the point of Brüning's dubiously improvised government and showed little grasp of the way the Nazi period had transformed the country's politics. So little did he value the interdenominational cooperation supposedly facilitated by his cartel that neither the CDU's subsequent electoral successes nor its refusal to be captured by Hugenberg-style reactionaries could convince him to abandon the Center.

With the official refounding of the Center at Soest, Catholics were now divided into two adversarial parties. To discredit the Christian Democratic claim to Centrist ideals, Centrists shrilly associated the CDP/CDU with the old alliance of Hitler and Hugenberg, the Harzburg Front. By contrast, the first major Christian Democratic leaflet after Soest spoke of "a few well-meaning friends from the old Center party" who were making a "mistake." Whereas the Center had always strived to incorporate all Christians politically, a neo-Centrist "splinter," the leaflet stated, would be a "purely confessional party." Interdenominational cooperation could not be sacrificed to a "petty quarrel over the Center," for in these dangerous times, there were "more important things to do." "The ideals of the Center party will also live on in the Christian Democratic party," most of whose leaders had been Centrists; the CDP would consider its traditions "a holy bequest."[60]

Unlike Strunk in his letter to Hamacher, the CDP's Cologne founding group was still reluctant to admit that the Center had disgraced itself in 1933. According to trade union secretary Karl Zimmermann, the current "change of name" did not constitute a criticism of the old party, for the "unshakable" western and southern resistance to the Nazis had been due not just to the Catholic religion, but to the Centrist legacy of "political education." What had changed, however, was Protestantism. No longer did Catholics face a powerful state Church; indeed, said Zimmermann, the Confessing Church had suffered even more at Nazi hands than had the Catholic. From these facts, Zimmermann drew a conclusion opposite to Hamacher's: absent an organized, militantly anti-Catholic, Protestant political grouping, a "Catholic defense party" was no longer appropriate. The Center's mission had been fulfilled; its time had past; and "Protestants in today's Germany actually have a right no longer to be reminded of things like the Kulturkampf."[61]

In quick succession, Zimmermann thus attacked two of the old Center party's most cherished rhetorical traditions: its claim that it was not a Catholic confessional party, and its habit of invoking the Kulturkampf to maintain unity and élan. Furthermore, he depicted interdenominational union as a "new goal," not as the realization of an old Centrist goal. For Zimmermann, the development of a truly interdenominational party was not, as for Julius Bachem, the culmination of the return from exile, but the aftermath. He advocated such a party not to end the last vestiges of the Kulturkampf, but because those vestiges were already gone.

Zimmermann's ruminations are indicative of the process of transition from a Centrist to a Christian Democratic loyalty. But as his continued talk of a name change shows, that process was threatened after Soest by the need to convince wavering Catholics that the CDP was the true repository of Centrist tradition. This issue tempted the CDP to blur its message of boldness and newness and reinforced the element of ambiguity in its rhetoric.

What the party still needed was a leader who was both less sentimental about the old attachment and less utopian about the purpose of the new party than was the original founding group. While giving perfunctory respect to the old party, such a leader would answer the new Center's attacks not by trying to out-Center it, but by cold-bloodedly moving to discredit the new Center with Catholics while exploiting its presence to profile the distinctiveness of the CDP to Protestants. Born with a fanfare of idealism, the CDP now required shrewd, hard-nosed pragmatism. It needed a seasoned leader who based political decisions on a calculation of what was likely to succeed, who possessed proven administrative and political skills, and who could provide steady, clearheaded, "in-this-world" leadership that Catholics and Protestants alike would respect. In short, it needed a person who thought not of a political home, but of a political party.

That person was Konrad Adenauer.

8   The CDU of Konrad Adenauer

Seventy years old, in good health, his prestige intact, Konrad Adenauer stood out early among surviving Centrists as the kind of person who could lend the new Christian Democratic Party instant respectability. The Düsseldorf circle had broached the possibility of making him Rhenish party chairman as early as August 1945, but Leo Schwering's circle had been reluctant to yield control. Then, on October 6, the British suddenly removed Adenauer as Mayor of Cologne and barred him from political activity. Two months later, with as little explanation as when they had imposed the ban, they lifted it. On January 22, 1946, Adenauer was elected provisional chairman of the party (now called the CDU) in the British zone. Two weeks later, he replaced Schwering as Rhenish chairman, and on March 1, he became permanent zonal chairman. With the party a going concern, Adenauer was moving quickly to consolidate his hold.[1]

Adenauer's Initial Conception

It is ironic that Adenauer, whose ascent was eventually to mean the end of Christian socialist predominance in the CDU, began his rise with the support of key Christian social leaders such as Düsseldorf's Karl Arnold. Several factors underlay that support. First, the new party needed his administrative and organizational experience. Second, mindful of the need to recruit workers, Adenauer seemed likely to respect their interests. He told Wilhelm Hamacher that the CDP could win far more labor support than the Center; he told the liberal Protestant Mayor of Hamburg, Rudolf Petersen, that the demise of the Christian trade unions necessitated the word "Christian" in the new party's name. Third, Adenauer's broad name recognition and proven political acumen were assets in combating the new Center. He met immediately with Hamacher upon becoming Rhenish chairman, and blamed Schwering's tactlessness for alienating him. At the same time, he shared the trade unionists' concern that portraying the CDP/CDU as the Center's heir would endanger the bridge to Protestants. On November 24, 1945, Arnold contrasted the old, "confession-delimited" Center to the "new beginning" represented by the CDP. Much more categorically than the Cologne founders, Adenauer too was insisting as early as September that the CDP was an entirely new party.[2]

It soon became apparent, however, that Adenauer's vision of the role of the new party in the future party system varied from that of his trade union sponsors. While Arnold expected a partnership or Grand Coalition of Christian Democrats and Social Democrats, Adenauer from the beginning envisioned a polar rivalry. On August 21, 1945, he wrote Munich Mayor Karl Scharnagl that the SPD was likely to be swallowed by the Communists, that a "strong alliance" was being forged between those "a-Christian parties," and that only a concentration of Christians in one party, eventually including some Social Democratic defectors, could resist the "threatening danger from the East." Ten days later, he wrote Petersen that the development of the party system might well "result in the end in the materialistically based parties standing on one side, [and] on the other side, the Christian Democratic party."[3]

Adenauer's clear and early two-bloc conception distinguished him not only from Arnold but also from a prominent conservative Protestant: ex-German Nationalist and former cabinet official Hans Schlange-Schöningen. In a series of circulars during January 1946, Schlange outlined his concept of a true three-party system consisting of the KPD on the left, the SPD in the middle, and, perhaps in coalition with the latter, a Christian Democratic "gathering party" *(Sammelpartei)* on the right. In one of his first acts as zonal chairman, Adenauer rebuked Schlange for this "misleading" and "incorrect picture of our party." The CDU, wrote Adenauer, was neither a "right party" nor a "gathering party"; it was not a lumping together of old groups, but a new party "with a new program of its own." He distinguished between the positive function of building a party of the Christian Weltanschauung and the sterility of seeking a "gathering" *(Sammlung)* for its own sake: "No new party can be built upon a foundation of 'gathering' because 'gathering' does not indicate any particular pathway into the future."[4]

Schlange's rhetoric, Adenauer feared, would play into the hands of those (including both Johannes Brockmann and the SPD) who complained that the Christian Democratic movement was a revival of the reactionary Harzburg Front or a Papen-style cover for an antilabor Bürgerblock.[5] The CDU would thereby throw away its chance to win moderate voters, to cut into the SPD's constituency, and to obviate the need for a Grand Coalition. Likewise, Adenauer objected to Schlange's "wish" that the SPD emulate the British Labour Party's success in using moderation and a clear stand against the Communists to become *the* large party of workers, for the CDU had "at least as much right as the SPD" to working-class support. Indeed, wrote Adenauer, "insofar as a comparison between parties of different countries is possible," the parallel was closer between the Labour Party and the CDU. Adenauer thus invoked Arnold's progressive profile of the CDU to counter a scenario for a Grand Coalition that was coming from a right-wing source.

Adenauer had a second objection to Schlange's circulars: they spoke of two separate Christian Democratic parties, the CDU in Catholic regions and the "Christian Democratic Party of Construction" in northern Protestant regions. While the two might merge later, their separateness was "justified for the time being because a significant part of the Protestant electorate glimpses in the CDU the old Center, in spite of its loosening from an ultramontane connection." Such passages were anathema to Adenauer on three counts. First, the reference to Centrist ultramontanism was pejorative in the German context; by injuring the prospects for interdenominational cooperation, it heightened the neo-Centrist threat. Second, while Schlange denied that either of his "two" parties was "confessional," his formulation threatened to reopen this old Pandora's box. Third, identifying the CDU with the old Center both revived the thesis of the "change of name" and subverted the reason for the change. At a time when Adenauer was trying to profile the CDU as a new beginning unburdened by the Center's confessional association, he could hardly allow a Protestant colleague to make that association explicit again. Thus, in its first communique under Adenauer, the zonal organization boasted that the CDU was "the only party" that constituted "a fundamentally new manifestation" in German politics. In subsequent weeks, Adenauer repeatedly emphasized that the CDU was "a new party, not a continuation of an old party from an era that is dead and gone." In contrast to Schwering's circle, he generally refrained from citing the Center as a precursor or referring to Windthorst, Bachem, Stegerwald, or even his own speech about interdenominationalism at the Catholic convocation of 1922. When he did mention the old Center, his purpose was to deny its tradition to the new Center, not to claim it for the CDU per se.[6]

For Adenauer, then, the SPD was an old and shopworn party that was in danger of becoming an appendage of the Communists, while the CDU was a new, democratic, moderate, coherent, and genuinely interdenominational movement. The party system would not consist of left versus right, but it would consist of two clear camps. Yet, rather than leaving the CDU isolated and overwhelmed (as a right party or a camouflaged Centrist revival would have been), such a party system might well result in a Christian Democratic majority. Freed of non-Marxist competitors and attractive to younger Social Democrats who rejected Communism, the CDU would shake off the old mentality of minority-group politics and subcultural splintering and pursue a majority "Christian" strategy instead.

Just as Adenauer became zonal chairman, this vision seemed to require some correction. Although the Marxist parties were moving toward a shotgun wedding in the Soviet zone, their relations were increasingly tense in the West, where the strongly anti-Communist concentration camp survivor, Kurt Schumacher, was emerging as the Social Democratic leader. Furthermore, the CDU in the British zone now faced two non-Marxist rivals: the new Center, which explicitly denied the felicity of a bipolar party system, and the Free Democratic Party (FDP), the partisan liberal vehicle whose emergence Adenauer had hoped to forestall during his northern trip of the previous July (Chapter 7). Adenauer would have to adapt his vision to these emerging realities—or he would have to change the realities to match his vision.

Adenauer, Weltanschauung, and the SPD

In late January 1946, the first local elections were held in American-occupied southern Germany. Adenauer could feel gratified by the results: surprising almost everyone, the CDU/CSU outpolled the two Marxist parties combined.[7] But the elections also produced another surprise: for every vote garnered by the Communists, eight went to Social Democrats. Not coincidentally, this result came just as Schumacher was fighting to prevent the Soviet-mandated Socialist-Communist merger in the Soviet zone. With the subsequent formation there of the Socialist Unity Party (SED), the SPD found itself banned from its former eastern strongholds and confined to Berlin and the West. In effect, the SPD became the first battlefield of the Cold War.

Having sensed that the divergent development of East and West might result in separate party systems, Adenauer had earlier opposed the CDP's adoption of the eastern party's name ("Union" instead of "Party") for fear that the eastern CDU's actions under Soviet pressure might discredit the western party.[8] Now, it was the western KPD that was apparently discredited, while the SPD had emerged as the CDU's most formidable western competitor. Adenauer swiftly turned it into his chief political target.

In a major speech on March 24, 1946, Adenauer asserted that resistance to the rise of Nazism in Germany had been strongest where Marxism had been weakest ("this is an irrefutable fact!"). Likening Schumacher's attacks on the "ruthless and reactionary" CDU to Nazi tactics, he rejected the claim that the CDU's Christianity was a facade for the opportunistic pursuit of power and asked how Social Democrats would feel were their own socialist convictions to be similarly dismissed. He thus set the stage for his main point: the socialism of the SPD was not a socioeconomic or political program, but (like Chistianity) a Weltanschauung; hence, it had to be opposed by a party that explicitly championed the Christian Weltanschauung.[9]

To illustrate the need for the CDU, Adenauer contrasted the situation in England. Whereas all English parties had many Christian members, the German system had always contained parties that "purposefully fought Christianity." While he would be "overjoyed were the SPD to declare that it is just as Christian in its conviction as the CDU," prudence required an unequivocally Christian counterpart. Schumacher's claim that Social Democratic strength was the measure of democracy in Germany showed that he had "not yet" understood democracy, whose "essence" was "respect for the convictions of other parties." For a party to claim leadership of the state because it alone possessed the "correct" Weltanschauung, said Adenauer, was "incompatible with the nature of democracy." He advised the SPD to give up the "materialistic Weltanschauung," which was based on the undemocratic premise of class struggle, and to become a democratic party of social reform.[10]

Adenauer's remonstrance against intolerance based on Weltanschauung in a democracy would have made a good argument for keeping the issue of Weltanschauung out of politics altogether. It should have followed that if the SPD were to prove it was tolerant and democratic, then a specifically Christian party would cease to be needed. Instead, Adenauer made a sweeping assertion in the opposite direction: democracy itself derived from Christian principle, and this too necessitated the formation of a party that championed the Christian Weltanschauung. The world, he said, faced a struggle between this Weltanschauung, which emphasized the freedom and worth of the individual, and the "materialist Weltanschauung" spawned by the industrial revolution, whose emphasis on collectivism, be it fascist or Marxist, had led to totalitarian deification of the state.[11] For Adenauer, then, the only true democracy was Christian Democracy. Although he avoided concluding that the CDU would have to stay in power indefinitely, he implied that the SPD could safely come to power only after giving up its own Weltanschauung and embracing the Christian-inspired conception of individual freedom. In the meantime, he was making the same monopolistic claim about Weltanschauung and democracy for the CDU for which he had just chastised the SPD.

Adenauer, Weltanschauung, and the FDP

Although he insisted on the importance of Weltanschauung in the German party system, Adenauer dwelled neither on subcultural concerns (as the old Center had) nor on Christianity for its own sake, but on an allegedly derivative principle that one might just as easily have associated with traditional liberalism: the integrity of the individual. Had it not been for the Kulturkampf, Adenauer remarked early in 1945, only two parties would have developed alongside the SPD: an agrarian-conservative eastern party, and an industrial-liberal western party (to which he, a westerner of liberal inclination, would presumably have belonged). Accordingly, he supported a postwar effort to persuade former staffers of the *KV* and the liberal *KZ* to produce one newspaper for both liberals and Catholics.[12] Despite denying that the CDU was a gathering party, he was fully capable of arguing that in the bipolar battle between the Christian and Marxist Weltanschauungen, liberals should join the CDU.

Adenauer thus set out in 1946 to swallow up the FDP. Proceeding regionally, he told the chairman of the Lower Saxon FDP on February 14 that the C in the CDU's name was not a blurring of religion and politics, but an indication that the party was open to all who opposed the "materialistic outlook" and believed in the "Christian-*humanistic*

Weltanschauung." Four months later, he was ready to call the Hamburg CDU the "Union of Christian and Free Democrats." Meanwhile, he minimized the importance of the FDP as one of two small parties (with the KPD) in a system dominated by the "only two" large parties: CDU and SPD.[13] When he failed to coax the FDP into a fusion, however, he rediscovered the difference in Weltanschauung between the two groups. The CDU, he recommended at the end of the year, must emphasize Weltanschauung to stem the FDP's growth.[14]

Adenauer next tried to turn the apparent viability of the FDP to his advantage. Since the FDP was likely to "hold the balance," he recommended steering toward a "sensible relationship" with it. Here he was able to build on the experience of the intervening months in the new administrative unit (and future federal state) of North Rhine-Westphalia. During the summer of 1946, the British had summoned an appointed Landtag and sanctioned the formation in Düsseldorf of an all-party government. But the two big parties had quarreled over the Interior Ministry, and the Center, allegedly fearing "Harzburg" influence over the police, had opposed even Karl Arnold for the post. A government without the CDU had thereupon been formed, with Rudolf Amelunxen, soon to join the Center, as Minister-President (and Hamacher as Transportation Minister). Local elections in the fall, however, confirmed the CDU's drawing power: the new party topped the poll, averaging 48.5 percent of the vote. The British then insisted that the CDU be brought into the government and reapportioned the Landtag to approximate the election results, giving the CDU and FDP a majority. With the FDP on most noncultural matters seemingly to the right of the CDU, Adenauer commented that the FDP was breathing a sigh of relief to have company against the left within the all-party government.[15]

Adenauer and the Center

As the CDU's caucus chairman and floor leader in the Landtag, Adenauer too must have been breathing a sigh of relief, for the Center had been using the summertime events in Düsseldorf to charge his party with DNVP-style oppositional intransigence. Comparing the Center's "long history" of "responsibility-consciousness" with the CDU's current "flight from" it, the only currently licensed Center party newspaper, Karl Spiecker's *Rhein-Ruhr Zeitung (RRZ)*, recalled that "true democratic parties" had not sought "flimsy reasons" to evade responsibility in 1918–1919. Adenauer replied that the CDU was not in the Amelunxen government because the insidious Spiecker preferred Carl Severing's Social Democratic son-in-law from Berlin over a lifelong Rhinelander and trade unionist (Arnold) as Interior Minister. He minimized the importance of the CDU's oppositional stance—this was not yet a democratically chosen cabinet anyway—and promised that the CDU never would engage in "opposition for opposition's sake."[16]

As the polemics over the Amelunxen government showed, Adenauer's concern now was not just that the new Center was frivolously dividing the Christian camp, but that it was deliberately augmenting the Marxist forces. The strongly left-leaning positions taken by Spiecker and by the Center's floor leader, Brockmann, seemed to be more than just tactics to differentiate the party from the CDU. Accordingly, Adenauer's public approach to the new Center was to proceed as if he were unmasking it.

The background to Adenauer's rhetoric in the summer and fall of 1946 was his prior effort (which had aroused Protestant anxiety)[17] to woo Hamacher. Interjecting himself into this process, Spiecker told Adenauer on March 14, 1946, that the purpose of a "political" party (the Center) was to bring together a majority in support of a policy; basing a party (the CDU) on the "Christian Weltanschauung" (or any Weltanschauung) was a mistake and cut off others willing to work for the same policies. Adenauer countered that Hamacher's position was diametrically the opposite: for him, the CDU was "not Catholic enough," and interdenominationalism served no purpose. Spiecker replied that while Hamacher had not entirely freed himself from his old mentality, he now agreed with Spiecker. Predicting that the Center would eventually absorb the left wing of the CDU and the right wing of the SPD, he put Adenauer on notice that the Center represented a whole different concept of how to structure the party system.[18]

Informed via telephone by Adenauer of what Spiecker had said, Hamacher replied that he was willing to meet again, though not with Spiecker present. But Hamacher was now in full retreat. On April 9, the three men did meet, along with some members of the clergy. Reading from a prepared text, Spiecker outlined his arguments for the new Center based on removing religion and Weltanschauung from politics. The old Center too, he claimed, had been this sort of party. Asked if he shared these views, Hamacher sheepishly said that he did. If so, came the reply, then Hamacher and Spiecker ought to call their party the "Free Democratic Party." When the Centrists nonetheless suggested a working partnership *(Arbeitsgemeinschaft)* with the CDU, Adenauer responded, "No; between a party that consciously and willfully expunges the word 'Christian' and us, there can only be struggle!"[19]

All this was grist for Adenauer's mill. While he had failed to recruit Hamacher, he had demonstrated to the clergy the preeminence within the Center of Spiecker's outlook. Adenauer now studded his speeches with references to the "astonishing" course of a party that used the name of the old Center while denying the relationship of Weltanschauung and politics. Even so, he avoided becoming overly strident, for he was worried as the fall elections approached that the dispute might cause some Christian voters to stay home. Thus, when the Spiecker-controlled *RRZ* unleashed a flood of anti-CDU polemics (even calling Adenauer "the Führer in Cologne"), Adenauer's response was crisp but measured: he denounced as demagogic the assertion that the CDU was harboring reactionaries, pointed out that Spiecker was calling for a separation of politics and Weltanschauung, asked the doubters in his audience to investigate the matter for themselves, and concluded that the "Neo-Center" had "absolutely nothing in common" with the old party.[20]

Adenauer's shrewd mixture of firmness and conciliation contrasted sharply with Spiecker's shrill polemics. On July 28, Adenauer told one audience that he would be fascinated to know which was the true face of the new Center: "Is it that of Spiecker, [or] is it that of Hamacher? For the two are fundamentally different." On August 24, he told another gathering: "If his adherents knew how Herr Spiecker really stands on the Christian Weltanschauung in politics, they would not follow him any more. You must all make sure that everyone learns about this. We don't want to polemicize against his adherents in a malicious or spiteful way; they have been led astray. When they come back to us—and they will . . .—we want to accept them with open arms." Masterfully taking the high road, he followed up in the pious Centrist stronghold of Münster on September 8:

Herr Spiecker wants his party not to stand on the basis of the Christian Weltanschauung . . . [Yet] a member of the Executive Board of the party, *Studienrat* Laube, declares that the foundation of the Center party is the Christian Weltanschauung. These are such diametrical contradictions that one really cannot have too much confidence in the future development of this party. (Heckler: . . . you know full

well that we in the Center want to see the Christian standpoint realized.) The heckler is absolutely right . . . But, my honored member of
this party, please direct yourself not to me, but direct yourself to
Herr Spiecker. ([Cries of] "very true," "bravo," intense applause.) I
have cited for you word for word what Herr Spiecker said . . . I really don't want to speak to you polemically; check for yourself . . . I
beg you . . . do think it over once again . . . Calmly think it over once
again and don't be in a hurry to heckle. I repeat, I don't want a row
with you . . . I believe that you will indeed come to the conviction
that exactly those members of your party who want to see the Christian demands realized will have to say to themselves: no, every splintering is harmful and damages the cause . . . ([Cries of] "bravo" and
intense applause.)[21]

Thus, Adenauer proceeded by cajoling the Centrist electorate and trying to separate it from its leaders, concentrating his fire always on
Spiecker. By contrast, he portrayed Hamacher in the same way as the
voters he was trying to cajole: the Center's chairman was simply the
most prominent of Spiecker's victims, the archetype of the duped
voter.

The CDU's massive victory in the first round of local elections (September 15) confirmed Adenauer in this strategy. When Father Caspar
Schulte on September 30 offered to mediate, Adenauer politely
thanked him, writing on October 13 (the day of the CDU's equally
impressive showing in the second round) that the best strategy now
was to wait for the Center to fall apart. The two agreed that whereas
the prospects for winning the Centrist leaders were dim, progress on
the local level was more likely and should be a priority. The wisdom
of this course seemed confirmed when Hamacher was taken ill and
relieved of his duties by the more intransigent Brockmann.[22]

Though in early December Adenauer was optimistic about eliminating the Center before the first Landtag elections in the spring,[23] by
February of 1947 he was worried again. The British and Americans by
then had merged their zones and were about to create the first cross-
zonal German institution, the Frankfurt Economic Council (FEC).
Were the Soviets to respond by playing the German unity card, Adenauer expected a relicensed SPD to get an overwhelming majority in
the Soviet zone; by adding victories in Schleswig-Holstein and Lower
Saxony, the SPD, if not checked in North Rhine-Westphalia, could
become the dominant party in all of Germany and build a socialist
state. A Christian Democratic majority in North Rhine-Westphalia

was therefore vital; the key, said Adenauer, was fusion with the Center, even if the fusion had to be negotiated with Spiecker.[24] In this all-German scenario, Adenauer briefly pondered whether fusion did not belong at the heart of his entire agenda.

A group of priests now prevailed upon Brockmann to meet quietly with Adenauer and try to conclude an election accord. Such an accord was important, since seats were to be awarded according to a mixed system: proportional representation would be in force, but candidates who finished first in local districts would be deemed elected regardless of the effect on the proportions. In frustrating and time-consuming negotiations (Brockmann stood up Adenauer at least once), Adenauer failed to get an agreement to limit direct competition in key districts. From Brockmann's standpoint, acceptance would have lent credence to the CDU's old charge that the Center was frivolously splintering the Christian camp and had no raison d'être; besides, Brockmann wanted to position his party to be pivotal in passing progressive social legislation. Having entered the negotiations under clerical pressure, Brockmann used a news leak as an excuse to call them off.[25]

Adenauer and Coalition Politics

As the Düsseldorf Landtag prepared to debate the issue of socialization, Adenauer's paper majority of FDP and CDU meant little. Since a withdrawal by the FDP would not bring down the all-party government, the CDU's trade unionists would be undeterred from siding often with the SPD. Indeed, in late January 1947, some trade unionists even threatened secession.[26]

Adenauer therefore made a two-stage tactical concession. In February 1947, he agreed to support a more "social" program for his party—the famous Ahlen Program. Originally drafted primarily by Johannes Albers, the program foresaw a mixed economy in which private capital, labor, and the state would share ownership and guidance of key industries. On this basis, Adenauer's Landtag delegation introduced its own mild socialization bill. The bill provided that no single stockholder could own more than 10 percent of the stock of the large mining, iron, and chemical concerns, that nonprivate capital would control an absolute majority of votes at general business meetings, and that workers would have codetermination rights through representation on company boards. In order to block the left-wing parties' more sweeping bill, the FDP agreed to vote for the CDU's bill, thus assuring its passage. Since the western occupation authorities were unlikely to allow the regions to decide the final disposition of issues so fundamental, Adenauer could reckon that even this relatively modest bill would never be implemented.[27] More important than the actual text of the bill and the Ahlen Program, then, was the function they performed. By fashioning an alternative to the social legislation of the Marxist parties—and by replacing the phrase "Christian socialism" with the more neutral phrase "community economy" *(Gemeinwirtschaft)*—they helped prepare even the trade union wing of the CDU for a future relationship with the SPD of government and opposition.

During this early socialization debate, the Center sided with the SPD. This development seemed to justify the CDU's fear, reiterated by Adenauer on March 21, that the Center might fill out a majority co-alition for the two Marxist parties.[28] With the Landtag elections on April 20, this fear became greater still. The Christian Democratic vote was one-fifth lower than it had been in the local elections of the previous fall. With 38 percent of the vote, the CDU still beat out the SPD (32 percent). But the Center (10 percent) nearly doubled its share, finishing ahead of the FDP (6 percent) and just behind the KPD (14 percent). Several factors may have aided the Center: its soft-pedaling of Spiecker's anti-Weltanschauung line and its renewed emphasis on the schools question (recent concessions on schools by the CDU in Hesse, together with the eastern CDU's apparent preference for inter-denominational schools, allowed the Center to claim that the CDU was "unreliable" on this issue);[29] the prestige of having the sitting Minister-President (Amelunxen, a known *Kulturpolitiker*); and, on the Christian Democratic side, a normal falloff after the first blush of interest in a new party. Thanks to the election system, the CDU, with 92 out of 216 seats, was proportionally overrepresented; even so, it no longer could form a majority with the FDP alone (12 seats). Were the Center (20 seats) to join forces with the SPD (64) and KPD (28), a majority without the CDU was possible.

The subsequent coalitional negotiations, involving all five parties, dragged on for two months. The central issue was socialization. In effect, the SPD, KPD, and Center tried to get the provisions they had failed to pass during the Landtag session. Adenauer, with the FDP and most of the CDU, opposed concessions. But Arnold was operating from a different agenda. To the British, he was just the man to head the new government: he came from the largest party, yet was a pro-gressive whose campaign rhetoric (unlike Adenauer's) had been conciliatory toward the SPD. Social Democrats by now could find little fault with Arnold, who was emerging as Adenauer's bane and who shared their view that the FDP was the home of reactionary economic liberalism.

In a letter to Arnold on May 23, Adenauer insisted that there be no coalition without the FDP. But in a meeting that day, leading Centrists, Social Democrats, and Communists increased the pressure on Arnold to make his own progressive agenda clear. In the face of a four-party coalition dominated by the SPD and the left wing of the CDU, it was Adenauer's wing of the CDU that now favored an all-party government. When success proved impossible, Adenauer tried vainly to interest Brockmann in a coalition of just the CDU and the Center.[30]

On June 17, Arnold formed a four-party government of CDU, SPD, KPD, and Center. Then, in a governmental address before a session of the Landtag in which Adenauer's seat sat empty, Arnold promised socioeconomic restructuring that went beyond the Ahlen Program. By eliminating the role foreseen for private capital in some industries, Arnold in effect capitulated to the SPD. His address caused an uproar in the CDU party caucus, whose meetings for the rest of the year were marred by factional battles between Minister-President Arnold and caucus chairman Adenauer.[31]

Adenauer was in no position at the moment to work his will with Arnold. The April election results had been disappointing throughout the British zone: fulfilling Adenauer's fears of the previous February, the SPD had emerged as the largest party in Schleswig-Holstein and Lower Saxony, and governments without the CDU were possible everywhere. Yet Adenauer continued to believe that time was on his side. It was in settings like the Frankfurt Economic Council that the socioeconomic system, and perhaps also the party system, would finally be shaped; and it was in Frankfurt that Adenauer spent the day of Arnold's governmental address, successfully laying the groundwork on a bizonal level for what he had hitherto failed to achieve in North Rhine-Westphalia: a two-sided alignment of CDU-led "responsible" parties and SPD-led "opposition."[32]

By June 1947, then, two competing models of the future party system had taken concrete form: in Düsseldorf, the Grand Coalition of CDU and SPD; in Frankfurt, the less formal alignment of CDU and FDP against SPD and KPD. The situation in Frankfurt, however, remained precarious. The occupying powers had decreed that seats in the 52-member Council be distributed as follows: 20 each for the CDU/CSU and SPD, 4 for the FDP, 3 for the KPD, 2 each for the Center and the small northern conservative German Party (DP), and 1 for another minor nonsocialist party, the Union of Economic Construction (WAV). Since the CDU/CSU, FDP, DP, and WAV together held a majority only barely, the small parties would be sorely tempted to take advantage of their indispensability.

This situation confirmed Adenauer's sense that what the country really needed was not an anti-SPD coalition but a true two-party system. In a major speech to the zonal party congress in Recklinghausen on August 14, he put this to the public. Coalitions, he asserted, should be exceptions in politics—time-constrained arrangements in unusual circumstances to achieve specific and overriding goals. Coalitions of indefinite duration between inconsonant partners were inherently unstable; such "coalition forming at any price" had brought down the Weimar Republic. Party systems should therefore contain only two large but coherent parties, one of which formed the government while the other provided the loyal, "constructive opposition."[33]

To promote such a party system, Adenauer went on, the CDU favored single-member, single-ballot districts over proportional representation. He applauded the functioning of such a first-past-the-post electoral system in Schleswig-Holstein, where the SPD had achieved a parliamentary majority and formed the government alone. Such a system, he said, fostered clear accountability: at the end of the current Landtag, voters could pass judgment on the Socialist government. Of course, Adenauer's "defense" of the SPD was largely a defense of himself, for it was he who had insisted (in May) that the CDU withdraw from the Grand Coalition in Schleswig-Holstein. Likewise, Adenauer defended the SPD's decision to go into opposition in Frankfurt.

To insure that both government and opposition had a clear sense of direction, Adenauer emphasized the contrasting Weltanschauungen of the two big parties and identified that contrast with specific differences in policy. He accentuated policy differences not just because of the substantive point at issue but also because of his bipolar conception of a successful democratic party system. For both reasons, Adenauer deplored Arnold's eagerness to make concessions on socialization to the SPD.

As former members of resistance circles, Arnold and Kaiser had worked with Social Democrats in an idealistic cause. They combined this experience with that of Weimar to conclude that a broad democratic concentration was both possible and necessary. If such a concentration could not be achieved in one democratic, socialist, but non-Marxist "bridge" party (Kaiser's original conception), then it should be advanced through a Grand Coalition (Arnold); in the East, Kaiser even allowed at first that *Blockpolitik*—the Soviet-mandated system of compulsory solidarity among all the parties and mass organizations—had to be given a loyal test. For Adenauer, on the other hand, the lesson of Germany's recent past was that the road to a healthy democracy was not democratic concentration, but a distinct relationship, between two democratic parties, of government and opposition.

9   The CDU and Jakob Kaiser

It is ironic that the most memorable battle over self-image in the young CDU was fought not between Catholic and Protestant factions but between two factions led by Catholics who had made their names in Cologne. Compounding the irony, the leader of the more "conservative" faction, Konrad Adenauer, was operating in the region with the greatest concentration of Christian labor voters, while the leader of the more "progressive" faction, Jakob Kaiser, was initially operating in the region where the CDU was most dependent on conservative Protestant support. Yet, while the rivalry between Kaiser and Adenauer on social and national issues has frequently been noted, less attention has been given to the change in their relations after December 1947, when the Soviets tired of Kaiser's independent-mindedness and forced him to relinquish leadership of the eastern party. What Kaiser's experience with conservative Protestants did not do, his experience with the Soviets did: it convinced him not just of Communist perfidy, but of Social Democratic complicity. By the time of the first federal election campaign and coalitional negotiations in 1949, Kaiser, as deputy for Essen and chairman of the Christian Democratic Social Committees, opposed Karl Arnold's desire for a Grand Coalition of CDU and SPD. Kaiser's policy differences with Adenauer were by no means over. But on the basic issue of how to structure the party system, the two men had come to be allies. The alternative to *Blockpolitik,* in Kaiser's view now as in Adenauer's, was a bipolar system of government and opposition.

Kaiser, Adenauer, and the Roots of Convergence

While one would have been hard-pressed to predict this outcome in 1946, certain early points of common ground suggest the basis on which the paths of Adenauer and Kaiser would later converge. First,

194

both men emphasized Weltanschauung as the principal mark of distinction between the CDU and its rivals. Second, both refused to become trapped in Centrist-style rhetorical disputes and insisted that the CDU was an entirely new party. Indeed, like Stegerwald, Kaiser maligned the old Center for more than its confessionalism: "It had— today we can say it openly—no economic program of its own and was therefore basically an unpolitical party. For this reason alone a simple revival of this party would be out of the question."[1] Even more significant, just as Adenauer tried to woo secular liberals and to fuse the CDU with the FDP, Kaiser tried to prevent the founding of the LDP and to woo freethinkers to the CDU. The logic of a Christian-liberal union, however, pointed toward an eventual adversarial relationship between Christian and Marxist parties—especially if the Marxist parties also fused, as they did in the Soviet zone.

Kaiser and Adenauer's most celebrated bone of contention was the East-West question, but even here one can discern the roots of convergence. Kaiser's theory of Germany as a unified "bridge" or "synthesis" between East and West was anathema to Adenauer, who believed that synthesis would only lead to Communism. Playing to federalist sentiment within the CDU, Adenauer skillfully blocked Kaiser from asserting Berlin's control over the party and its program. Yet, despite Kaiser's lingering resentment over this development, the original disagreement largely resolved itself. Kaiser's own fate at the hands of the Soviets was the best proof of Adenauer's greater realism. While Kaiser might continue to prize German unification over western consolidation, he had to concede that the second would have to precede the first.[2]

More difficult to resolve were differences over the domestic merits (rather than the geopolitics) of Christian socialism. To Adenauer, the term was a non sequitur, since Christianity and socialism were competing Weltanschauungen. He countered Kaiser's repeated insistence that the "bourgeois age was over" and the "socialist age" had begun by saying that since men would always aspire to personal freedom and property, the "bourgeois age will never come to an end." To Kaiser, however, socialism was not a Weltanschauung, but a pragmatic socio-economic consensus that counterposed social justice and economic planning to untrammeled socioeconomic liberalism. After the "fiasco" produced by the latter, all parties, in his view, would join the socialist socioeconomic consensus. What Germany needed was "honest tolerance" between the Christian socialists and the heretofore dogmatic Marxist socialists so that the "several socialistic streams" could flow harmoniously alongside one another. On this basis, Kaiser was initially prepared to accept *Blockpolitik*.[3]

Yet, even in this area, Adenauer and Kaiser had common ground. If both the SED and the CDU were pursuing socialism, then Weltanschauung, in Kaiser's view, was precisely the reason to vote for one of these parties rather than the other. Indeed, despite his talk of synthesis, Kaiser insisted that Christianity and Marxism were mutually exclusive. Like Adenauer, he said that Christianity's "highest law" was freedom of the individual; this law distinguished Christian socialism's pursuit of the common good from dogmatic Marxist "collectivism." "Social and economic" (that is, nondogmatic) socialists could join "only an outspokenly Christian party," since the SED and SPD were again embracing intolerant Weltanschauung-based principles (class struggle, anticlericalism). For Kaiser as well as Adenauer, then, the Christian Weltanschauung was the basis on which the CDU could carry on an adversarial relationship with its one large rival—even within the Soviet-mandated all-party bloc.[4]

Just as the socialist economic system was not limited in Kaiser's view to any one Weltanschauung, the Christian Weltanschauung was not limited to any one economic system. Christians thus could freely follow the "trend toward a socialistic order" that was sweeping the world. If Kaiser could use this argument now to justify socialism, however, he could use it later to justify some other socioeconomic system. In the summer of 1948, he would accept the lifting of economic controls and the crucial currency reform that launched Ludwig Erhard's neoliberal "social-market economy." By the summer of 1949, Kaiser would even assert that it was only "a secondary question" whether one chose a "free market with state regulation and social security" or a "moderately socialized economy including genuine entrepreneurial initiative."[5] The glibness of this transition reflects the fact that Kaiser's usage of the term "socialism" was never very rigorous or specific.

Generally speaking, "socialism" for Kaiser was a synonym for "progress." Hence, in 1945, he argued that the early socialists' doctrinaire rejection of religion could not be an essential attribute of socialism, since such a doctrine was regressive. Strikingly, nearly every point on his list of the essential attributes of socialism could be converted into an argument for social-meliorative liberalism. Socialism, he wrote, was "social progress," "social vision," "social justice"—that is, "guaranteeing each person a humane existence." Socialism was "the victory of reason in the economy," by which he meant not authoritarian planning, but using the latest scientific knowledge in production. Socialism was community ownership of essential raw materials; yet even Adenauer conceded mixed ownership in the subsequent Ahlen Program. Moreover, said Kaiser, "'socialism' is not . . . the same thing as 'socialization of all means of production,'" but meant taking account of the "social effect" of all actions. "Socialism is cosmopolitanism": international agreements should regulate production; this was the proper Christian attitude. Socialism was "the rejection of imperialism and militarism," a vaguely Wilsonian goal with which Erhard would not have disagreed. Furthermore, Kaiser occasionally even left the impression that he saw socialism as a temporary response to the current socioeconomic emergency.[6]

Although Kaiser had not abandoned his dream of following the example of what he called the "mature" party systems of other countries and forming a Labour Party that transcended Weltanschauung, he believed that "the hour for such a further development has not yet come." Despite occasionally echoing those neo-Centrists who feared trivializing Christianity by excessively invoking it in politics, he asserted that Weltanschauung properly played a bigger role in politics, which involved issues of national morality and freedom of conscience, than it did in the trade unions, whose goals were purely socioeconomic. Having argued, however, that the divisive effects of Weltanschauung among the trade unions had contributed to the rise of Nazism, he was vulnerable to the SED's argument that what was good for the trade unions was good for the party system.[7]

Of course, Kaiser could respond that while the aim of a trade union was to foster the solidarity of its members against an outside adversary, the aim of a party system was to foster a healthy competition of ideas and policies among its member parties. It was precisely this argument, however, that the Communists in the Soviet zone could not abide, for it implied the possibility of opposition. Indeed, even in the trade unions, Kaiser was warning by November 1946 that he had kept silent as long as he could about the SED's high-handed domination.[8] If the CDU too were not to be effaced, he was soon to realize, then it would have to challenge the constraints of *Blockpolitik* by asserting its right to go into opposition.

From *Blockpolitik* to Loyal Opposition

During 1947, as Kaiser's stance toward the SED and the Soviets grew increasingly defiant, Cold War tension escalated. In March, responding to Communist pressure on Greece and Turkey, the United States announced the Truman Doctrine and launched the policy of containment. Two months later, the Moscow conference of foreign ministers collapsed in disagreement over Germany. The United States and Britain then proceeded with their bizonal Frankfurt Economic Council (FEC). On June 5, the Americans proposed the Marshall Plan; Soviet rejection four weeks later effectively sealed the division of Europe. On June 7, the Munich conference of German minister-presidents collapsed amidst an atmosphere that caused one observer to label the participants "little Molotovs and little Marshalls."[9]

Operating in the Soviet zone against this background, Kaiser feared for the continued independence of his party. By the summer, his newspaper was flatly contradicting the Soviet-inspired notion that the obligatory solidarity of *Blockpolitik* (officially, the "Anti-Fascist Unity Front") produced a more genuine form of democracy than did the fluidity of contingent coalitions. On July 12, Kaiser criticized attitudes in the West as a lead-in to a discussion of the inequities of the bloc. Germans in the West, he said, were allowing the nation to slip toward division. Blinded by the hope that western European integration might bring prosperity, they were panicking as rumors and refugees poured in from the East. "Opinion about the role of non-Marxist parties in the eastern zone," he went on, "is already poisoned"; people were saying that the eastern CDU was a "fig leaf." The blame for this he placed squarely on the Communists. The bloc, he stated, was limiting political freedom; by bringing the SED-controlled trade unions and other mass organizations into its meetings, the SED was pressuring the non-Communist parties to go against their principles. While the CDU wanted "honest cooperation," he concluded, it could not proffer such cooperation at the price of its independence.[10]

At the CDU party congress in Berlin on September 6, Kaiser, despite Soviet pressure, went even further. The bloc, he said, was a consequence of the "special situation" in eastern Germany; it was provisional in nature, and only "one of the possible forms of loyal cooperation of the parties during an extraordinary time." Declaring that he would have preferred another form, he accepted the bloc "so long and insofar as it is not used by one party to secure its own ideological and practical hegemony." It would be "nonsensical" to hold up *Blockpolitik* as the "only sanctifying form of political cooperation"; "only dogmatists" would consider its acceptance a "moral law." Like Adenauer at Recklinghausen the previous month (Chapter 8), Kaiser then expounded on the need for a loyal opposition in a democracy.

That Germans did not understand the legitimate task of an opposition, he said, was another of the "deplorable" legacies of Weimar, where the role of opposition had been abused. Opposition was not equivalent to reaction, and Germans must tolerate rather than defame those with different views. "Even in *Blockpolitik*," he asserted, "a healthy, a regulating opposition can exist and must exist," for only then could a democracy avoid "suffocat[ing] in self-satisfaction."[11]

Going from principle to practice, Kaiser now attacked by name his party's partner in the bloc. The SED's "defamation of those with different political views," he charged, was a tactic used by parties with "totalitarian inclinations." At stake was the choice "between dogmatic Marxism, with its totalitarian will, and a world for which personal liberty and the rights of the individual constitute the highest law. That goes for politics and for economics." The CDU was "the breakwater against dogmatic Marxism and its totalitarian tendencies." The Soviets had repeatedly stated that their goal was not to Sovietize Germany; "we would like to be convinced" that the German people would be allowed "to go their own way. We, the [Christian Democratic] Union, stand for this own way. And we can only wish that the SED will stop trying to overwhelm the Union with its totalitarian and revolutionary will. It will then be all the easier for everybody" to interact in the spirit of true democracy.

By identifying the SED with "Sovietization" and his own party with self-determination, Kaiser was not just making a declaration of loyal opposition, but was calling for the ascendancy of the CDU as the only legitimate voice of Germany. (As for the SPD, he dismissed it as absent in the East and dogmatic under Kurt Schumacher in the West.)[12] Kaiser's previous argument—that those who traveled different "socialist streams" could harmonize their policies without compromising their Weltanschauungen—had rested on a distinction between matters of conscience and matters of socioeconomic policy. Once Kaiser identified class struggle, collectivism, and individual economic freedom as matters of Weltanschauung, however, he had to strain to continue to justify both Weltanschauung parties and *Blockpolitik*. For the aim he had imputed to the bloc—that of striking the proper "balance [between] freedom and [social] obligation"—he had now rendered the exclusive ideological property of the CDU.

This exclusivity, of course, had always been a latent aspect of his position (for what else was Christian socialism?). But its consequences were now explicit; and chief among them was that Christian tolerance would have to vanquish Marxist totalitarian intolerance. As the SED was wont to put it, Christian socialism was no longer a bridge but a bridgehead.[13] Yet Kaiser continued to declare that he could adopt an oppositional stance inside the bloc—the purpose of which would be to block the policies of his partner in the bloc! Logically and practically, this was an untenable position. It had to lead to a final confrontation, which duly took place at the end of the year. On December 20, after another four-power conference over Germany had collapsed in London, the Soviets forced the removal of Kaiser and Ernst Lemmer from the leadership of the zonal CDU. Purged and shorn of its independence, the emasculated party was to remain as window dressing in the official Unity Front throughout the life of the East German state.[14]

Kaiser and the SPD

Meanwhile, the Cold War had also affected Kaiser's relations with the SPD. In March 1947, when the upcoming Moscow Conference seemed likely to decide Germany's fate, Kaiser called for the creation of an all-party interzonal committee to deal with the occupying powers and prepare the way for a National Assembly. The newly formed interzonal coordinating body of the CDU/CSU endorsed the plan (though Adenauer distanced himself from it) and invited the leaders of the other major parties to a meeting. But the SPD, under Schumacher, made its approval contingent on the right of all parties to be licensed in all zones. Since the SED claimed to be a merger of the KPD and the SPD, it rejected this condition, and the plan died. Kaiser henceforth held the SPD responsible for having torpedoed, at a decisive moment and for allegedly partisan purposes, a patriotic initiative that might have stopped the drift toward Germany's partition.[15]

While Kaiser did not hold Adenauer faultless ("Germany will not become healthy by setting up a liberal system against the Marxist danger and then building a wall between them"), it was Schumacher, from Kaiser's perspective, who consistently added insult to injury. Throughout Kaiser's interzonal initiative, Schumacher refused to meet with him. Calling Kaiser a "Trojan horse," Schumacher attacked the CDU for profiting from the absence of the SPD in the eastern zone. Kaiser responded that he could not understand why taking votes from the SED should be a cause for complaint. He added that it was not the CDU's fault if leading Social Democrats had merged their eastern party with the KPD.[16]

In his antibloc speech on September 6, Kaiser actually devoted more time to attacking the "totalitarian bent" of Schumacher's SPD than to attacking the SED. He ascribed the failure to form a Grand Coalition in Frankfurt to Schumacher's "tireless effort . . . to monopolize all the significant posts." Just as in his "attempts to defame" the CDU over the interzonal all-party committee, Schumacher had put his "passionate desire to be the strongest party at any price" over the national interest. His "dictatorial gestures" were impeding the SPD's "honest struggle" to overcome "Marxist dogmatism" in favor of "true tolerance" and were preventing the "understanding" that "progressive forces of all parties" wanted.[17]

Though sharp, these comments were as sorrowful as they were polemical. As the London Conference approached, however, Kaiser took the gloves off: "Schumacher rejects joint consultations because the SPD is not represented in the eastern zone. Why, then, is it not represented? Because almost *all its responsible leaders succumbed to merger-mania (Verschmelzungsfieber)* . . . The responsibility of the Union for the noncommunist forces of the eastern zone thereby only became greater. All the world knows this. Only Herr Schumacher appears not to know it." Two weeks later, Kaiser heaped scorn on Schumacher's efforts to defame the eastern CDU's "honorable struggle" when the SPD had been the party that had caved in to Communist pressure. Now, said Kaiser, the SPD wanted to be sure it had "51 percent of the votes in Germany" before it would approve an all-German committee; "I can only hope, for the sake of our people, that it does not achieve this 51 percent":

> Some of my best friends were Social Democrats. In the Hitler period, we honestly tried to come to a settlement *(Ausgleich)* of our political and social outlooks. We discovered . . . that there can be a settlement. But it appears to me that broad circles in the SPD still have not found the way from Marxism to a free socialistic will. It appears to me that there still lurks quite a lot of the propensity toward totalitarian and dictatorial forms . . . not only [in] the brother of the left, the Communist Party, . . . [but also] in the SPD . . . We cannot desire any totalitarian methods in Germany. We want freedom of decision for every individual.[18]

Kaiser's tone was regretful. But in drawing totalitarian parallels between the two Marxist "brothers" while contrasting Christian Democratic respect for the individual, he was speaking the language of Konrad Adenauer.

By the end of 1947, Kaiser's resistance-era vision of high-minded cooperation with Social Democrats had given way to growing antipathy toward a party that had dashed his expectations. In the new year, Kaiser vacillated between the hope that the SPD might yet help shape the path between Marxism and neoliberalism and the assertion that only the CDU, as part of a European Christian Democratic front, could stand up to Communism and build a progressive and moderate Germany. By December 1948, Kaiser would have to choose: he would have to decide, after municipal elections in Berlin, the only city where the SPD and SED coexisted, whether he preferred a coalition of SPD and CDU or an adversarial relationship between them. The backdrop for his decision would be the now certain partition of Germany. For 1948 would be the year in which the occupying powers initiated steps to form two separate German governments. Nowhere was the impact more immediate than in the four-power island in the Soviet sea, Kaiser's adopted home of Berlin.

Kaiser and Coalition Politics

A new round of Cold War escalation began in late November 1947, when the SED, under Soviet pressure, called for the convening of a People's Congress, to be made up of the parties and the "coordinated" mass organizations. This People's Congress was to send an uninvited delegation to the upcoming London Conference. Believing that such a zonal (as opposed to an interzonal) initiative only further jeopardized German unity, Kaiser and Lemmer refused to participate. This was the act of defiance that sealed their fate.

After the December collapse of the London Conference and the Soviet-mandated removal of Kaiser and Lemmer from their zonal party posts, Kaiser delivered a fiery speech (January 10, 1948) likening the new order in the eastern zone to the dictatorship of Hitler. The Soviets responded by banning Kaiser from speaking in Soviet-occupied territory. The CDU/CSU interzonal committee then declared that it still considered Kaiser and Lemmer the official representatives of the eastern party. In mid-February, Kaiser's Berlin CDU separated from the decapitated zonal party.[19]

Meanwhile, the western powers took the first step toward organizing a West German parliament by doubling the size of the FEC and giving it new legislative authority. The KPD's chairman in North Rhine-Westphalia responded by asserting that the CDU's support for this step treasonously abetted the American monopoly capitalists' plan to split the country. This statement led to the ejection of the KPD from Arnold's coalition government.[20] Then, in March, eastern zonal authorities convened a Second People's Congress, which summoned a People's Council and instructed it to write a constitution.

As these events were unfolding, a Communist coup in neighboring democratic Czechoslovakia sent shock waves throughout western Europe. In the resultant atmosphere of siege, the French resolved in April to support the establishment of a trizonal West German government. (At this point, Heinrich Strunk began to prepare a western base for Kaiser in Essen.) The London Recommendations, transmitted to the minister-presidents of the German states as the Frankfurt Documents on July 1, called for a western constituent assembly; an appointed Parliamentary Council then convened in September to write the so-called Basic Law. The words "constituent assembly" and "constitution" were avoided in order to indicate that the West German state was to be provisional pending the accession of the East.

With inflation running rampant and the Soviets having walked out of the four-power Allied Control Commission, the western powers decided in June to authorize an immediate currency reform in their zones, including West Berlin. The Soviet response was to blockade Berlin. The Cold War now was on the verge of turning hot. Against all odds, the subsequent western airlift succeeded, but the blockade and the war scare persisted until May 1949. The Berlin elections in the fall of 1948 thus came in the midst of the crisis and during the deliberations of the Parliamentary Council. Moreover, during the election campaign, the SED staged a coup in the Soviet sector of the city. This coup completed the political partition of Berlin and set the stage for the definitive partition of the nation the next year.

Throughout 1948, Kaiser had been repeating his view that the CDU, thanks to the moral power of Christianity, had proven it could stand up to Communism, while the SPD, having failed to outgrow its hard-left tradition, had proven it could not. True social progress, he had lectured the SPD in October, would be achieved not through pettiness and destructiveness in Frankfurt, but through loyal cooperation or, failing that, through loyal and constructive opposition. Kaiser had also reinforced Adenauer's attacks on the revived Center party in North Rhine-Westphalia by labeling as "irresponsible" its support for the SPD's latest socialization bill over Arnold's more moderate proposal.[21] Now, during the Berlin campaign, Kaiser charged that the SPD's dogmatic Marxism endangered the anti-Communist front, while its former leaders "have their breakfast today in the ranks of the SED." The SPD got 64.5 percent of the vote in Berlin; the CDU got 19.4 percent and the LDP got 16.1 percent. Thus, the SPD could have governed alone. In view of the crisis, however, it formed a tripartite government. The CDU agreed to participate—but only over Kaiser's objections.[22]

Kaiser thus had finally made his choice in favor of an adversarial rather than a cooperative model of the party system. By the time of the federal election campaign in the spring and summer of 1949, he was the point man for Christian Democratic attacks on the SPD. With Schumacher posing in the Parliamentary Council as the defender of German national interests against the western powers and the overly deferential CDU, Kaiser echoed Adenauer's complaint that the SPD, which Adenauer compared to the anti-"fulfillment" and constitutionally obstructive DNVP of 1918, was recklessly appealing to demagogic nationalism.[23] Coming out foursquare for a West German "core state" to battle Communism, Kaiser energetically opposed a last-minute KPD proposal for a conference between members of the Parliamentary Council and the People's Congress to arrange an all-party government. Yet he also reiterated Social Democratic responsibility for having destroyed his 1947 interzonal plan, which he characterized as the best and most timely opportunity for Germany to have stayed whole.[24] Schumacher fired back that Kaiser's plan was "stupid" and blasted the "bridge builders" who "wanted to be celebrated as fighters and resistance heroes." But Kaiser, campaigning with Adenauer, retorted, "It remains a historical fact: the capitulation of the SPD to the KPD according to [east-SPD chairman Otto] Grotewohl's slogan, 'Birds of a feather [*Blut will zu Blut*],' was the decisive weakening of the German power of resistance against Soviet Communism. And what happened in Hungary, in Czechoslovakia? Everywhere the same capitulation [by socialist parties]: delivery of the state to Communism."[25]

Kaiser scorchingly summarized his position in a speech before the Christian Democratic Social Committees on July 23. The SPD, he said, now dared to play the martyr, but its capitulation to the Communists was inherent in its "disastrous attitude" from the very beginning. Far from making a clean break with Marxism, the SPD had joined the KPD in a statement of "armed brotherhood" in June 1945, leaving it to the CDU to fight Marxism alone. The string of comparable socialist capitulations elsewhere should leave no one in a hurry to put the SPD to a similar test in West Germany.[26]

Kaiser went on to defend the currency reform as "a liberation" and to blast Social Democratic attacks on the "big capitalism" of Erhard's Frankfurt policies as simpleminded sloganeering. "A constructive opposition party," he scolded, "could have fulfilled truly positive tasks" in Frankfurt; instead, the SPD had indulged in rhetoric "fatally close" to that of Moscow. Christian workers, said Kaiser, were moderate enough to accept the CDU's new economic program, the Düsseldorf Guidelines of July 15, as a market-economy elaboration of the social principles of Ahlen. Kaiser thus came into accord with Adenauer's position on a matter that as recently as February had caused a clash between Adenauer and Albers in the Zonal Committee—a clash that Kaiser had chosen to mediate rather than to enter on the side of Albers. Since the Düsseldorf Guidelines, which codified Erhard's social market economy, amounted to a scrapping of Ahlen's mixed economy, Kaiser, in accepting them, was buying into what was soon to be Adenauer's justification for a government without the SPD: by voting for the CDU, the electorate was voicing its preference for parties that supported the liberal Frankfurt policies over a policy of socialization.[27]

The electoral system melded proportional representation with the British system of local constituencies. Out of 402 seats, 242 were direct mandates, with the rest distributed to bring the parties up to their proper proportions. If a party won too high a proportion directly, it kept the excess and the number of total seats was raised accordingly. To relieve the Weimar problem of excessive splintering, a party had to win either one direct mandate in a state or 5 percent of the state's voters in order to receive its proportion of seats. (In later elections, this 5 percent hurdle was made more stringent by basing it on the vote nationwide.) On August 14, 1949, the CDU/CSU won 114 direct mandates and 139 seats overall, while the SPD won 97 direct mandates and 131 seats overall. The rest of the seats were: FDP, 52; DP, 17; the particularist Bavarian Party (BP), 17; KPD, 15; WAV, 12; Center, 10; others, 9. A CDU-led majority thus required either a Grand Coalition with the SPD (270/402) or a so-called Small Coalition with the FDP and DP (208/402).

Adenauer's task now was to outflank those in his party who still favored the former choice. A step in this direction was an unofficial but pivotal Sunday conference on August 21 at his country home in Rhöndorf. The CSU's strident opposition to a Grand Coalition gave Adenauer a trump card, since the CDU without the CSU's 24 seats would no longer be the largest parliamentary grouping. Adenauer further improved his hand by carefully selecting two representatives of Christian labor to invite to the conference. One, Theodor Blank, was a member of the Frankfurt Council, where he had developed a profound distaste for Social Democratic behavior and a firm belief in the efficacy of Erhard's policies. The other labor representative was Kaiser. Arnold, now the likeliest head of a federal Grand Coalition, was not invited. He first learned of the gathering from the press.[28]

Kaiser took a prominent role at Rhöndorf, at one point conferring privately with Adenauer and speaking in favor of the Small Coalition. The next day, he prepared a newspaper article that, while mildly critical of the SPD, justified the coalition primarily on the basis of the need in a democracy for a healthy adversarial relationship of government and opposition.[29] Sending Adenauer a copy of this article, Kaiser addressed him not with the customary formality—"Sehr geehrter Herr Dr. Adenauer"—but with the unusually familiar "Lieber Herr Dr. Adenauer," a striking indication of the improvement in their relations. Kaiser assured Adenauer that he would try to bring Albers and others around.[30]

In a memorandum for the Social Committees on August 29, Kaiser detailed the reasons for his coalitional choice. But for the SPD's stridency, he wrote, a coalition between the two large "pillars of German democracy" would have been natural. If "politicians of the middle" (that is, if Jakob Kaiser) now favored a "British"-style system of government and opposition, they were simply following the SPD's lead—though the SPD had not foreseen that it would be the party in opposition, and "though its opposition was anything but constructive." Kaiser granted that such a system was risky in a young and fragile democracy and could lead to a "government against labor." But he countered these fears with a vision: should Christian workers succeed in becoming "the social conscience and the social motor" of the Small Coalition, then the workers, the trade unions, and even the SPD would benefit, for such a government would compel the otherwise obstinate SPD to reform itself. Sounding like his old mentor and Franconian compatriot Adam Stegerwald, Kaiser threw down the gauntlet: "We have a socially minded economic policy to execute, if not with the SPD, then without it."[31]

Like Stegerwald years before, Kaiser was asserting that only through cooperation and moderation, not arrogance and zealotry, could the SPD constructively contribute to the progressive cause. Regrettably, the SPD had failed to learn this lesson from its days in the wilderness; the labor wing of the CDU thus had to seize the initiative. Properly built up, the Social Committees of the CDU could become the key element of labor representation in the new Federal Parliament (Bundestag). Kaiser thus cast the Social Committees and the CDU, respectively, in much the same roles as Stegerwald had once cast the Christian trade unions and his projected Essen party. Once again, Christian workers and their organizations were the key to a stable, socially progressive democracy; and once again, whether this development proceeded via coalition or opposition between the Christian and Socialist parties was a secondary matter. This time, however, the Christians, wrote Kaiser, had the upper hand.

Kaiser thus had come to the conclusion that while conditions in 1949 were more conducive to a socially minded democracy than they had been after World War I, the stilling of the right had yet to be complemented by the taming of the left. Those Social Democrats who lacked the experience of broad cooperation in the resistance were still living in their "reactionary" Marxist world; it was up to a progressive CDU to prepare them a lesson. Terms for any future coalition must be toughly set by the CDU alone; in the meantime, progress required the arrangements favored not by Arnold but by Adenauer. Kaiser concluded his memorandum of August 29 by stating: the Federal Chancellor must be Adenauer.[32]

The Adversarial Party System

On August 31, 1949, Adenauer met with the thirty labor deputies of the CDU/CSU Bundestag delegation and assured them that the CDU would continue "the same as before" to be guided by the principles of Ahlen. The deputies thereupon agreed to the Small Coalition.[33] Never would the relationship between Kaiser and Adenauer be so good or matter so much.[34] The next day, on Kaiser's motion, the CDU/CSU Bundestag delegation unanimously made Adenauer its candidate for Chancellor.[35]

To negotiate the terms of coalition with the FDP and the DP, the caucus designated its chairman, Adenauer, and his two vice-chairmen, Fritz Schäffer (CSU) and Kaiser. The latter's selection linked the

Christian trade unionists publicly to the Small Coalition and showed Kaiser's willingness to be so linked. Kaiser and others subsequently denied press reports of unhappiness among Catholic labor over the coalition.[36] As Erich Kosthorst has documented, these denials deserve the observation that where there is smoke, there is usually fire;[37] nevertheless, the salient feature here, in contrast to the still smoldering camp being tended by Karl Arnold, was Kaiser's own eagerness to put the fire out.

Why had Kaiser turned so decisively on the SPD? At first glance, his vehemence might seem out of proportion to the provocation: it was almost as if Schumacher and the SPD had become the available object for venting a fury more rightly directed at the SED. Yet Kaiser's behavior stemmed not just from hurt feelings or personal antagonism,[38] but from a political vision.

Instead of forming a Labour Party with Kaiser, eastern Social Democrats had fused with the Communists. To Kaiser, this disastrous step was due not to outside pressure but to the arrogant refusal of Social Democrats to overcome their history of Marxist parochialism. Although Schumacher had resisted the eastern party's course, he had also refused to take the only action that might have stopped it in its tracks: cooperation with progressive forces in the CDU. To Kaiser, Schumacher's insistence on his party's exclusive right to shape the new Germany showed a determination even greater than Adenauer's that the two large parties should be adversaries. Together, then, the formation of the SED in the East and the domination of Schumacher over a refounded SPD in the West produced a party system that both split the German nation and alienated Christian labor, doubly frustrating Kaiser's vision. Since a strongly progressive CDU was his fallback option, Kaiser had to aim to keep workers out of the Schumacher-SPD. Christian Democracy and Social Democracy thus ineluctably assumed for him an adversarial relationship.

It is instructive to compare Kaiser's position here with those of Arnold, Adenauer, and Spiecker. Within the CDU, Kaiser aimed for union not just across religious lines but also across social lines. Although Arnold shared this aim, he placed more of the burden of social bridging on the governmental coalition. Since Arnold's experience with multi-Weltanschauung collaboration was more reassuring than Kaiser's (the North Rhine-Westphalian SPD was serving under him, a Christian Democrat), the image of harmoniously flowing socialist streams, not the image of the breakwater against Marxism, was still the operative one for Arnold. Furthermore, whereas a party devoted to interdenominational bridging had been Kaiser's second choice, Arnold had emphasized interdenominationalism from the beginning—not because social union was a lesser priority, but because it would be largely fulfilled through the coalition. Thus, Arnold could not indefinitely defer a Grand Coalition with the alacrity that Kaiser could.[39]

A convinced advocate of a two-party system, Adenauer believed that only when tamed could the SPD be a tolerable party of alternation in power; since alternation should take place only over relatively long periods,[40] the CDU would have time to do the taming. By contrast, Kaiser embraced a system based on alternation in power in much the same way he had embraced the CDU itself: as a fallback position in the event his earlier plans should fail. Thus, a part of him clung to the hope of a relatively early collaboration with a post-Schumacher SPD. Nevertheless, once committed to something, Kaiser was not the type to look back. Like the new party, the new coalition was less a temporary arrangement for him than an alternate one. If it resulted in eventual collaboration with the SPD, that was good; but one must not wait for this to happen. Instead, one must build up the Social Committees so that a socially progressive course could still be pursued.

Unlike Kaiser, the other major advocate of a Labour Party, Karl Spiecker, saw his fallback party as a temporary rather than as an alternate way to align the party system: the Center for him was a provisional step toward the future left-center catch-all party that remained his ultimate goal. By 1949, however, Spiecker too would have to take stock, with consequences for both big parties. The Center's development in the early postwar years is thus doubly important: it sheds light both on the potential for alternatives to the stabilizing party system and on the process of stabilization itself. Fittingly, then, the story of the role of political Catholicism in the emergence of the modern German party system requires a return to the year 1946 to trace the tumultuous last chapter in the history of the Center.

10   The Center Party and Karl Spiecker

Just as the western CDU pushed aside its founding circle and placed itself by 1946 in the hands of a new and bolder leader (Konrad Adenauer), the Center too seemed on such a course with the unofficial rise of Karl Spiecker. Despite the Center's subcultural homogeneity, however, this process, and the associated one of developing a clear political profile, proved more divisive in the Center than it did in the CDU.

In a party whose seventy-five-year tradition was allegedly unbroken even by the Hitler era, novelty was controversial. Yet, like all postwar parties, the Center had to respond to and assimilate the lessons of the traumatic recent past. Indeed, contrary to what Adenauer and others claimed, the refounding of the Center grew out of more than just misplaced and exaggerated loyalty: it was a response to that recent past. United by their belief that the democracy of Weimar had run aground on the false hope that Protestant conservatives could be tamed to act responsibly, neo-Centrists could see only folly in repeating that mistake. Nor did the folly seem lessened if based on the uncompleted path laid out by Adam Stegerwald rather than on the disastrously diverted one laid out by Franz von Papen and the Catholic Committee of the DNVP (especially since the connection to Martin Spahn seemed palpable in both cases). According to one Centrist leaflet, the CDU revealed its reactionary colors by citing Stegerwald as its precursor: after his rumored letter to Hitler (Chapter 7) and his urgings to the bishops to "make peace" with the Nazi leader, "we would never have tolerated Stegerwald any longer in the Center." Going further, Spiecker's group cited Joseph Wirth as the inspiration for what it proudly and repeatedly called, in the words of Spiecker's young aide Rainer Barzel, the only wing remaining in the Center: "the left wing."[1]

Centrist traditionalists who believed in the old party thus found themselves thrown together with the heirs of Wirth's brand of innovation. For if all the Weimar-era efforts to gather Christians had contributed to the rise of Nazi evil, then one might question whether the Christian Weltanschauung, or any Weltanschauung, properly belonged at the core of the process of building partisan alignments. In this view, not a Catholic-Protestant union to oppose the Marxist Weltanschauung but a variegated progressive union to oppose reactionary despotism was the order of the day. One was back to the position once formulated by Heinrich Teipel, which had led to his expulsion from the old Center: what mattered were not metaphysical *(weltanschauliche)* but political likenesses and differences. Whereas Centrists once had argued about the ramifications of the claim that theirs was a political, not a confessional party, the deceased Teipel's former colleague, Spiecker, now embroiled his party in a new controversy: the Center, he asserted, was a political, not a weltanschauliche party.

In the Center, such a premise could not simply be asserted, but had to be "proven" through references to past tradition. This was all the more necessary once Adenauer began attacking the new Center as a fraud. As an unabashedly new party, the CDU was not dependent on a similar excavation of tradition; Adenauer could make his charge and then stand away from the fray. The reform-minded Spiecker, no less than the traditionalist Wilhelm Hamacher, thus found himself arguing on the basis not just of current political efficacy but also of dredged-up, philosophically dissected, scholastically analyzed precedents. In short, one was back in the morass of subtle distinctions, distant historical references, and arcane rhetorical debate that had weighed down the old Center.

Spiecker's view of the new Center as a step toward progressive union was just as logical a consequence of the suspicion of Protestant conservatism as was Hamacher's Catholic triumphalism. Yet, especially in light of Teipel's old expulsion, Spiecker's conception exceeded in novelty even that of the CDU. Leading Centrists now would have to reconcile the differing conceptions of their innovators and traditionalists—or they would have to hold the party together even as the two orientations continued to coexist.

Spiecker's Conception

In championing his vision of the new Center, Spiecker had one major advantage: he controlled what for most of 1946 remained the party's only major organ, the Essen-based, twice-weekly *Rhein-Ruhr-Zeitung (RRZ)*. In view of the paper shortage and the Center's apparent smallness, the British military government awarded the party only one newspaper license in the Rhineland. Two groups vied for the license. One, in Essen, was led by Spiecker, his earlier business colleague Heinrich Steffensmeier, and the writer Richard Muckermann (brother of an émigré Jesuit); the other, oriented toward Wilhelm Hamacher, was led by the more conservative former editor of the *Düsseldorfer Tageblatt* and the General Secretary of the revived party, Karl Klein. Aided, perhaps, by Spiecker's ties to the British, the Esseners were awarded the license. Edited by Muckermann, the *RRZ* first appeared in May 1946. As party chairman, Hamacher now joined Spiecker and Steffensmeier as co-licensee, but since Hamacher was neither effective nor present in Essen (and since his Düsseldorf allies soon went over in disgust to the CDU), Spiecker and his colleagues had little trouble making the paper the principal outlet for what came to be known as the "Essen orientation" *(Essener Richtung)*.

At the heart of the Esseners' conception was the notion that it was a "misuse" of Weltanschauung to place it in the forefront of political life. Religion and Weltanschauung, wrote Spiecker, were "values unto themselves," whereas politics consisted of "methods, detours, and expediencies." The more inviolable one's Weltanschauung, the more one had to reject its perversion as a label in a sphere of activity whose essence was the fashioning of compromises. Accordingly, "in contrast to the Christian Democrats," the task of the Center was "to prove that a political party . . . may be defined and guided by political [policy] goals instead of by motives of Weltanschauung."[2]

In reply to the taunting of Adenauer, the Esseners insisted that their party was "indeed the old Center and not a New Center." Through a series of historical articles, they tried to demonstrate that the CDU, like the DNVP, Papen, and the Nazis, was slandering the Center using the same contradictory charges employed since the days of Bishop Ketteler: that the Center was both "too Catholic" and "no longer on a Christian footing." By dating the previous year's refounding of the Westphalian Center not from October 14 (Soest) but from July 15 (the date of the inconclusive Lippstadt meeting), the Esseners even argued that their first provincial founding predated the CDP's (September 2). Whereas the CDP/CDU, allegedly due to eastern Protestant pressure, had stopped depicting itself as a renamed Center and now declared that it was something new, "the Center is and remains the old party as it was [when] founded by the Reichenspergers, Mallinckrodt, and Windthorst."[3]

According to the Esseners, the Weimar Center's attempt to substitute a "common Weltanschauung" for a "common political conviction" had "contradict[ed] the nature of the Center" and enabled people like Papen to stay on board by cloaking themselves in Catholicism. "From time immemorial," Spiecker contended, "no German party" had tried "more vigorously" to separate Weltanschauung and politics. Though Carl Bachem had used the phrase "Christian Weltanschauung," his purpose had been to underscore that the party was not based on the "Catholic Weltanschauung," since Catholicism was "not a political Weltanschauung." Bachem's argument that Catholicism mandated no particular position on most political issues also applied to Christianity. In keeping with its Windthorstian and Bachemite heritage, therefore, the Center today "asks no one what his Weltanschauung is if he is determined to help realize [its] political goals."[4]

The old Bachemite assertion that the Center was "political, not confessional" the Esseners thus rendered "political, not weltanschaulich." In doing so, however, they often sounded more like Hermann Roeren than the Bachems. "If [one means] Christian Weltanschauung in the correct sense," said Spiecker, "then up to 99 percent of it must be the Catholic Weltanschauung"; it was a mistake to think that Weltanschauung was not the same thing as religion or confession. The Center now "reject[ed]" the "hazy and unclear" term "Christian Weltanschauung" because it wanted to "avoid the impression that it favors mixing and watering down the Catholic and Protestant Weltanschauung[en] for political purposes." Since both Catholics and Protestants eschewed a "general supraconfessional Christianity," there "certainly" could not be a "supraconfessional party" claiming a "Christian Weltanschauung." To Spiecker, the Center was "political," whereas the CDU was "double-confessional."[5]

In the face of unparalleled horrors and the need to rebuild, here was a group of reformers reviving and parsing rhetoric that dated from before not just the Second World War, but the First! In this preoccupation, Spiecker's party could indeed still claim, as Julius Bachem did in 1913, that the Center "is what it was."

Nevertheless, the Esseners were making an important and, in Germany, controversial assertion: stable democracy, marked by civility among the parties, required that policy lines be separated from Weltanschauung in determining partisan relations. In their view, the fundamental problem with the Weimar democracy had been not the excessive number of parties (this was symptom rather than cause), but the type. As long as parties persisted in reducing political discourse to posturing about philosophical first principles, neither a multiparty nor a two-party system could be stable, for the former merely reflected the multiplicity of Weltanschauungen in a modern pluralistic state, while the latter cheapened Weltanschauungen by artificially mixing or redefining them and then bandying them as covers for questions of policy. Either way, the Esseners believed, Weltanschauung prevented genuine political cooperation; it became a bank of irrelevant slogans presented as categorical imperatives. It was no accident, added Spiecker, that the heir to the Weimar system of Weltanschauung parties had been the manipulative and sloganeering NSDAP, itself trumpeting Weltanschauung.[6]

The immediate danger, from the Esseners' perspective, was a two-party Weltanschauung-based system. The CDU's strength in the North Rhine–Westphalian local elections of September 1946 caused Spiecker to sound the alarm. In other countries, he wrote, the prerequisite to a successful two-party system had been the removal of disputes over Weltanschauung from politics: the essence of a two-party system was alternation in power, whereas each side in a competition based on Weltanschauung sought total victory. Was the CDU "really prepared," asked Spiecker, "to alternate in government with a 'Marxist' block? Is it willing to allow the country to be governed one time by the CDU, another time by the SPD or SED?" If so, then Christianity would presumably be endangered whenever the CDU was out of power; if not, then the CDU would have to erect a partisan dictatorship "for the duration." This new dictatorship, however, would be established under false pretenses: having buried the first republic, the reactionaries were building a Bürgerblock and implying that anyone who did not belong was not a good Christian. So soon after the first dictatorship, a second could not last, and there could not be the "slightest doubt where . . . millions of people would [then] turn." The CDU's drive for a two-party system must lead to a massive, militant Communist movement, and thence "to civil war."[7]

For Spiecker, the Center provided the way out of this dilemma. As he told Adenauer in March 1946 (Chapter 8), both the SPD and CDU would split, their moderate factions joining the Center to form what Spiecker and Barzel later called the "Union of the Middle" (UdM). In other words, there would be a three-party system, with by far the largest party, freed of Weltanschauung, in the middle. Powerful enough to operate independently, this large, moderate catch-all party would compel the rump parties of right and left to emulate it and free themselves in turn of Weltanschauung. Either through this three-party system or through a subsequent, second realignment to produce a Weltanschauung-free two-party system on the Anglo-American model, German democracy would be stabilized.[8]

Consistent with this conception, Spiecker, though he wooed both Karl Arnold and Jakob Kaiser,[9] rejected the term "Christian socialism." "Our socialism," he said, meant the "socially just" regulation of the "natural right" to property; this "socialism" was neither "Christian" nor "Marxist," but "a system, an economic order, that corresponds to human reason, . . . natural law, and natural morality." By decoupling this "system" from either Weltanschauung, Spiecker hoped to draw the adherents of both. His unspoken model was clearly the British Labour Party.[10]

Indeed, though the *RRZ* defended Spiecker against the charge of Anglophilia, the paper continued to offer its readers lavishly Anglophilic civics lessons. Praising British Labour and the two-party system as practiced in Britain, the *RRZ* noted that the CDU and SPD "in no way correspond to the English Conservative and Labour Parties" because the latter "do not embody ideological contrasts but set different political goals." As a policy-based party, Labour contained Catholics and Protestants, Christians and Marxists; and English Catholics, in the words of their cardinal, "are represented in every party." When British subjects voted for a certain party, the *RRZ* concluded, they did so "for political reasons"; Christian versus non-Christian blocs were impossible. The system of government and loyal opposition operated like the sparring of two lawyers who had agreed beforehand on the rules of law and who both knew that tomorrow the roles of prosecution and defense could be reversed. Only when Germany had such British-style parties would a two-party system be safe.[11]

Despite Spiecker's claims to the contrary, his formulation went far beyond anything the old Center might have countenanced. His insistence that the Center (in contrast to its members) had no Weltanschauung was bound to lead to tension with those who believed that the lesson of Nazism was the need to maintain the kind of vigilance practiced during the Kulturkampf and for whom the designation "Christian" rather than "Catholic" was already too impious. Notwithstanding repeated denials of a new "orientation controversy" *(Richtungsstreit)*, therefore, the Center clearly contained a combustible mixture of elements. The only question was who would remain to pick up the pieces once the mixture exploded.

Wessel and Weltanschauung

For three reasons, the orientation controversy in the new Center proceeded for a time without the orgy of public polemics that had marked the Zentrumsstreit. First, while traditionalists surely outnumbered Esseners among the rank and file, their leadership was weak. Second, although the party acquired a second paper in the fall of 1946, the *Neue Westfälische Kurier (NWK)* was not an organ of the traditionalists but of the mediation-minded group around Helene Wessel. Third, working skillfully with Wessel to contain the quarrel was her former colleague in the Prussian Landtag, Johannes Brockmann.

By vocation a teacher, Brockmann, fifty-eight years old in 1946, was the Wilhelm Marx of the new Center. Called a "master of politics" by Rudolf Amelunxen, a "great parliamentarian" and "the great practical man" by the Center's later General Secretary Josef Rösing,[12] Brockmann was less interested in political theorizing than in crafting internal peace in his party and fashioning sturdy parliamentary alliances. Also like Marx, he was committed to a progressive social agenda, but his real thrust as a politician had always been on schools. Perhaps not accidentally, the largest surviving file in Brockmann's papers from the Weimar period is on the schools question, and Brockmann's private correspondence in the Nazi era was dominated by Church affairs.[13] Without adopting the Esseners' theories, Brockmann thus combined Spiecker's concern for parliamentary pragmatism with Hamacher's concern for Kulturpolitik.

If Brockmann was the Marx of the new Center, then Wessel was its Joos. Known as the party's "social conscience," the forty-eight-year-old former social worker had a gift for fusing the sociopolitical with the pious that made her the regular keynote speaker at Centrist gatherings and the frequent author of disquisitions on the party's nature and role. Although Wessel's creative mind and readiness to pursue innovation rendered her closer in temperament to Spiecker than to Hamacher, she used those attributes to blaze a fully independent, if intermediate, position.[14]

Like all Centrists, Wessel opposed a two-party system based on Weltanschauung and deemed the CDU a hiding place for reactionaries. Confessional bridging, she insisted, was a task for the churches, not for a political party. But while she did not share Hamacher's illusions about solo Catholic domination of the party system, she too distrusted Protestants for more than just their conservatism. Declaring that Protestants were not about to end their "narrow-minded" insistence on predominance in Germany, she concluded that difficulties were in store for the CDU.[15]

She did not, however, agree with Spiecker that the ideal was to get Weltanschauung completely out of politics. On October 18, 1945, she warned that Spiecker's desire "to make our outlook regarding Weltanschauung dependent" on the relative prospects for "political cooperation with other parties" was "very disastrous" and put the cart before the horse. Before one could work with other parties, she said, one had to amass one's own electorate. That task required an "entirely clear" outlook in all areas (political, social, and economic), but above all "precisely in the area of Weltanschauung." "These questions of Weltanschauung," she continued, "need not at all lead to an intolerant attitude vis-à-vis other parties."[16]

Unlike Spiecker, Wessel thus distinguished between fronts based on Weltanschauung, which she rejected, and parties based on Weltanschauung, which she did not. She agreed with Spiecker that a front based on Weltanschauung was "false" and "artificial" and risked discrediting Christianity by monolithically politicizing it. Moreover, such a front was ill-suited to the safeguarding of democracy—a task that required clear political fronts against the reactionary right, including the socially and morally oblivious laissez-faire liberals, as well as against the revolutionary left. But Wessel was convinced that in the aftermath of the war, the only parties that would prosper would be those that "look on politics from a spiritual point of view and . . . do not regard politics as an 'art to achieve what is attainable.'" Neither bourgeois gathering parties nor Marxist parties were the answer; "only from Christianity—seen, however, in its ultimate social demands on the human being"—would man again find happiness.[17]

What Wessel wanted was a party whose chief concern was social justice based on Christian (Catholic) precepts. To raise the political priority attached to issues of family, women, and youth, she characterized them not as gender issues but as universal matters of Kulturpolitik. Combining a traditional Catholic feminine piousness with a pioneering Catholic feminist activism, she defined Kulturpolitik to mean the development of a moral and institutional framework that would meliorate problems such as divorce, broken homes, and illegitimacy, whose spread she deemed a symptom of the social tensions of the industrial age. Solving the social question was to her both a Christian duty and a political exigency: "those parts of the people who no longer are Christian will only find their way back to the Church if the Christians recognize their present social tasks." It was neither sensible nor Christian, however, to refuse to cooperate with those whose motives differed but whose end was the same. Accordingly, Wessel called for a socially minded partnership of Center and SPD, but not for a unified, Weltanschauung-free party. The Center to her was by no means the provisional entity that it was to Spiecker.[18]

In demanding "political" rather than "weltanschauliche" alliances between parties and yet insisting on the need to fuse the social and moral issues into a coherent political philosophy for her own party, Wessel offered it a formula for unity. To end the dispute, though, both sides would have had to cease promulgating their own positions and to rally to Wessel's. This neither proved willing to do, and the dispute continued to fester.

The Orientation Controversy

On February 10, 1946, the refounded Center of the Rhenish town of Wuppertal held its first rally. As usual at such rallies, a Catholic schoolteacher played a central role. After the local party chairman explained that the decision to rebuild the party was not intended as a rebuff toward Protestants, the teacher, *Studienrat* Möhlig, elaborated: "Not all religions and confessions and Weltanschauungen are equally great and good. Precisely we Catholics are in the powerful position, we are so fortunate, that we have those powerful healing reserves the likes of which no other Weltanschauung has . . . Indeed, we have for ourselves the sacraments, we have for ourselves prayer, we have for ourselves the two-thousand-year tradition." The strength the nation needed, he went on, did not come from some "general Christianity"; "therefore, you see, we are of the conviction that we have to go back," away from the materialistic trend of modern times, to the "new idea" the Center had introduced seventy years before. That idea was that people must root themselves in religious life to overcome their troubles. For holding this view, the old Centrists had been maligned as ultramontanists, but if more people had followed their example and been guided by eternal values rather than day-to-day matters, then, "by God, we would not need to look out over fields of ruins today."[19]

Appeals such as this one pulled no punches: one should support the Center because one was Catholic. Indeed, this schoolteacher's confidence that Centrists were preferentially guided by values, his reference to religious practices (prayer, the sacraments) as political weapons, and his presumption of exclusive Catholic title to those religious practices suggest not just confessionalism but religious fundamentalism—in Catholic terms, integralism. It was natural that some should draw from Nazism the lesson that only a redoubled commitment to confessional purity as a guide to political behavior could assure the necessary vigilance against another such moral atrocity. All the more daunting, then, was the task that faced the Esseners, for only through converting local Catholic opinion leaders like this schoolteacher could they hope to gain popular support.

While the Essen wing decried the Weimar Center party for allowing Weltanschauung to distort the process of fashioning political alignments, the Hamacher group saw things just the other way around. In their view, the Weimar Center's preoccupation with its coalition-building function had obscured its weltanschaulichen compass; process had replaced substance. As Hamacher put it, only one thing in the old Center had not pleased him: for too many of its members, the first question to ask had always been what the parties of the left or right wanted, not what the Centrists themselves wanted.[20]

What the party needed now, wrote Karl Klein, was "a thoroughgoing weltanschauliche infusion": the Center, "without detriment to its character as a *political* party," could and should "hold unmistakably fast" to "the Catholic Weltanschauung." To Klein, "middle" was not just a locus on the political spectrum, but "a basic weltanschauliche attitude toward the problems and tasks of political life." Another Catholic teacher, Theodore Abele, stated, "we make no secret of the fact that *the political idea of the Center, especially its principle of the creative middle, . . . comes from Catholic tradition* . . . Insofar as Protestant Christians . . . live and think in this single Christian tradition, they can belong to the Center." Hamacher himself proclaimed: "the reproach of confessional narrowness . . . is as unjust and untruthful as anything can be. Not confessional narrowness, but confessional breadth is the correct phrase. For to be Catholic means to see the whole, not in confessional narrowness, but in catholic breadth." The Center's approach, then, was "not anti-Protestant but truly catholic— that is, taking the whole into account."[21]

For Hamacher and his friends, this claim to catholicity was not inconsistent with the Center's sectional function: "the cultural and churchly affairs of the Catholic part of the population," wrote Klein, were the "political . . . affair of the Center party now as in the past."

To Spiecker, however, the constrictive nature of this sort of "catholicity" was precisely the problem with a Weltanschauung party. Although he was not oblivious to Catholic sectional issues (chief among which, as always, stood the civil status of denominational schools), Spiecker argued that a mature political party should approach such issues not in the proprietary manner of a special-interest lobby but in the manner of a defender of a generally extendable political right. In other words, there was nothing Catholic about the Center; the cultural or churchly affairs of Catholics were neither more nor less its political affair than were the cultural or churchly affairs of anybody else. What *was* the Center's affair, however, was the universal political (not weltanschauliche) "fight for free human rights." It was for this sake and not as a "Kulturkampf party" that the Center had been founded; the fact that Catholics, as the first group whose rights had been in jeopardy, had been the party's first constituency was "a pure historical accident." Accordingly, rather than saying that the Center as a Weltanschauung party demanded denominational schools, the party ought to say that the schools issue was a matter *not* of Weltanschauung but of the civil right of parents to guide the education of their children. Indeed, the party need not explicitly mention denominational schools at all, but need only say that the "parents' right" *(Elternrecht)* was a "natural right" *(Naturrecht)*. Only such a generalized standpoint would entitle the Center Party to claim that it was "political and supraconfessional."[22]

To Spiecker, the ambiguity of the term "natural right" or "natural law" *(Naturrecht)* was precisely its recommendation. Every group could identify the term with its own moral principles, regardless of source; it encompassed both Catholic teachings and the secularized notion of the inalienable rights of man. By transcending differences in Weltanschauung, it facilitated political cooperation. After all, what mattered was not the difference in the philosophical motive for defending human rights, but the shared political belief in the primacy of defending them. If one could not convince adherents of another Weltanschauung to vote for a measure by referring to Church teachings but could by referring to "natural moral law" or the "natural rights of man," that was what one ought to do; "that is practical politics."[23]

As proof that a nonexclusive or Weltanschauung-free Center was not un-Christian, the *RRZ* cited Thomas Aquinas and a papal encyclical from 1937 acknowledging the authority of natural law. According to Spiecker, a political party could not demand that people recognize God's providence, but such a recognition for the sake of political cooperation was in any case unnecessary, because that providence existed just the same, regardless of its political label (for example, "rights of man").[24] The abstract nature of this argument, however, placed it well beyond the ken of the average voter.

After hearing Spiecker expound his position at a conference in Oberhausen, one clergyman commented that of course the people were in the Center for reasons of Weltanschauung, and politely asked if Spiecker did not mean his analysis to be "just ideas for a leadership stratum." Pulling fewer punches, a delegate to the party convention at Werl in November 1946 noted that the Center was not an academic debating society but an agency of practical politics. Another delegate complained that party spokesmen had had to devote half of each speech during the recent campaign trying to clarify Spiecker's position. A third added that Spiecker had not noticed that human nature could not be divided arbitrarily into political and religious components, nor did Spiecker seem to have asked himself the obvious question of "which voters we can win" (the answer, said the delegate, was ordinary churchgoing Catholics) and to have adjusted his line accordingly.[25]

For months before the Werl convention, local Centrists had been pleading with Hamacher to "stamp out the Spiecker heresy." The present moment, one local branch asserted, offered a "unique opportunity" to follow the example of Catholics in France, Holland, and elsewhere by creating a "Catholic State Party"; if Spiecker objected, he should be ejected from the party. The chairmen of fifteen of the most important local branches declared that they were "no longer prepared to tolerate" the presence "alongside the official party line" of a "Spiecker tendency" that controlled the Centrist press; they demanded that Spiecker publicly "renounce his erstwhile attitude" and stand up "unequivocally" for the party's "history, tradition, and Weltanschauung." Another writer pointed out that since "the character of the Center party has always been inherently problematic," it had been "a great mistake to have publicly broached this problem all over again." All that Spiecker had accomplished was to sow demoralization and confusion while giving Adenauer a weapon to "defame" the Center as non-Christian. By "removing and isolating the purely political character from the Weltanschauung character, one destroys the roots from which the Center party has grown in the people." As one clergyman put it, "We have always emphasized that the Center is the representative of the Catholic part of the population, even if we also know and desire that the Center is an interconfessional party . . . [People] vote for the Center because they are Catholic . . . and find in the party the expression of their religious conviction. That Weltan-schauung and politics have nothing to do with each other is indeed a false teaching of . . . liberalism and National Socialism."[26]

Such sentiment came to a head at Werl. Since the task of the convention was to approve a party program, not just political philosophy but concrete questions of policy were at stake, including the question of schools. As a result, Spiecker came under fire not just from stodgy traditionalists but also from the progressive but pious group from Münster—the place where the Church, under Bishop Clemens Graf von Galen, had been most prominent in resisting Nazi atrocities.

Defending his position that the Center should not directly demand denominational schools, Spiecker argued: "Let's get one thing straight. We are here to talk politics, and all liberties that we demand for ourselves must also be given to others . . . If we keep that in mind, then everything becomes clear." Only with the help of other parties could Church-state relations be favorably settled; the only way to secure that help was to stick to the principle of natural law and "not to abandon [it] even by one centimeter." If instead of demanding parents' rights the Center demanded denominational schools, then the Communists, even without strong and genuine parental support, could demand Communist schools. If the Center demanded a Catholic university, then the Communists could demand a Communist university. "What we should be doing is not to draw up a Christmas wish list. We are, rather, a political party." That meant "limit[ing] ourselves to what we can portray to outsiders as a reasonable, serious demand. That is decisive, if we as a political party do not want to come under the suspicion . . . of being ridiculous."[27]

That the most traditional of Centrist demands might fall into the category of the "ridiculous" was well beyond what the convention was prepared to accept. Even Fritz Stricker, a prominent member of the Münster contingent who was often sympathetic to Spiecker's positions, stated flatly that the words "denominational school" could not be missing from a program of the Center party. Although the chair (Brockmann) reminded the gathering that the issue was not whether but how to defend the schools, the fact was that something more fundamental was being debated. Spiecker was essentially arguing that a party could not maintain the primacy of Kulturpolitik and still claim to be a political, nonconfessional party. He was, in short, denying the assertion at the heart of the Center's entire history.

Leading the charge from Münster was the head of the Westphalian party, Bernhard Reismann: "Naturally we are a political party, . . . and naturally we allow everyone the right to his conviction . . . But it is also natural that the parents whom we represent will have no understanding that we mean to support denominational schools with this cop-out" *(Schlappheit)*. This statement was greeted with cheers. Reismann continued, "Why can't we . . . say: We demand denominational schools for our parents. I herewith move this addition." As the tumult continued, some of the leaders withdrew to hammer out a compromise. They returned with the following: "The demand by parents for denominational schools is based on natural law. *For that reason,* the Center party unreservedly supports denominational schools *wherever parents demand denominational schools.*" But the convention had a mind of its own, and Spiecker now could not get it to retain even the italicized clauses. Moreover, during the discussion, several participants talked openly of the existence of two orientations in the party. The animosity toward Spiecker was palpable.[28]

Spiecker did not leave Werl empty-handed: though he failed to get his way on schools, his social program easily passed. This too, however, was indicative of the Center's dilemma. For here was a party whose rank-and-file appeal resided above all in its name, its tradition, and its identification with the primacy of Kulturpolitik, yet much of whose leadership, even in Münster, wanted a social course more radical than any it had navigated in the past. Inevitably the question would arise whether a substantial constituency of zealously sectarian but socially radical Catholics even existed. The combination was not impossible, for it was based on the identification of Protestantism with reaction—an identification many Catholics could readily make, especially after Weimar. Nevertheless, there was a difference between rejecting the CDU because it was serious about being interdenominational and rejecting it because it was reactionary. The Werl program meant that only those who did both were potential Centrist voters.

This was not as Spiecker would have wished: his objection to the CDU was not that it actively welcomed Protestants, but that it made confessional (not political) reconciliation its raison d'être. In "the Center's good old days," Spiecker remarked, "'Christian Weltanschauung' in fact was identical to 'Catholic Weltanschauung'"; by distorting "the Center's interconfessional principle" to mean that

"Catholic plus Protestant equals Christian," the CDU was artificially creating its so-called Weltanschauung. Since Catholicism, Protestantism, and Christianity were not political categories, however, neither confessional reconciliation nor confessional solidarity were proper bases for a political party: "My friends, if we wanted to found a Catholic party, do you believe that even if we lived in a purely Catholic state, we would wind up with *one* party? Even in a Catholic religious state there would obviously be several parties. We are together today in the Center, Catholics and Protestants, because we have found our way to each other through a political common denominator." Spiecker denied that he believed that religion and politics had nothing to do with each other—for individuals. Since parties, however, were not spiritual brotherhoods but political associations of diverse individuals, the Center, to survive the Christian Democratic challenge, would have to learn to express itself in a manner that was "irreproachably political."[29]

Spiecker was of course correct to claim that the Christian Weltanschauung of the old Center had really been Catholicism. But this had reflected the real reason that the members of the old Center had "found their way to each other": they had all been Catholics who had felt threatened in a country with a Protestant majority. To say that Catholics in a purely Catholic country would not all belong to the same party was therefore beside the point: the Center had existed precisely because Germany was not a purely Catholic country. Thus, "Catholic" and "Protestant" really were political categories in Germany; the problem was how to make them cease to be so.

If, as Spiecker now said, it had been "a mistake" for the Center to continue to base its unity on Weltanschauung once the Kulturkampf was over, on what was its unity based today? The answer was the traditional Centrist desire that "social" and "cultural" Catholics mediate between "reactionary" Protestants and "atheistic" Socialists. But whereas Hamacher and Wessel agreed (for different reasons) that the Catholic identity of the mediating group was crucial, Spiecker, who saw Catholics as just the "accidental" seed group for a much larger union, could not tolerate the limits that an emphasis on Catholicism would impose on the growth of a party in a largely Protestant country. To Wessel, smallness was a positive recommendation: in France, she said, the lack of "smaller mediating groups" between the CDU's counterpart (the MRP) and the Marxist parties (Socialists and Communists) had led to chaos and constitutional crisis. She was satisfied that the "warning" of Weimar—"A democracy can be constructed only by convinced democrats!"—could be lastingly heeded via a coalition between her "smaller mediating group" and the SPD. Spiecker, however, had never believed that a small Catholic appendage to the SPD was "the last word . . . a final solution," for his concern was not to create a social Catholic check on Marxist excesses, but to cleanse the political spectrum of its whole unpolitical preoccupation with Weltanschauung.[30]

At Werl, Spiecker ran up squarely against the fact that, whatever else the Center was, it continued to be a confessional lobby. Confronted with this reality, his first reaction was to plead and to explain: "unfortunately," he lamented, "it remains the case even today that we still sometimes do not understand each other in these fundamental things." As time went by and the Center did not lose its "small party" mentality, however, his patience would begin to give out. If there was to be a "Union of the Middle," it clearly could not be confined to the narrow base prescribed by Werl; there would have to be overtures to groups outside the Center. Where was one to find these groups, and how was one to win them over?

The very word "Union" suggested the answer.

11　The Fusion Fiasco

Had anyone told Konrad Adenauer in 1946 that the fusion he desired between CDU and Center would come only with Karl Spiecker's faction rather than with Wilhelm Hamacher's, he might well have been alarmed. For Adenauer's motives in pursuing fusion seemed decidedly different from any that Spiecker might entertain. Where Adenauer wanted a bipolar contest between CDU and SPD, Spiecker wanted a party system dominated by a sizable third force; where Adenauer wanted a sharply adversarial relationship with the traditional left, Spiecker wanted cooperation; where Adenauer stressed Weltanschauung, Spiecker tried to banish it.

Nevertheless, in aiming for a majority party, Adenauer never excluded the possibility of an arrangement with Spiecker. To head him off from building up the Center, Adenauer even suggested at their meeting in March 1946 (Chapter 8) that Spiecker join the CDU and work from there to realize his conception. While Spiecker's rejoinder that his middle party would eventually rob the CDU of its left wing would have raised Adenauer's guard lest "fusion" mean splitting the CDU and creating a Union of the Middle, Adenauer made his suggestion in the firm expectation that, in any internal struggle over their two conceptions, Spiecker would lose. Thus, even though Adenauer subsequently went on the attack, his tone remained coolly reasonable, not passionately inflammatory. Never did he emulate the *RRZ*'s shrillness, nor did he forget that the purpose of his volleys, in contrast to those he directed at the SPD, was to speed a reconciliation.

On one point, Adenauer and Spiecker were agreed: both wanted fewer Weltanschauung-based partisan divisions. Though the difference between one such division and none is not trivial, quantifying it in this way is suggestive, given the anything but zealously religious way Adenauer employed the term "Christian Weltanschauung." The issue of Weltanschauung, however, concealed another: that of the

226

most desirable majority alignment within the new party system. Differing on this point, Spiecker and Adenauer could move toward fusion only if each expected to outflank the other.

Close to Spiecker in this contest was Karl Arnold, who was beginning to feel that he held a weak hand and needed Spiecker's reinforcements. The Esseners, however, would not join the CDU to buttress a weak Arnold against the conservative wing;[1] their refusal to do so was the reason they had not joined in the first place. They would join only if they perceived the Arnold wing to be in a position of strength. There had to be the prospect of a tight working coalition with the SPD that would approximate the alignment of forces Spiecker wanted to see in a Union of the Middle. Moreover, joining the CDU was supposed to be just a provisional solution. In just a few years, when the temporary emergency created by Soviet intimidation would be over, the most zealous and intolerant of all Weltanschauung parties, the SED, would be eliminated. Then would come the final nationwide realignment into a Weltanschauung-free system of moderate progressive and conservative parties.[2]

As his hopes faded for building up the Center, then, Spiecker was drawn to rethink his position regarding the CDU. Seeing none of the virtue Helene Wessel claimed to perceive in small parties, the ambitious repatriate did not want to be left standing on the sidelines when the first federal government was installed. What he did not fully grasp, however, was that even if the terms of fusion suited him, a majority of the Center might refuse to go along—for both traditionalist and "social" reasons. Furthermore, if Arnold, for whom the CDU was by no means provisional, appeared to be augmenting Spiecker's plan to split the party, the Minister-President would weaken himself and his cause in the CDU. With Arnold's maneuverability thus limited, Adenauer could afford to wait out the Esseners for the best terms.

The First Fusion Controversy

Spiecker's first serious overtures toward fusion came in the aftermath of the Düsseldorf coalitional discussions in June 1947, in which Arnold's views had prevailed over Adenauer's (Chapter 8). In light of Arnold's show of strength, the *RRZ* now significantly moderated its tone toward the CDU, praising Arnold regularly and even taking credit for the impact he was having. Without the Werl Program, the paper claimed, there would have been no Ahlen Program; and without the Center, there would have been no Arnold wing of the CDU.[3]

A June conversation between Adenauer and Spiecker on the occasion of the convening of the Frankfurt Economic Council[4] inaugurated a pattern of linkage between critical junctures in the Cold War and flurries of activity over fusion. A few weeks earlier, Richard Muckermann had lashed out at the Soviets and compared them to the Nazis.[5] The greater the sense of siege from the East, the more urgently the Esseners would seek a provisionally viable and congenial party system in the West.

Adenauer and Spiecker quietly met again on August 16, two days after Adenauer's Recklinghausen speech calling for a two-party system (Chapter 8). The day before, the *RRZ* had praised Arnold for saying that socialism was no more the exclusive property of the SPD than Christianity was of the CDU. According to the *RRZ*, Arnold had also conceded that the CDU should not have stayed out of the first North Rhine–Westphalian government. The *RRZ* seemed to feel both vindicated in its own stances and confirmed in its suspicion that a progressive wind was blowing through the CDU.[6]

In contrast to Johannes Brockmann, who had earlier avoided an election accord out of fear that any special arrangement between the Christian parties might sap the Center of its vitality (Chapter 8), Spiecker was willing to draw a distinction between the importance of maintaining the Center and the higher priority he attached to the shaping of the whole party system. That priority required not staunchness and rigidity, but adaptiveness to developments on all sides. Thus, at their meeting on August 16, Spiecker tried to reassure a properly skeptical Adenauer that he had never really favored a coalition in Düsseldorf of Center, SPD, and KPD; according to Adenauer, Spiecker even stated that he found the notion of a Center-CDU government attractive.[7] This was exactly the idea Adenauer had floated and Brockmann had exploded in early June. Spiecker in effect was telling Adenauer that he could do business with Spiecker.

Prodded by Adenauer to commit himself, Spiecker hesitated to forsake the SPD's trust, yet noted that the Center could not fuse with the CDU without a "visible external cause." He agreed that if a significant purely right-wing party were to arise, the CDU could wind up in the middle and the Center would lose its raison d'être. Another external cause, he mused, might be the breakup of the current coalition over the terms of the state constitution. The meeting ended inconclusively but cordially, the two men agreeing to "consult before decisions on important political questions."

Spiecker's sudden flexibility left Adenauer encouraged but very wary. When Arnold subsequently sponsored the selection of Spiecker to fill the North Rhine–Westphalian seat on the Executive Council at Frankfurt, Adenauer's understanding was that Spiecker had promised Arnold in return not to try to refound the Center in the southern states. On October 19, Adenauer complained to Spiecker that a planned meeting in Frankfurt to consider a Hessian founding violated their agreement. Spiecker hotly denied having made any such promise "in the form you claim," but he also denied involvement with a Frankfurt meeting or with any "south German foundings." Meanwhile the *RRZ,* which had generally avoided anti-CDU polemics since August, returned to the wars with an article by Fritz Stricker labeling fusion senseless as long as the CDU persisted in seeking a Weltanschauung-based two-party system. Privately, Spiecker expressed willingness to meet with Adenauer to clear the air.[8]

After receiving a new report of localized Hessian foundings, Adenauer asked for clarification from Arnold. The *RRZ* itself then produced the smoking gun: it reported that Stricker and Muckermann (thus, not Spiecker but his alter ego) spoke at the Frankfurt meeting, which took place on October 30 and resolved to found a Hessian Center. One month later, Arnold finally responded to Adenauer's letter: he had met again with Spiecker, who had reaffirmed his interest in an *eventual* unification *(Vereinigung)* of the CDU and Center. Spiecker had added that he was too busy with the Frankfurt Economic Council to engage in southern foundings, though the situation there was favorable (implying that his restraint showed goodwill). Arnold advised Adenauer to enter into discussions with Spiecker "again soon."[9]

His suspicions aroused, Adenauer held no further discussions. He later stated that party leaders decided at this point to cease all negotiations with Centrist leaders, since negotiations only seemed to strengthen their self-importance and their obstinacy. This decision did not mean that Adenauer now opposed fusion, but that he had an alternative strategy for pursuing it. By convincing the "individual local parties" to fuse "from below," the CDU would rob the Center of its base and force the leaders to settle.[10] Unbeknownst to Adenauer, however, Arnold continued to work on Spiecker.

The Esseners' interest in holding talks was kept alive by developments in the Cold War. The summoning of the People's Congress in the Soviet zone and the dismissal of Jakob Kaiser in December 1947 caused the *RRZ* to harden its line toward the Soviets. On January 6,

1948, the paper commented that Kaiser's fall, though predictable, had profoundly affected people's views well beyond the Soviet zone. Now, wrote Muckermann, only the churches stood in the Russians' way. Although Spiecker still eschewed a choice between East and West and called for a pan-European union, he also characterized the Marshall Plan as a step toward that union, embraced a western European union as a "jumping-off point," and rejected the neutralization of Germany.[11] Sooner or later, he would have to accept that western European union meant anti-Communist western integration.

The February coup in Czechoslovakia put the seal on this development. Asserting that the Czech events must open the eyes of even the greatest doubters as to the Soviets' intentions, the *RRZ* applauded the American President's announcement of a military buildup and hailed the signing of the Brussels Pact for the mutual defense of Britain, France, and the Benelux countries as a step toward European union. The Russians, the *RRZ* boasted, could no longer doubt western resolve.[12]

By the end of March, the *RRZ* was comparing Soviet demands on country after country to Hitler's demands in the 1930s. "We in the West," it added, "want no dictatorship, from any side." The paper began talking of the "struggle" of East against West, and of the need for "West Germany" to restore its economy through currency reform. Whereas the *RRZ* had warned as recently as February 10 that the weakening of the left due to the expulsion of the Communist ministers from the North Rhine–Westphalian government compelled the SPD, Center, and left-CDU to special alertness, all such fears vanished when Arnold gave one of the two vacated cabinet slots to the Social Democrats and the other to Spiecker himself. The *RRZ* welcomed the crystallization during April of the western powers' decision to form a West German government; by May, it was scoffing at the efforts of the American dove, Henry Wallace, to start a dialogue with Stalin. Like many in both the CDU and the SPD, the *RRZ* began to espouse the so-called "magnet theory": a democratic and socially minded West German state would eventually attract and attach the eastern zone. Spiecker now asserted categorically, "The fact is . . . that no bridge can be built between the interpretation of democracy in East and in West"; and Germany could not but choose Europe and the West over the Asiatic, Soviet East.[13]

Meanwhile, Spiecker continued his double game of either splitting the CDU from without or transforming it from within. On April 27, the *RRZ* again editorialized against trying "to unite all Christians in one great political party" and asserted that Germany needed "a clear right, an independent middle, and a stable left." But the paper also commented that the entire situation right of the SPD was in flux, and that the "necessary cleaning up and decamouflaging" had begun and would continue. This sign of confidence in the CDU's progressives was corroborated one week later by a reference to a democratic and socially minded West German state. The *RRZ* also reported Adenauer's declaration on May 3 that, despite past failures, he wanted to try again to reach an understanding with the Center. This declaration was occasioned by the disclosure of renewed efforts (dating from February) by Father Caspar Schulte and his revived KAV to get fusion talks started. Eschewing the usual polemics, the *RRZ* replied by citing Spiecker's general willingness to come together with all parties, though the paper did not neglect to add Brockmann's speculation that the CDU might split and presumably cleanse itself in that way.[14]

Three weeks later came the bombshell. On May 26, 1948, Arnold's *Rheinische Post (RP)* published an exchange of letters between Arnold and Spiecker. Arnold initiated the exchange on May 22 by writing that he could find no "political" reason why the two parties were separate. He assured Spiecker that the purpose of his party's name was not to suggest that nonmembers could not be good Christians, but to indicate its general programmatic or moral direction and its commitment to western cultural values. In this way, it hoped to overcome outmoded prejudices in order to pursue "a truly social, democratic, and in every respect progressive policy." Since Spiecker shared these goals, the two men had a "moral duty," in light of the weighty tasks facing Germany and Europe, to consider how this "partisan split among politically like-thinking men" could be "removed."[15]

Spiecker's reply two days later was upbeat: he agreed with what he called Arnold's view that a "political" party had to be made up of people with "common political aims," that anything "genuinely weltanschaulich" did not separate people but brought them together, that the "correct" political standard was the "balancing . . . middle," and that *"all politically like-minded"* people who wanted an "equitabl[y] balance[d]" and "progressive economic order . . . *do indeed belong together.*" Spiecker thus transliterated Arnold's phrases into his own conceptual language. Previously, he had stated that since the Christian legacy should be used not to separate people into adversarial political camps but for "reconciliation and unity," the Center rejected a "Christian bloc."[16] By transforming the premise of this idea now from a criticism of the CDU into the basis of agreement with the author of a fusion initiative, Spiecker signaled a major political reshuffling; by emphasizing that *"all"* the like-minded belonged together, he kept open the possibility that this reshuffling might eventually involve the SPD.

Publication of the two letters created a sensation. Speculation promptly focused on what sort of understanding was intended, and at whose expense. One paper surmised that Arnold's intent was to declare war on the CDU's reactionaries. This impression was augmented by Arnold's press secretary (and Spiecker's friend), Hermann Katzenberger, who released the letters on May 25 with the comment that fusion might well lead to "splits within both" the CDU and Center.[17]

The fact was that the chairmen of both parties had been taken by surprise. Brockmann, who first learned of the exchange during a caucus in the Landtag on May 25, insisted that it must under no circumstances become public, that no negotiations were allowed without the approval of the party's Executive Board, and that fusion was flatly out of the question. The next day, confronted with publication, he stated publicly that speculation about fusion negotiations was baseless.[18]

Adenauer at first was more flexible. In two statements on May 26, he interpreted Arnold as having emphasized Weltanschauung and Spiecker as having accepted this emphasis; on this basis, he welcomed Arnold's initiative and expressed satisfaction that the two parties might finally reach an understanding. Privately, he told Arnold that while he had no objection in principle to Spiecker's phrase "party of the middle," it might be objectionable in some Christian Democratic quarters (surely the ones against which, according to the press, Arnold had declared war). In a confidential tone, he warned Arnold that "the writings of Herr Spiecker have to be read and deciphered with caution." But he added that his concerns were not serious and that he would be "very glad if your initiative were to succeed in finally moving the matter a good piece forward."[19]

This initially mild response shows again that Adenauer was serious about fusion, if obtainable without sacrificing the emphasis on Weltanschauung that was both a drawing card and a fragile bond of trust between Catholics and Protestants. But his reaction had come without knowledge of Katzenberger's remarks. A flood of anxious telephone calls, especially from Protestants, soon put the matter in a different light. Indeed, not only had Katzenberger toyed publicly in Arnold's name with the possibility that the CDU might split, but he had also speculated that the fused party might retain only the word "Union" in its name. Making matters worse, Spiecker now sharply rebutted Adenauer's remark that Spiecker had accepted an emphasis on Weltanschauung, saying that Adenauer was trying to kill the understanding and "revive the poisoning quarrel." After Adenauer's positive-sounding public response, Spiecker's remarks gave the impression that he was going out of his way to direct the initiative not just against Protestant "reactionaries" but against Adenauer himself.[20] This could only confirm Adenauer's impression that what was afoot was not the expansion of the CDU but its division and transformation into a Weltanschauung-free Union of the Middle (UdM).

On May 27, Adenauer wrote to Arnold, told him about the telephone calls he was getting, and asked him not to engage in further negotiations until the Executive Board of the zonal party could assess the matter. The new letter was firm but diplomatic, and ended with a solicitously conciliatory postscript: "What, in your opinion, should happen now?" But Arnold did not answer, and Adenauer's patience gave out. In a long letter on June 2, he complained as party chairman that he had been kept in the dark during negotiations that Arnold had "apparently been conducting for some time." The behavior of Katzenberger, who had emphasized that he spoke personally for Arnold, earned Adenauer's special wrath. He complained that Katzenberger's talk of a split and a name change had led the press to ascribe these positions to the leadership of the statewide CDU, while the Center persisted in its uncompromising stance. He spelled out for Arnold the disastrous impression this must leave on the Protestants of the northern states (at a time, he might have added, when the CDU faced its first real challenge from the fledgling conservative DP). Reminding Arnold of the earlier decision not to negotiate with Centrist leaders but to pursue fusion on the local level, Adenauer demanded in the name of the zonal party's Executive Board that Arnold cease his "separate politics" and act only in conjunction with the proper party authorities. This letter earned no reply. Neither did a note on June 11 ("May I be permitted to request an answer to my letter of May 27?") nor a note on July 13.[21]

By this time, talks (the so-called Bottrop Discussions) were under way between nine Centrists and seven Christian Democrats. Neither party officially recognized the talks. The Executive Board of the Center issued a statement on July 10 "reject[ing] every amalgamation with another party" and asserting that discussions among individual party members had a "purely private character." Having become aware of Adenauer's efforts to bypass the statewide Centrist leaders, the ever vigilant Brockmann circulated a note to all party bureaus interpreting the Executive's statement as forbidding any local negotiations. Inviting the left wing of the CDU in each state to leave that party and form its own as a prelude to joining "Ludwig Windthorst's Center" was as far as he would go.[22]

For his part, Adenauer, as he had made clear on June 2, continued to favor his alternative approach to fusion. Armed by his experiences with Hamacher (mid-1946), Brockmann (early 1947), and Spiecker (late 1947), he understood the pitfalls of allowing the Center always to be the courted party. Yet, once an initiative for fusing the Christian parties had become public, Adenauer, having repeatedly called for fusion himself, could not simply oppose it; nor did he want to be accused of "torpedoing"[23] an initiative that had the backing of the clergy of the KAV. What he could continue to do, though, was to resist any attempt to get the CDU to drop its Christian badge of honor.

On July 20, Adenauer obtained a unanimous vote in the North Rhine Committee of the CDU that tampering with the party's Christian name was impermissible (in Adenauer's words) "under any circumstances." Two weeks later (August 2), he assured the Westphalian KAV veteran and former provincial governor, Johannes Gronowski, that the negotiations would be "continued most keenly"; but he added that whereas "certain gentlemen" were inclined "to give in" to Spiecker's demand to strike the word "Christian" from the name, he considered that "impossible." Writing to Arnold the same day, Adenauer was far more harsh. Citing the groups that had urged him to intervene to secure the party's name, he virtually demanded that negotiations cease.[24]

Arnold rejected the demand.[25] The Bottrop conferees then signed a protocol agreeing to "merge the two parties into a 'UdM.'" According to rumor, the "Adenauer-Lehr" rump CDU (a reference to the conservative Protestant and former Mayor of Düsseldorf, Robert Lehr) would then give way to an unambiguously conservative party, thus completing the construction of a three-party system (SPD, UdM, Conservatives).[26] The scene was now set for a major confrontation. In the CDU Zonal Committee on August 3, Adenauer charged that

Spiecker's only aim was to split the party in order to pave the way for a Labour Party. Denying the charge, Arnold said that fusion could not be allowed to founder just because of the party's name. But not one member of the Committee supported him.[27]

Four days later, Arnold suddenly broke off the talks. The reason was not just Adenauer's pressure, but new and unexpected tension with the Centrists. On August 6, a Social Democratic bill calling for the socialization of the coal mining industry came to a vote in the Landtag. Amendments by Arnold's government allowing some mixed ownership were the price of CDU support. A compromise did not seem impossible, for the more pragmatic Social Democrats and trade unionists believed that only a broad show of consensus for socialization would induce the western occupying powers to accept it. But the Social Democrats on the relevant parliamentary committee, and then the leaders of the caucus, refused to accept the amendments. The CDU thereupon repackaged the compromise version as its own bill, with Adenauer joining Arnold as a sponsor.

The Center thus found itself in a pivotal position. On the one hand, Adenauer's sponsoring signature on a socialization measure was a gain worth securing, especially in the weeks just after the currency reform and the implementation of Ludwig Erhard's Frankfurt policies. On the other hand, Centrist support of the CDU's bill would have resulted in the passage of a socialization provision against the votes of the Marxist parties. From Adenauer's standpoint, the CDU would have gained credit among Christian labor even while distancing itself from the SPD and dealing another blow to the Grand Coalition—all over a bill the occupying powers were likely to veto. For the Centrists, however, socialization in defiance of the Socialist party was simply unthinkable; to force the moderate left into opposition was to repeat a major mistake of the Weimar era. The Center voted for the Social Democratic bill, which passed. To save face and party unity, the CDU abstained.[28]

Arnold was crestfallen. Having tried to keep the fragile partnership of CDU and SPD intact, he thought that he had managed to compel Adenauer's cooperation, only to be slapped in the face by the SPD and left in the lurch by the Center. Having committed his prestige to the compromise bill, he had seen the Center's stand as a test of good faith, and the Center had failed the test. Thanking Adenauer for his parliamentary support, Arnold cut off the fusion negotiations "for the time being."[29]

Adenauer had won another round. Henceforth, Spiecker would insist that Adenauer be included in any new fusion talks, lest Spiecker again be embarrassed in his own party by lending his prestige to a failed effort. Nor was a chastened Arnold eager to be isolated again between these two more wily players. In short, there could be no fusion that did not go through Adenauer—which meant that fusion would have to be on Adenauer's terms. Those terms entailed not the transformation of the CDU, but the absorption of any willing Centrists. Above all, the name question was off the table.

Motivating Adenauer was not so much the wish to prevent Arnold from acquiring reinforcements within the *statewide* CDU on the social question[30] but the fear that replacing the "Christian Democratic" Union with an entity not based on Weltanschauung would destroy the *interzonal* prospect of a non-Marxist majority party. As the Ahlen Program and even the Düsseldorf coalitional negotiations had shown, Adenauer was willing to go quite far to keep the social wing of his party in the fold, since a majority party was otherwise impossible. As long as every added Christian Democrat was one less anti-Christian Democrat, Adenauer could not begrudge Arnold his search for reinforcements. The problem, however, was that these particular reinforcements, if allowed to set their own terms, were likely not to make the party bigger but to shatter it, whether or not that was their intention (and Adenauer believed it was). Whereas ecumenical Christianity provided an ideal to people who needed one, the notion of a party free of Weltanschauung was alien and difficult to understand. With Catholic-Protestant political cooperation in its infancy, a name change (especially to accommodate Centrists) would have destroyed tenuous bonds of trust; nor was compensation likely via the SPD's dissolution (an expectation that to Adenauer seemed fantastic). Besides fearing northern Protestant defections, Adenauer told the Zonal Committee on August 3 that a name change to UdM would lead within four weeks to a Catholic exodus and the formation of a purely Catholic party.[31] Thus, the danger Adenauer perceived was not a more "social" or pro-Arnold CDU/UdM but the CDU's profitless destruction.

By backing the SPD over the CDU when the chips were down, the leaders of the Center seemed to confirm Adenauer's view that there was little sense at the moment in discussing fusion with them.[32] Adenauer's long-term strategy, however, remained intact: to use local fusions to put pressure on the party leaders to meet his terms. Essentially, he was turning Spiecker's strategy on its head: instead of using fusion to split the CDU, he wanted to use it to splinter the Center. Afterward, the CDU could defeat or absorb the pieces separately, until all that would be left of the Center would be an empty shell.

That strategy soon paid dividends. Although the Executive Board of the Center decided on September 25 against any local election accords with the CDU (despite the newly instituted 5 percent clause—see Chapter 9), several local Christian Democratic organizations convinced their Centrist counterparts to accept places on the CDU's local list. Campaigning in one such locale, the anti-Spiecker stronghold of Leverkusen, Adenauer hailed this show of "self-reliance" and drew cries of *"Pfui"* toward the Center party leaders who had forbidden the accord.[33]

Spiecker himself emerged from the summer fiasco not just embarrassed but disoriented. Still signaling an interest in fusion, he wrote on August 9 that the CDU's abstention on the Social Democratic socialization bill, as well as Adenauer's signature on the CDU's proposals, showed that the party no longer rejected the basic idea.[34] By September, however, he was again in doubt. It was hard for him to believe, he lamented, that there was truly common ground between the parties when the CDU's "readiness for an understanding collapses at the first puff of wind." His path, he said on October 11, was clear: "It remains the Center, and we will vote Center!"[35]

As usual, the waxings and wanings of Spiecker's interest in fusion were in phase with the state of his belief in the strength of the left wing of the CDU. Beneath these declarations, however, Spiecker was becoming desperate, for he had lost the initiative to Adenauer. The Parliamentary Council had opened on September 1, presided over by the CDU chairman; little time remained to adjust the party spectrum before federal elections might be called and a federal government formed. When that happened, Spiecker would not want to find himself consigned to a tiny regional party. Adenauer in effect was stonewalling Spiecker—or, rather, he was starving him out of his tower. Faced with this situation, Spiecker resolved on a bold attempt to secure a new shelter. In mid-October 1948, he journeyed south to meet his old friend Joseph Wirth, who had finally returned from exile in Switzerland. Together with the disgruntled former chairman of the Württemberg-Baden CDU, Arthur Ketterer, they launched a trial balloon. At a rally in Stuttgart on October 23, they hailed the founding of a "Union of the Middle."

The Union of the Middle

One month before the Stuttgart rally, the Executive Board of the Center, having rejected election accords with the CDU, considered having regional sister parties under other names. As Brockmann put it, "We do not want to dictate to the Bavarians or the Württembergers under which name they wish [to support] us."[36] This was a concession to reality: there was no nationwide Center party, and the state party would need allies if it was to have an impact in federal elections. Yet few Centrists were prepared for the sudden appearance of a southern UdM.

Even more surprising was the sudden reappearance of Wirth. In exile, the former Chancellor had participated with former Minister-President Otto Braun (SPD) in Democratic Germany, a movement Wirth had hoped would give rise to a unified democratic party after the war. By 1939, however, Wirth, mired in alcoholism, was enmeshed in constant feuding; as one Social Democrat put it, he was "talking nonsense and doing great damage." When the war ended, the French, perhaps remembering the attempt under Wirth's chancellorship to counter their influence through the Rapallo treaty with the Soviets, blocked him from returning to Germany. From exile, he tried without success to assist Ernst Föhr in refounding the south German Center party; he tried again when he finally did return to Freiburg in 1948.[37] Then, with the collapse of the fusion initiative, Wirth joined Spiecker in the effort to launch the UdM.

The new party, Wirth explained in an interview, would bring to fruition his Weimar-era plan for a large Republican Union, a plan thwarted by the murder of his intended partner, Walther Rathenau. Rathenau's colleague in the old DDP, ex–Vice Chancellor (under Heinrich Brüning) Hermann Dietrich, was a "guest" at the Stuttgart meeting. But the Centrist rank and file seemed unimpressed. One local chairman, Augustinus Kalisch, wanted to know where Wirth had been for three years while Germany was going hungry; another southern Catholic grumbled that nobody wanted anything to do with Wirth because he was a known opponent of Brüning.[38]

Concern over Spiecker's role was just as great. The suspicions of party traditionalists had already been aggravated by the *RRZ*'s latest outrage: on September 1, the paper had replaced on its masthead the venerable Centrist slogan "For Truth, Justice, and Freedom," with "The Organ of the Political Middle." The Stuttgart rally thus seemed another stroke in a design to shunt aside the old party. How, asked Hamacher's friend Theodore Abele, could a leader of the Center be simultaneously a cofounder of another party—indeed, a party that (paraphrasing the *RRZ*) proclaimed itself a "new party . . . free of all ties of ideology or Weltanschauung"? "I see now," Abele concluded, "that Brüning was correct when he held Spiecker to be an adventurer." Nor was Kalisch the only local traditionalist who became alarmed when he learned that the fledgling Mannheim Center party was planning to change its name to "UdM" and that the "party of the middle" that was about to be founded in Wiesbaden would not be named the Center. Kalisch was at a loss as to whether Spiecker had acted with the approval of the Center party's Executive Board or whether he was pursuing (in the grand style of Wirth) a quixotic wildcat action.[39] Could this really be the beginning of an expansion? Surely it looked more like a secession!

What Spiecker really wanted was, as usual, more complicated. Spurred on by Ketterer, local branches of the southwestern CDU would go over to the UdM. With this move, the long-awaited transformation of the party system would begin. By adding UdMs in Hesse and Württemberg to the Center parties in North Rhine–Westphalia and Lower Saxony, Spiecker would tempt Arnold to take the one step that would allow him to bypass Adenauer and create a viable three-party system: secession from the CDU. As Muckermann put it, the UdM was proof that a "propitious political evolution" was under way; it "takes the wind out of the sails" of those who had accused the Center of "narrowness" and "splintering." The UdM was "a great chance" for "friends in the CDU as well as the SPD" who were committed to "the idea of the middle." Indeed, stated an Essener periodical, "Reshufflings *(Umbildungen)* are unavoidable not only on the right but also on the left."[40]

Despite this show of optimism, the North Rhine–Westphalian community elections of October 17 only confirmed the sense in Essen that time was running out. Statewide, the Center drew 9.6 percent of the vote, down slightly from its share in the Landtag elections eighteen months before. But the Esseners could no longer be satisfied just to hold their own. "The Center party," an Essener pamphlet later recalled, "went into the community elections . . . with high expectations. In light of the temporary difficulties of the Frankfurt economic policy, the prospects seemed more favorable than ever before . . . [But] the election was a disappointment. In many places the number of

votes went backwards. Thus, the Center in Essen lost 3,000 votes."
These elections had been "the great test,"[41] and the Center had not
passed. The moment of crisis had arrived.

When the Center party congress met in Essen-Kupferdreh in early
December, Spiecker came carefully prepared for the occasion. Having
packed the hall with enthusiastic supporters from the Center's refounded youth clubs (Windthorst Leagues), he used Brockmann's
concentration of party offices (party chairman, state chairman, caucus
chairman in the Landtag, delegate—with Wessel—to the Parliamentary Council) to insinuate that Brockmann bore responsibility for the
poor state of the party's finances. With the currency reform and the
community elections, the Center had exhausted its resources, and it
was anybody's guess how it was to fund a federal election campaign
the next year. While Brockmann had been ready to yield the party
chairmanship to Stricker, Spiecker in effect campaigned for the job
himself. Lest he take his press, his prestige as chairman of the Frankfurt Executive Council, and his young supporters with him, he was
accommodated. Brockmann was given a cover story—he had stepped
down for health reasons—but neither the *RRZ* nor the new Essener
newsletter, the *Kurier der Mitte,* tried to conceal their glee.[42]

The deteriorating personal and financial situation was manifest
when the party's Executive Board next met, on December 19. "I assume without further ado," began Spiecker, "that those present are
resolved to continue to belong to the Executive. It must be determined
whether those not present who did not excuse themselves beforehand
intend to do the same." A member of the Executive then asserted that
since the party's debts had been run up almost exclusively by the
North Rhine–Westphalian branch, the Lower Saxon rank and file
would resist paying them. This was just the kind of provincialism
Spiecker, who was trying to build a national party, could not abide.
He reminded the assembled that the debts included the costs for the
Windthorst Leagues and the skeletal party organizations in Hesse,
Bremen, and Schleswig-Holstein. Without more money, he went on,
the party would be confined to two states during the Bundestag elec-
tions, on which everything depended. Only a good showing in those
elections would "free us of the current worries."[43]

Spiecker was hardly being realistic in considering expansion at a
time when even the two established state organizations were inade-
quately funded. But his comments to the Executive illuminated the
difference between him and others in the party's inner circle. The

party's later General Secretary, Josef Rösing, subsequently stated that Spiecker gave up on the Center because of the financial situation.[44] But this was just the visible symptom of the deeper problem. To the traditionalists, the choice of political party was a matter of long-term loyalty; one did not abandon a political home because of financial problems. To Spiecker, however, the choice of party was a matter of political effectiveness: what one did not abandon was not a political home, but a political conception. In Spiecker's conception, there was no sense in having the party at all if it was to have a minimal impact in just one or two states.

The situation in the party only worsened in the weeks that followed. Spiecker had played his UdM card, and he had lost: the Center party was hardly at his beck and call, the CDU had not split, no consequential southern support had materialized, and Spiecker lacked the means to fund an expansion. As the year came to a close, neither the Center nor the phantom UdM was in any position to mount a credible challenge in the federal election campaign. There now seemed little choice remaining. If Spiecker still wanted to cooperate with progressives like Arnold, he would have to do it from within the CDU.

The New Fusion Initiative

On January 3, 1949, Arnold met Spiecker in Frankfurt and proposed a new round of fusion talks. When Spiecker agreed, Arnold, this time after consulting Adenauer, quickly prepared a letter. Spiecker's acceptance of the letter's terms represented victory for Adenauer's strategy.

The earlier talks, wrote Arnold, had shown agreement that the "best foundation" for rebuilding Germany was "politics based on Christian responsibility" without "misus[ing] Weltanschauung." Although pride and petty politics had heretofore prevented fusion, the immensity of Germany's problems required "a courageous and statesmanlike decision": "Let us join together in the Christian Democratic Union . . . rest assured that you and your political friends can represent your political ideas in the CDU with the same freedom . . . as you have done heretofore . . . I have talked over the content of this letter thoroughly with the chairman of the CDU in the British zone, Dr. Adenauer. Dr. Adenauer agrees with my suggestion to you, as you will see from his co-signature on this letter." And indeed, Adenauer did co-sign the letter, for it was as clear about the identity of the fused party as the May initiative had been ambiguous.[45]

Two days later, Spiecker met with Adenauer, who assured him that Centrists would receive a proportional number of safe places on the CDU's list and that he would accept a constitutional clause allowing religious provisions to be appealed through referendum (an approach Spiecker somehow deemed less partisan). Spiecker then recommended to the Center party's Executive Board that it accept the Arnold-Adenauer offer, and the Executive summoned a party congress for January 30 in Oberhausen to decide the matter.[46]

Developments in the Cold War again contributed to Spiecker's decision. The last three months of 1948 had seen a crisis in France sparked by domestic Communist pressure, the rounding up of Catholic priests in Communist Romania, the SED's Berlin Putsch, and the arrest on Christmas Day of the Hungarian Primate, Cardinal Joseph Mindszenty. Breathlessly reporting these events, the *RRZ* added that the U.S. Congress's Un-American Activities Committee had determined that religion was "Communist Enemy Number One."[47]

Another factor in Spiecker's decision was a round of confrontations in the Parliamentary Council during December over cultural issues, especially schools and the validity of Hitler's concordat of 1933. Here, the Center and the CDU opposed the FDP and the SPD.[48] The Center thus had faced a choice: either it could emphasize the need for Christian solidarity, thereby echoing the slogan through which the CDU had been maligning the Center as a splinter party, or it could try to distinguish itself by claiming to be the more earnest and vigorous defender of Catholic-Christian interests. This choice had not been a happy one for Spiecker, whose concept of a party system free of Weltanschauung seemed undermined in either case.

The two Centrists on the Council, Brockmann and Wessel, had chosen the second strategy. This meant that they had had to take a very hard line, using any sign that the CDU was inclined to reach a compromise as an occasion to cast aspersions on its Christian commitment. Though they had regretted having to suspend cooperation with the SPD, this was where Wessel's point of 1945 had become operative: preventing Weltanschauung fronts did not mean abandoning Weltanschauung parties; one could not sacrifice core principles for the sake of a coalitional concept.

This position, however, simultaneously strained relations with both big parties at a critical juncture in the constitutional work. This could hardly sit well with Spiecker, who viewed it as his party's mission to bring together those in all parties who desired a broader progressive consensus. Thus, when Brockmann asked the Executive Board on December 19 for a vote of confidence in his and Wessel's work, Spiecker complained that the Parliamentary Council was venturing beyond properly constitutional areas into "all sorts of other matters, such as matters of Weltanschauung." That these issues (which ought to be settled via referendum) had come up in Bonn was "regrettable," but if they had to be discussed, then one had to be accommodating and to refrain from following the example of the Church in "raising demands that are virtually ultimata." A demand that was registered in the language of civil rights, said Spiecker, was properly a constitutional matter; a demand that was registered in the language of Kulturpolitik, being the desire of one interest group, was not. Indeed, said the *Kurier der Mitte,* the Center, as the *non*-Weltanschauung party in the middle of this dispute, was perfectly situated to mediate and to restore cooperation between the Weltanschauung parties.[49]

In rhetoric, this position was very far from that of Adenauer and the CDU; in practice, the gap was much more narrow. Spiecker deemed it imperative in the face of the eastern danger to defend the "civil rights" of Christians; but since those rights could not be upheld without a stabilizing constitutional consensus, the prompt achievement of the latter had to be the priority. For Adenauer too, Kulturpolitik could neither be advanced through an overly hard line in Bonn nor allowed to prevent a speedy constitutional consensus.

To Adenauer, the Christian Weltanschauung had never been primarily a matter of promoting Kulturpolitik, but of supporting individual dignity, combating totalitarianism, and advancing the integration of "Christian" western Europe. Confronted with a Parliamentary Council containing an irremovable but not immovable antichurch majority, he realistically avoided excessive posturing (which could be delayed until the election campaign) and sought an acceptable constitutional settlement. Recognizing that there could be no dichotomy of government and loyal opposition without a prior constitutional consensus, Adenauer was more accommodating and less partisan as President of the Parliamentary Council than he would later be as head of government. Of course, his flexibility was also due to differences within his own interdenominational party. But his willingness to make concessions to Protestant opinion was a variation on the same theme: without the CDU, there could be no two-party system; if the price of obtaining such a system was to downgrade the old primacy of Kulturpolitik, Adenauer was willing to pay the price.

With Spiecker encouraging the CDU in exactly those efforts to find an accommodation with the SPD that Brockmann and Wessel derided, the battles over Kulturpolitik in the Parliamentary Council contributed to Spiecker's decision in January 1949 to seek fusion with the CDU.[50] As for his old fear that the battle over Weltanschauung would be exacerbated by a two-party system, Spiecker comforted himself with the thought that fusion, by strengthening Arnold and facilitating cooperation between the CDU and the SPD, might help free party politics from Weltanschauung.[51] With the seventy-three-year-old Adenauer thought to be headed for the Federal Presidency, Arnold might well wind up Chancellor, heading a coalition of CDU and SPD; perhaps the office might even fall to Spiecker himself, as rumors in the popular new news magazine *Der Spiegel* indeed had it. If industrialists in the CDU who disliked Spiecker's and Arnold's social emphasis were then to go over to the FDP, the result, however imperfect, would approach what Spiecker wanted: a three-party system (with the CDU in the middle) where political loyalties were determined by social policy rather than Weltanschauung.[52]

But then the bubble burst. In the week before the party congress in Oberhausen, signs of impending mutiny mounted. By January 27, every one of the fledgling Centrist state organizations outside of North Rhine–Westphalia was on record as opposing fusion; the handful of Bremen Centrists even went over to the SPD. The *Frankfurter Rundschau* reported that the party leaders for North Rhine–Westphalia had been so inundated by antifusion sentiment in that state that they wanted nothing more to do with the idea.[53]

At the Oberhausen congress on January 30, Spiecker gave his reasons for recommending now what he had earlier rejected. The financial situation, he declared, would confine the Center essentially to North Rhine–Westphalia—precisely the place where the CDU most resembled the Center. Under Arnold, that state's CDU was engaged in a difficult battle to set the tone for the entire party. Its initiative in seeking fusion was a cry for help in that cause. It made little sense, said Spiecker, for the Center to be absent where the CDU was dominated by its more questionable elements and yet to continue the fight where the CDU was most progressive. Moreover, with the imminent creation of a federal parliament, political decisions could no longer be postponed until some better future.[54]

To Spiecker, a small Center was worse than no Center. He argued that the party would get no more than 2 percent of the vote in the first federal elections and would be isolated and ineffective during a four-year period that would tip the scales in the Cold War and decide the fate of all of Europe. Without a coalition of forces that could keep Europe from becoming Asiatic, the first federal elections might be the last. Given these stakes and the Center's limited prospects, the party could not justify persisting in what had become a "ghetto struggle." While Arnold's battle in the CDU was not yet won, the Minister-President had proven that he had the personal tenacity, the political integrity, and the political base to advance the cause. Spiecker deemed Adenauer's signature on Arnold's letter to be another sign of Arnold's strength: he had wrenched a commitment from the reluctant party chairman not to "wreck" the negotiations "again." Moreover, Adenauer had conceded that Centrist caucuses in state and local assemblies would continue to exist until the next elections.[55] This meant added leverage for the Centrists: if dissatisfied with the CDU's course, they could threaten to call off the fusion.

Spiecker's analysis failed to persuade his audience. Even the head of the North Rhine–Westphalian state organization and the member of the Münster contingent closest to Spiecker, Fritz Stricker, insisted that Spiecker had departed from the Bottrop conception. Fusion, said Stricker, must be predicated upon rejection of a Christian versus non-Christian political dichotomy; it must give prominent emphasis to "the idea of the middle"; it must aim to lure half a million Catholics from the SPD; and it must document the fact that the resultant entity was a new party by giving that party a new name. In short, fusion must mean "acknowledgment of the ideas especially emphasized by the Center party." The entry at one stroke of all 600,000 Centrist voters would "give the whole CDU an entirely different orientation"; anything short of this, Stricker said he had told Arnold on January 12, would be rejected by 90 percent of local Centrist leaders. After visiting many local organizations, said Stricker, he had gone back to Arnold on January 26 and had told him that fusion was now out of the question. For even if it were to carry by a slim majority, the result would be not the wholesale transferral of the Centrist electorate, but the division and destruction of the Center and its goals.[56]

To Spiecker, the Center's rejection of his arguments showed that the party had become a stubborn corps of traditionalists *(eine Traditionskompanie)* who let nostalgia for shopworn constructs overpower political considerations. Stricker countered that it was the CDU that was bound to politics as usual, and the Center that was trying to build something new. The failure of the attempt at Bottrop to create the new entity was no reason to "take a step backwards." Not nostalgia but realpolitik demanded the rejection of Arnold's initiative in order to "keep our people together . . . for new political actions." The current crisis would spur the membership to repair the party's financial footing; the Center must use the next four years to attract compatible groups from other parties.[57]

Seconding Stricker, Wessel recalled Spiecker's old admonition not to "abandon the political middle" in favor of a two-party system based on "Christian versus non-Christian" or "*bürgerlich* versus anti-*bürgerlich*." But she added that a party founded on unambiguously clear concepts "has a significant advantage over other parties, even if [those parties] are significantly larger." Size, then, continued not to concern her as it did Spiecker. On questions of Weltanschauung, Bonn had shown that other parties, particularly the SPD, were not free of past constraints; moreover, "if, as Dr. Spiecker says, the next four years will decide if we become European or Asiatic," the deciding factor would be the "social course on which this people is led." In combining social and cultural concerns, then, the Center was both a distinctive and an influential entity in the party system, regardless of its size. The party was not a corps of traditionalists, but a political necessity whose mission was to "save the political middle."[58]

When the floor was opened for statements from the local branches of the party, the tide was overwhelmingly against fusion. Motives were mixed: one delegate was "sick of the orientation controversy" and was "clear about the fact" that the Center "is a party with a Weltanschauung bond"; another found his local CDU "impossible . . . to work with, . . . too dictatorial, too undemocratic, . . . too unsocial." Several delegates stated that their branch would refuse to merge with the CDU even if the congress voted otherwise; one, a priest, concluded: "I believe that we here are all de-Nazified; now it is time that we finally de-CDU-ize ourselves." The congress then voted 239 to 26 to reject fusion. Saying that the delegates had chosen an unsalvageable anachronism over an effective political concept, Spiecker resigned the party chairmanship and stormed out of the hall.[59]

On February 8, Muckermann, Heinrich Steffensmeier, and two colleagues withdrew from the Center's Landtag caucus; five days later, the Center party's Executive Board expelled them and Spiecker from the party. Three of the four Centrists on the Frankfurt Economic Council thereupon went over to the CDU. The fourth, Stricker, became chairman of the Center, and the polemics with the CDU were renewed.

From Fusion to Understanding

If Spiecker and Muckermann were to have an impact in the CDU, they would have to demonstrate that they brought with them a constituency. Before entering, they launched a drive to win over as many of their former party colleagues as they could. Rank and file queries regarding what to do received this standard reply: form a small committee, make contact with a comparable committee from the local CDU, and negotiate on the basis of Arnold's letter; avoid individual initiatives, act in groups, and send the names and addresses of the members to the *RRZ*.[60]

The word "fusion" having become too charged, the Esseners now spoke instead of "understanding" *(Verständigung)*. Thus, Muckermann stated on February 16 that they had been expelled from the Center "because we did not reject an honestly proffered hand of understanding." Opening a "Central Office of Friends of an Understanding between the Christian Democratic Union and the Center," they began to disseminate pro-"understanding" literature using Christian Democratic funds. Like election campaigners, they barnstormed through Catholic towns, bringing their message to the rank and file. Meanwhile, they eased their way into the CDU through a series of meetings in Recklinghausen with the leaders of the CDU's Rhenish organization.[61]

The Esseners justified their new stand by switching their emphasis from the Center as the *"party* of the middle" to the goal of realizing "a *politics* of the middle" through the CDU. As Muckermann put it on February 16, this "cherished Centrist ideal" was too valuable to be tied to the "very uncertain fate of a small party." He added that three years of work in building up the Center had not been in vain: the party, particularly "its last chairman, Dr. Spiecker," had performed "the lasting service" of "preserving" and "winning new adherents" for the "political . . . idea of the middle." The result, Muckermann told the first Recklinghausen meeting one week later, was that the CDU had accepted many Centrist positions it had once rejected, including "natural law," "referendum in questions of belief and conscience," and a more progressive socioeconomic policy. The CDU thus had proved by 1949 what could not have been apparent in 1945: it was not a right-wing party.[62]

The CDU's business manager in the Rhineland, Hans Schreiber, responded that a "Christian" policy by its very essence rejected extremes and emphasized "mediation, balance, and reconciliation." The

CDU, said Schreiber, had no difficulty accepting the formula "politics of the middle" and had objected to the slogan "party of the middle" only to avoid raising Protestant suspicions that the CDU was a camouflage for the old Center. Muckermann by now was entirely sensitive to such concerns, telling the meeting even before Schreiber spoke that the goal was to build "a broader platform for a politics of the middle (not for a party of the middle)."

Even so, the Esseners continued to appeal to wavering Centrists by hinting that the CDU, like the West German government, was only provisional. Immediately after Oberhausen, Spiecker said: "We will soon be electing the first, but also the last Bundestag in this form. Four years from now [presumably after German reunification], we will be facing entirely new and differently constituted problems, and then the problem of the parties will be broached once again from the ground up." Muckermann agreed: events could well result within a few years in "essentially different groupings"; this was "especially" true "for a party like the CDU," which was "obviously not yet a homogeneous" structure. "The forces of the middle will find each other more easily" in the new Bundestag, and "from there out" would realign the rank and file.[63]

In explaining why one provisionally needed the CDU, the Esseners came dangerously close to admitting (though only as a temporary proposition) what Adenauer had argued all along: that the existence of anti-Christian Weltanschauung parties (above all, the SED) required the existence of pro-Christian ones. Yet a full admission would have undermined their own long insistence that a two-party system where both parties were Weltanschauung parties was the worst situation of all. Again, it was the Cold War that had brought them to this precipice. In justifying "understanding," Muckermann noted that the debates in the Parliamentary Council had shown what happened when 31 Christian votes were pitted against 34 non-Christian votes; it was important to see to it that something similar did not happen in the Bundestag. His concern, however, was not with Kulturpolitik per se, but with his belief that the decisions of the next four years could decide the future of Europe and the world.[64] When Muckermann now talked of "Christian" and "non-Christian," the issues he had in mind were exactly the ones that Adenauer cited: the Cold War and the reorganization of Europe.

Yet despite suggesting that there was a Christian component to this argument, Muckermann continued to deny even after he entered the CDU that its goal was a "Christian unity front." On April 10, at a large, well-publicized love fest in Essen of 170 Esseners and 50 pro-Arnold Christian Democrats (including Arnold himself), Muckermann reiterated that "there are Christians in all parties." But if persons whose basic outlook was Christian shared "the same political goals," then they should be able to work together; that was what they did in the CDU.[65]

For his part, Spiecker continued to try to avoid invoking Christianity altogether. At the meeting of April 10, he just did manage to do so: "Now, as all the great decisions converge upon us, now, when the future of Germany and Europe is at stake, there is no longer time . . . for petty ideological skirmishing. The time has come for the ideas we have in common with the CDU to become reality in the new Germany and in the new Europe . . . [For] in three or four years, everything will be over with. In three or four years, either we will have a new Germany, a new Europe, or we will all be in the SED." Once again, then, it was that most virulent of Weltanschauung parties, the SED, that made it necessary, as an emergency measure, to accept the CDU. Yet, rather than calling this the Christian solution, Spiecker said that he had embraced the CDU because it had shown the potential to overcome an emphasis on Weltanschauung. When Arnold was queried from the floor as to why the CDU was not prepared to change its name, Spiecker stepped in to say that it was sufficient for now that the party had issued a statement rejecting "every misuse of Weltanschauung and every misuse of the Christian name." The key to the CDU's potential was to win the internal battle for the party's soul: it was "*this* CDU of North Rhine–Westphalia and Lower Saxony" with which Centrists should come to an understanding. "My friends, we must make *this* CDU, which is embodied in Arnold . . . and Strunk . . . and all the friends who are here today, strong. We must help the CDU to become the way our friends in the CDU themselves would like to see it shaped." At the Recklinghausen meeting of April 29, Spiecker stated that he had entered the CDU for reasons that were political, not weltanschaulich, and he considered it a "compliment" to the CDU to say so. He added a second "compliment": at upcoming Christian Democratic rallies, he intended to give one of his old speeches.[66]

The Mission of Middleness

In complaining on February 2 that a Center limited to North Rhine–Westphalia and Lower Saxony was renouncing its "mission" of spreading "the idea of the political middle," Karl Spiecker accorded to middleness a transcendental moral significance. This style of argument had a pedigree. Long before, Julius Bachem had spoken of the Center's Christian commitment to the moral quality of national mediation as the glue that would compensate for the downplaying of Catholicism in holding the party together; later, Wilhelm Marx and others had emphasized that this moral quality uniquely endowed the Center to assume political leadership. Yet, in writing that "one can no longer fulfill today's political tasks" through "piously cultivate[d] nostalgic societies,"[67] Spiecker separated the mission of the middle from the cultivation of Centrist tradition. He thus completed the rupture of the three elements—Christian Weltanschauung, middleness, Centrist tradition—whose indivisibility had been an article of faith within the Center's old Cologne school.

To be sure, the union of the three elements had always involved contradictions—between isolation and integration, between opportunism and idealism, between staunchness and cravenness. The nonconfessional character of the party was both an inertial claim and a formula for change; middleness was both an inward mechanism of Catholic defensive solidarity and an outward assertion of the capacity for political responsibility. And behind both the myth and the reality of the "political, not confessional" party stood the unchanging fact of the party's Catholic bond.

What was different after 1945 was that the contradictions were explicit in the new Center from the very beginning. This was so for two reasons. First, the old Center had been shipwrecked due to those contradictions, so they could not be ignored. Second, the CDU had taken away the excuses. No longer could one say "Christian" when one meant "Catholic" or "national mediation" when one meant "confessional solidarity." Since the realization via the CDU of Bachem's dream had left a lingering Centrist presence alongside the new interdenominational party, the question Bachem had tried to preempt now had to be explicitly answered: why was there a Center?

Spiecker's original answer in 1946 had been that the Center existed because "national mediation" or "the idea of the middle" was a political value in its own right, quite apart from Christianity. Furthermore, the Center existed because the CDU's "Christian" facilitation of interconfessional reconciliation was at best a misguided motive for a political party, and at worst a mantle that draped the forces not of the middle but of social reaction. Spiecker thus had justified the new Center by arguing that it was progressive while the CDU was not—even though the Center was a revival while the CDU was an innovation.

The truth, however, was that political mediation was not a principle but a function. When stripped of its Christian justification and made to stand alone, it was an uninspiring raison d'être for a political party. Indeed, though the leading Centrists of the Weimar era had been proud (and jealous) of their pivotal role in the party system, they had seen their mediating function not as a drawing card but as an electoral disadvantage, a sacrifice. By the fall of 1946, the orientation controversy and the flare-up at Werl over schools had demonstrated that the idea of the middle in Centrist tradition could not be divorced from its origins in the service of Catholic defense. Two years later, the failure of the UdM proved the unattractiveness of middleness when separated from Centrist tradition and presented as a cause of its own.

The Arnold-Ahlen CDU, on the other hand, was showing an unexpected capacity for social moderation and progress. With the Cold War and the SED seemingly precluding the end of Weltanschauung in the all-German party system and with the Center's failure to establish itself across state lines in time for the federal elections, Spiecker pragmatically concluded that the mission of middleness could be provisionally transferred to the CDU. Rather than continuing to insist (like Bachem earlier) that his proposed innovations were actually assertions of Centrist tradition, Spiecker pitted the idea of the middle against tradition and chose between them. It remained to be seen whether his innovations would take hold in his new party, which, after all, was now also a going concern. But Spiecker at least was finally able to do what earlier Centrist innovators, including Wirth and Stegerwald, could not: seeing that the Center would not change, he was able to take his leave of it.

For Helene Wessel, this process was to take somewhat longer.

12 Helene Wessel and the Christian Opposition

Of the Centrist leaders who remained after Oberhausen, the one who stood out was Helene Wessel. Beyond the mere novelty of being a woman who was prominent in politics, Wessel had established herself through her keynote addresses at Centrist congresses and rallies as one of the most original thinkers in her party. A committed political Catholic and a social progressive, she was at once adaptive and persistent, idealistic and pragmatic. Whatever her male colleagues thought of having to share power with a woman,[1] there were few who did not respect her strength of character, her levelheadedness, and her political skills. When it came to coordinating the affairs of the party, she often deferred to Johannes Brockmann and Fritz Stricker. But when it came to formulating and articulating a political vision, she took a back seat to no one.

As Centrist co-delegate to the Parliamentary Council and then in the first Bundestag as party chair, Wessel would be the person who would steer a course for the party on the federal level in the years to come. During her period at the helm, she would continue to show consistency and strength of purpose, yet a willingness to consider new ways to reach her aims. But the course she chose would take the Center party on an unusual odyssey. As she tried to guide her tradition-minded party in its response to issues and contexts that were very different from those of the past, she would not always find it ready to follow her. In the end, she too would have to choose between her tradition and her vision. Her choice was to prove even more startling to contemporaries than Spiecker's had been.

The Social and the Cultural

"Windthorst's words, often cited by Herr Muckermann—may one never say of the Center, 'By its enemies not vanquished but by its friends forsaken'—are today as valid as ever! That was proven in

252

Oberhausen and is being proven in the purification and firming of the Center party since Oberhausen!" Thus did a Centrist leaflet celebrate the demise of the Spiecker heresy. Insisting that two parties could defend the same Weltanschauung while pursuing different political goals, the leaflet proclaimed: *"The Center is not a party without a Weltanschauung bond! . . . If doubts were ever possible, occasioned by . . . Dr. Spiecker, they are definitively removed by his exit from the Center party."*[2]

With the departure or expulsion of the Esseners, those who held sentiments like these could triumphantly come forward. But while this leaflet was written under the eye of Wilhelm Hamacher,[3] the sentiments it expressed were not confined to traditionalists. In October 1947, Wessel, like Karl Spiecker, had argued that a two-party system was appropriate only in countries where the parties were "not Weltanschauung parties but political parties"; elsewhere, a middle party was needed as a "regulator." She now repeated this view. But the point on which she had always differed from Spiecker now became central to the entire discussion: the middle party too was a Weltanschauung party.[4]

In a flurry of articles and speeches, Wessel laid out her position. The lesson of the battles in the Parliamentary Council over Kulturpolitik, she said, was that Germany was fated to have Weltanschauung parties. The hope of freeing the "SPD, KPD, and Democrats" of their traditional "anticlerical attitude" had been "severely disappointed"; Bonn had "shown how necessary a party is that fights with the decisiveness of the Center for the preservation and anchoring of Christian cultural values in the state."[5] Not only was the CDU less vigilant in Kulturpolitik than the Center, but it was a right-wing party whose absorption of the Center would speed the destruction of Christianity by pushing the SPD to merge with the KPD, just as in the East. Such a result would be especially tragic for being so eminently avoidable: many Social Democrats neither knew nor cared for Marxism, but were motivated only by the social question.[6] "More than ever," one needed a party that could "gather those citizens who, besides wanting a clearly democratic and socially progressive Germany, also want to preserve for the people the cultural values of the Christian West."[7]

For Wessel, it was this combination of the "social" and the "cultural" that made the Center unique and necessary. On both scores, the CDU fell short. Spiecker's argument that the North Rhine–Westphalian CDU had proven socially progressive, wrote Wessel, was true only of a small group around Karl Arnold. Only the existence of the Center had compelled the CDU to join a coalition that included the SPD, and only the fear of losing voters to the Center kept the CDU from moving further rightward.[8] As for the cultural, if the promised preparliamentary referendum on Kulturpolitik were carried out in a polarized two-party system, the voter might afterwards be induced to believe that "he no longer needs to consider grounds of Weltanschauung in choosing his party and could now, merely on social-political grounds, also join a left party." Once again, the merger of CDU and Center would have "weakened rather than strengthened the Christian front."[9]

Wessel's melding of the social and the cultural was certainly more congenial to Centrist voters than the line once championed by Spiecker; her accession to his former role as the Center's leading spokesperson undoubtedly eased its rhetorical problems. Even so, the fusion fiasco had taken a significant toll. Though few in number, Spiecker's followers were political activists; they were overrepresented among Centrists who held elective office. Their exodus on the local level thus often seemed dramatic. Moreover, it was augmented by the departure of many non-Esseners for whom the fiasco was the final proof that the party was going nowhere. After watching Wessel and Hamacher at a local rally on February 15, 1949, one Christian Democratic observer concluded that the Center's leaders were demoralized and the party would soon disintegrate. By March 11, three hundred local Centrist deputies were reported to have come to terms of one kind or another with the CDU.[10]

Nothing was more natural for the Center than to resort to its most traditional issue to try to stem this tide. Again events in the Parliamentary Council provided the opening. Proclerical forces were actually faring quite well in Bonn: the separation of church and state was defeated, and the Basic Law ultimately included the clauses of the Weimar constitution that protected the corporate status and historical privileges of the churches in public law, including the right to levy their own taxes using the civil tax rolls. The issue that continued to disturb, however, was schools.

In mid-February, Konrad Adenauer and the CDU accepted a compromise: although the term "parents' rights" *(Elternrecht)* would not appear in the Basic Law's enumeration of fundamental human rights, another article would guarantee the right to found "private" but (to the chagrin of some Catholics) "state-supervised" denominational schools that would have official parity with interdenominational schools in places where the latter were the norm. In light of the free-thinking majority in the Parliamentary Council, this was a generous settlement. Attached to it, however, was the so-called Bremen Clause, whereby the school provisions in the Basic Law would not apply to states (like Bremen) that had passed different provisions before January 1, 1949. The High Committee of the Parliamentary Council adopted the Bremen Clause by a vote of twelve to five. The ayes included all eight Social Democrats, both Free Democrats, the single Communist delegate, and one of the eight Christian Democrats; the nays came from the single delegates of the German party and the Center, and three Christian Democrats. Four Christian Democrats abstained.[11]

Had the Christian Democrats not split, the Bremen Clause would still have passed. In any event, it was part of the compromise package, which helps account for the abstentions. But the split vote also reflected the difficulty of getting an interdenominational party to adopt a common line on an issue that had divided Christians, particularly Protestants, for decades. Wessel now maintained that these events confirmed that the Center was more reliable on questions of Weltanschauung than the CDU was. The CDU's flexibility on schools during the earlier debates in Bremen and Hesse, she charged on March 4, had tied its hands in Bonn; if the Center instead of the CDU had twenty-seven deputies in Bonn, more would have been achieved. On March 6, the Center announced that it would vote against ratification of the Basic Law if it did not include an unequivocal affirmation of the principle of parents' rights.[12]

Wessel's polemic of March 4 ignored two facts. First, the tiny Center party in Bremen had itself defected to the anti–parents' rights SPD (Chapter 11). Second, if the CDU's interdenominationalism was the reason for the flexibility Wessel derided, it was also the reason it had as many seats as it did. To chastize the CDU for not doing with that strength what the Center, as a purely Catholic party, might have done with it was thus to indulge in sheer fantasy.

Nevertheless, Centrist leaders knew their issue when they saw it. On March 12, Stricker circulated a flyer "by a well-known Catholic cultural politician" (Brockmann) to the Catholic clergy throughout North Rhine–Westphalia. Entitled "The Defeat in Bonn!", the flyer shrilly attacked the CDU for not obtaining ironclad guarantees on schools. The "defeat" was said to demonstrate what the Center had argued all along: if a two-party system were instituted where one party was Christian and the other non-Christian, then Christian interests would suffer. For such a system required that one party command and the other oppose, assuring that no understanding on questions of Weltanschauung could be reached. Only an alternate strategy, possible for the Center but not for a conservative gathering party, might have prevented the "defeat in Bonn": by trading social for cultural concessions, a Christian party might have pried the SPD away from the FDP and broken up the non-Christian majority. This, according to the flyer, is what the Center had done in 1919, thereby achieving more in cultural policy (and a Christian social policy) than the numerically larger CDU had achieved today.[13]

Two months later, the Basic Law came up for final passage. Hoping to open a last avenue for changing the church-state provisions, the Center promoted a clause allowing referendums. But Spiecker's support for the February compromise permitted Adenauer, who distrusted referendums in light of their abuse under the first republic, to oppose the Centrist bill. When a last-minute amendment on parents' rights was also defeated, the two Centrist delegates lived up to their word and voted against ratification.[14]

Adenauer's position again showed his priorities and his nonparochial definition of the Christian Weltanschauung. Yet, despite Brockmann's denial,[15] he and Wessel too would doubtless have voted to ratify the Basic Law had it not been assured of passage; they even praised it in announcing they would vote against it.[16] To some extent, then, they were posturing on schools in an effort to revitalize their party. In light of the CDU's other cultural successes in Bonn, such posturing was not very effective. Nor was a parley between Center and SPD on a shortened, "purely functional" Basic Law that would have left (among other things) the schools issue open.[17] The bulk of the CSU, for reasons primarily of federalism but not uninfluenced by Kulturpolitik, also voted against the Basic Law, but since no serious rift between the Union parties developed, the Center could take little comfort from this. Meanwhile, the CDU could argue that the real lesson of Bonn was the need to rally to the party of Christian solidarity in time for the August elections to the first federal parliament.

From Parliamentary Council to Federal Parliament

As the elections approached, the Center and the CDU again were pressured by the clergy to moderate their feud. But although party leaders agreed to hold talks, their motives clashed. For the Center, anything smacking of fusion, or even of an election accord, had to be avoided: as Stricker told the clerical intermediary Wilhelm Böhler, his party must not appear to be just "an appendage of the CDU."[18] The only subject open to negotiation, then, was a set of ground rules to keep the campaign from becoming too virulent. Stricker's real aim here was to get the CDU to stifle Richard Muckermann's Essen operation, which was seriously affecting morale. But if Adenauer could not get an election accord turning the Center into a Christian Democratic client, then he had to convince the Catholic electorate of the Center's lack of viability. An agreement might be useful if it lowered the Center's profile, but not if the price was the Essen operation.

Sure enough, Stricker was soon complaining to Böhler that Christian Democratic sources were leaking the talks and portraying them as a step toward fusion. Stricker insisted that Christian voters must be given "a true choice" between two Christian parties with differing political programs if they were not to wander to parties where the Church would not like to see them. He labeled as "parasitic" Adenauer's (generally accurate) claim that the clergy was for the CDU, and professed little confidence that negotiations with Adenauer could succeed.[19] Nevertheless, he did meet with Adenauer on June 30.

After the meeting, Böhler drafted a set of campaign guidelines and sent them first to Stricker. The guidelines provided that the two parties avoid actions that might harm the prospects of electing as many Christian deputies as possible. Neither party was to use the statements of clergy to suggest that it was more faithful to the Church than was the other; nor was either to accuse the other of "unreliability on Weltanschauung"; nor was either to cite the position of the other on the Basic Law as an indication of such unreliability. The two parties would agree to campaign "in a fair way." "They recognize each other as equally entitled political factors. The fusion efforts will cease." A committee consisting of a Centrist, a Christian Democrat, and a neutral would enforce the agreement.[20]

On July 2, Stricker wrote to Böhler to accept—provided the CDU "renounce all fusion activity for the duration" and neither "exploit [n]or portray" the agreement as an instrument of fusion. Furthermore, priests and Catholic organizations were not to favor one party over the other, and the Center reserved the right to profile in a "positive" way its reasons for voting against the Basic Law.[21] Stricker would have had good reason to be satisfied with such an agreement: it would have demanded virtually nothing from his party while blunting the CDU's advantage with the clergy and closing down Mucker-mann's operation. Before he could send his letter, however, tragedy struck. On July 3, Stricker died in an automobile accident.

As acting chair, Wessel delivered the letter to Böhler, who passed it to Adenauer on July 9 with the comment that Wessel and Brockmann were prepared to hold talks immediately. But Adenauer complained that the guidelines included conditions not mentioned on June 30. He could never agree, he said, that the clergy must treat the Center and CDU as equals. Furthermore, he demanded that the sentences on mutual recognition and ending fusion efforts be stricken, since they amounted to "a disavowal" of Centrists who had gone over to the CDU.[22]

Adenauer also complained about another document that had come into his possession. Drafted by Stricker in late June, it was a sketch for a standard stump speech for Centrist candidates. The draft speech chided the CDU for its failure to support a referendum provision, attacked the "catastrophic" Frankfurt economic policy, and threatened to file a complaint with the Federal Constitutional Court against anyone who tried to involve the occupying powers in the matter of the election law (a reference to an attempt by the Christian Democratic Minister-Presidents to procure an end to proportionality and the list system). An attachment, entitled "What ought to be treated in every speech," contained several additional points: (1) since Adenauer had defamed the Center as "un-Christian" because of Spiecker, Adenauer must now apply this charge to the CDU; (2) a two-party system would risk the fate of the Church on that of one political party; (3) only a socially progressive political course would assure the cultural viability of the Christian West; (4) the Center had been true to its principles on parents' rights while the CDU had compromised.[23]

Adenauer seized upon this document to avoid an agreement he did not want. Stricker, he told Böhler, had been trying to deceive him; he had been planning strident attacks on the CDU while professing to be seeking a truce. The smoking gun, marked in Adenauer's copy with three bold pencil strokes, was the passage on the Frankfurt economic policy. Adenauer reminded Böhler that Stricker had given assurances on June 30 of Centrist support in the first Bundestag for a policy he had all the while been plotting to attack as "catastrophic." Adenauer concluded that any assurances that came from the Center were worthless.[24]

The subsequent campaign between CDU and Center was a relatively low-key affair. Exceeding expectations, the Center managed to field candidates in all but one district in three states: North Rhine-

Westphalia, Lower Saxony, and Schleswig-Holstein. But the Christian feud was overshadowed by the first interzonal battle of CDU and SPD.[25] On August 14, as Spiecker had foreseen, the Center, barely mustering 3 percent of the federal vote, garnered only 10 seats, all in North Rhine–Westphalia. Its 601,435 votes in that state represented 8.9 percent of the vote there, a drop from 9.7 percent in the local elections of the previous fall. The 113,464 Centrist votes in Lower Saxony and 12,590 votes in Schleswig-Holstein fell below the state-based 5 percent barrier and were lost. Even so, had the votes for the Center been cast instead for the CDU, the distribution of Christian to non-Christian seats would have been virtually unchanged. In North Rhine–Westphalia, the CDU received 43 seats, while the SPD got 37, the Center and FDP 10 each, and the KPD 9. Without the Center, the distribution would have been: CDU 54 (one more than CDU and Center), SPD 36, FDP 10, KPD 9.[26]

There was indeed a difference, however, between CDU and Center. Once Wessel formally ascertained from Adenauer that the path of Frankfurt would be continued, neither of them reckoned on their joint participation in a coalition.[27] After Adenauer was elected Chancellor on September 15, the Center faced a situation wholly novel in its history. Neither the pivotal party of government nor the principled party of opposition against Kulturkampf-minded Protestants and anticlerical liberals, the self-styled middle party and Christian party of national mediation found itself aligned with Socialists in opposition to a coalition whose senior partner, while conservative, was a moderate and democratic catch-all party that was firmly allied with the churches. In contrast to 1919, this alignment could hardly be explained as necessitated by the primacy of subcultural defense.[28] Nor could one credibly compare the Center's current oppositional role (though some tried) to that of 1932: the massive CDU of Adenauer, Kaiser, Arnold, and Spiecker (Papen's enemy at *Germania* in the 1920s) was simply not the same sort of entity as Papen's reactionary fringe group of Centrist renegades. How, then, was the Center going to justify its current political status to its tradition-minded constituency?

The Christian Opposition

On October 15, 1949, Helene Wessel officially became the first woman ever to chair a German parliamentary party. She used the occasion to discuss the new self-image her party wished to recommend to its voters. According to Wessel, Adenauer's justification for a government without the SPD—"the German people must accustom themselves to having one large party take over the leadership and the other the opposition"—was actually "the best justification" for rejecting a "Christian 'unity party'": "For where ought the adherents of a Christian unity party to go, if they no longer agree with the policies of this party, and there is no Center? Their only choice . . . would be either not to vote, or to vote for a left party." Wessel here was presenting her own dilemma: only the presence of a "Christian opposition" would save voters like herself from having to vote for the SPD.[29]

The idea of a Christian opposition was a long way from the idea of a middle party inside a governing coalition, tempering the polarizing predilections of its partner. But it answered the dilemma of a Catholic Center party that had to compete and coexist with a Christian and democratic rival. If Kulturpolitik was not the reason for going into opposition, it did determine the vehicle of that opposition. It was a negative rather than a positive constraint: not sufficient to cause Centrists to become Christian Democrats, it was sufficient to prevent them from becoming Social Democrats. The underlying presumption here, however, was that one's natural political affinities lay with the party to which one was closest not on cultural but on social policy. This attitude stood in marked contrast to the rhetoric of sacrifice that had accompanied the Weimar coalition, or to the belief of many Centrists in those days that their party was closer in conviction *(Gesinnung)* to its "Christian" opponents than to its "atheist" partners (Chapter 3).

To be sure, at the Center's eightieth anniversary celebration in Soest in October 1950, Wessel was still resisting the conclusion that her party was a kind of fellow traveler *(Gesinnungsgenosse)* of the SPD. Indeed, while she continued to reserve her big guns for the CDU ("an outspokenly restorative party with all the dangers that we have to see in that"), she was disappointed in the SPD. In the spring, it had tried to block a Center-CDU proposal to include a particularly sweeping parents' rights provision in the North Rhine–Westphalian constitution. Now, after that constitution had been approved by referendum, Wessel lamented the SPD's seeming inability to "free itself" of Marxism and "its anti-Christian complex": "How differently post-1945 politics would have proceeded, had the SPD acknowledged . . . parents' rights in the Parliamentary Council and had it therefore not lost the federal election campaign."[30] Yet this criticism reveals how the gap had narrowed between herself and the SPD: thinking she was scolding that party, she was actually expressing regret that it had lost an election.

Wessel's chief preoccupation thus was not Kulturpolitik per se, but the effect of the SPD's cultural stance on the larger political picture. For one year, Adenauer had been trying to "coordinate" the North Rhine–Westphalian government—to bring the Düsseldorf coalition into line with that in Bonn—while Arnold had been trying to do the reverse.[31] One of Arnold's tools had been the upper chamber of the Federal Parliament, the Bundesrat. This body was composed of delegates from the state governments; heading the North Rhine–Westphalian delegation was Arnold's Minister for Federal Affairs, Karl Spiecker. In the fall of 1949, with the votes of the SPD, Arnold had spoiled Adenauer's plan to give the CSU the presidency of the Bundesrat and had claimed this prize for himself. Since many areas of federal legislation required the Bundesrat's approval, advocates of a Grand Coalition, including Arnold and Spiecker, had hoped to use the Bundesrat as a sort of countergovernment to, or regulator of, the government of Adenauer. But after the state elections and North Rhine–Westphalian constitutional referendum in June 1950, Arnold was able to prevent a Bonn-style coalition of CDU and FDP in Düsseldorf only by getting Brockmann to accept a last-minute coalition of CDU and Center. While this was not exactly what Adenauer wanted, it was much closer to his ideal than to Arnold's (or Brockmann's). Wessel now complained that the SPD's behavior on Kulturpolitik, by providing an excuse to exclude the SPD from the state government, had yielded to "restorative forces" political territory that might have been denied them.[32]

Had the SPD made the desired cultural concessions, should Wessel not then have led her party into a fusion with it? Although she glimpsed this logic,[33] she was reluctant to accept it. For the moment, her conclusion was the same as during the Parliamentary Council: neither of the two big parties was an acceptable political home for voters like herself. But whereas during the Böhler negotiations she had been exploring the possibility of peaceful coexistence with the CDU, her focus now was on defining the relationship with the SPD. The North Rhine–Westphalian coalition was a setback, but it was the Center's leader in the Landtag, Brockmann, who would have to deal with that. In the Bundestag, both the SPD and the Center were in opposition. Both espoused the so-called "magnet theory," whereby the eastern zone would be won back only by an attractive social welfare state. Furthermore, both were critical of Adenauer's emerging foreign and security policies. In short, Wessel's natural partner was increasingly the SPD.

Indeed, in security policy, Wessel sometimes sounded even more opposed to Adenauer's policies than did Kurt Schumacher. "Whether we like it or not," she had said in October 1949, "West Germany will have to take up contact with East Germany and . . . shape an all-German solution." Wessel thus repudiated from the start a notion at the core of Adenauer's policy: the isolation of the East German regime. Schumacher was more difficult to pin down. While he believed that any overtures from the East should be explored, he referred to the government in East Berlin as "the Pankow marionettes." Never had he believed in a solution negotiated between German states or parties (recall his reaction to Jakob Kaiser's earlier suggestions); the real players were the occupying powers. To negotiate peace with them, a government based on free all-German elections was needed. The speedy attainment of such a government was the priority; everything about security policy had to be measured against that aim.[34]

Accordingly, when the issue of rearmament arose, Schumacher was its more formidable but Wessel its more unequivocal opponent. In 1948, the Soviets deployed militarized German police units (the Volkspolizei) in their zone; in the fall of 1949, they exploded their first atomic bomb. These developments prompted Adenauer to hint in December that West Germany, if asked by the western powers, would consider rearming "in the framework of a European federation." Then, in June 1950, Communist North Korea attacked South Korea. Fearing what this portended in divided Germany, Adenauer in August openly proposed rearmament. He was opposed by the SPD on three grounds: the young democracy was not vibrant enough to control a revived military; rearmament would threaten prospects for reunification; and rearmament, in case of attack, would facilitate a tactical retreat by the western powers (in order to regroup and strike back) while Germany was overrun and Germans did the fighting. Schumacher did not flatly reject rearmament, but insisted on two prerequisites: forward basing of western allied troops at the German-German border (to lower the chance of a tactical retreat), and the prior restoration of German sovereignty (whereas Adenauer saw rearmament as leading to sovereignty). By contrast, after a speech by Wessel in June, one Catholic newspaper commented that the Center's position against remilitarization, unlike that of other parties who "leave the back door open," was absolute.[35]

Though western-oriented and anti-Communist, Wessel accepted

military neutrality as the road to social progress and reunification—whereas Schumacher argued that only his terms would prevent rearmament from resulting either in permanent division or in a wave of neutralist sentiment and eventual Soviet domination. Practically, however, Schumacher's terms for rearmament were so unrealistic as to constitute a prescription for opposing it. Indeed, with much of his party supporting the concurrent *"Ohne mich"* ("count me out") movement of young people opposed to conscription, it is unlikely that the SPD would have supported rearmament even if Schumacher's terms had been granted. Moreover, when Pastor Martin Niemöller of the Confessing Church, an outright neutralist, called upon the clergy in October 1950 to oppose rearmament, Schumacher pointedly met with him, for the Social Democratic leader was not about to miss a chance to play on the potential for a Catholic-Protestant split within the CDU. Further augmenting this potential, Gustav Heinemann of Essen, the leader of the Protestant synod and a future President of the Federal Republic, chose this moment to protest the government's rearmament policy by resigning as Adenauer's Interior Minister.[36]

Also in October, the French Defense Minister, René Pleven, proposed the creation of a European Defense Community (EDC) that would include West German contingents. As high-level rearmament talks commenced in Bonn and Paris, Adenauer was gratified: here was progress toward the restoration of German freedom and respectability, yet in a context that replaced nationalism with the new ideal of Europeanism. Only in alliance with the West, Adenauer believed, could (or should) Germany be reunified. Moreover, western integration was a pragmatic way to defend the culture of the Christian West against the savage doctrine from the East. Both on pragmatic and idealistic grounds, then, Adenauer's western-oriented foreign policy, with its symbiosis between rearmament and Europeanism, was at the core of what he meant by the Christian Weltanschauung. But Wessel, who could never grant that a policy of rearmament was at the core of what was Christian, endorsed Heinemann's stand and used the issue to make concrete what she meant by "Christian opposition."[37]

Innovation and Tradition

In the weeks that followed, the East German premier, Otto Grotewohl, wrote a series of notes to the government in Bonn proposing a joint constituent assembly. Although Adenauer firmly rejected this initiative (and even Schumacher was wary), it further stoked the fires set by Niemöller and Heinemann. On November 30, Ernst Föhr, the Badenese Catholic prelate and associate of Joseph Wirth, wrote an article that gave the last rites to the CDU. Protestants, he said, were now dispersing to the SPD and the "Democrats" (FDP), partly as a result of Niemöller; the next step should be a "return" of Catholics to the Center and the creation by its side of a Protestant "Christian Social" party. In effect, Föhr's was a two-Center solution, complete with Hamacher's (and Hermann Roeren's) old slogan, "divided we march, united we strike," but inspired by the Wirth rather than the Brüning tradition.[38]

A few days later, according to an internal Center party newsletter, Heinemann privately denied rumors that he was considering starting "a new Weltanschauung party—that is, an outspokenly Protestant party," because

> the existing parties are much too bound by Weltanschauung. What is missing is a party of practical political and social work . . . Christian and social . . . but not confessional. [Heinemann] by no means wants a Catholic and a Protestant Center. Asked to make an official statement to this effect or to deny the reports about his plans to found a party, Heinemann declared: not yet . . . "let these trial balloons fly freely and have an effect for a while, so that we can see what the reaction is."

If Heinemann's aim was not in line with Föhr's, then what exactly did he intend? Wessel decided to find out. In January 1951, with the four powers exploring the possibility of new negotiations, Heinemann and Wessel held a long discussion "of especially current significance and importance."[39]

Wessel, however, had a problem. Many Centrists either leaned more toward Adenauer's position than her own or simply believed that security policy and the German question were not the issues on which the party should establish its political profile. This was particularly the case since the Church hierarchy favored rearmament, and since the CDU and Center in North Rhine–Westphalia were now partners in a culture-oriented coalition. While the state constitution guaranteed parents' rights, it left the further regulation of schools and the curriculum to the Landtag. As the legislative term progressed, Brockmann, under constant pressure from the clergy (without whose good graces the party seemed doomed), became more and more committed to his working partnership with Arnold. Brockmann and Wessel were thus increasingly at cross-purposes. As the relationship between them deteriorated, Wessel found herself becoming isolated within her party, for she was the one whose nontraditional activities were risking Brockmann's work on schools and the Center's standing with the clergy.[40]

Brockmann was now using the North Rhine–Westphalian Center not to moderate the SPD, as he once had planned, but to moderate the CDU. By discouraging it from forming a coalition with the FDP, he was doing what he could to prevent a complete rout by the Adenauer forces over those of Arnold. But his cultural agenda put him in a weak position for achieving anything more. With school legislation pending in the fall of 1951, by-elections in Hamm and Wiedenbrück assumed critical importance, for the majority of CDU and Center over the three anticlerical parties was a scant three votes. Not only did Brockmann now seriously pursue an election accord for the first time, but he even conceded privately that if the CDU were to refuse an accord, the Center would have to refrain from putting up candidates.[41] Moreover, the Center's poor showing in the state election of 1950—its share of the vote had fallen by nearly a quarter, to 7.5 percent—had led some local branches to conclude that the only way to save the party was to distinguish it from the CDU through a retreat into overt confessionalism. These branches repeatedly called for more emphasis on the party's "Catholic character," or even a change of name to "Catholic People's Party." Thus, just when Wessel was becoming increasingly bold in her policies, Centrist leaders on the state level were increasingly reluctant to provoke the CDU, while part of the rank and file (to Brockmann's chagrin) was flirting with integralism.[42]

At the party congress in November 1951, things came to a head. In a thinly veiled power play, Brockmann proposed the establishment of a new party organ, a five-member Presidium, which for all intents and purposes would preempt Wessel's functions as chair. He even proposed who the five members should be: Wessel, Otto Krapp (chairman in Lower Saxony), Brockmann himself, and two reliable allies, Rudolf Amelunxen and Peter Tollmann (Hamacher had died in July). Brockmann recalled his own recent statement that "it would be impossible to allow ourselves the luxury of another party leader now": such a move was precluded by the foreign policy situation, the recent withdrawal from the party of one of its Bundestag deputies, and the spate of outside attacks on the chairperson.[43] Even while denying that he wanted Wessel's job, Brockmann was thus divesting it of significance; even while denying that there was tension between them, he listed the points of tension.

Brockmann's proposal was approved. It was now but a matter of time before the other shoe would drop. Wessel had continued to develop her relationship with Heinemann through a new organization, the Emergency Community for Peace and Freedom (Notgemeinschaft für Frieden und Freiheit), whose aim was to mobilize the opposition to rearmament and to prevent the permanent division of Germany. In January 1952, the Center Party Committee told Wessel that if she did not wish to dedicate herself exclusively to her tasks as party leader, she should resign. She did so, saying that her work for the Emergency Community was now more important.[44]

Having been criticized for taking her party into uncharted waters that had nothing to do with its tradition, Wessel had proved that she had meant it when she had rebutted Spiecker's charge at Oberhausen that the Center was nothing but a corps of traditionalists. Like Spiecker before her, however, she had discovered that the old dog did not wish to learn new tricks. Though she stayed on in the party until the end of 1952, her activities on its behalf were essentially at an end. Thus, Brockmann was virtually all that remained of the original group of leaders.

Struggling to keep his remaining Centrist fragment alive, Brockmann felt compelled in 1953 to seek a federal election accord with the CDU. This Bundestag election was the first in which the 5 percent clause applied to the overall vote rather than to the vote in one state. Since a party not getting 5 percent would still receive its proportional allotment of seats in any state in which it won one direct mandate, the CDU was asked to withdraw its candidate from one district and to throw its support to a Centrist. Had the CDU refused, the Center would not have survived at all on the federal level. Displaying his usual shrewdness, Adenauer favored an accord (albeit a tough one), arguing that Centrists who were forced to become CDU "guests" would soon become CDU deputies and bring their voters with them. Even so, Brockmann had to issue dire threats about the fate of the Düsseldorf coalition before the CDU would come to terms, for many Christian Democrats would just as soon have seen the demise of the Center in the Bundestag.[45]

With 0.8 percent of the federal vote (down from 3 percent four years earlier), the Center emerged from the September election with only three seats. Two of the three—all but Brockmann himself—did indeed become guests, and later members, of the CDU. As the Center licked its wounds at a meeting in October, some members asked the obvious: How could a party fight the Chancellor's policies for the better part of four years and then tell its voters to enter into an accord that had some of them voting for the CDU? Others went further, wondering aloud what the party's purpose or function nowadays was, and why it continued to exist.[46]

The Third Force

With the events of 1952–1953, the Center's back was broken. No longer a presence on the national scene, the party, from Arnold's perspective, was still worth propping up in Düsseldorf if he could thereby avoid the coalition he dreaded with the FDP. But when the Centrist vote (despite an arrangement with the CDU) dropped to 4 percent in the Landtag elections of 1954, the CDU-Center coalition, now with 99 out of 200 seats, lost its majority.

While the subsequent Bonn-style coalition was troubling to Arnold,[47] its collapse in 1956 was even worse. Angered when the CDU in the Bundestag introduced a bill that would have limited proportional representation, the Düsseldorf FDP formed an alliance of convenience with the SPD to topple Arnold. Although the Center did not vote for the motion of no confidence, it let the sponsors know it would cooperate in a new government, and Amelunxen subsequently received a ministry. Forced as a result to run virtually on its own (with the fading Bavarian Party) in the federal elections of 1957 (an attempt to interest the SPD in an accord got nowhere), the Center garnered only 70,000 votes (one-tenth as many as in 1949) and no seats. Meanwhile, an embittered Arnold, warning that a coalition of SPD and FDP was being planned in Bonn, joined Adenauer in championing his "Christian" party against the "Marxist" SPD.[48]

Even more than Kaiser, Arnold never completely abandoned his dream (now deferred) of a Grand Coalition. After Schumacher's death (1952), Kaiser had launched a trial balloon during the 1953 campaign, but it had quickly been exploded by Adenauer. With both a regional and a class base, Arnold stood in a potentially stronger position than did Kaiser, who was constrained by his membership in the cabinet. Having paid in Düsseldorf in 1956 for the party's sins in Bonn, Arnold was owed compensation by his party. Still young enough to reckon on someday succeeding the octogenarian Chancellor, Arnold busily gathered party posts to solidify his power for the future. His day, however, was never to come. Campaigning to win back the minister-presidency during the Landtag elections of 1958, Arnold suffered a fatal heart attack just days before the CDU obtained an absolute majority.

For its part, the federal-level CDU/CSU in 1957 became the first (and still the only) party in German history ever to win an absolute majority in a free national election. The following April, citing Kulturpolitik, schools, and their own lack of numbers, seven of the nine Centrists in the Landtag went over to the CDU. By the federal elections of 1961, if anyone was still listening, Brockmann counseled any remaining Centrist stalwarts to give their votes to the FDP, apparently on the premise that it was all that remained of the "idea of the middle." The Center never again returned a deputy to Bonn or Düsseldorf.[49]

As for Wessel, after resigning the party chairmanship in 1952, she had embarked on a new effort to create a viable Christian opposition. On November 13 of that year, the Center's General Secretary, Josef Rösing, announced that Wessel, believing she would "find a better and broader platform for her foreign policy views in a coming new party," had withdrawn from the Center. Rösing went on to say that anyone who supported either the Emergency Community for Peace and Freedom or the "coming new party" would be automatically expelled from the Center.[50]

Wessel's move had been widely expected, for these were the months in which the debate over rearmament had reached its climax. On May 26, Adenauer had signed the General Treaty. Contingent on western European ratification of the EDC, this pact extended West German sovereignty to all issues but Berlin, reunification, and a peace treaty, with the western occupying powers retaining the right to resume control if democracy were threatened. To Adenauer, the treaty proved that rearmament and western integration were indeed the keys to restoring German sovereignty, and most members of the Center by now agreed.[51] Like the Social Democrats, however, Wessel was convinced that the treaties meant the permanent division of Germany, remilitarization of both German states, and the indefinite perpetuation of occupation. She felt reinforced in these views by the famous series of Soviet notes starting in March 1952. Motivated by the hope of heading off West German rearmament and the EDC, the notes offered a step-by-step process of reunification and neutralization under a provisional all-German government composed of representatives of the two existing regimes. While even the Social Democrats were skeptical of the notes (they continued to insist that free elections must precede, not follow, the other steps), they were intrigued enough to argue that the opening ought to be explored. Wessel and Heinemann were even more positive. But Adenauer successfully urged the western powers to reject the Soviet initiative.[52]

Dismayed but undaunted, Wessel and Heinemann laid plans for their new party. In the summer, Wessel commissioned a state-by-state analysis of the prospects for a "third force."[53] Subsequent discussions generated a network of contacts and a series of draft manifestos under various suggested party names. In these manifestos, the preoccupation with international affairs pervaded even the sections on domestic policy: "The worldwide danger of Communism cannot be overcome through the force of weapons, but only through a reform of the western social order." The CDU had "slap[ped] in the face" all who had believed in the Ahlen Program; the SPD had lost sight of fundamental reform and was bogged down again in Marxism.[54]

On November 30, 1952, Wessel and Heinemann launched the new "All-German People's Party" (Gesamtdeutsche Volkspartei, GVP). This party was to be what the Center was not: a supraconfessional alliance, a broad partnership of Catholic and Protestant men and women who held a common political position. In alleged contrast to the CDU, the basis of this alliance was to be not Weltanschauung but a policy conception, for the CDU's attempt to turn Christianity into a political ideology only "falsified" Christianity and condemned the Christians of the eastern zone to "persecution and extermination." Cemented by policies that were social, democratic, progressive, and antimilitarist, the GVP aimed to attract individuals of genuine Christian spirit; theirs would be a "resistance out of Christian responsibility." But never would this party do what it claimed the CDU had done: never would it pursue special interest under cover of Weltanschauung.[55]

These statements show where Wessel had landed: while her continuing emphasis on the social and the cultural precluded her entry into the SPD, she had moved from the concept of Weltanschauung party to that of policy party. In a sense, she was cutting back toward the path once paved by Spiecker. But this path was now rendered far more concrete, due to two factors: the GVP was genuinely interdenominational (as embodied by the association of Wessel and Heinemann), and it had a specific political and moral issue, not just the "idea of the middle." Moreover, while the GVP denied being preoccupied with the bonding of policy to Weltanschauung, the fact remained that one motive in its founding was the reluctance of its Christian leaders to make their political home in the SPD.

That reluctance, however, produced no outpouring of support for the new entity. For as the Cold War persisted, the linkage among rearmament, West German respectability, and western integration increased the public's sense of the wisdom of Adenauer's policies. The bloody suppression of demonstrations in East Berlin just three months before the federal elections of September 1953 helped Adenauer. He was further helped by the thriving economy, for which Adenauer, with his Europeanism and his pro-Americanism, and Ludwig Erhard, with his social-market policies, claimed credit. To the extent that there was economic dissatisfaction, it was channeled either into the SPD, with its skepticism about "Europe Inc.," or into the new League of Expellees and Dispossessed (BHE), a refugees' protest party that had what the GVP lacked: a bread and butter issue and a natural core constituency. Yet, after some initial successes on the state level (23 percent in Schleswig-Holstein in 1950, 15 percent in Lower Saxony in 1951), even the BHE faded in the face of the economic miracle and the resulting smooth assimilation of the refugees.[56]

As an oppositional alternative to the SPD, the GVP was further hurt by its election accord with a rather dubious entity: the League of Germans (Bund der Deutschen, BdD). Founded by Wirth and the old Christian trade unionist Wilhelm Elfes, the BdD was the latest in a series of efforts dating from 1951 to organize a citizens' movement against a one-sided western orientation and in favor of the "spirit of Rapallo." The analogy to 1922 (when Wirth had been Chancellor) was ill conceived, for the Soviet Union then had been a prostrate power, while France had been demanding German reparations payments and would soon be invading the Ruhr. Nevertheless, Wirth and Elfes now advocated a drive to achieve unification and democracy through reconciliation with Moscow and direct negotiations with the East German regime. Over a two-year period, they became what Wirth called "pilgrims" to East Berlin, with one of their trips, and an audience with Otto Grotewohl, taking place just days before the 1953 election. Their private diplomacy earned them the attention of the Ministry of the Interior, which had earlier concluded that a precursor of the BdD was a Communist front and was probably financed by the SED.[57]

The 1953 elections were a fiasco for the GVP. Proving that Bonn was not Weimar, the leading government party, instead of losing votes (as had happened in every Weimar election), rose by an astounding 50 percent. In going from 31 percent to 45 percent, the CDU/CSU was the only contestant from 1949 to post a gain. Even the new BHE, with 5.9 percent, fell below expectations. Together, the SPD and CDU/CSU now had 74 percent of the vote, up from 60 percent in 1949. The CDU/CSU's success thus reinforced the impression that the country was headed toward a two-party system. As for the GVP, it got 1.2 percent of the vote and no seats.

With the formation of the GVP, Wessel and Heinemann seemed to have crossed their Rubicon; with its failure, they seemed to have arrived in the political wilderness. Though they tried for three more years to advance their party, the GVP was clearly going nowhere. One option remained open to them. Only a country without Weltanschauung parties, Wessel had said in 1949, could have a two-party system; but if German parties downplayed Weltanschauung, then any Christian could simply join the SPD. At the time, she had meant these lines as justification for maintaining the Center: she was rejecting Spiecker's fusion project by conjuring up a horror. As the elections of 1957 approached, however, she drew a different conclusion. She and Heinemann wanted an election accord with the SPD, but the Social Democratic leaders countered that the GVP's candidates should simply enter the SPD. After several weeks of hesitation, Wessel and Heinemann agreed. On May 19, 1957, the GVP officially dissolved. Its two leaders received high places on the SPD's candidate list and subsequently reentered the Bundestag.[58]

Epilogue: The End of Weltanschauung?

Our concern . . . [is to] overcome the old gap between Christian voters and the SPD.

Gustav Heinemann, March 1957

On February 27, 1949, a correspondent of Richard Muckermann's, P. H. Rohs, warned the former Centrist that he and Karl Spiecker were deluding themselves if they thought that joining the CDU would advance the goals they cherished. In their new party, Rohs predicted, they would find themselves without influence; Adenauer would only use them to try to tear the Center apart. If Muckermann claimed that one must join the CDU to be its social conscience, others could claim that one must enter the SPD in order to Christianize it.[1]

Rohs's warnings were justified. Hoping to outlast their conservative rivals in a post-SED Germany and produce a progressive realignment of the party system, the Esseners were shipwrecked even before they could set sail. Their inability after the Oberhausen fiasco to deliver the Centrist rank and file destroyed their usefulness to Karl Arnold in his promotion of a federal Grand Coalition but left intact their value to Adenauer: by documenting the turmoil in the Center, they enhanced the credibility of his alternative. They thus contributed to the achievement of the very thing Spiecker thought was still in the future: the final consolidation of the party system. Moreover, their belief that things were still in flux in the party system was based on the belief that things were also still in flux on the German question. But post-SED Germany, for this generation, never came; and Spiecker, like his new party, proved unwilling to let European integration be held hostage. Since the SPD resisted this ordering of priorities, Spiecker, until his

273

death in 1954, had to watch the existing bipolar party system move not toward realignment but toward entrenchment.

As for Rohs's second point, another Centrist innovator, Helene Wessel, did indeed join the SPD—though only after eight years, and only after first trying to gather a counter-CDU. Her reasons for hesitating could only have been due to Weltanschauung. What requires explanation, then, is why the opponent of Weltanschauung parties, Spiecker, joined the explicitly Christian CDU, while the proponent of Weltanschauung parties, Wessel, eventually joined the SPD.

Spiecker was not being disingenuous when he told one of the fusion conferences in 1949 that his reasons for joining the CDU were political, not weltanschaulich.[2] It seemed impossible at that point to convince Social Democrats to favor a non-Weltanschauung-based realignment on the British model unless there was clearly a progressive constituency to be gained; the weakness of the Center convinced Spiecker that the only way to rally that constituency was to build up the social wing of the CDU. Wessel, however, had never believed that the CDU had a genuine social potential; by 1957, she had had plenty of time to confirm her suspicions. But she also had had time to see that the SPD itself was evolving toward Labour Party–style moderation and doctrinal tolerance, even without a general realignment. With large numbers of Catholic workers voting regularly for the SPD, even the Church, while never even-handed, did take a markedly more balanced position toward the two big parties as the decade progressed.[3] Having argued for years that the Catholic religion would be the loser if the anti-"social" CDU were allowed to claim a monopoly on Christianity, Wessel now convinced herself that it was imperative for workers to see active Christians in the leadership of the SPD.

Yet in the last analysis Wessel joined the SPD not because she was driven to Christianize it; rather, she decided that she had to render it acceptable to practicing Christians because other factors compelled her to join. The year before, Gustav Heinemann, who once had stated flatly that "Christian forces [could] find no home" in the SPD, had come to see the removal from power of the CDU as his political priority, and the SPD as the core of any alternative. Now Wessel emphasized that she was in the SPD for "policy" reasons: on foreign policy, social policy, and economic policy, she agreed with its positions.[4]

Wessel's self-justifications to a nun and to other Catholic correspondents reveal how deeply she had had to search her soul. She was helping those within the SPD, she wrote, who wanted to free the party from Marxism and open it to Christians; while she was aware of the responsibility she was bearing, her conscience was clear before God.[5] In short, she was not abandoning the Christian opposition, but was relocating it within the SPD. It was "necessary," she said, to have a circle of religious Social Democrats "who help form the physiognomy of the SPD—not a weltanschaulich but a clear political physiognomy, in which a Christian also finds his place."[6] But whereas Spiecker had once tried to discredit the Christian-monopoly claims of the CDU because he wanted a party system free of Weltanschauung, Wessel had come around to a party system free of Weltanschauung because it seemed the only remaining way to discredit the Christian-monopoly claims of the CDU. Only then, it appeared, might Christian voters cease to feel obliged to vote for Adenauer and contribute to a change of governmental policy.

Despite Wessel and Heinemann's efforts, the CDU won the greatest victory in German political history in 1957 (in the process eliminating the BHE and using an election accord to reduce the DP to dependency) after a campaign replete with anti-Marxist bluster and pro-Christian tirades—including Adenauer's famous prophecy that a victory of the SPD would mean "the downfall of Germany."[7] Yet this campaign turned out to mark the swan song of Weltanschauung parties in Germany. Coming just months after the Soviet invasion of Hungary, the "red scare" rhetoric was certainly effective. It was clear—indeed, Wessel had argued all along—that the SPD would get nowhere unless it could distance itself convincingly from Marxism. But the CDU won these elections not because of its Christian *Weltanschauung,* but because it had a successful set of economic and foreign *policies* that the voters wanted to see continued. However much the CDU may have wanted to equate the Weltanschauung with the policies, it was perfectly possible to separate them.

Indeed, no sooner were the elections over than the SPD drew exactly this lesson and entered into the process of renovation that was to lead in November 1959 to the Godesberg Program. At Godesberg, the party formally abandoned its (in any case moribund) Marxist Weltanschauung and accepted as a fait accompli the basic framework of the CDU state—its social-market economy, its new army, and its role within the institutions of western integration (including the Common Market and, as was made explicit by Herbert Wehner in June 1960, the NATO alliance). Henceforth, the SPD's role would be to reform, not to overturn. Having thus documented its entry into the growing consensus that lay at the base of Bonn's success, the SPD was ready to profit when Christian Democratic policies in the 1960s no longer seemed as successful as they had in the 1950s. For Godesberg was not a sellout, but a coming to terms. It made the SPD not a clone of the CDU, but a potential successor; it offered not an alternative to the popular CDU state, but an alternative way to fashion it. Godesberg was thus a long step toward the two-party alternation of government and opposition that was to follow.

Godesberg, however, was not the first step. For the official "de-Weltanschauunging" of the SPD was a response to the unofficial de-Weltanschauunging of its rival. The CDU, in other words, had already had its Godesberg. Prophesied in a general way by Spiecker,[8] its specific realization was the work of Adenauer himself. For it was he above all who transformed the Christian Weltanschauung from a euphemism for defending sectional Catholic interests into a formula for a novel and comprehensive set of policies leading to western European integration. Under cover of a Weltanschauung, Adenauer built a party unlike the old subculturally exclusive Weltanschauung parties of the pre-Nazi era—a party bonded not by the exclusory rhetoric of subcultural principle but by the inclusive rhetoric of policy tenets. Indeed, his desire for a bipolar party system had necessitated such a switch from the beginning, even before the specific outlines of his policy became clear. For a majority party could not be a subcultural party. From the moment Adenauer had taken control of the CDU, then, he had placed his party, and (as it turned out) the whole party system, on the path to Godesberg.[9]

To be sure, Adenauer never fully conceded this point, for he tried to transcend Centrist tradition not by rejecting the notion of Weltanschauung but by redefining it to suit his purposes. Hence his early denial of Hans Schlange-Schöningen's "directionless" assertion that the CDU was a "gathering party"; hence too his perennial insistence that Germany's development, being fundamentally different from England's, required all German parties to be Weltanschauung parties, even in a two-party system. Maintaining that democracy in Germany was not possible except as a derivative of Christianity, he was able to argue from election to election that the CDU had to rule until its values became the consensus, rolling back those of the SED and SPD.

By defining Weltanschauung not in sectarian terms but in the grandiose language of western cultural preservation, Adenauer identified his party with a noble international cause that was larger than itself.

This was important: at a time not only of a clear and present danger from the East but also of eagerness to deny the once-prized notion of Germany's cultural uniqueness (which had now become an international argument for Germany's unique depravity), Adenauer glimpsed the prospect of rehabilitation into the western comity of nations; by asserting that rehabilitation was inevitable not for Germany's sake but for Europe's, he soothed German consciences and provided a moral pathway for building a new political consensus in his psychologically shell-shocked people. In so doing, he transformed the concept of Weltanschauung from an instrument of subcultural division into an instrument of political integration.

That process of integration, however, was not confined to the CDU: the SPD, with its long democratic tradition, was certainly no less "western" than its rival. And although Adenauer was correct that Germany's development differed from England's, that development now included Nazism, massive war-induced dislocations, and the travails of the Cold War, all of which lowered subcultural barriers and raised the sense of a common fate. Indeed, the Cold War and economic miracle nurtured a sense of West German solidarity and privilege in respect to the East that crossed party lines. After all, the fate of the SPD in the eastern zone was one of the West German grievances; and western Social Democratic workers were participants in the economic miracle. The resultant social mobility and consumer culture further loosened subcultural bonds, while the new mass medium, television, radiated the process throughout society.

By embedding and diffusing the basic Bonn consensus, these factors weakened the impulse to view West German partisan differences as uncompromisable philosophical ideals. Indeed, as reflected at Godesberg, not only was Adenauer correct about the new republic's need for a legitimizing consensus, but he was also proved correct that the general consensus would be specifically shaped by the CDU. The consensus, however, was a matter not of Christianity, but of policy. It was, as Spiecker would have said, "political, not weltanschaulich." In the last analysis, Adenauer did not require the SPD to become Christian, or even to cease its advocacy of significant social and economic reforms. What he did require was that it accept the basic tenet that Federal Germany was a firmly integrated partner in the booming market-oriented but socially minded West.

In a sense, of course, the East-West battle of individualism versus collectivism, if not Christianity versus materialism, was indeed a battle of Weltanschauungen. But the SPD of the 1960s would have accepted none of these four designations—individualism, collectivism, Christianity, materialism—for itself. This did not daunt Adenauer: he concluded that the CDU was the only reliable Weltanschauung party left in Germany; and the SPD, "a party with no Weltanschauung foundation," would prove no match for the Communists.[10] As early as 1946, one CDU pamphlet had stated that the American parties too were Weltanschauung parties, but since they shared the same "western, . . . Greek, and Christian" Weltanschauung, they generally did not emphasize it except "when dealing with Communist or Fascist opponents."[11] If this analogy was any indication, Weltanschauung now meant nothing more than the difference between totalitarianism and democracy. As time went on, however, Adenauer would find his credibility at greater and greater risk when he tried to place the SPD in anywhere but the latter category.

In the end, Adenauer's answer to Spiecker's rhetorical question of September 1946—were the Christian Democratic advocates of a two-party system really prepared to alternate in power with a Marxist bloc?—was more complicated than a simple yes or no. Rather, it involved a series of calculations. First, Adenauer desired an electoral system based on single-member, single-ballot districts, not proportional representation; aided by this first-past-the-post system, he expected to unify the non-Marxist vote behind the CDU. Second, using the label "Christian Weltanschauung" to define his vision, he expected to deflect the charge that his was just a right-wing catch-all party whose sole bond was hostility toward the vision of the left. Third, with the Weimar experience as his guide, he counted on the Marxists failing to muster 50 percent of the vote. The CDU would thus emerge as the majority party and maintain a long period of predominance. Rather than leading to dictatorship (as the neo-Centrists predicted), such predominance would assure a healthy democracy. Under Allied and ex-Centrist mentoring, governmental conservatives would have less opportunity or incentive for mischief than they would in the role of opposition; the palpable Communist threat would further strengthen their commitment to the democratic status quo. Meanwhile, with the SPD the prime opposition, Adenauer could rest assured, his own flights of red-baiting notwithstanding, that the opposition too would be loyally democratic. Finally, a long period in opposition, far from pushing the SPD toward the Communists (another neo-Centrist fear), might wean the SPD away from Marxism: forced either to accept the basic Christian Democratic construct or to remain out of power indefinitely, the SPD would tame itself. Alternation in power might indeed take place, but only over long periods of time (as was normal in healthy democracies),[12] and only once the necessary policy consensus was secure.

As the 1960s opened, virtually all the points of this scenario had come true. The major exception was that Adenauer had failed to get a first-past-the-post election law, with the result that the FDP continued to contest the non-Socialist vote. The 5 percent clause, however, was nearly as effective: there were, if not two parties, at least no more than three. Meanwhile, as Godesberg had shown, the SPD was indeed tamed. While this did not preclude further policy debate, it did mean that Adenauer, by the time of federal elections in 1961, need not have feared, as he had professed to fear four years earlier, that a Social Democratic victory would mean the downfall of his conception of Germany.

Yet Adenauer remained uneasy. Though one could hardly have expected the leader of the CDU to recommend that his party now relinquish power and let the opposition govern, the eighty-five-year-old Chancellor seemed unconvinced that he could entrust the state even to his Christian Democratic heir apparent. Having agreed in 1959 to stand for President so that Ludwig Erhard could become Chancellor, Adenauer had then reversed himself. In this way, and in full public view, the succession problem had emerged two full years before the elections. By the time those elections arrived, additional complications had arisen. On August 13, 1961, a Sunday morning in the midst of the campaign, Berliners awoke to find a wall dividing their city.

The new Berlin crisis was the rite of passage of the post-Godesberg party system. By failing to act or promptly to visit the city, Adenauer seemed to betray his own consensus. Indeed, it was one of the movers of Godesberg, the SPD's young candidate for Chancellor and mayor of West Berlin, Willy Brandt, who seemed the more resolute. The ineffectual Allied response appeared to discredit Adenauer's notion that a western "policy of strength" would cause the Russians to allow reunification on good terms. By contrast, Brandt's dramatic letter of appeal to U.S. President John F. Kennedy reinforced the SPD's identification with the West and completed its legitimation as a party to the Bonn consensus. Brandt could now advance a new policy toward the East while standing firmly on the soil of the Atlantic alliance (whose senior partner, the United States, was also seeking the path to détente). Adenauer's "Christian" foreign policy had inadvertently made the West German provisional state permanent; this was now clear for all to see; and Brandt was now prepared to construct a policy that, while different from Adenauer's, built upon it, and was its logical successor.

In a sign that much of the electorate understood this, the Social Democratic vote in 1961 rose proportionally by 13 percent (from 31.8 percent to 36.2 percent), while the self-styled representative of the Christian West suffered its first great proportional setback (from 50.2 percent to 45.3 percent). Equally significant, many other non-Marxist voters who were still skeptical of the SPD deserted the Christian CDU in favor of the anticlerical FDP. The third party's share of the vote jumped by two-thirds, from 7.7 percent to 12.8 percent—a record that still stands.[13] Worried about the capacity of the political system to survive him, Adenauer again pondered ways to guarantee his legacy.

His solution has shocked and puzzled observers ever since. For fourteen years, Adenauer had maintained that a Grand Coalition would risk instability and a flight to the political extremes; he had even "coordinated" the state governments of his party colleagues who thought otherwise. Now, in 1961, Adenauer held informal talks with the SPD before forming a coalition with the FDP. Since Brandt had publicly called for an all-party government after the building of the Wall, the CDU-SPD talks could be justified to the public as a response to an emergency. The resumption of talks one year later, however, could not be so readily explained.[14] Werner Kaltefleiter has concluded that these flirtations, as well as Adenauer's support for a Grand Coalition in 1966, show that Adenauer had never understood the importance of the government-opposition dichotomy in prompting the consolidation of the party system.[15] But there is so much evidence to the contrary that one is led to another explanation.

One must begin with the immediate cause: the electoral setback of 1961 had cost the CDU its free hand, leaving it dependent, for the first time since the mid-1950s, on the resuscitated FDP. Flexing its new muscles, this party, after trying to procure Adenauer's retirement in favor of Erhard, accepted Adenauer as Chancellor only after extracting two concessions: a coalitional committee would henceforth pass judgment on all proposals before they were taken up by the cabinet; and Adenauer would leave office within two years. Even this agreement unraveled during the *Spiegel* affair one year later, in which Adenauer was implicated. The problem began when the Defense Minister, Franz Josef Strauss (CSU), bypassed the Free Democratic Minister of Justice and ordered the arrest of a *Spiegel* editor for "treasonously" publishing details of NATO strategy. The FDP's response was to withdraw its ministers from the government and to demand not just the resignation of Strauss but a specific retirement date for Adenauer.

Chancellor Adenauer now set out to rid himself of the FDP once and for all. The means would be a new election law, anchored in the constitution, that would end proportional representation in favor of first-past-the-post districts. Since a constitutional amendment required a two-thirds majority, it could be passed only if the two big parties joined forces; in any case, only they stood to gain from such a law. Furthermore, only a Grand Coalition gave Adenauer any hope of staying to the end of his term as Chancellor. The cunning CDU chairman must also have calculated that it would be more difficult for the untrusted Erhard to succeed him after a coalition whose creation Erhard opposed. Beyond these motives, Adenauer could add one other: if the SPD were ever to come to power, better that it be under his own hand, where he himself could check its foreign policy, commit it to his conception, and tame it. Only then could he be sure of the triumph of the Christian Weltanschauung.

There was nothing inconsistent in Adenauer's decision to rid himself of the FDP. After all, he had aimed from the beginning for a two-party system, and he had resigned himself to the presence of the FDP only after failing to arrange a fusion or a change in the election law. Although he had managed to procure advantage from the "two-and-a-half-party system," the North Rhine–Westphalian events of 1956 (when the FDP had toppled Arnold) had shown its dangers. Indeed, the instability of coalitions that depended on splinter or swing parties, a recurring theme in his speeches of the 1940s against all the minor parties, again exercised him during the 1961 campaign.[16] With the CDU's federal and North Rhine–Westphalian absolute majorities in 1957 and 1958, the transition to a true two-party system had seemed but a matter of time. In the 1960s, however, the FDP's willingness to use its new strength dramatized for Adenauer the fact that his original vision was not yet fulfilled. He now determined to fulfill it—to assure through a Grand Coalition in the 1960s the two-party system he had failed to complete in the 1940s and 1950s.

Intending to "crown his political life's work," Adenauer wanted a brief Grand Coalition not as a precedent but (in the words of an aide) as a onetime expedient to achieve "the definitive establishment of free democratic conditions in the Federal Republic" by "clos[ing] all the still open gaps" and rendering German democracy "fail-safe" *(krisenfest)*.[17] In 1947, Adenauer had argued that all coalitions should be the exception in politics, undertaken only for very specific purposes. Two years later, as President of the Parliamentary Council, he had acted from the explicit premise that constitution-writing gatherings were exceptional bodies; since their purpose was not to promulgate detailed political programs but to set the rules of the process, they had to aim for broad agreement.[18] In the last analysis, it was this sort of task Adenauer now wanted to undertake; this was why he could now contemplate a Grand Coalition. In effect, what he meant by "closing gaps" was to institutionalize, constitutionally, party-system reform.

But Germany no longer needed party-system reform. A democratic consensus was already in place, and the existing parties all functioned responsibly therein; on this score above all, Bonn was not Weimar. Furthermore, the two-and-a-half-party system was at least as centripetal as a two-party system would have been. Pending the fuller growth of a pool of swing voters (a pool that would reach the level of one-fifth of the electorate only in the 1970s),[19] the FDP helped to ease the path of voters who wished to endorse the bulk of the policies of one of the big parties but who still hesitated due to Weltanschauung to vote directly for that party. As Spiecker had discovered with his UdM, a party with such a mediating function could never be a large party; as Wessel had discovered with her social and cultural Center, a small party of Weltanschauung-oriented affirmation could not fulfill this function. A swing party had to be available to a variety of voters holding differing doctrinal biases. Unlike the Center, then, the FDP could survive in the "Godesberged" party system because it was not a rigid tower of subcultural defense, but a fluid conduit between the two big parties. From 1949 to 1961, its presence worked to the advantage of the CDU: policy-minded voters to whom clerical black was still anathema could endorse the bulk of the CDU's policies while checking its cultural proclivities by voting for the FDP. What the 1961 election hinted was that the analogous phenomenon—anti-"red" voters endorsing the bulk of the SPD's policies while checking its radical proclivities—could make the FDP a conduit to the SPD.

This was what Adenauer wanted to prevent. In terms of his own notions of government and opposition, there was in fact no democratic gap that needed closing. But there was a threat—to Adenauer's personal power, and to that of his party. Adenauer's one hesitation about the talks with the Social Democrats, his feeling that they would in the end back away from changing the electoral system, would later (in 1966) prove fully justified. It was not this, however, but the SPD's reluctance to commit itself to his own continuation as Chancellor that brought the talks of 1962 to an end. The upshot was a return to a government of CDU and FDP, and a definite date in 1963 for Adenauer's replacement by Erhard.

The talk in the Chancellery of "closing gaps" cannot but recall an earlier case of an embattled, long-tenured German Chancellor who self-servingly spoke of constitutional gaps. In the 1860s, Bismarck had asserted that the King, as the promulgator of the Prussian constitution, had the right to fill the alleged "gap" regarding the resolution of constitutional disputes between monarch and parliament. Similarly arguing a quarter-century later that what the German princes give the German princes can take away, Bismarck made it clear that he would not shrink from a coup *(Staatsstreich)* against his own creation, the imperial constitution, in order to assure his own and his class's continued rule. Having seen his earlier handiwork fail to produce the predicted and desired results, Bismarck was rather transparently concocting a rationale to justify a new, purer beginning. Can such a charge be leveled at Adenauer?

The analogy, of course, must not be taken too far; the difference between a Grand Coalition and a coup hardly needs to be stressed.[20] There is, however, a more telling point here. While Bismarck acted out of fear that his constitutional system had unleashed forces beyond his control, his real problem was that his system had succeeded too well. Though it did not conform to what he ideally would have liked, it was stable and produced reasonably effective government. Despite the failure of Bismarck's repressive policies against the SPD and Center, the flourishing pariah parties, though the cause of much foreboding, did not really threaten to bring down his constitutional system, which adapted and survived right up to the end of the First World War. Similarly, Adenauer's problem was that his system also had succeeded too well. It had tamed the SPD, and it seemed on the verge of producing what it was supposed to produce: a healthy alternation in power. Meanwhile, thanks to Adenauer's toying with a Grand Coalition, the SPD's claim to being "capable of governing" *(regierungsfähig)* had implicitly been endorsed by the Chancellor himself. It was this inadvertent endorsement that was the true crowning of Adenauer's political life's work.

Yet the analogy ultimately breaks down. It is not insignificant that Adenauer chose to abet the coming to power of his opponents (albeit under his personal aegis), while Bismarck wished to repress them. In other words, it matters that Adenauer, unlike Bismarck, left behind no defiantly unintegrated "enemies of the state" *(Reichsfeinde)*—not even the Communists, who lacked genuine popular support. In this sense, Adenauer's system was not just stable, but (unlike Bismarck's) was operating in keeping with his original aims. Old enough to remember Bismarck and what Bismarck's methods had meant for Catholics like himself, Adenauer consciously set out to overcome what he deemed to be Bismarck's great mistake: his persecution, rather than assimilation, of potentially cooperative subcultural minorities.[21] The way to do so was neither to pander nor to humiliate, but to tame—to integrate affirmatively, as a consequence of a successful and embraceable set of policies. It was because Adenauer succeeded in this aim— hugely aided, of course, by the favorable contextual circumstances and by the exemplary moderation and shared democratic values of the SPD—that a Grand Coalition under him was now conceivable. It was also why such a coalition was not really needed.

The difference regarding Reichsfeinde is the reason why party-system reform was on the German agenda not just in 1945 and 1918, but as early as 1900—yet not in 1962. The problems that had motivated Julius Bachem and Adam Stegerwald, while not yet pressing or even realistically solvable at the turn of the century, were genuine nonetheless. But whereas Bachem's initiative seemed premature, Adenauer's seemed anachronistic.

The flashes of apocalyptic rhetoric that accompanied the prolonged coalitional crisis of 1961–1962—the fears that Bonn might be Weimar after all—reappeared late in 1966 after a mild encounter with another spectre of Weimar: economic recession. The result, endorsed by the CDU's ninety-one-year-old honorary chairman in the last year of his life, was finally a Grand Coalition (without Erhard). But no change in the election law ensued: the constitutional "gap" persisted, and the FDP remained a player.[22] Indeed, the federal Grand Coalition seemed to feed the growth of extremist movements on both the left and the right, just as its opponents of the 1940s had predicted. The lesson was not lost on the major parties, which have not, to date, repeated the experiment.

The trend already visible on the state level—the swing to coalitions of SPD and FDP—now reached the federal level. In March 1969 (six months before Helene Wessel's death) the two parties elected Heinemann to the presidency. After parliamentary elections in the fall, they formed the first federal Social-Liberal coalition. In 1972, the SPD passed the CDU/CSU in percentage of the vote, and Social-Liberal governments eventually remained in power for nearly as long as had Adenauer himself.

Both Bismarck and Adenauer were dominating figures. Both worked within constitutional regimes they had done their best to tailor to themselves. Both revitalized the conservatism of their time. And both managed to avoid unwanted Social Democratic interference. Yet in the end Adenauer's conservative democracy was more equilibrated and flexible than Bismarck's conservative authoritarianism. As a result, it could survive and even outgrow its founder in a way that Bismarck's system could not: it could be entrusted to the opposition.

While the SPD's grim twelve-year exile under Bismarck fanned the party's élan, its milder yet longer exile under Adenauer only fanned the party's frustration, making leaders like Herbert Wehner hungry to participate. If there is a parallel to Wehner in the Kaiserreich, it is certainly not the SPD's defiant leader, August Bebel, but the hungry leader of the other pariah party, the Center's Ernst Lieber. Yet Lieber, however pivotal his party, could never become a welcome figure in polite society (as the former Centrist Adenauer well knew), and the Center, right up to the wartime crisis of 1917, could never participate directly in government; whereas Wehner in 1969 saw his party come smoothly into power, pursuing its own policy initiatives free of Christian Democratic oversight, with Wehner himself the floor leader of a parliamentary majority and his protégé Brandt as Chancellor. In the end, Bismarck departed while advocating a coup against his own system in order to keep the SPD out; Adenauer departed while seeking the least disruptive way to bring the SPD in. That his efforts were superfluous is only further testimony to the fundamental healthiness of the system Adenauer had done so much to fashion.

Abbreviations

Parties and Institutions

BdD	Bund der Deutschen (League of Germans)
BdL	Bund der Landwirte (Farmers' League)
BHE	Block der Heimatvertriebenen und Entrechteten (League of Expellees and Dispossessed)
BP	Bayerische Partei (Bavarian Party)
BVP	Bayerische Volkspartei (Bavarian People's Party)
CDP	Christlich-Demokratische Partei (Christian Democratic Party)
CDU	Christlich-Demokratische Union (Christian Democratic Union)
CNVP	Christlich-Nationale Volkspartei (Christian National People's Party)
CSU	Christlich-Soziale Union (Christian Social Union)
CSVD	Christlich-Sozialer Volksdienst (Christian Social People's Service)
CVD	Christlicher Volksdienst (Christian People's Service)
DDGB	Deutsch-Demokratischer Gewerkschaftsbund (German Democratic Labor Federation)
DDP	Deutsche Demokratische Partei (German Democratic Party)
DGB	Deutscher Gewerkschaftsbund (German Labor Federation)
DHV	Deutschnationaler Handlungsgehilfen-Verband (German National Association of Commercial Employees)
DNVP	Deutschnationale Volkspartei (German National People's Party)
DP	Deutsche Partei (German Party)
DVP	Deutsche Volkspartei (German People's Party)
EDC	European Defense Community

EV	Evangelische Volksgemeinschaft (Protestant People's Community)
FDP	Freie Demokratische Partei (Free Democratic Party)
FEC	Frankfurt Economic Council
GVP	Gesamtdeutsche Volkspartei (All-German People's Party)
JDO	Jungdeutscher Orden (Young German Order)
KAV	Katholische Arbeitervereine (Catholic Labor Leagues)
KPD	Kommunistische Partei Deutschlands (Communist Party of Germany)
LDP	Liberale Demokratische Partei (Liberal Democratic Party)
MRP	Mouvement Républicain Populaire (Popular Republican Movement)
MSPD	Majority Socialists
NSDAP	Nationalsozialistische Deutsche Arbeiterpartei (National Socialist German Workers'—Nazi—Party)
RA	Republikanische Arbeitsgemeinschaft (Republican Working Group)
SED	Sozialistische Einheitspartei Deutschlands (Socialist Unity Party of Germany)
SPD	Sozialdemokratische Partei Deutschlands (Social Democratic Party of Germany)
UdM	Union der Mitte (Union of the Middle)
USPD	Unabhängige Sozialdemokratische Partei Deutschlands (Independent Social Democratic Party of Germany)
WAV	Wirtschaftliche Aufbau-Vereinigung (Union of Economic Construction)
WDR	Westdeutsche Rundfunk (West German Radio)

Archives, Archival Sources, Printed Sources

ACDPStA	Archiv für Christlich-Demokratische Politik, St. Augustin
AHR	American Historical Review
ARK	Akten der Reichskanzlei, BAK, R43/I
AS	Adam Stegerwald papers, ACDPStA, I-206
BAK	Bundesarchiv Koblenz
BRZ	*Bericht über die Verhandlungen des Parteitages der Rheinischen Zentrumspartei in Köln, 15.–18. September 1919* (Cologne, 1919)
BS	Bruno Six papers, HStAD, RWN-75
BT	*Berliner Tageblatt*
CB	Carl Bachem papers, HAStK, 1006
CDU-LVR	CDU Landesverband Rheinland, HStAD, RWV-26

CEH	*Central European History*
CT	Christine Teusch papers, HAStK, 1187
DR	*Die Deutsche Republik*
DS	Deutsche Sammlung, BAK, ZSg.1-E/127
FESB	Archiv der sozialen Demokratie, Friedrich Ebert Stiftung, Bonn
FZ	*Frankfurter Zeitung*
HAStK	Historisches Archiv der Stadt Köln
Hen	Walter Hensel papers, HStAD, RWN-88
HP	Hermann Pünder papers, BAK, 5
HPB	*Historisch-Politische Blätter*
HStAD	Hauptstaatsarchiv Düsseldorf
HW	Helene Wessel papers, FESB
JB	Johannes Brockmann papers, BAK, 240
JK	Jakob Kaiser papers, BAK, 18
KA	Konrad Adenauer papers, StBKAH
KA-CDU-BBZ	Helmut Pütz, ed. *Konrad Adenauer und die CDU der britischen Besatzungszone 1946–1949. Dokumente zur Grundgeschichte der CDU Deutschlands* (Bonn, 1975)
KBr	Klaus Brauda papers, HStAD, RWN-71
KBZ	Karl (Carl) Bachem, *Vorgeschichte, Geschichte und Politik der Deutschen Zentrumspartei,* nine volumes (Cologne, 1926–1932)
KS	Karl Spiecker papers, BAK, 147
KV	*Kölnische Volkszeitung*
KZ	*Kölnische Zeitung*
LS	Leo Schwering papers, HAStK, 1193
ME	Matthias Erzberger papers, BAK, 97
NRWStAM	Nordrhein-Westfälisches Staatsarchiv Münster
NWK	*Neue Westfälische Kurier*
OB	*Offizieller Bericht des 1. [2., 4., 5.] Reichsparteitages der Deutschen Zentrumspartei* (Berlin, 1920 [Berlin, 1922; Berlin, 1925; Trier, 1928])
PJ	Georg Schreiber, ed., *Politisches Jahrbuch 1925 [1926, 1927/28]. Politik des Deutschen Reiches* (Mönchengladbach, 1925 [1927; 1928])
PZ-1	Rudolf Morsey and Karsten Ruppert, eds. *Die Protokolle der Reichstagsfraktion der Deutschen Zentrumspartei 1920–1925* (Mainz, 1981)
PZ-2	Rudolf Morsey, ed. *Die Protokolle der Reichstagsfraktion und des Fraktionsvorstands der Deutschen Zentrumspartei 1926–1933* (Mainz, 1969)
RM	Richard Muckermann papers, HStAD, RWN-125

RMV	*Rhein-Mainische Volkszeitung*
RP	*Rheinische Post*
RRZ	*Rhein-Ruhr-Zeitung*
RTH	Rudolf ten Hompel papers, BAK
StBKAH	Archiv der Stiftung Bundeskanzler-Adenauer-Haus, Rhöndorf
VfZ	*Vierteljahrshefte für Zeitgeschichte*
VIZ	*Vertrauliche Information der Zentrumspartei*
WAZ	*Westdeutsche Arbeiter-Zeitung*
WH	Wilhelm Hamacher papers, HStAD, RWN-48
WM	Wilhelm Marx papers, HAStK, 1070
ZB	*Zentralblatt der Christlichen Gewerkschaften Deutschlands*
ZD	Zentrumspartei Depository, NRWStAM
ZS	*Der Zusammenschluss*

Notes

Introduction

1. The Italian Partito Popolare (PPI) arose only after World War I and was immediately challenged for its Catholic constituency by the Fascists: see John N. Molony, *The Emergence of Political Catholicism in Italy. Partito Popolare 1919–1926* (Totowa, 1977).

2. The regional peculiarities of the Bavarian issue are generally excluded from this study. See Klaus Schoenhoven, *Die Bayerische Volkspartei, 1924–1932* (Düsseldorf, 1972); Karl Schwend, "Die Bayerische Volkspartei," in Erich Matthias and Rudolf Morsey, eds., *Das Ende der Parteien 1933* (Düsseldorf, 1960); Alf Mintzel, *Die CSU: Anatomie einer konservativen Partei 1945–1972* (Opladen, 1975); Ilse Unger, *Die Bayernpartei: Geschichte und Struktur 1945–1957* (Stuttgart, 1979).

3. See Margaret L. Anderson, *Windthorst: A Political Biography* (Oxford, 1981).

4. Ibid., p. 249.

5. M. Rainer Lepsius, "Parteiensystem und Sozialstruktur: zum Problem der Demokratisierung der Deutschen Gesellschaft," in G. A. Ritter, ed., *Die Deutschen Parteien vor 1918* (Cologne, 1973), pp. 56–80.

6. On the Free Democratic liberal rump, see Chapters 8, 9, and 12, and the Epilogue of this volume.

7. For a few basic references and a brief discussion of the role of Nazism as a catalyst for integrative catch-all politics, see the introduction to Part IV, this volume.

8. On the systemic change from Weltanschauung parties to catch-all parties see Otto Kirchheimer, "The Transformation of Western European Party Systems," in J. LaPalombara and M. Weiner, eds., *Political Parties and Political Development* (Princeton, 1969); and Gordon Smith, "The German Volkspartei and the Career of the Catch-All Concept," in Herbert Döring and Gordon Smith, eds., *Party Government and Political Culture in Western Germany* (New York, 1982), pp. 59–76.

9. KA-02.03.

10. "Partei ohne Geschichte," WDR, March 3, 1964, LS-355.

I. The Center Party and Interdenominationalism in the Kaiserreich, 1870–1917

1. Margaret Anderson, "History in the Comic Mode: Jonathan Sperber's 1848," *CEH*, 25 (1992): 337.

1. The Enemy of the State

1. Ronald Ross, *Beleaguered Tower: The Dilemma of Political Catholicism in Wilhelmine Germany* (Notre Dame, 1976), pp. 1–15; Margaret Anderson, *Windthorst: A Political Biography* (Oxford, 1981), p. 45.
2. Rudolph Stadelmann, *Social and Political History of the German 1848 Revolution* (Athens, Ohio, 1975); William Langer, *Political and Social Upheaval 1832–1852* (New York, 1969); Jonathan Sperber, *Rhineland Radicals: The Democratic Movement and the Revolution of 1848–1849* (Princeton, 1991).
3. See George Windell, *The Catholics and German Unity 1866–1871* (Minneapolis, 1954), and Otto Pflanze, *Bismarck and the Development of Germany*, vol. 1, *The Period of Unification, 1815–1871* (Princeton, 1990).
4. Pflanze, *Bismarck*, p. 335.
5. See Lothar Gall, *Bismarck: The White Revolutionary* (London, 1986), vol. 2, pp. 12–20, and Karl Buchheim, "Die Frage nach der katholischen Partei," *Zeitschrift für Politik*, series 2, 10 (1963): 63–77.
6. Anderson, *Windthorst*; Wilfried Loth, *Katholiken im Kaiserreich* (Düsseldorf, 1984); Heinrich Bornkamm, "Die Staatsidee im Kulturkampf," *Historische Zeitschrift*, 170 (1950): 41–72, 273–306.
7. Anderson, *Windthorst*, pp. 146–200.
8. Ibid., pp. 217, 249, 374–375.
9. See Helmut Böhme, *Deutschlands Weg zur Grossmacht* (Cologne, 1966); and Gordon Craig, *Germany 1866–1945* (New York, 1978), pp. 140–144.
10. Anderson, *Windthorst*, pp. 187, 225.
11. Ibid., pp. 335–358; see also *KBZ-4*, pp. 148–217.
12. Anderson, *Windthorst*, pp. 280, 359–366.
13. But, this Catholic (Peter Wust) argued, the most significant strides came only as a result of World War I. Karl Hoeber, ed., *Die Rückkehr aus dem Exil: Dokumente der Beurteilung des deutschen Katholizismus der Gegenwart* (Düsseldorf, 1926).
14. See Anderson, *Windthorst*, p. 281.
15. See Craig, *Germany*, pp. 140–144, 157, 171–179.
16. Windthorst in his last years did explore the possibility of an accommo-

dation with Bismarck and even supported Caprivi's first army bill (but see Anderson, *Windthorst,* pp. 384–406).

17. *KBZ-5,* pp. 290–294; Rudolf Morsey, "Die Deutschen Katholiken und der Nationalstaat zwischen Kulturkampf und ersten Weltkrieg," *Historisches Jahrbuch,* 90 (1970): 49; John Zeender, *The German Center Party, 1890–1906* (Philadelphia, 1976), pp. 28–47; David Blackbourn, *Class, Religion and Local Politics in Wilhelmine Germany* (New Haven, 1980), pp. 44–48.

18. Morsey, "Deutschen Katholiken," pp. 31–64; Blackbourn, *Class,* pp. 50–52; Eckart Kehr, *Battleship Building and Party Politics in Germany, 1894–1901* (Chicago, 1975); Hans-Ulrich Wehler, *The German Empire, 1871–1918* (Dover, N.H., 1985); compare Geoff Eley, "Sammlungspolitik, Social Imperialism and the Navy Law of 1898," *Militärgeschichtliche Mitteilungen,* 15 (1974).

2. Labor, Party, and Zentrumsstreit

1. *KV,* no. 665, August 13, 1905.
2. Rhenanus (pseudonym for Heinrich Brauns), *Christliche Gewerkschaften oder Fachabteilungen in katholischen Arbeitervereinen?* (Cologne, 1904), p. 11.
3. J. Carbonarius (pseudonym for Jakob Treitz), *Kann und darf ich für eine Arbeiter-Bewegung auf katholischer Grundlage eintreten?* (Trier, 1904), p. 25.
4. Eric Brose, *Christian Labor and the Politics of Frustration in Imperial Germany* (Washington, 1985); Michael Schneider, *Die christlichen Gewerkschaften 1894–1933* (Bonn, 1982); Horstwalter Heitzer, *Der Volksverein für das katholische Deutschland im Kaiserreich* (Mainz, 1979); F. J. Stegmann, "Geschichte der sozialen Ideen im deutschen Katholizismus," in Helga Grebing, ed., *Geschichte der sozialen Ideen in Deutschland* (Munich, 1969), pp. 325–560; Wilhelm Spael, *Das katholische Deutschland im 20. Jahrhundert* (Würzburg, 1964); Emil Ritter, *Die katholisch-soziale Bewegung und der Volksverein* (Cologne, 1954); Oswald Wachtling, *Joseph Joos* (Mainz, 1974); Joos, *Die KAB in der Geschichte der christlichen Arbeiterbewegung Deutschland* (Cologne, 1963); Joos, *Am Räderwerk der Zeit* (Augsburg, 1951).
5. Giesberts, *Die christlichen Gewerkschaften in der Arbeiterbewegung, der Volkswirtschaft und im öffentlichen Leben* (Cologne, 1907), p. 35.
6. Brose, *Christian Labor,* pp. 159–232; David Blackbourn, *Class, Religion, and Local Politics in Wilhelmine Germany* (New Haven, 1980), pp. 52–53; Klaus Epstein, *Matthias Erzberger and the Dilemma of German Democracy* (Princeton, 1959), pp. 52–72; John Zeender, *The German Center Party, 1890–1906* (Philadelphia, 1976), pp. 104–114;

George Crothers, *The German Elections of 1907* (New York, 1941); *KBZ-6; KBZ-7.*

7. Giesberts, *Christlichen Gewerkschaften,* p. 35; Brose, *Christian Labor,* pp. 195–200, 209, 219–220, 230–231; Martin Spahn, *Das Deutsche Zentrum* (Mainz, 1906).

8. Brose, *Christian Labor,* chap. 5; *Germania,* no. 106, May 10, 1902; Carbonarius (Treitz), *Arbeiter-Bewegung,* pp. 51–63; Heinrich Pesch, *Ein Wort zum Frieden in der Gewerkschaftsfrage* (Trier, 1908), p. 45.

9. Carbonarius, *Arbeiter-Bewegung,* p. 23; Pesch, *Frieden,* p. 26.

10. Rhenanus, *Christliche Gewerkschaften,* pp. 8–11 (Ruhr), 15 ("possible"), 82 (windfalls); *KV,* no. 984 (quotation) and no. 1002, November 17 and 23, 1906; *Germania,* no. 106, May 10, 1902 (quoting union spokesman on separate factories); *KV,* no. 363, April 23, 1902 (hurting religion). By contrast, the Sitz Berlin organ *Der Arbeiter* reported that the pope had warned a Dutch cleric not to copy the German attempt "to withdraw the economic movement from the influence of the Church": *KV,* no. 111, February 8, 1906.

11. Text in August Erdmann, *Die christlichen Gewerkschaften, insbesondere ihr Verhältnis zu Zentrum und Kirche* (Stuttgart, 1914), pp. 154–159.

12. Stegerwald to Joos, November 10, 1912, speech draft, and Schulte-Stegerwald correspondence, AS-001/1; Brose, *Christian Labor,* pp. 276–279, 318–321. Of 330,000 Christian trade unionists in 1914, roughly 270,000 were Catholics. Membership in the craft associations was 120,000. Another 800,000 Catholics belonged to Social Democratic unions. Ronald Ross, *Beleaguered Tower: The Dilemma of Political Catholicism in Wilhelmine Germany* (Notre Dame, 1976), pp. 87, 94, 162. Karl Buchheim states, and William Patch implies, that *Singulari quadam* forced union opponents to stop their attacks: Buchheim, *Geschichte der christlichen Parteien in Deutschland* (Munich, 1953), p. 320; Patch, *Christian Trade Unions in the Weimar Republic, 1918–1933* (New Haven, 1985), p. 23. But on December 1, Kopp wrote Schulte and again attacked the unions. His letter was made public in early 1914, and the dispute flared again. The formal truce in the trade union controversy came only in 1919.

13. See Joos, *KAB,* p. 57; Joos, *Räderwerk,* pp. 60–61; Joos, "Die von unten kommen," WDR, November 13, 1963, Cologne University Library, pp. 11, 14–15.

14. See Stegerwald's own statements in this regard: Erich Kosthorst, *Jakob Kaiser: Der Arbeiterführer* (Stuttgart, 1967), p. 43; Stegerwald, *25 Jahre christliche Gewerkschaftsbewegung* (Berlin, 1924).

15. Ernst Deuerlein, "Verlauf und Ergebnis des Zentrumsstreits," *Stimmen der Zeit,* 156 (1955): 108–110; Ross, *Tower,* pp. 23–32.

16. Julius Bachem, "Wir müssen aus dem Turm heraus!" *HPB,* 137 (1906): 376–386.

17. After the colonial scandal, Bachem even stated that the "education of Catholics" into national participation would be remembered as "the most important and most difficult colonial and world-political act achieved by German politics": *KV,* no. 436, May 19, 1907, reprinted in H. M. Krueckemeyer, *Zentrum und Katholizismus* (Amsterdam, 1913), p. 109.

18. *Westdeutsche Volkszeitung,* no. 212, September 14, 1907 (CB-277). Even Bachem's associate Karl Trimborn commented as late as 1921 that "every Catholic belongs to the Center from the moment of his christening." Rudolf Morsey, *Die Deutsche Zentrumspartei 1917–1923* (Düsseldorf, 1966), p. 48.

19. Hermann Roeren, *Zentrum und Kölner Richtung* (Trier, 1913), pp. 40–41.

20. Julius Bachem, *Das Zentrum, wie es war, ist und bleibt* (Cologne, 1913), pp. 28–29 (quoting Reichstag deputy, 1909); *KV,* no. 928, October 30, 1906.

21. Details in Noel D. Cary, "Political Catholicism and the Reform of the German Party System" (Ph.D. diss., University of California, Berkeley, 1988), section 2.3.

22. Spahn praised the Center's evolution away from what he termed its antinational and confessional course during the Kulturkampf, a characterization too extreme for Bachem. See Spahn, *Zentrum; Hochland,* 4/2 (1907): 221–229 (Hertling), 461–465 (Bachem), 465–466 (Hertling); *Hochland,* 8 (1911): 416–430 (Spahn). However, the *KV* was not loathe to say, "The prerequisite to the realization of all Centrist demands would be a broader [*allgemeineres*] Center, as the originators of the slogan 'Get Out of the Tower!' clearly had in mind." *KV,* no. 628, July 22, 1907.

23. CB-284a.

24. Karl Hoeber, *Der Streit um den Zentrumscharakter* (Cologne, 1912), p. 50 ("private"); Krueckemeyer, *Zentrum,* p. 173 (forty years); *KV,* nos. 636 ("Windthorst," "completely new"), 639 ("old"), July 30, 31, 1909; Deuerlein, "Verlauf," p. 120 (quoting Roeren).

25. *KBZ-7,* pp. 237–245; Edmund Schopen, *"Köln": Eine innere Gefahr für den Katholizismus* (Berlin, 1910).

26. Quoted by Heinz Brauweiler, "Der Kern und die Bedeutung des Zentrumsstreits," *Hochland,* 11 (1914): 86.

27. See *KV,* no. 436, May 19, 1907; *Hochland,* 4/2 (1907): 221–229, 461–466; Hoeber, *Streit,* pp. 23, 59, 71; and the title of Bachem's final pamphlet, *Das Zentrum, wie es war, ist, und bleibt* (Cologne, 1913).

28. Roeren, *Zentrum,* pp. 5–8, 26–28, 35, 56–73; also Krueckemeyer, *Zentrum,* p. 157: "A Christian Weltanschauung as you [Cologne] want,

there is not." To illustrate how the meaning of the programmatic points in party platforms depended on Weltanschauung, Roeren noted (pp. 44–45) that "religious freedom" to the National Liberals meant freeing Catholics from the pope in Rome via the May Laws.

29. *KBZ-7*, pp. 230–231. See also Carl Bachem, *Zentrum, katholische Weltanschauung und praktische Politik* (Krefeld, 1914), esp. pp. 8–13.

30. J. Bachem, *Zentrum*, pp. 40–41, 46 (creed); J. Bachem in *KV*, no. 280, April 3, 1906 ("justice") and in *Hochland*, 4/2 (1907): 463 (neglected tradition, "defame"); *KV*, no. 454, May 26, 1907.

31. Compare Buchheim, *Christlichen Parteien*, p. 315, and Deuerlein, "Verlauf," pp. 103–105, with Zeender, "German Catholics and the Concept of an Interconfessional Party," *Journal of Central European Affairs*, 23 (1964): 424–439, and Ross, *Tower*, pp. 34–39. The third view is that of Brose, *Christian Labor*, pp. 203–209. See the historiographical discussion in Cary, "Political Catholicism," prologue and section 2.4; also Margaret Anderson, "Interdenominationalism, Clericalism, Pluralism: The Zentrumsstreit and the Dilemma of Catholicism in Wilhelmine Germany," *CEH*, 21 (December 1988): 350–378.

32. Hence Hoeber's list of explanations for the timing of the tower article: *Streit*, pp. 9–16.

33. Brose tells this story, seemingly without grasping its significance: *Christian Labor*, p. 219.

34. Easter Tuesday minutes, CB-284a (see also *KBZ-7*, p. 207); Krueckemeyer, *Zentrum*, p. 155; C. Bachem, *Zentrum*, p. 19. However, the Easter Tuesday program did include a provision to rein in the Volksverein.

35. *KBZ-7*, pp. 165–168. The contrast may be compared to that between some black power advocates and mainstream integrationists within the American civil rights movement in the late 1960s.

36. J. Bachem, "Nochmals: Wir müssen aus dem Turm heraus!" *HPB*, 137 (1906): 503–513.

37. Ibid. This puts a very different light on the rhetorical significance of the sequel article, which Brose remarks "went no farther" than the original (*Christian Labor*, p. 205).

38. Krueckemeyer, "Müssen wir aus dem Turm heraus?" *HPB*, 137 (1906): 686; *Germania*, nos. 59 (quotations), 75, 84, March 14, April 1, April 12, 1906.

39. *Germania*, nos. 59 ("desire," "isolation"), 75, 84 ("academic"), March 14, April 1, April 12, 1906.

40. Compare Ross, *Tower*, especially pp. 34–39.

41. *Germania*, no. 84, April 12, 1906; Roeren, *Veränderte Lage des Zentrumsstreits* (Trier, 1914), pp. 60–63; also Krueckemeyer, "Der Streit um den Zentrumscharakter," *HPB*, 150 (1912): 70–73 ("the

tower article had absolutely nothing to do" with these "undoubtedly correct" tactics).

42. *KV*, no. 617, July 19, 1906.

43. By 1914, 270,000 Catholics belonged to Christian trade unions, while 800,000 belonged to Social Democratic unions. The Rhenish SPD gained 84,000 votes in 1912 over 1907, while the Center gained only 14,000. Ross, *Tower*, pp. 87, 94, 162. Notoriously stable, the Center held 73 of the 104 Reichstag districts that never changed hands between 1874 and 1912. Thus, its loss of 14 seats in 1912—just under half its seats beyond the solid 73—was for it an unprecedented and staggering defeat.

44. The unions reluctantly approved the accord of 1912 out of fear of Social Democratic electoral gains and lack of an alternative. The resultant frustration set off a leftward drift in the unions on the eve of the war: see Brose, *Christian Labor*, chapter 11. Thus Brose's claim (p. 299) that the accord of 1912 was among the "crowning accomplishments of the politics of Christian labor" is a serious distortion.

45. See note 22.

46. WM-222, September 11, 1915.

47. CB-851; WM-222; Bachem to Prince Carl zu Löwenstein, February 18, 1922, in Hugo Stehkaemper, *Konrad Adenauer als Katholikentagspräsident 1922* (Mainz, 1977), p. 89.

48. CB-464, January 19, 1917.

49. CB-464, April 5, 1917.

50. See *KBZ*, Bachem's nine-volume history of the party.

3. Defeat, Revolution, Reorientation

1. Rudolf Morsey, *Die Deutsche Zentrumspartei 1917–1923* (Düsseldorf, 1966), pp. 66–68; Helga Grebing, *"Zentrum und katholische Arbeiterschaft 1918–1933"* (Ph.D. diss., Berlin, 1953), pp. 15–18.

2. *KV*, no. 525, July 6, 1918. The guidelines are summarized in Morsey, *Zentrum*, pp. 70–71.

3. Adam Stegerwald, *Arbeiterwähler und Zentrumspartei* (Krefeld, 1918), pp. 3–9. Similarly (September 29): the Center lacked a "coherent political manner of thinking." Quoted in *KV*, no. 771, September 30, 1918.

4. Stegerwald, *Arbeiterwähler*, pp. 17–25.

5. Ibid., pp. 40, 44–46.

6. Ibid., pp. 25–39. Founded by East Elbian grain magnates in the 1890s, the BdL was not just a lobby but a powerful electoral machine. See Hans-Jürgen Puhle, *Agrarische Interessenpolitik und Preussischer Konservatismus im Wilhelminischen Reich* (Hanover, 1966).

7. As Stegerwald later reiterated, "Equal suffrage in Prussia is coming because in this world-historical hour it is no longer to be held up. A con-

troversy over it in the Center party is a vain waste of energy." Quoted in *KV*, no. 771, September 30, 1918.

8. Finding his train from Cologne overcrowded, Brauns perched perilously in an open doorway. WM-49, p. 17; Brauns to Bertram Kastert, November 19, 1918, WM-222; Hubert Mockenhaupt, *Weg und Wirken des geistlichen Sozialpolitikers Heinrich Brauns* (Munich, 1977), p. 116; Klaus Epstein, *Matthias Erzberger and the Dilemma of German Democracy* (Princeton, 1959), pp. 257–283; Morsey, *Zentrum,* pp. 83–92, 105.

9. Brauns to Marx and Kastert, November 13, 1918, WM-222. Brauns's proposed program included heavy taxation of war profits, a democratic (but preferably monarchical) constitution, proportional representation, equal suffrage, women's suffrage, federal reform, absorption of German-speaking Austria, expanded social programs, and religious protections.

10. Indeed, Erzberger's recent musings to Munich Archbishop Michael von Faulhaber about a postwar "Catholic Renaissance" were hardly in keeping with the Christian trade unionists' hopes for interconfessional conciliation: "As an intellectual and spiritual power, Protestantism totally collapsed in the war; it accomplished nothing for the reconciliation of the nations; it died in its [four hundredth] anniversary year." ME-45, December 27, 1917.

11. CB-463, January 12, 1919, citing Heim, November 12, 1918; *KV,* nos. 898, 904 *("fusion"),* 912 ("shared"), November 14, 16, 19, 1918; Mockenhaupt, *Brauns,* p. 115 (quoting Marx); also WM-228 and Morsey, *Zentrum,* pp. 87–88, 99. In the end, the Center would be the only major non-Socialist party *not* to change its name.

12. *KV,* no. 909, November 18, 1918 (citing the left-liberal *Vossische Zeitung*); see also William Patch, *Christian Trade Unions in the Weimar Republic, 1918–1933* (New Haven, 1985), pp. 38–39. During the war, Meinecke, Stegerwald, and Gustav Bauer of the free unions had sponsored the People's League for Freedom and the Fatherland (Volksbund) to counter the Fatherland Party's annexationist agitation: Patch, pp. 28–29. Naumann, who had long advocated that liberalism meet the Social Democratic challenge by adopting a more religious and social bent, was a sympathetic figure to Stegerwald in much the way the conservative Adolf Stöcker had been.

13. *KV,* no. 904, November 16, 1918. Meanwhile, an undated memorandum to Erzberger suggested that the Center form a "cartel" with the merged liberal parties and the Austrian Christian Social party: ME-32a.

14. See Larry Eugene Jones, *German Liberalism and the Dissolution of the Weimar Party System, 1918–1933* (Chapel Hill, 1988), pp. 8–25. *KV,* no. 925, November 24, cited a report that Stegerwald and Giesberts had signed the proclamation of the DDP: Morsey, *Zentrum,* p. 102.

15. Julius Stocky (the *KV*'s printer) to Trimborn, October 12, 1918, CB-853; compare Marx (1935), WM-222, and *Für den Reichsgedanken: Historisch-politische Aufsätze 1915–1934: Festschrift für Martin Spahn zum 60. Geburtstag* (Berlin, 1936), p. 387. There is no record that Stegerwald showed interest in Stadtler's project.

16. See Becker to Stegerwald, November 19, 1918, WM-222.

17. Ibid. A veteran of the trade union controversy, Becker favored the subtitle "Free German People's Party" over "Christian People's Party": "experience shows that this word Christian would immediately give the Church hierarchy occasion again to mix into things that are none of its immediate business."

18. Contrast Morsey, *Zentrum*, p. 95, who argues that Stegerwald dropped the idea of a new party because his energies were absorbed in the union merger.

19. *KV*, nos. 915 and 917, November 20 and 21, 1918.

20. Fear of a "Farmers' Party" movement persisted one year later: *BRZ*, p. 273; *OB*-1, pp. 73–75.

21. *KV*, nos. 915 (Cologne draft) and 997, November 20 and December 20, 1918; *KV*, no. 4, January 2, 1919; Max Pfeiffer, *Zentrum und politische Neuordnung: Ein Programm* (Berlin, 1918); Morsey, *Zentrum*, pp. 128–132. Marx later commented that Hoffmann deserved thanks for having roused even the "most drowsy Catholics" (p. 113).

22. *KV*, nos. 4 and 25, January 2 and 10, 1919.

23. *KV*, no. 974, December 11, 1918; similarly no. 993, December 18.

24. Morsey, *Zentrum*, pp. 115–116, 135–136; *KV*, no. 6, January 3, 1919.

25. *KV*, no. 6, January 3, 1919.

26. *KV*, nos. 12, 32, 48 (election eve), January 5, 12, 18, 1919. *KV*, no. 48, called the revolution an act of treasonous partisanship.

27. *KV*, nos. 36, 42 (Schwering), 50 (League), January 14, 16, 18, 1919.

28. Bruno Gebhardt, *Handbuch der Deutschen Geschichte*, 9th ed., vol. 22 (Munich, 1982), pp. 390, 392; Morsey, *Zentrum*, pp. 145–147. *Germania*'s exaggerated claim of half a million Protestant votes apparently includes 240,000 votes accrued through a list arrangement with the Hanoverians: see Herbert Hömig, *Das Preussische Zentrum in der Weimarer Republik* (Mainz, 1979), p. 34.

29. See *KV*, no. 67, January 24, 1919.

30. *KV*, nos. 60, 64 ("taint"), 103 ("reservations"), January 22, 23, February 6, 1919. Provisional "black-red" coalitions had operated since November in Baden and Württemberg.

31. *KV*, no. 119, February 12, 1919.

32. *KV*, nos. 103, 105, 119, 153 ("all-or-nothing"), 162 ("chasm," "boundary"), 163, 193 *("Vernunftehe")*, February 6, 7, 12, 24, 27, 27, March 10, 1919. Trimborn later told the party's first national convention that

the coalition had forced the SPD temporarily to abandon the class struggle: *OB*-1, p. 7.

33. *BRZ,* pp. 71–76, 81–83; *OB*-1, pp. 19–20, 24–25, 29; Morsey, *Zentrum,* pp. 275–277.

34. Morsey, *Zentrum,* pp. 180–195, 208–219; Hömig, *Preussische Zentrum,* pp. 49–63; Günther Grünthal, *Reichsschulgesetz und Zentrumspartei in der Weimarer Republik* (Düsseldorf, 1968).

35. *BRZ,* pp. 45–48; *OB*-1, pp. 5–17. In another context, Joos later stated, "No German would ever forgive the German Catholics if the Reich were to fall apart because of them." Hugo Stehkämper, *Konrad Adenauer als Katholikentagspräsident 1922* (Mainz, 1977), p. 78.

36. *BRZ,* p. 149.

37. *OB*-1, pp. 8 (Trimborn), 26 (Wirth), 32 ("no ideal"); also *BRZ,* p. 45 (Trimborn: one had to avoid "the disastrous mistakes of the French Catholics" after 1870), and Morsey, *Zentrum,* p. 241 (Giesberts, July 1919: "It is not at all necessary to become a republican" in order to support the new regime).

38. *KV,* no. 57, January 21, 1920.

39. CB-850.

40. *BRZ,* pp. 66–67.

41. *KV,* no. 525, July 9, 1922.

42. For example, see *BRZ,* pp. 71–73 (Joos), 76, 113, 123; Morsey, *Zentrum,* p. 312 (Giesberts); *KV,* no. 119, February 12, 1919 (Bergmann, quoted earlier). Compare Generalsekretariat der Christliche Volkspartei, ed., *Die Christliche Volkspartei* (Koblenz, 1920), pp. 11–13 (complaints).

43. Worse yet, if the Center's obligation to facilitate a majority was a function not of shared values but of the need for order, then this Weltanschauung party might feel obligated to fill out a future majority for any party momentarily in ascendance, regardless of its values or its Weltanschauung. A policy intended to insure order could thus result in a blank check for those who prized order less than the Center did. The bill would be tendered a dozen years later, when the Weimar coalition would be spuriously used as a precedent for Nazi-Center coalitional negotiations (Chapter 6).

44. Teipel, *Krisis in der Zentrumspartei?* (Opladen, 1920), pp. 15–19, 28–31, 48 (WM-233).

45. Proclamation, Christliche Volkspartei, WM-233 and *KV,* no. 297, April 18, 1920.

46. CB-850.

47. CB-465, April 20, 1920.

48. WM-230, May 12 and May 20, 1919. Haecker publicly withdrew from the Center in June, saying that joining had been "a mistake": Gottfried

Mehnert, *Evangelische Kirche und Politik 1917–1919* (Düsseldorf, 1959), p. 171.

49. *BRZ*, pp. 83–85, 326–328; *OB-1*, pp. 75–76, 81–82. It was "a crime against our nation!" to "poison political life with confessional conflict" at such a critical juncture in the country's history; the same went for those who would "sift city and country, entrepreneur and worker as a matter of principle into different political parties." *OB-1*, pp. 75–76.

50. *OB-1*, pp. 75–76, 82; *BRZ*, pp. 85–86, 325–329, 380.

51. *OB-1*, p. 96; *KV*, no. 57, January 21, 1920.

52. *OB-1*, pp. 46–49.

53. *OB-1*, pp. 69–70.

54. *OB-1*, pp. 49–51.

55. *BRZ*, pp. 71–73 (Joos), 92–94 (Stegerwald). Compare Ellen Evans's claim that Stegerwald "obstinate[ly] reject[ed] any accommodation with the Social Democratic party." *AHR*, 90 (1985): 1220.

56. The distribution between SPD and Center of posts in the western provincial bureaucracies evoked considerable resentment at the Rhenish convention, avowedly because of its impact on the administration of cultural policy. But Stegerwald told the convention that the SPD, like the Center, had been barred from such posts under the old regime and had a right to call for them now. To insist that no predominantly Catholic region have a Social Democratic regional president would be to give the largest party none of the regional presidencies, a situation that one must understand would be intolerable. *BRZ*, pp. 91–92.

57. *OB-1*, p. 51. Stegerwald's use of the phrase "Christian People's Party" evoked the reformers' usage of 1918–1919 and predated the attempted cooptation of the phrase by the Rhenish secessionists mentioned earlier.

4. The Essen Program and Its Aftermath

1. Percentage of seats (not votes), 1920 (1919): DNVP, 15.5 (10.6); DVP, 14.2 (4.5); Center, 13.9 (21.6); separate BVP, 4.6 (—); DDP, 8.5 (17.8); SPD, 22.2 (38.7); USPD, 18.3 (5.2); Communist Party (KPD), 0.9 (—). The BVP's short-lived Rhenish ally drew 65,300 votes, or about 1.4 percent of non-Bavarian Centrist voters of 1919 (WM-233).

2. William Patch, *Christian Trade Unions in the Weimar Republic, 1918–1933* (New Haven, 1985), p. 58.

3. Lorenz Sedlmayr, "Her mit der christlich-nationalen Volkspartei!" ("Bring on the Christian National People's Party!") *Deutsche Arbeit*, 5, no. 4 (April 1920), pp. 137–142.

4. Oswald Wachtling, *Joseph Joos* (Mainz, 1974), p. 82.

5. AS-001/2-102 ("middle way," April 25, 1920), AS-001/2-104 ("bloc party," May 28), AS-001/2-106 ("foolish," May 31).

6. *PZ-1*, pp. 11–14 (June 23, 1920).

7. Larry Eugene Jones, "Adam Stegerwald und die Krise des Deutschen Parteiensystems," *VfZ*, 27 (1979): 11.

8. AS-001/2. The memorandum seems to have resulted from brainstorming by Stegerwald, Heinrich Brüning, Brauer, and Brauns. Brüning's later claim to authorship of the Essen speech (HP-613, November 14, 1945) may have been based on this memorandum. Leo Schwering, who was present at Essen, recalled that the self-educated Stegerwald often had an intellectual work up his ideas; if Brüning and Brauer formulated the speech, they got their instructions from Stegerwald: "Stegerwalds und Brünings Vorstellungen über Parteireform und Parteiensystem," in Ferdinand Hermes and Theodor Schieder, eds., *Staat, Wirtschaft und Politik in der Weimarer Republik: Festschrift für Heinrich Brüning* (Berlin, 1967), pp. 26–27. Brauns, whom Brüning consulted (Brüning, *Memoiren 1918–1934* [Stuttgart, 1970], pp. 70–71), told the cabinet on September 9 that new elections would produce a political realignment: Rudolf Morsey, *Die Deutsche Zentrumspartei 1917–1923* (Düsseldorf, 1966), p. 342. For Martin Spahn's role see Jones, "Stegerwald," pp. 13–14.

9. See Karl Hoeber, *Der Streit um den Zentrumscharakter* (Cologne, 1912), p. 23.

10. *PZ-1*, p. 56.

11. See Klaus Epstein, *Matthias Erzberger and the Dilemma of German Democracy* (Princeton, 1959), pp. 349–372.

12. *PZ-1*, pp. 49–56.

13. *PZ-1*, pp. 55–60. Erzberger's warning of a split was no empty threat. In the spring campaign, workers had carried Erzberger around on their shoulders: Morsey, *Zentrum*, p. 301. On October 31, Badenese party chairman Joseph Schofer worried that indiscretions in negotiations with Erzberger could lead to a Baden-Württemberg breakaway alongside the Bavarian breakaway ("a Neckar-line alongside the Main-line"): RTH-16, p. 90.

14. *PZ-1*, pp. 58–59.

15. Hans Goslar, quoted by Epstein, *Erzberger*, p. 339.

16. *PZ-1*, pp. 70–72. The "economic service" proposal would have been especially startling in light of Leon Trotsky's recent draconian proposal to militarize all industrial labor in revolutionary Russia.

17. In two pamphlets, Erzberger went beyond the Christian unions' traditional demand for dual direction by labor and management of industrial concerns *(Mitbestimmung)* and advocated that workers acquire fifty percent of a firm's stock through gradual purchases funded by half the firm's dividends beyond the first six percent. Epstein, *Erzberger*, pp. 374–378.

18. Pesch, *Liberalismus, Sozialismus und christliche Gesellschaftsordnung*

(Freiburg, 1896), and *Nicht kommunistischer, sondern christlicher Sozialismus! Die Volkswirtschaft der Zukunft* (published by the newly-founded, Erzberger-inspired party secretariat in Berlin, December, 1918); David Barclay, *Rudolf Wissell als Sozialpolitiker, 1890–1933* (Berlin, 1984), pp. 75–158; Gerald Feldman, *Iron and Steel in the German Inflation, 1916–1923* (Princeton, 1977), pp. 100–109.

19. *PZ-1*, pp. 71–72.
20. *PZ-1*, p. 66 (for Hitze's even stronger opposition to Erzberger see Epstein, *Erzberger*, p. 383); RTH-16, pp. 88–92, 110–111; Morsey, *Zentrum*, pp. 364–365.
21. RTH-16, pp. 95–98.
22. Ibid., pp. 99–100.
23. Ibid., pp. 101–105.
24. Ibid., pp. 105–106.
25. Compare Morsey, *Zentrum*, p. 367. Interestingly in light of later events (Chapter 5), Stegerwald's ally, Johannes Becker, asserted that a properly formulated program would find Wirth and Stegerwald in agreement: RTH-16, p. 116.
26. RTH-16, pp. 106–109. Intriguingly in light of events after 1945, the respected Centrist Georg Schreiber said that some kind of liberal bloc would remain even if the Brauns-Stegerwald project succeeded—a point Brauns conceded but discounted (pp. 112–113).
27. Ibid., p. 114.
28. Compare Morsey, *Zentrum*, pp. 368–369.
29. Stegerwald, *Deutsche Lebensfragen: Vortrag gehalten auf dem X. Kongress der christlichen Gewerkschaften Deutschlands am 21. November 1920 in Essen* (Berlin, 1921), pp. 3–24, 36. The French experience left Stegerwald unconvinced that social issues fared better in a centralized liberal democracy: "From time immemorial, plutocratic thinking ruled in France under the mask of the democratic." France was ruled by "bankers and pensioners who let others work for them" (p. 18).
30. Ibid., p. 15.
31. Ibid., pp. 38–42. Although postwar liberal historiography has echoed many elements of this diagnosis, Stegerwald's biting phraseology has caused confusion and controversy. Wachtling finds little difference between Stegerwald's "repeated attacks on the allegedly un-German 'formal democracy' imported from the West" and "comparable comments by prominent politicians of the 'national right'" (*Joos*, pp. 65–66); Ellen Evans even characterizes Stegerwald as "near-fascist": *AHR*, 90 (1985): 1220. Yet, despite his unfortunate predilection for phrases that were provocative when taken out of context, Stegerwald's consistent point was the need to stabilize democracy through integrative political institutions that would break subcultural and social barriers and engender a greater

sense of nationhood. Moreover, some of his socioeconomic proposals, such as a labor bank to fund a collective stock purchase plan that would guard against entrepreneurs reacquiring the shares during recessions, were not far from later proposals by Erzberger: Stegerwald, *Lebensfragen,* pp. 25, 33–38, and note 17 above. Compare Rudolf Uertz, *Christentum und Sozialismus in der frühen CDU* (Stuttgart, 1981), pp. 138–140, where he deems the Essen speech "a downright classic" expression of "solidarism in the sense of Heinrich Pesch," with Epstein, *Erzberger,* pp. 373–378, where Epstein ties Erzberger to Pesch and deems Stegerwald the greatest opponent of Erzberger's conception. Stegerwald understood that a stable democratic order was impossible unless conservatives had a place in it. Although this insight led him to overestimate the readiness of the right to adjust, his agenda was not that of a fascist, but of a reform-minded conservative democrat.

32. Stegerwald, *Lebensfragen,* pp. 41–52.

33. Ibid., pp. 45–47, 50, 55–56, 59.

34. *KV,* nos. 912, 917, 920, November 22, 23, 24, 1920.

35. *KV,* no. 920, November 24, 1920.

36. *KV,* no. 920, November 24, 1920 (citing, inter alia, *Dortmunder Tremonia,* no. 323, November 24); *KV,* no. 926, November 26 (citing, inter alia, *Badische Beobachter,* no. 271). *Tremonia* took refuge in the most time-tested formula for Centrist inertia: "we hold fast unswervingly to the old . . . Center"; it had "no need to be ashamed of its past"; its doors were open "to everyone who stands on the basis of the Christian *Weltanschauung*"; "it is an interconfessional party."

37. *Neue Preussische (Kreuz)Zeitung,* no. 554, November 25, 1920; *KZ,* no. 986, November 24; *FZ,* no. 869, November 24. Citing the *FZ* and a later reform proposal by Anton Erkelenz, William Patch sweepingly concludes that "the liberal press responded enthusiastically" to the Essen program: *Christian Trade Unions,* p. 68. But Erkelenz, a leader of the Hirsch-Duncker unions, was a special case whose views were not representative of DDP reaction; indeed, the *FZ* deemed Erkelenz's own reform proposal unrealistic (no. 504, July 10, 1921). Unlike Stegerwald, Erkelenz called for a straight merger of the Center, the BVP, the DVP, and the DDP to produce a party bonded not by the Christian *Weltanschauung* but by the fulfillment policy in foreign affairs.

38. *Rheinische Volkswacht,* no. 428, November 26, 1920, citing *Germania,* November 25; *KV,* no. 934, November 29, quoting Giesberts (but see also Patch, *Christian Trade Unions,* pp. 68–69).

39. *WAZ,* no. 49, December 4, 1920. Quotations from this article appeared in the *KV* immediately following the issue that reported on Giesberts: *KV,* no. 935, November 29.

40. *KV,* no. 959, December 7, 1920.

41. *KV,* no. 975, December 13, 1920.
42. Ibid. Stegerwald later said that Essen was not intended to aggrandize an existing party, whereas Julius Bachem's initiative resembled the DNVP's effort to attach a "Catholic committee" to itself: *Der Deutsche,* no. 130, June 9, 1922.
43. *KV,* no. 975, December 13, 1920. *Tremonia's* Lambert Lensing replied that these ideas "still" were "nothing new"; Centrists had "always . . . placed the Fatherland above the party"; it was "not we who had sharpened confessional antagonisms." Lensing's remarks were greeted with "applause and agreement." *KV,* no. 976, December 13.
44. Dated December 27, in *KV,* no. 1023, December 30, 1920.
45. Quoted in *Westdeutsche Landeszeitung,* no. 2, January 4, 1921 (AS-002/1-132).
46. *KV,* no. 26, January 11, 1921.
47. Ibid. Giesberts at that point abandoned ship. Expressing satisfaction with Trimborn's answer, he asserted that the interconfessional character of the Center was beyond doubt, and pronounced the question "completely settled": *KV,* no. 27, January 11, 1921. Centrist solidarity, he said, was pivotal to Germany's future: *KV,* no. 30, January 12.
48. *KV,* no. 30, January 12, 1921.
49. Brauns had told the cabinet that new elections would produce a political realignment (see note 8).
50. *KV,* no. 694, September 27, 1921.
51. Brüning to Stegerwald, August 4, 1921, AS-018/4.
52. Extensive documentation in AS-002/1, AS-002/2 (quotation: AS-002/3-258); see also Patch, *Christian Trade Unions,* pp. 70–71, and Herbert Hömig, *Das Preussische Zentrum in der Weimarer Republik* (Mainz, 1979), pp. 96–116.
53. Morsey, *Zentrum,* pp. 379–386; Hugo Stehkämper, "Konrad Adenauer und das Reichskanzleramt während der Weimarer Zeit," in Stehkämper, ed., *Konrad Adenauer: Oberbürgermeister von Köln* (Cologne, 1976), pp. 405–412, 427.
54. RTH-16, pp. 77–78 (June 29, 1921).
55. *Germania,* no. 686, November 8, 1921; see also Stegerwald to Joos, September 22, AS-018/4; *Der Deutsche,* no. 150, September 24 (AS-002/2-207).
56. That is, a democracy requires the support of, and gathering places for, both a viable right and a viable left. Compare Karl-Dietrich Bracher, *Die Auflösung der Weimarer Republik* (Düsseldorf, 1955), who deems the Weimar coalition the Republic's only hope, with Josef Becker, "Joseph Wirth und die Krise des Zentrums," *Zeitschrift für die Geschichte des Oberrheins,* 106 (1961): 361–479, who regrets left-Catholic undermining of the moderate-right alternative coalition he sees emerging in 1927–1928.

57. On June 29, 1921, Erzberger boasted to the Reich Party Committee: "[I] was the only one who preserved the Center during the revolution, when many were of the opinion that the Center must transform itself . . . [I] never proclaimed the slogan of founding a new party." RTH-16, pp. 69–70.

58. In that context, the Center's own coalitional flexibility was a sign not of boldness but of subcultural defensiveness (see Chapters 3 and 6). Ironically (and poignantly), this flexibility only further isolated the party: few others were consistently inclined to take responsibility when it could so readily be passed along to those they derided as Catholic opportunists.

59. Spahn, "Mein Wechsel der politischen Partei," *Das Neue Reich*, no. 8, November 20, 1921, pp. 136–139; Stegerwald in *Der Deutsche*, no. 136, September 8 (AS-002/2-197), and *BT*, September 8 (AS-002/2-192); see also AS-002/2-199; Patch, *Christian Trade Unions*, pp. 71–73; Wachtling, *Joos*, pp. 88–89; and later Spahn-Stegerwald polemics: AS-003/3-427, 431 (from 1926); AS-004/2-521 to 524 (from 1928).

60. Clippings in AS-002/3-258, 260.

61. AS-002/3-279.

62. *KV*, no. 584, July 30, 1922.

63. *Germania*, nos. 393 and 395, July 16 and 18, 1922.

64. The Center's Executive Board may never have approved the strong wording of the published resolution: Morsey, *Zentrum*, p. 474.

65. See Hugo Stehkämper, *Konrad Adenauer als Katholikentagspräsident 1922* (Mainz, 1977).

66. *KV*, no. 594, August 3, 1922.

67. Stegerwald, *Zusammenbruch und Wiederaufbau* (Berlin, 1922).

68. *KV*, nos. 622 (Marx) and 635 (Marx and Joos), August 13 and 18, 1922. Marx even said (no. 622) that the party would continue to represent the "Catholic Weltanschauung," and that any Protestant who was willing to defend denominational schools with "Catholic ardor" was welcome.

69. Morsey, *Zentrum*, p. 482; Wachtling, *Joas*, pp. 83–84 (epigraph to Part II, this volume).

5. Political Mavericks and Catholic Consciousness

1. Lewis Hertzman, *DNVP: Right-Wing Opposition in the Weimar Republic, 1918–1924* (Lincoln, 1963); Robert Grathwol, *Stresemann and the DNVP* (Lawrence, 1980).

2. Noel D. Cary, "The Making of the Reich President 1925: German Conservatism and the Nomination of Paul von Hindenburg," *CEH*, 23 (1990): 179–204.

3. *Kreuzzeitung*, no. 116, March 10, 1925; *Deutsche Tageszeitung*, nos.

116 and 117, March 10 and 11; *FZ*, nos. 181 and 182, March 9; *RMV*, March 10; *KV*, no. 183, March 10.

4. *Der Deutsche*, no. 23, January 27, 1924; Stegerwald, *Aus meinem Leben* (Berlin, 1924), pp. 15–17.

5. *KV*, no. 123, February 16, 1925 (see also *Germania*, March 1, 1925). There was a prodemocratic logic, then, to what Wirth called Stegerwald's "pendulum politics" of these years.

6. *PJ-1925*, p. 55.

7. Ellen Evans, *The German Center Party 1870–1933* (Carbondale, 1981), p. 295.

8. "Der Bürgerblock" (September 1924), in Wirth, *Unsere politische Linie im Deutschen Volksstaat: Gesammelte Reden und Schriften zur Deutschen Politik der Nachkriegszeit Nr. 1* (Berlin, 1924), pp. 85–86.

9. Wirth to Marx, August 21, 1925, WM-237.

10. Cary, "Reich President"; Herbert Hömig, *Das Preussische Zentrum in der Weimarer Republik* (Mainz, 1979), pp. 121–143; Jürgen Bach, *Franz von Papen in der Weimarer Republik: Aktivitäten in Politik und Presse 1918–1932* (Düsseldorf, 1977), pp. 62–96.

11. *KV*, nos. 147 and 148, February 25, 1925; Port, "Zweiparteiensystem und Zentrum," *Hochland*, 22/2 (1925): 369–377.

12. *Germania*, nos. 363 (Papen), 388 (Röder), 416 (Papen), August 6, 21, September 6, 1925; Röder, *Der Weg des Zentrums: Gesammelte Reden und Schriften zur Deutschen Politik der Nachkriegszeit Nr. 3* (Berlin, 1925); Bach, *Papen*, pp. 102–114.

13. Teipel, *Wir müssen aus dem Turm heraus! Gedanken zur Krise des Deutschen Parteiwesens* (Berlin, 1925), pp. 17–18.

14. Ibid., pp. 4–8, 31–32.

15. Ibid., pp. 18–22, 46–47.

16. Ibid., pp. 50–54. Hence, Teipel criticized the Essen program because its real goal was to foster the unity of the DGB, a goal for the sake of which none of the existing "bourgeois" parties could be interested in dissolving (p. 3).

17. Ibid., pp. 34–44.

18. Ibid., pp. 42–43.

19. Friedrich Dessauer to Wilhelm Marx, September 28, 1925 (also letters by Joseph Joos and Heinrich Vockel), WM-237.

20. *OB-4*, p. 37.

21. *OB-4*, pp. 31–48, 68–78, 84–85, 91–93, 114.

22. *Germania*, no. 305, July 5, 1926.

23. Ibid.; *Sächsische Volkszeitung*, December 22, 1925 (AS-003/2-394); *KZ*, September 7, 1926 (AS-003/3-415).

24. Marx memoir, WM-236; BAK-R45-II/3; *PJ-1926*, pp. 68, 78–81; Larry Eugene Jones, *German Liberalism and the Dissolution of the Weimar Party System, 1918–1933* (Chapel Hill, 1988), pp. 275–277.

25. *BT,* July 20, 1926; Wirth, ed., *Der Aufbruch: Republikanische Flugschriften* (Berlin, 1926), pp. 7–18.
26. *PJ-1926,* p. 81, and *ZS,* 1, no. 8, November 1926; *ZS,* 1, no. 5 (Thimme), August 1926; Wirth, ed., *Der Aufbruch,* p. 18; Dessauer, *idem,* p. 42. See also Heinz Blankenberg, *Politischer Katholizismus in Frankfurt am Main, 1918–1933* (Mainz, 1981), pp. 122, 161–162, and Bruno Lowitsch, *Der Kreis um die Rhein-Mainische Volkszeitung* (Frankfurt, 1980).
27. *DR,* 1, no. 1, October 28, 1926 (quotations); also Wirth, ed., *Der Aufbruch,* p. 49 (on Kulturpolitik), and *DR,* 1, no. 14, January 27, 1927 (on republican movement's primacy). In later refusing to vote with his party for Marx's Center-right government, Wirth reiterated: "I put the republican movement above the partisan." *DR,* 1, no. 16, February 9.
28. *Germania,* no. 510, November 2, 1926. Compare Joos's original trepidations about the Union: Blankenberg, *Frankfurt,* p. 161.
29. *DR,* 1, no. 8, December 16, 1926.
30. *DR,* 1, no. 9, December 23, 1926.
31. *DR,* 1, nos. 12–17, January 13–February 17, 1927; *PZ-2,* pp. 86–105; Marx memoir, *WM-236; PJ-1927/28; RMV,* nos. 32 and 34, February 9 and 11, 1927; Josef Becker, "Joseph Wirth und die Krise des Zentrums," *Zeitschrift für die Geschichte des Oberrheins,* 106 (1961): 373–377. According to William Patch, Stegerwald had urged Wirth to "sharpen the language" of his manifesto: *Christian Trade Unions in the Weimar Republic, 1918–1933* (New Haven, 1985), p. 115. Stegerwald publicly called for a Grand Coalition as late as January 4 (AS-004/1-445); he still expressed this preference even after the rightist government was formed (*DR,* 1, no. 16, February 10). Opposing Stegerwald, Brüning and Brauns worked for a Bürgerblock.
32. Becker, "Wirth," pp. 379–380 ("shoddy"); *DR,* 1, no. 30 ("higher unity"), May 19, 1927. Two-thirds of the German National deputies were absent during the vote to renew the Law for the Protection of the Republic: *BT,* no. 230, May 17, 1927.
33. *DR,* 1, nos. 31 (Teipel), 32 (dare), 33 (threat), May 26, June 2, 9, 1927.
34. *WM-265, WM-1059,* and Thomas Knapp, "Joseph Wirth and the Democratic Left in the German Center Party 1914–1928" (Ph.D. diss., Catholic University, 1967), pp. 174–180.
35. Evans, *Center,* pp. 236–240, 316–335.
36. *DR,* 1, no. 34, June 16, 1927; Lowitsch, *Kreis,* p. 55; Becker, "Wirth," pp. 391–392.
37. *Dortmunder Tremonia,* no. 227, August 20, 1927.
38. *DR,* 1, nos. 29 and 45, May 12 and September 2, 1927.
39. *KV,* no. 653, September 5, 1927, and Becker, "Wirth," pp. 392–394 (Kaas); *FZ,* no. 660, September 6 (Teipel); *BT,* September 10.

40. *DR*, 1, no. 11, January 6, 1927.
41. *BT*, no. 124, March 15, 1927.
42. Ibid.; *DR*, 1, nos. 21 *(Zweckgemeinschaften)* and 26 (presidential election), March 18 and April 21, 1927; *DR*, 2, no. 16, January 20, 1928 ("impossible").
43. *DR*, 2, nos. 4 ("Weimar front"), 5 ("Arbeitsgemeinschaften"), 9 ("misuse"), 18 ("Zentrumsstreit"), October 28, November 4, December 2, 1927, February 3, 1928; *DR*, 1, no. 38 (Teipel), July 15, 1927.
44. *DR*, 2, no. 21, February 24, 1928.
45. Imbusch to Marx, November 12, 1927, WM-241; Patch, *Christian Trade Unions*, pp. 119–122; Karsten Ruppert, *Im Dienst am Staat von Weimar: Das Zentrum als regierende Partei in der Weimarer Demokratie, 1923–1930* (Düsseldorf, 1992), pp. 274–287; Helmut Schorr, *Adam Stegerwald* (Recklinghausen, 1966), pp. 121–124.
46. Stegerwald, *Westfälisches Volksblatt*, no. 21, January 25, 1928 (AS-004/2-518).
47. Franz Focke, *Sozialismus aus christlicher Verantwortung: Die Idee eines christlichen Sozialismus in der katholisch-sozialen Bewegung und in der CDU* (Wuppertal, 1978), pp. 115–172; Evans, *Center*, pp. 337–339.
48. AS-004/1-488 (Catholic convocation); Schorr, *Stegerwald*, pp. 114–115 ("Christian politics," May 6, 1927); AS-003/3-431 (on Spahn). Of course, Stegerwald's support for Wirth's candidacy was not mere altruism. He did not want to lose pro-Wirth workers to the SPD or to see a splinter party or DDP candidacy for Wirth (broached in Marx's own Düsseldorf district: WM-236).
49. Patch, *Christian Trade Unions*, pp. 135–137.
50. AS-004/2-520–524 (March 4, 1928); Patch, *Christian Trade Unions*, p. 135 (July 2); AS-004/2-539 (September).
51. *DR*, 2, nos. 38 and 40, June 22 and July 6, 1928.
52. *DR*, 2, no. 48, August 31, 1928.
53. *Germania*, no. 108, March 4, 1928. Compare Wirth: "We must finally come to the clear relationship: here the government; there the opposition!" *Germania*, no. 152, March 30.
54. Joos, *Die politische Ideenwelt des Zentrums* (Karlsruhe, 1928), pp. 1, 35–38; *Germania*, June 10 (quotations).
55. WM-247 (Mönnig); *Der Deutsche*, December 10, 1928.
56. Mönnig to Marx, November 5, 1928, WM-247.
57. *Abendland*, no. 3, December, 1928 (Joos); *Germania*, no. 561A, December 3; *KV*, no. 875, December 4.
58. *OB-5*, pp. 8 (Austrian), 28 (political but Catholic), 34 (Baumhoff), 41 (Marx).
59. Jakob Kaiser, "Aufzeichnungen zur Wahl des 1. Vorsitzenden" (January 12, 1929), AS-005/1-606; *OB-5*, pp. 42–44; *KV*, no. 890, December 9,

1928; Marx memoir, WM-247; Patch, *Christian Trade Unions,*
pp. 138–139; Oswald Wachtling, *Joseph Joos* (Mainz, 1974), pp. 127–
132.

60. Stegerwald, *Zentrumspartei, Arbeiterschaft, Volk und Staat* (Berlin,
1928), p. 17.

61. *KV,* no. 907, December 15, 1928; similarly *Der Deutsche Weg* (coedited
by Joos), December 13.

62. *Mitteilungsblatt für die Mitglieder der "Politischen Vereinigung
Deutscher Katholiken"* 4 (October–December 1928), WM-235.

63. *KV,* no. 891, December 10, 1928.

64. *DR,* 3, nos. 12 and 13, December 21 and 28, 1928; Stegerwald,
Zentrumspartei, pp. 7–8.

65. *Deutsche Weg,* December 13, 1928; *KV,* nos. 894, 897, 910 (quotation),
December 11, 12, 17; *WAZ,* no. 52, December 29.

66. Patch, *Christian Trade Unions,* pp. 146–153.

67. Quoted by Patch, *Christian Trade Unions,* p. 141.

68. See Evans, *Center,* pp. 341–342.

69. *KV,* no. 926, December 23, 1928.

70. Beyond the *Manchester Guardian* affair, note especially the *Panzer-
kreuzer* affair of 1928–1929, when the SPD opposed construction of
battleships approved by its own Chancellor. For Wirth and Teipel's dismay, see *DR,* 3, nos. 19 and 30, February 8 and April 20, 1929.

71. Kaas to Richard Bornemann, February 8, 1929, WM-230.

6. The Fall of the Tower

1. See Noel D. Cary, "Political Catholicism and the Reform of the German
Party System, 1900–1957" (Ph.D. diss., University of California, Berkeley, 1988), pp. 143–145.

2. Eduard Stadtler in *Das Grossdeutsche Reich,* no. 50, December 3, 1928
(see epigraph to Part III of this volume).

3. Günter Opitz, *Der Christlich-Soziale Volksdienst: Versuch einer pro-
testantischen Partei in der Weimarer Republik* (Düsseldorf, 1969).

4. *ZS,* 1, no. 6, September 1926 (Bornemann); *DR,* 1, no. 40, July 29,
1927, and *FZ,* no. 660, September 6 (Teipel); Röder, *Der Weg des
Zentrums* (Berlin, 1925); *ZS,* 2, no. 4, July 1927 (Thimme).

5. WM-230; *ZS,* 2, no. 4, July 1927 (Thimme).

6. Opitz, *CSVD,* pp. 35–124.

7. WM-230; *ZS,* 2, no. 11, and *ZS,* 3, no. 2, February and May 1928
(Thimme).

8. *ZS,* 3, no. 3, June–July 1928; WM-230.

9. WM-230.

10. Ibid. Bornemann did get one concession: a committee would be set up to

discuss the confessional issue, and he would be allowed to suggest its Protestant members. There is no record that this committee ever convened.

11. Ellen Evans, *The German Center Party, 1870–1933* (Carbondale, 1981), pp. 351–354; Stewart Stehlin, *Weimar and the Vatican, 1919–1933* (Princeton, 1983), pp. 412–429.

12. Hajo Holborn, *A History of Modern Germany, 1840–1945* (New York, 1969), p. 669.

13. See Brüning to Stegerwald, August 4, 1921: the Essen goal of creating "a great national middle party . . . can only be realized by exploding the German National party. I'm working on this with all my strength." AS-018/4. Also see Erasmus Jonas, *Die Volkskonservativen 1928–1933* (Düsseldorf, 1965), and Treviranus, *Das Ende von Weimar: Heinrich Brüning und seine Zeit* (Düsseldorf, 1968).

14. Brüning seems to have told more to Hitler and Hugenberg than to his own party. See Brüning, *Memoiren 1918–1934* (Stuttgart, 1970), pp. 146–147, 191–197, 209–210, 372–378, 453–463, 511–513, 577–580. Though portions of Brüning's memoirs are of questionable authenticity, these themes are generally corroborated by Brüning's public comments after his fall—e.g., *KV*, nos. 208 and 289, July 31 and October 20, 1932—and by John Wheeler-Bennett, *Wooden Titan* (New York, 1936), a book based on information supplied by Brüning while he was a houseguest of the author after fleeing the Third Reich.

15. See Thomas Childers, *The Nazi Voter* (Chapel Hill, 1983).

16. After the election, former Chancellor Hans Luther, long an advocate of constitutional reform, said that the proper means would be via Grand Coalitions in both Prussia and the Reich. While this suggestion was by now impossible, this was not why Brüning rejected it. Rather, he believed it to be "a backward step, since I wanted to hold at any price to the principle of a government not bound by parties, in order to propel the evolution toward a . . . government in the sense of the Bismarckian constitution." Brüning, *Memoiren*, p. 290. Brüning also wrote that at the time of his original appointment, he refused an offer from Rudolf Breitscheid (SPD) to join his government (pp. 166–167). Whether true or not, the statement is revealing. Brüning was determined to defy inconvenient political realities and to proceed "at any price" along the course he had charted. One of those realities was his government's need for an organized base of mass support. In advancing party-system reform, Brüning claimed to understand this; in robbing it of its preconditions and bypassing the parties, he proved he did not.

17. Brüning, *Memoiren*, pp. 195–196, 375–376, 460–461, 504, 515, 568–570; *KV*, no. 184, July 4, 1932. Compare Stegerwald, AS-009/1-1017, December 8, 1931; also see William Patch, *Christian Trade Unions in*

the Weimar Republic, 1918–1933 (New Haven, 1985), pp. 205–206. In late 1931, Brüning, Kaas, and Stegerwald disingenuously denied Nazi-Center "coalition rumors" before their party's Reich Committee: *Rheinische Zeitung,* no. 265, November 6.

18. See Patch, *Christian Trade Unions,* pp. 159–187.

19. Brüning, *Memoiren,* pp. 379–385, 399–402, 446; *KV,* nos. 133, 150–152, 183, May 13, May 31–June 2, July 3, 1932; see also Detlef Junker, *Die Deutsche Zentrumspartei und Hitler 1932–1933* (Stuttgart, 1969), and Rudolf Morsey, *Der Untergang des politischen Katholizismus* (Stuttgart, 1977).

20. *KV,* nos. 151, 153, 159 (Joos), 181 (civil war), 199 (Joos), June 1, 3, 9, July 1, 22, 1932; on workers, *KV,* nos. 201, 202, 206, July 24, 25, 29; see also Joos to Franz von Galen, August 5, in Rudolf Morsey, "Die Deutsche Zentrumspartei," in Erich Matthias and Rudolf Morsey, eds., *Das Ende der Parteien 1933* (Düsseldorf, 1960), pp. 424–425.

21. *Nicht rückwärts—vorwärts! Rede des Prälaten Kaas M.d.R. (Trier)* (Berlin, 1931), ARK-2659.

22. *KV,* nos. 112 (Joos: "fever") and 152, April 22 and June 2, 1932.

23. The *FZ* endorsed the Center anyway. *KV,* nos. 129 (Joos), 176 (Protestant pro-Center appeal), 183 (State party again rejected, "Führer"), 199 (*FZ* endorsement), 203 (Hugenberg), May 9, June 26, July 3, 22, 26, 1932; Opitz, *CSVD,* pp. 243–286.

24. *KV,* no. 263, September 24, 1932 (Stegerwald); Junker, *Zentrum,* Morsey, *Untergang,* and *KV,* nos. 220–249, August 12–September 10 (Nazi-Center talks); *Das Zentrum,* 1–3, 1930–1932, and *KV,* nos. 113, 186, 200, 207, April 23, July 6, 23, 30, 1932 (Nazi Weltanschauung).

25. *Das Zentrum,* 2, no. 9/10/11, December 1931.

26. *KV,* nos. 220, 248 (Joos), 263, 280, August 12, September 9, 24, October 11, 1932.

27. *KV,* nos. 334, 340, 344, December 4, 10, 14, 1932; *KV,* nos. 24, 25, 29, 30, January 24, 25, 29, 30, 1933; Kaas to Schleicher, January 26, 1933, in Matthias and Morsey, *Ende,* pp. 428–429; Patch, *Christian Trade Unions,* pp. 212–216. Junker, *Zentrum,* argues that the "constitution party" should have approved Schleicher's request, since only an unconstitutional interlude could have stabilized or reformed the regime.

28. *KV,* nos. 31–34, 39 (Joos), January 31–February 3, 8, 1933; Morsey, "Hitlers Verhandlungen mit der Zentrumsführung am 31. Januar 1933," *VfZ,* 9 (1961): 183–194; Matthias and Morsey, *Ende,* pp. 339–345; Morsey, "The Center Party between the Fronts," in John Conway, trans., *The Path to Dictatorship, 1918–1933* (Garden City, 1966), pp. 77–78.

29. *KV,* no. 54, February 23, 1933.

30. Bachem memorandum, March 25, 1933, in Matthias and Morsey, *Ende,* pp. 431–432.

31. Documents in Matthias and Morsey, *Ende,* pp. 429–431.
32. Rudolf Morsey, *Das "Ermächtigungsgesetz" vom 24. März 1933* (Göttingen, 1968), pp. 27–30. Seven days later, however, Joos met with Papen and, according to Patch, agreed that Catholics "should avoid political uproar, because toppling the current government would most likely result in a Communist dictatorship." *Christian Trade Unions,* pp. 222–223.
33. "Hitler-Regierung und Zentrum," April 10, 1933, WM-231; Marx memoir, spring 1934, WM-228. Junker, *Zentrum,* examines the role of Leonine tradition in detail; Morsey, *Untergang,* rather tortuously rejects its relevance.
34. Brentano, "Was ich in Wirths Aufruf vermisse," in Wirth, ed., *Der Aufbruch: Republikanische Flugschriften* (Berlin, 1926), p. 49.
35. *KV,* nos. 98, 101 (Joos), 112, 115, April 11, 14, 26, 29, 1933. The *KV,* which underwent *Gleichschaltung* more slowly than *Germania,* is the more reliable barometer of the Center's desired public face.
36. *KV,* nos. 124 and 133, May 10 and 19, 1933; Bachem memorandum, July 7, in Matthias and Morsey, *Ende,* pp. 443–452.
37. *KV,* nos. 118, 123, 125, 128, 137, 141, 143, May 4, 9, 11, 14, 23, 27, 29, 1933 ("Selbstbesinnung"); *KV,* nos. 162, 164, 170, 173 (Goebbels), June 18, 20, 26, 29.
38. *KV,* nos. 179–184, 193, 196, July 5–10, 19, 22, 1933; Matthias and Morsey, *Ende,* pp. 398–411; Stehlin, *Weimar and Vatican,* pp. 431–447. For the controversy over the concordat's role, see John Jay Hughes, "The Reich Concordat of 1933: Capitulation or Compromise?" *Australian Journal of Politics and History,* 20 (1974): 164–175; Junker, *Zentrum;* Konrad Repgen, "Über die Entstehung des Reichskonkordats Offerte im Frühjahr 1933 und die Bedeutung des Reichskonkordats," *VfZ,* 25 (1978): 499–534; Klaus Scholder, *Die Kirchen und das Dritte Reich* (Berlin, 1977); Scholder, "Altes und neues zur Vorgeschichte des Reichskonkordats," *VfZ,* 25 (1978): 535–570; Ludwig Volk, *Das Reichskonkordat vom 20. Juli 1933* (Mainz, 1972). Scholder argues that even the vote for the Enabling Act was due to the Vatican's desire for a concordat.
39. John Conway, *The Nazi Persecution of the Churches, 1933–1945* (London, 1968); Ian Kershaw, *Popular Opinion and Political Dissent in the Third Reich* (Oxford, 1983); Guenter Lewy, *The Catholic Church and Nazi Germany* (New York, 1965); Scholder, *Kirchen.*
40. Compare Evans, *Center,* p. 400: "in spite of the interest shown among Catholics," interdenominational initiatives had failed because Protestants were not interested.
41. See Chapter 5, notes 30, 70. Wirth also delivered the government's response to the SPD's motion to override Brüning's decrees in July 1930,

the events that led to the Nazi breakthrough elections: *Stenographische Berichte des Deutschen Reichstages* 428, Fourth Reichstag, 204th session, July 18, 1930, pp. 6505–6508.

42. *Der Deutsche,* no. 55, March 5, 1933; *ZB,* 33, no. 7, April 1, 1933; and Chapter 7 of this volume.

43. *KV,* no. 184, July 4, 1932.

IV. Reshaping Party Politics, 1945–1957

1. Compare David Schoenbaum, *Hitler's Social Revolution* (New York, 1966), and Ralf Dahrendorf, *Society and Democracy in Germany* (New York, 1967), with Tim Mason, "The Workers' Opposition in Nazi Germany," *History Workshop,* 11 (1981): 120–137; David Welch, ed., *Nazi Propaganda* (London, 1983); Ian Kershaw, *Popular Opinion and Political Dissent in the Third Reich* (Oxford, 1983); Detlev Peukert, *Inside Nazi Germany* (New Haven, 1987).

2. Local religious tensions in the decade after the war are just beginning to be studied. See Karen Gatz, "East Prussian and Sudeten German Expellees in West Germany, 1945–1960: A Comparison of their Social and Cultural Integration" (Ph.D. diss., Indiana University, 1989). The League of Expellees and Dispossessed (BHE), a mostly Protestant refugee party of the 1950s, had no explicit religious orientation. In contrast to the CDU, "the BHE was *par excellence* the party of non-integration": Gordon Smith, *Democracy in Western Germany,* 3rd ed. (New York, 1986), p. 111. See Stephen Fisher, *Minor Parties of the Federal Republic of Germany* (Hague, 1974), pp. 94–107, and Franz Neumann, *Der Block der Heimatvertriebenen und Entrechteten 1950–1960* (Meisenheim am Glan, 1968).

3. The British, for example, at first favored a reemergence of the Center party over some kind of new Christian party (see Chapter 7), and rumors that they had favored a Labour-style party at the expense of both the SPD and CDU were still making the rounds in the 1950s. Even the Soviets influenced but did not originally determine the form taken by the non-Marxist parties they tolerated.

4. According to the Nazi definition, "resistance" included both active anti-Nazi conspiracy and membership in adjunct discussion circles on postwar institutions.

5. See Henry Krisch, *German Politics under Soviet Occupation* (New York, 1974).

6. Peter Hoffmann, *The History of the German Resistance 1933–1945* (Cambridge, 1977); Hans Mommsen, "Social Views and Constitutional Plans of the Resistance," in Hermann Graml et al., *The German Resistance to Hitler* (Berkeley, 1970).

7. Kershaw, *Popular Opinion,* pp. 156–223, 331–357. But see also Shelley Baranowski, *The Confessing Church, Conservative Elites, and the Nazi State* (Lewiston, 1986), and Victoria Barnett, *For the Soul of the People: Protestant Protest against Hitler* (New York, 1992).

8. See Elfriede Nebgen, *Jakob Kaiser: Der Widerstandskämpfer* (Stuttgart, 1967), and Werner Conze, *Jakob Kaiser: Politiker zwischen Ost und West, 1945–1949* (Stuttgart, 1969).

9. LS-540 (Schwering diary), September 4, 1945; LS-544 (Rudolf Heinen), August 26, 1947; *Aachener Volkszeitung,* no. 25, March 29, 1947 (Schwering); Schwering, *Frühgeschichte der Christlich-Demokratischen Union* (Recklinghausen, 1963), p. 135; WH-7 (Heinrich Strunk), November 21, 1945; KA-07.20 (Heinen to Adenauer), October 12, 1948; CT-30 (H. W. Zech-Nenntwich to Adenauer), January 13, 1950.

7. Catholics at the Zero Hour

1. Hofmann (1962), based on notes from 1945, LS-342.2.

2. See Werner Conze, *Jakob Kaiser: Politiker zwischen Ost und West, 1945–1949* (Stuttgart, 1969), pp. 10–25.

3. "CDUD-Sondermaterial," KA-08.54/1.

4. Ibid.; similarly LS-361.1 (Hermes, July 22).

5. Conze, *Kaiser,* pp. 25, 45–57. Kaiser too refused to endorse the reform, but since the decision predated his chairmanship, the Soviets, wishing to avoid conflict with a labor figure, did not discipline him (though they forbade further agitation).

6. Hamacher, "Zur Geschichte der Wiederbegründung des Zentrums," WH-7; Hamacher-Brockmann correspondence, November 1945, JB-1.

7. WM-250.

8. "CDUD-Agitationsmaterial, Folge X," KA-08.56/1.

9. AS-011/3-1211.

10. Helmut Schorr, *Adam Stegerwald* (Recklinghausen, 1966), pp. 287, 292; Alf Mintzel, "The Christian Social Union in Bavaria: Analytical Notes on Its Development, Role, and Political Success," in Max Kaase and Klaus von Beyme, eds., *German Political Studies 3: Elections and Parties* (Beverly Hills, 1978), pp. 193–194, 201–203.

11. Stegerwald, *"Wo stehen wir?"* and *"Wohin gehen wir?"* (Würzburg, 1945); see also AS-011/3-1209, 1235.

12. Stegerwald, *Gehen,* pp. 49–54; similarly 61: "Protestant adherents are not an appendage, but full members of the Christian Social Union, which is a new party and not, perchance, a continuation of the earlier Center party."

13. Schorr, *Stegerwald,* p. 296 (Severing); Stegerwald, *Deutsche Lebens-*

fragen (Berlin, 1921), pp. 39–40; AS-021 ("force," September 15); Stegerwald, *Gehen*, pp. 7–8 ("dilettantism").

14. Communication from Engelbert Hommel (StBKAH). A draft neo-Centrist leaflet (1946) stated that Thomas Esser possessed a copy of such a letter (1943): JB-5.

15. Ellen Evans, *AHR*, 90 (1985): 1220.

16. *Der Deutsche*, no. 55, March 5, 1933 ("civilized"); *ZB*, 33 no. 7, April 1, 1933, pp. 73, 83–84.

17. Quoted in Schorr, *Stegerwald*, p. 264.

18. Several letters from 1938 and 1941 to Nazi officials on the pension matter are in AS-018/3. According to an official notation dated November 21, 1941, Hitler personally decided to maintain Stegerwald's pension at the disputed low level.

19. See Rudolf Morsey, "Adenauer und Nazismus," in Hugo Stehkämpfer, ed., *Konrad Adenauer: Oberbürgermeister von Köln* (Cologne, 1976), pp. 460–468.

20. *Der Deutsche*, no. 55, March 5, 1933; Stegerwald to Hackelsberger, July 14, AS-014/1-22.

21. Peter Hoffmann, *The History of the German Resistance 1933–1945* (Cambridge, 1977), p. 368 (cabinet list); Elfriede Nebgen, *Jakob Kaiser: Der Widerstandskämpfer* (Stuttgart, 1967), pp. 33–34, 41; Schorr, *Stegerwald*, pp. 266–280; AS-011/2-1199.

22. Stegerwald, *Stehen*, pp. 8–12.

23. Stegerwald, *Gehen*, pp. 36–37, 27.

24. *Das Deutsche Volk*, no. 41, December 12, 1926.

25. Stegerwald, *Stehen*, p. 24. "What is democracy? First, a few words about what democracy is not. Democracy is not what we did in Germany after the First World War," when proportional representation, the list system, the persistence of old power bastions, and the lack of social consciousness produced no change beyond "the nomination of candidates by thirty to forty parties and the rise of profiteer gangs instead of political parties." *Stehen*, p. 22.

26. Stegerwald, *Gehen*, pp. 8–9, 18; *Stehen*, pp. 25–27.

27. Stegerwald, *Stehen*, pp. 15–18; *Gehen*, pp. 37–38, 46–48, 54–55, 65.

28. Rudolf Uertz, *Christentum und Sozialismus in der frühen CDU* (Stuttgart, 1981), pp. 32–33, 65.

29. For Bavarian developments after Stegerwald's death see Alf Mintzel, *Die CSU: Anatomie einer konservativen Partei 1945–1972* (Opladen, 1975), and Ilse Unger, *Die Bayernpartei: Geschichte und Struktur 1945–1957* (Stuttgart, 1979).

30. Detlev Hüwel, *Karl Arnold* (Wuppertal, 1980), p. 55; Uertz, *Christentum*, pp. 23–24.

31. Schwering, notes from 1945, LS-342.1, LS-342.6, LS-342.7 (1958 tran-

scription), LS-349; Hans Georg Wieck, *Die Entstehung der CDU und die Wiedergründung des Zentrums im Jahre 1945* (Düsseldorf, 1953), p. 58 (quoting Schwering's diary paraphrasing Warsch); compare the melodramatic account, affected by later battles with the revived Center, in Schwering, *Frühgeschichte der Christlich-Demokratischen Union* (Recklinghausen, 1963), pp. 9–13, 34–40.

32. LS-342.1, LS-342.6, LS-342.7; Schwering, *Früh,* pp. 14–15. Schwering later claimed that Adenauer was decidedly cool toward the early initiatives to found the CDP. But his complaints in the summer of 1945 about Adenauer's "continued meddling" (LS-349) show that the Mayor was far from inactive in the party's early history. For Adenauer's "internal emigration," see Hans-Peter Schwarz, *Adenauer, Der Aufstieg: 1876–1952* (Stuttgart, 1986), pp. 343–424; for Adenauer's tactical and strategic considerations regarding the early CDP, see Schwarz, pp. 478–493.

33. LS-343.2a (June 1 draft, with corrections).

34. Compare Hamacher on June 6: since the Center had never been a confessional party, there was no need for something new. Hofmann, LS-342.2.

35. Welty, "Was nun?" pp. 26–31 (KA-08.06).

36. Kölner Leitsätze, *KA-CDU-BBZ,* pp. 105–109.

37. LS-342.6, LS-342.7.

38. LS-342.6, LS-342.7 ("danger"); LS-348.7, August 19, 1945 ("struggle"). Schwering added that solidarism, not mechanistic socialism, was to be the basis of the social order. Two weeks later, he contrasted the CDP to the Socialist-Communist "front": LS-347.3. Calling Schwering "an adherent of Christian socialism," Uertz accepts Schwering's claim that only the party's name, not the concept, was at issue in Walberberg: Uertz, *Christentum,* pp. 9, 24–30; Schwering, *Die Entstehung der CDU* (Cologne, 1946), p. 18. Undoubtedly, Schwering admired Welty, whom he credited with negotiating much of the final wording of the guidelines (*Früh,* p. 83). In saying that only the name was at issue, however, what Schwering emphasized about the concept was that it was opposed to "Marxism, class struggle, dictatorship of the proletariat, [and a] materialistic outlook," it was an "intellectual dam" against collectivist ideas, it put "explicit emphasis on the value of private property and individual initiative," it "reject[ed] socialization of the means of production," and it upheld "civil" or "bourgeois" *(bürgerliche)* society and culture (Schwering, *Entstehung,* pp. 17–18). Although Schwering was a progressive, his orientation, as Peter Hüttenberger notes, "was Christianbürgerlich": *Nordrhein-Westfalen und die Entstehung seiner parlamentarischen Demokratie* (Siegburg, 1973), p. 51.

39. LS-342.6, LS-342.7. Morsey dates Adenauer's commitment only from August 31; Schwarz says "during August at the latest": Morsey, "Der politische Aufstieg Konrad Adenauers," in Klaus Gotto et al., *Konrad*

Adenauer, seine Deutschland- und Aussenpolitik 1945–1963 (Munich, 1975), p. 40; Schwarz, *Adenauer,* pp. 490–491.

40. LS-342.6, LS-342.7.
41. LS-348.7.
42. Ibid.
43. E.g., *Union in Deutschland,* no. 93, November 22, 1952 (LS-545); *Rheinisches Monatsblatt,* September 1962; Schwering, *Früh,* p. 40.
44. "Weltanschauung und Politik," CDU flyer, Essen, September 22, 1946, and Karl Zimmermann, "Zur Gründung des neuen Zentrums," *CDP des Rheinlands. Rundbrief 1/45* (Cologne, October 23, 1945), RM-46; *KV,* no. 628, July 22, 1907.
45. Hüwel, *Arnold,* pp. 62–63; Lensing, "Der Wattenscheider Kreis," *Ruhr-Nachrichten,* no. 203, September 2, 1955 (LS-359.4); Hüttenberger, *Nordrhein-Westfalen,* pp. 54–55; Wieck, *Entstehung,* pp. 76–79, 105–108; Schwering, *Früh,* pp. 64–67.
46. LS-342.6, LS-342.7; Wieck, *Entstehung,* pp. 108–115, 134–135.
47. Wieck, *Entstehung,* pp. 124–125 (emphasis added).
48. "Protokoll der Gründungsversammlung der CDP Rheinland," LS-347.1, LS-347.2.
49. "Protokoll," LS-347.1, LS-347.2.
50. Hamacher to Adenauer, August 26, 1945, WH-29; similar orally to Hugo Mönnig, September 2, 1945, cited in Hamacher, "Zur Geschichte der Wiederbegründung des Zentrums" [1948], WH-7. On June 6, 1945, Hamacher told Hofmann that the Catholic Reich of the thirteenth century should be the prototype for a pivotal Germany between England and the Soviet Union: LS-342.2. In magnanimous Roerenesque fashion, he told Karl Horster that Catholics would now shape Germany according to their own principles; the Center could then be truly tolerant and open its doors to all (i.e., Protestants could join an outspokenly Catholic Center): WH-51, March 5, 1946.
51. Hamacher to Adenauer, WH-29 ("Holland"); "Protokoll," LS-347.1 and LS-347.2, and Schwering, *Früh,* p. 105 (Brüning). Both sides invoked Brüning in the early postwar debate, much as both sides in Centrist debates had traditionally invoked Windthorst.
52. "Protokoll," LS-347.1, LS-347.2; Schwering, *Früh,* p. 195 (September 9). Having left the room at Schwering's request to speak with his venerable mentor Hugo Mönnig, Hamacher suspected a ploy to allow the vote to take place without him: Hamacher, "Zur Geschichte," WH-7.
53. Schulte, "Gedanken zur Bildung von Parteien im christlichen Volksteil," WH-12; Hamacher, February 10, 1946, WH-6.
54. Brockmann to Hamacher, September 2, 1945, with enclosure "Welche Partei?" WH-35.
55. Hamacher to Adenauer, September 24, 1945, RM-49.

56. Brockmann, "Welche Partei?" WH-35.
57. RM-11; printed as *Warum Zentrum? Die Soester Rede von Dr. Wilhelm Hamacher auf der Jubiläums- und Gründungstagung der Zentrumspartei am 14. Oktober 1945* (Düsseldorf, 1946).
58. Ibid.; also Hamacher to Adenauer, September 24, 1945, RM-49.
59. WH-7, September 23, 1945 (Gilsing) and November 21 (Strunk); WH-39, October 20 (Esser); HP-613, November 1945 and January 1, 1946 (Brüning to Johannes Maier).
60. Josef Kannengiesser, "Liebe Freunde!" (October 1945), WH-7. Brockmann responded that the new party was "nothing but a political hope," while the Center was a seventy-five-year-old "fact." Saying that loyalty to this preexisting party splintered the Christian front was as "absurd" as saying that reactivating the SPD splintered the socialist front. The CDP was not an expansion but a discarding of the Center. "Warum Zentrum," JB-19. For examples of the Harzburg charge see CDU-LVR-199; Wessel, *Der Weg der deutschen Demokratie* (Hattingen, 1946), RM-28; Brockmann, September 1, 1946, RM-11; *RRZ*, nos. 20 and 33, July 19 and September 3, 1946. Hamacher complained at Soest that the CDP welcomed those who had put Hitler in the saddle: RM-11. To procure a press license for the Center, he invoked the Harzburg charge in a letter to the British: WH-9, January 9, 1946. Christian Democrats (including Adenauer) typically answered much like Kannengiesser: the party's doors were open to the little man—the fellow traveler who had been deceived by Hitler, but who himself had done nothing wrong and who should now be left in peace—but not to war criminals or reactionaries.
61. Zimmermann, "Warum nicht Zentrum, sondern Sammlung der christlichen Demokraten Deutschlands," November 1945, LS-542.

8. *The CDU of Konrad Adenauer*

1. Details in Rudolf Morsey, "Der politische Aufstieg Konrad Adenauers, 1945–1949," in Klaus Gotto et al., eds., *Konrad Adenauer: Seine Deutschland- und Aussenpolitik 1945–1963* (Munich, 1975), pp. 39–53; Hans-Peter Schwarz, *Adenauer, Der Aufstieg: 1876–1952* (Stuttgart, 1986), pp. 439–509; Toni Diderich, "Adenauer als Kölner Oberbürgermeister von Mai bis Oktober 1945," in Hugo Stehkämper, ed., *Konrad Adenauer: Oberbürgermeister von Köln* (Cologne, 1976), pp. 518–530; Morsey, "Adenauer und der Nationalsozialismus," in Stehkämper, ed., *Adenauer Oberbürgermeister,* pp. 494–495. Reflecting the distrust in 1945 toward Weimar-era politicians with conservative reputations, each of the three original occupying powers dismissed from

office and tried to bar from politics its leading Christian Democratic politician (Adenauer, Andreas Hermes, and Fritz Schäffer).

2. "Notiz," September 13, 1945, WH-7; Adenauer to Petersen, September 1, 1945, KA-08.05; memorandum, May 15, 1946 (Adenauer-Hamacher meeting of February 5, 1946), WH-12 and KA-08.55/4; KA-02.03, May 5, 1946 (on Schwering's tactlessness—see also Schwering, *Frühgeschichte der Christlich-Demokratischen Union* (Recklinghausen, 1963), pp. 130–135, and Peter Hüttenberger, *Nordrhein-Westfalen und die Entstehung seiner parlamentarischen Demokratie* (Siegburg, 1973), pp. 77–78); Rainer Barzel, ed., *Karl Arnold: Grundlagen christlich-demokratischer Politik in Deutschland: Eine Dokumentation* (Bonn, 1960), p. 207 ("new beginning"); Adenauer-van Eyck exchange, September 14 and 25, 1945, KA-08.05. In June 1968, Arnold's friend Walter Hensel explained that the Düsseldorf circle had favored Adenauer because he was a good drawing card: Hen-3. Arnold's colleague Bruno Six told Hüttenberger that Adenauer was better able than Schwering to rise above Centrist tradition, yet more capable of winning the neo-Centrists: BS, October 13, 1967.

3. Adenauer to Scharnagl, printed in Morsey, "Vom Kommunalpolitiker zum Kanzler," Konrad-Adenauer-Stiftung, ed., *Konrad Adenauer, Ziele und Wege* (Mainz, 1972), pp. 76–79; Adenauer to Petersen, KA-08.05.

4. KA-08.57, January 29, 1946, with Schlange's circulars. See also John Farquharson, "The Consensus that Never Came: Hans Schlange-Schöningen and the CDU, 1945–9," *European History Quarterly,* 19 (1989): 353–383.

5. In a radio address on March 6, Adenauer stated: "We are not a Sammelpartei; we do not want to gather everything right of Social Democracy. We are not a right party; we are also not a moderate left party. We are a Weltanschauung party with its own character and its own stamp." KA-02.03.

6. Schlange, KA-08.57; Herford communique, January 1946, CT-42; speech of March 6, 1946, KA-02.03. Adenauer did argue (July 28) that the true bearers of Centrist tradition were the former Centrists in the CDU, but not that Centrist tradition was borne by the CDU itself. He himself, he stated, had decided to "depart from an old tradition" (May 5); he had "bid farewell to the Center" (May 12).

7. Adenauer repeatedly cited these elections as proof of his party's potential: Adenauer, *Reden 1917–1967: Eine Auswahl,* H. P. Schwarz, ed. (Stuttgart, 1975), p. 100 (March 24, 1946); also KA-02.03, April 7, May 5, May 12.

8. Adenauer to Petersen, September 1, 1945, KA-08.05.

9. Adenauer, *Reden,* pp. 86, 89, 95–97. Thus, Adenauer rejected the term

"Christian socialism," since Christianity and socialism were competing Weltanschauungen.

10. Ibid., pp. 88–89, 101–102.
11. Ibid., pp. 85–87.
12. Josef Hofmann (1962), based on notes from 1945, LS-342.3.
13. Adenauer to Wilhelm Heile, February 14, 1946, KA-08.68 (emphasis added); KA-08.54, June 11; KA-02.03, May 5.
14. Adenauer to Zonal Committee, December 17, 1946, KA-02.03.
15. Ibid. On the governmental negotiations see Hüttenberger, *Nordrhein-Westfalen,* pp. 227–240, and Detlev Hüwel, *Karl Arnold* (Wuppertal, 1980), pp. 105–109.
16. *RRZ,* no. 29, August 20, 1946; KA-02.03, September 8.
17. Otto Schmidt to Adenauer and reply, March 9 and 23, 1946, KA-08.53.
18. Adenauer memorandum, March 15, 1946, KA-08.55/4. Although Spiecker complained on April 3 that the memorandum was misleading, it corresponds with his later public position (Chapter 10).
19. Adenauer's notes, March 18 (telephone) and April 13 ("struggle"), 1946, and Deacon Schreiber's memo, May 15 ("Free"), KA-08.55/4.
20. KA-07.10, July 6, 1946 (voter abstention); *RRZ* no. 20, July 19 ("Führer"); speeches in KA-02.03, including May 5 ("astonishing") and (in Hamacher's home district) September 3 ("nothing in common").
21. KA-02.03.
22. KA-07.12. Efforts to woo Hamacher had continued until his illness: WH-67; KA-07.10. In April, Schulte had proposed another conference to promote cooperation; Hamacher had favored it and Brockmann had not: WH-35. On this score, nothing had changed since the Hamacher-Hermes conference the previous November (Chapter 7).
23. Adenauer to Schulte, December 3, 1946, KA-07.12.
24. Adenauer to Executive Board of Rhenish CDU, CDU-LVR-1025, February 11, 1947. Arnold had discussed fusion with another leading Centrist, Fritz Stricker, just six days before this meeting: JB-12.
25. JB-12, February 22, 1947; KA-07.13, March 7; KA-07.14, March 21; ZD-102, March 14; CDU-LVR-199, March 14 and 20; KA-08.55/4, April 15.
26. Hüwel, *Arnold,* pp. 129–131.
27. Schwering, *Früh,* pp. 228–233 (Ahlen text); Rudolf Uertz, *Christentum und Sozialismus in der frühen CDU* (Stuttgart, 1981), pp. 89–111, 166–204; Hüwel, *Arnold,* pp. 130–131. On June 5, 1947, Adenauer wrote the American consul in Bremen, Maurice Altaffer, that the Ahlen Program was "especially directed against the socialization endeavors of the SPD": KA-07.13.
28. Adenauer to Franz von Galen, KA-07.14.

29. See *RRZ,* nos. 15, 25 ("unreliable"), 30, February 21, March 28, April 15, 1947.

30. Adenauer, "Verhandlungen über die Bildung einer Regierung in Nordrhein-Westfalen," May 23, 1947, and Adenauer to Arnold, May 23 and June 3, KA-08.63; Adenauer to Brockmann, June 4, CT-44, with reply, June 6, KA-08.53. Hüwel states incorrectly that Adenauer's proposal to Brockmann was for a three-party government with the FDP: *Arnold,* pp. 112–116.

31. Arnold, "Der Weg in die Zukunft: Regierungserklärung 17.6.1947" (Düsseldorf, 1947); Adenauer, "Verhandlungen," and Adenauer-Arnold correspondence, KA-08.63; Adenauer to Robert Lehr, July 18, KA-07.15; Adenauer to Heinrich von Brentano, September 2, KA-08.59; Hüwel, *Arnold,* pp. 116–119.

32. See Hüwel, *Arnold,* pp. 117–118.

33. *KA-CDU-BBZ,* pp. 330–351.

9. The CDU and Jakob Kaiser

1. JK-454 [late 1945].

2. See Werner Conze, *Jakob Kaiser: Politiker zwischen Ost und West, 1945–1949* (Stuttgart, 1969).

3. Conze, *Kaiser,* pp. 37–38 (quoting Adenauer); JK-93, February 13, 1946 ("streams"), and May 17, 1947 ("fiasco"); see also JK-136, March 29, 1946; JK-93, June 16, 1946; JK-93, April 16, 1947. In the West, Walter Dirks's Frankfurt group also subscribed to the thesis of an all-party socialist consensus: Dirks, *Die Zweite Republik* (Frankfurt, 1947).

4. JK-93, February 13, 1946 ("law"), June 16 (mutually exclusive); JK-136, March 31 ("outspokenly Christian"); see also *Neue Zeit,* no. 187, August 11, 1946. To Kaiser's argument (June 16) that no party had a monopoly on socialism, the SED retorted that no party had a monopoly on Christianity and claimed that its program was consonant with Christian moral law: Conze, *Kaiser,* pp. 100–101. But the SED's efforts to quash the notion that Weltanschauung was a legitimate way to contest elections only made Kaiser more adamant.

5. JK-136, March 29, 1946 ("trend"); KA-08.56, October 17, 1948; JK-93, July 23, 1949 ("secondary"). After 1959, many Social Democrats adopted a similar position, but they came to it much more slowly, since the issue for them did involve Weltanschauung.

6. JK-93, February 13, 1946 ("social effect"); JK-454 [1945] (other quotations); JK-93, February 2, JK-136, March 29, JK-148, November 6 (temporary response). Conze writes that Kaiser used the phrase "Christian socialism" only in a "pragmatic sense," without concerning himself with its theological foundations or economic or constitutional consequences:

Kaiser, p. 41. One is left wondering what consequences he did consider, and in what sense this can be called "pragmatic." (Kaiser would surely have denied that he used the phrase only to get along with the Soviets.) Kaiser began regularly using the phrase "Christian socialism" in late 1945, well after his western trade-union counterparts.

7. JK-93, October 1945 ("hour"); JK-136, March 29 ("mature"), March 31 ("trivialize"), 1946. In her 1967 biography, Kaiser's widow saw the just-formed Grand Coalition as a kind of fruition of the resistance-era plans of Kaiser, Leuschner, and Habermann. Elfriede Nebgen, *Jakob Kaiser: Der Widerstandskämpfer* (Stuttgart, 1967), pp. 51–52.

8. JK-148, November 6, 1946.

9. Quoted in Conze, *Kaiser,* pp. 151–152.

10. Ibid., pp. 154–158.

11. JK-93.

12. "In the debate over ideological principles," he asserted further, the election trend in both East and West had shown a majority against Marxism and for a political course based on "the moral principles of the Christian Occident": JK-93.

13. *Täglische Rundschau* (SED), September 16, 1947 (Conze, *Kaiser,* p. 174).

14. On Kaiser's fall, his replacement by the more pliable Otto Nuschke, and the "coordination" of the eastern CDU, see Winfried Becker, *CDU und CSU 1945–1950* (Mainz, 1987), pp. 210–213, and Conze, *Kaiser,* pp. 182–214.

15. Conze, *Kaiser,* pp. 133–148.

16. Ibid., pp. 144 ("Trojan horse"), 188 ("wall"); JK-93, September 6, 1947.

17. JK-93. Even in March 1947, when Kaiser still hoped for "successful co-operation within a [CDU-SPD] coalition," he asserted (like Adenauer) that "much will depend on whether the Union succeeds in becoming the strongest party": "Protokoll der ersten Sitzung des Vorstands der Arbeitsgemeinschaft der CDU und CSU Deutschlands in Berlin . . . vom 13. bis 15. März 1947," KA-08.59.

18. JK-93, November 16 and 30, 1947.

19. Conze, *Kaiser,* pp. 211–221.

20. Detlev Hüwel, *Karl Arnold* (Wuppertal, 1980), pp. 120–124.

21. KA-08.56, October 17, 1948; on the Center, see Kaiser's remarks in "Protokoll über die Konferenz des Vorstandes der Arbeitsgemeinschaft . . . am 20.8.48 in Königstein," KA-08.60, and Kaiser to Adenauer, October 19, KA-08.56 (quotation). Indeed, in the internal jockeying over these matters (Chapter 11), Kaiser seemed to line up with Adenauer rather than Arnold.

22. Conze, *Kaiser,* pp. 248–250.

23. KA-02.05, April 21, 1949 (Adenauer); Erich Kosthorst, *Jakob Kaiser: Bundesminister für Gesamtdeutsche Fragen, 1949–1957* (Stuttgart, 1972), p. 30 (Kaiser, May 15).

24. Conze, *Kaiser*, p. 253; Kosthorst, *Kaiser*, p. 30.

25. Kosthorst, *Kaiser*, pp. 57–58.

26. JK-93.

27. Ibid.; Rudolf Uertz, *Christentum und Sozialismus in der frühen CDU* (Stuttgart, 1981), pp. 201–202 (on February clash).

28. Rudolf Morsey, "Die Bildung der ersten Regierungskoalition 1949," *Aus Politik und Zeitgeschichte*, B 34/78 (supplement to *Das Parlament*), August 26, 1978; Kosthorst, *Kaiser*, pp. 65–75; Arnold Heidenheimer, *Adenauer and the CDU* (Hague, 1960), pp. 179–182; Hüwel, *Arnold*, pp. 207–208.

29. "The Christian Democrats are not cut from the wood of totalitarian parties. They will not make it difficult for positive forces in the SPD to practice loyal opposition. They will let it be manifest in their political attitude that they see in the opposition of today the potential bearer of political responsibility of tomorrow." KA-08.56.

30. Indeed, Kaiser's secretary hurriedly typed simply "Lieber Adenauer," a breach of etiquette for which Kaiser apologized with a second letter— "Lieber Herr Dr. Adenauer"—the next day. KA-08.56.

31. "Die Stellung der christlich-demokratischen Arbeiterschaft zur Koalitionsbildung," JK-414.

32. Ibid. ("Der Kanzler kann nach Lage der Dinge nur Konrad Adenauer heissen"); JK-93, July 23, 1949 ("reactionary").

33. Kosthorst, *Kaiser*, pp. 75, 362.

34. For later clashes, see ibid.; Hans-Peter Schwarz, *Adenauer, Der Aufstieg: 1876–1952* (Stuttgart, 1986); Schwarz, *Adenauer, Der Staatsmann: 1952–1967* (Stuttgart, 1991).

35. Caucus minutes, JK-248, September 1, 1949.

36. JK-248, October 26, 1949 (Kaiser) and December 18, 1970 (Elfriede Nebgen, citing Walther Schreiber).

37. Kosthorst, *Kaiser*, pp. 74–79.

38. Contrast Heidenheimer, *Adenauer*, p. 155.

39. The result was their estrangement: Kosthorst, *Kaiser*, p. 75.

40. Adenauer to Cardinal Josef Frings, November 1, 1948, KA-07.05.

10. The Center Party and Karl Spiecker

1. In 1972, Barzel was the CDU's emphatically non-leftist Chancellor candidate. Draft leaflet [by Johannes Brockmann?], JB-5; Barzel, *Die geistigen Grundlagen der politischen Parteien* (Bonn, 1947), p. 158. See also "Zentrum und Christlich-Demokratische Partei" (Essen leaflet, De-

cember 1945), RM-46; *RRZ,* nos. 17, 19, 28, July 9, 16, August 16, 1946; *RRZ,* no. 16, February 25, 1947 (which linked and attacked Stegerwald and Spahn); *RRZ,* no. 36, May 6. *RRZ,* no. 31, August 27, 1946, compared Adenauer's attacks on Spiecker to German National incitement of Matthias Erzberger's assassination!

2. "Zentrum und Christlich-Demokratische Partei" ("misuse," "contrast"); *RRZ,* no. 2, May 17, 1946 ("values," "detours," "prove").

3. *RRZ,* nos. 1 ("old Center"), 18 ("Christian footing"), 28 (eastern Protestant pressure), May 14, July 12, August 16, 1946; Zonal Executive Board, July 4, in *RRZ,* no. 17, July 9 ("Windthorst"); see also *Das Zentrum im Kampf* (Essen [1946]), JB-19. In dating the refounding from the Lippstadt meeting, the Esseners naturally were joined by Johannes Brockmann, an instigator of the meeting (*RRZ,* nos. 20 and 43, July 19 and October 8, 1946), but not by Hamacher, who was still unhappily attending Christian Democratic meetings on September 2, 1945, when first contacted by Brockmann.

4. *Das Zentrum im Kampf* ("common"); "Zentrum und Christlich-Demokratische Partei" ("contradict," Papen, Windthorst); Spiecker in *RRZ,* no. 2, May 17, 1946 ("immemorial," Bachem, "asks no one") and CDU-LVR-199, January 13, 1947 (Bachem, "not a political Weltanschauung"); also Fritz Stricker in *RRZ,* no. 86, October 24, 1947 (Bachem argument applied to Christianity).

5. CDU-LVR-199, January 13, 1947 ("99 percent"); *RRZ,* no. 27, August 13, 1946 (mistake); Zonal Executive Board, July 4, in *RRZ,* no. 17, July 9 ("hazy"); Spiecker in *RRZ,* no. 2, May 17 ("mixing"); *Das Zentrum im Kampf* ("supra"); Spiecker at Werl party congress, November 17, RM-49, pp. 47–50 ("double-confessional").

6. *RRZ,* no. 2, May 17, 1946.

7. *RRZ,* no. 38, September 20, 1946; similarly no. 39, September 24, and October leaflet, CDU-LVR-199. In a two-party system, Spiecker warned the Oberhausen clergy on January 13, 1947, a CDU majority might write a "Christian" constitution, but five years later, when the left was voted into power vowing to reverse the Christian provisions, the CDU would feel compelled to rule by dictatorship (CDU-LVR-199).

8. KA-08.55/4, March 15, 1946; *RRZ,* nos. 29 and 38, August 20 and September 20, 1946. On UdM see Spiecker to Alois Klöcker, July 15, 1946, KA-08.56; CDU-LVR-199, January 13, 1947; Barzel, *Grundlagen,* pp. 158–159; and Chapter 11 of this volume.

9. On Arnold, see Chapter 11, this volume; on Kaiser, see *New Yorker Staatszeitung und Herald,* no. 228, September 23, 1946 (JB-6); Adenauer before British Zonal Committee of CDU, December 17, KA-02.03; CDU-LVR-199, January 13, 1947; and a furious confrontation between Adenauer and Kaiser (January) over Kaiser's alleged contacts with Spiecker,

KA-08.56. Adenauer documented feelers through a Spiecker-Kaiser intermediary (Klöcker) who seems, however, to have overstated his influence.

10. *RRZ,* no. 18, July 12, 1946; likewise Spiecker to Rhenish party convention, Düsseldorf, June 1–2, RM-11. *RRZ,* no. 11, June 18, equated Walter Dirks's call for a permanent Grand Coalition with both a Labour party and the plans of the Center.

11. *RRZ,* no. 21, July 23, 1946 (British two-party system, sparring); *RRZ,* no. 46, October 18 ("correspond"); *RRZ,* no. 66, August 19, 1947 (cardinal, "political reasons"); *RRZ,* no. 82, October 14 (denying Anglophilia). For additional praise of British Labour, see *RRZ,* no. 10, June 14, 1946; *RRZ,* no. 43, May 30, 1947 (which added that a cofounder of Holland's new Labour Party was a Catholic); *RRZ,* no. 89, November 7 (Barzel).

12. Paul Ludwig, "Johannes Brockmann," in Walter Först, ed., *Aus dreisig Jahre: Rheinisch-Westfälische Politiker-Porträts* (Cologne, 1979), p. 154 (quoting Amelunxen); Rösing interviewed December 6, 1982.

13. JB-40–42. Brockmann's work in the Parliamentary Council (1948–1949) would also be mostly on the schools issue.

14. *NWK,* no. 42, April 8, 1949 (quotation). Contrast Walter Schlangen, "Zentrum," in Schlangen, ed., *Die Deutschen Parteien im Überblick* (Königstein, 1979), p. 173, who reckons Wessel to the Essen wing.

15. Wessel, *Der Weg der Deutschen Demokratie* (Hattingen, 1946), pp. 16–22.

16. Wessel to Brockmann and others, October 18, 1945, JB-1.

17. Ibid. ("only from Christianity"); Wessel, *Weg,* pp. 4 ("spiritual"), 14 ("false"), 21 ("artificial"); compare Spiecker in *RRZ,* no. 2, May 17, 1946: politics consisted of "methods, detours, and expediencies."

18. Wessel, *Weg,* pp. 26 (quotation), 29. On the role of gender in Wessel's political activity, see Elisabeth Friese, "Helene Wessel und die Deutsche Zentrumspartei in der Nachkriegszeit" (M.A. thesis, University of Cologne, 1983).

19. WH-25.

20. WH-6, February 10, 1946.

21. Ibid. ("narrowness"); Hamacher to Heribert Aretz, February 23, 1946, WH-7 ("not anti-Protestant"); Klein (March), WH-8; Abele to Hamacher, April 4, WH-28.

22. Klein (March 1946), WH-8; *RRZ,* no. 18, July 12, 1946 ("accident"); "Protokoll," Werl party congress, November 17, 1946, RM-49 ("supra").

23. *RRZ,* no. 11, June 18, 1946; see also *RRZ,* no. 16, February 25, 1947.

24. *RRZ,* no. 6, May 31, 1946 (encyclical); *RRZ,* no. 2, May 17 (hence,

"there exists no more universal . . . Catholic . . . and Christian law than natural law").

25. CDU-LVR-199, January 13, 1947; "Protokoll" (Werl), RM-49.

26. Stadtgruppe Leverkusen to Hamacher, July 28, 1946, WH-9 ("heresy," "State Party"); July resolution of fifteen local chairman (including those of Düsseldorf, Siegkreis, Wuppertal, Duisburg, Mönchengladbach, Bonn, and Krefeld), WH-9; essay [September or October], WH-6 ("mistake," "roots"); Provost Koenen (Mönchengladbach) to Hamacher, May 26, WH-7 ("false teaching"), with other similar letters. Hamacher agreed that "liberalism, that is, the estrangement of politics and economics from religion and ethics, is the accursed paver of the way for National Socialism": Hamacher to Heribert Aretz, February 23, 1946, WH-7.

27. "Protokoll" (Werl), RM-49.

28. Ibid. (emphasis added). This dispute was left out of the official pamphlet on the convention: *Bericht über den Parteitag der Deutschen Zentrumspartei in Werl am 16. und 17. November 1946* (Essen, 1946), RM-28.

29. "Protokoll" (Werl), RM-49.

30. Wessel, speech at Werl convention, November 16, 1946, RM-11; Spiecker to Alois Klöcker, July 15, 1946, KA-08.56. Opposed by de Gaulle (but *not* by the MRP), a new French constitution was rejected by referendum in May 1946. A second version passed in October, but French politics remained turbulent. Wessel's apparent dismissal of the MRP as a mediating force is striking in light of its left-Catholic origins in the French resistance.

11. The Fusion Fiasco

1. Compare Detlev Hüwel, *Karl Arnold* (Wuppertal, 1980).

2. See Spiecker, "Meine Antwort," *RRZ*, no. 15, February 2, 1949, reprinted in *Kampf oder Verständigung? Dokumente zum Thema: Zusammenschluss CDU-Zentrum* (Essen, 1949), p. 21 (LS-548); Richard Muckermann to Max Schäfer, March 1, 1949, RM-2; speech draft, RM-3; and *Reicht Euch die Hände! Die Konferenz von Essen am 10. April 1949* (Essen, 1949), pp. 7–8 (KA-08.70).

3. *RRZ*, no. 82, October 14, 1947; see also nos. 49, 65, 73, June 20, August 15, September 12.

4. See Adenauer to Spiecker, July 30, 1947, and reply, August 4, KA-08.55/4.

5. *RRZ*, no. 29, April 11, 1947.

6. *RRZ*, no. 65, August 15, 1947.

7. KA-08.55/4.

8. Adenauer to Arnold, September 1, 1947, KA-08.63; Adenauer to Spiecker, October 19, and reply, October 25, KA-08.55/4; *RRZ*, no. 86, October 24.

9. Business Manager Wagner (Hesse-CDU) to Adenauer, November 3, 1947, Adenauer to Arnold, November 4, and reply, December 5, KA-08.55/4; *RRZ*, no. 88, November 4.

10. Adenauer to Arnold, June 2, 1948, KA-08.63.

11. *RRZ*, no. 2, January 6, 1948 (Muckermann); *RRZ*, no. 8, January 27, 1948, and Deutsche Zentrumspartei, Geschäftsstelle des Direktoriums, ed., *Bericht über den Parteitag der Deutschen Zentrumspartei in Recklinghausen am 24. und 25. Januar 1948* (Essen, 1948), pp. 48–53. Spiecker had contrasted neutralization to Europeanization as early as January 6, 1947, but he would not then hear of European union without Russia. Spiecker to Schumacher, KS-4.

12. *RRZ*, nos. 16 and 23, February 24 and March 19, 1948.

13. *RRZ*, nos. 12, 26 ("dictatorship"), 28 ("West Germany"), 29, 30, 36 (attract), 37 ("no bridge"), 41 (Wallace), February 10, March 31, April 6, 9, 13, May 4, 8, 21, 1948.

14. *RRZ*, nos. 34 and 36, April 27 and May 4, 1948; KA-08.55/4 (KAV initiative).

15. *RP*, May 26, 1948 (also *RRZ*, no. 43, May 29; *Kampf oder Verständigung?*, pp. 5–6; and CT-30).

16. *RRZ*, nos. 38 ("reconciliation") and 39 ("Christian bloc"), September 20 and 24, 1946.

17. *Die Welt*, May 27, 1948, cited in "Vorgänge Briefwechsel Dr. Spiecker-Arnold," ZD-103 (declare war); typed excerpt from *Tagesspiegel*, May 26, 1948, KA-08.55/4 (Katzenberger).

18. "Vorgänge," ZD-103 (caucus); *RRZ*, no. 43, May 29, 1948.

19. News releases and Adenauer to Arnold, May 26, 1948, KA-08.55/4.

20. Thus, said Spiecker, the question was not "whether Adenauer is a just as good or better Catholic than I am," but only whether their political views coincided—something that was the case for Spiecker and Arnold: *RRZ*, no. 43, May 29, 1948. Adenauer to Arnold, May 27, KA-08.55/4 (on telephone calls); typed excerpt from *Tagesspiegel* and *Westdeutsche Rundschau*, May 26, KA-08.55/4, and Adenauer to Arnold, June 2, KA-08.63 (on Katzenberger).

21. KA-08.55/4 and (June 2) KA-08.63. The DP had been licensed only since 1947. Apparently, so low had the Arnold-Adenauer relationship sunk by mid-1948 that the two most prominent Christian Democrats in the state managed not to speak to each other during arguably the most critical five-week span in postwar German history—the period of the currency reform, the start of the Berlin crisis, and the Frankfurt Documents.

22. *RRZ*, no. 60, July 12, 1948 ("private"—similarly Direktorium, June 12,

WH-8); Brockmann note, July 15, ZD-33; Brockmann speech
("Windthorst"), cited in Brockmann to Hamacher, July 21, WH-35.
Brockmann told Hamacher he was sure the Centrist membership was
"not prepared to go along with the Spiecker course." Among the sixteen
Bottrop discussants were Spiecker, Heinrich Steffensmeier, Stricker, Ru-
dolf Amelunxen, and Wessel (for the Center); and Arnold, Johannes Al-
bers, Christine Teusch, and Heinrich Lübke (for the CDU). *Kampf oder
Verständigung?*, p. 7.

23. Adenauer to Albert Lotz, July 22, 1948, KA-07.17.
24. KA-07.19 (to Gronowski); KA-08.63 (to Arnold, including reference to
    July 20 vote).
25. Arnold to Adenauer, August 2, 1948, KA-08.63.
26. *Westdeutsche Allgemeine Zeitung,* no. 54, August 3 (HW-3).
27. Hüwel, *Arnold,* p. 155.
28. *RP,* no. 32, August 7, 1948; *RRZ,* no. 72, August 9. The British voided
    the bill. On socialization see Rolf Steininger, "Reform und Realität:
    Ruhrfrage und Sozialisierung in der Anglo-Amerikanischen Deutsch-
    landpolitik 1947–48," *VfZ,* 27 (1979): 167–240.
29. Arnold to Adenauer, August 7, 1948, KA-08.63; see also Hüwel, *Ar-
    nold,* pp. 134–137, 156.
30. Compare Hüwel, *Arnold,* p. 153.
31. Ibid., p. 155.
32. Adenauer to Arbeitsgemeinschaft katholischer Frauen, August 16,
    1948, KA-07.17; similarly "Protokoll," Arbeitsgemeinschaft CDU/CSU,
    Königstein, August 20, KA-08.60 (where Adenauer was strongly sec-
    onded by Kaiser).
33. ZD-4, September 25, 1948; KA-02.04, October 14. Arnold's *RP* (no. 40,
    October 2) also lambasted the Center for rejecting local election accords
    and denounced the Center's behavior on the socialization bill. The Cen-
    trist chairman in the city of Hanover was expelled after his organization
    got its members to vote for the CDU. Similar local initiatives in
    Düsseldorf, Duisburg, and elsewhere were thwarted by intervention
    from the top. Yet, in many places, the Center joined post-election coali-
    tions with the SPD. CDU-LVR-137, January 20, 1949.
34. *RRZ,* no. 72, August 9, 1948. *RP,* no. 35, August 28, seemed to recipro-
    cate the signal when it again explained that the "C" in CDU indicated no
    monopoly on Christianity.
35. *RRZ,* nos. 84 and 99, September 6 and October 11, 1948.
36. ZD-4, September 25, 1948.
37. Garnot Erler and Karl-Otto Sattler, *Die unterlassene Ehrung des
    Reichskanzlers Joseph Wirth* (Freiburg, 1980), pp. 129, 162 (quoting
    Friedrich Stampfer), 171.
38. *RRZ,* nos. 105, 106 (interview), October 25, 27, 1948; Kalisch to Center

Business Office, October 28, RM-58; southern Catholic cited in Theodore Abele to Hamacher, November 8, WH-28.

39. Abele to Hamacher, October 27, 1948, WH-28; Kalisch, October 28,
RM-58; see also Hessian Center, November 27, ZD-69, and Johannes
Stevens to editors of *RRZ*, October 26, RM-58. Regarding the masthead, see Hamacher to Spiecker, September 8, WH-9; also Stevens.
Hamacher had been unhappy all year about the increasing emphasis on
"the middle" rather than on the Windthorstian and Christian "character
of the Center": Hamacher to Brockmann, January 17, February 11, May
19, WH-35.

40. Muckermann, October 13, 1948 (after the announcement that a southern UdM would file for licensing), *RRZ*, no. 101, October 15; *Kurier der
Mitte*, no. 7, December, 1948 (LS-547). On October 16, the former Centrist Karl Klein wrote in Arnold's *RP* (no. 42) that Spiecker's plan to
create a new middle party out of the SPD's right wing, the CDU's left
wing, and the Center would fail because the SPD lacked an incentive,
since its interests were already being served by the Center.

41. *Kampf oder Verständigung?*, pp. 7–8. The election results, from *RRZ*,
no. 102, October 19, 1948: CDU, 37.8 percent (+0.2 percent over April
of 1947); Center, 9.6 percent (−0.1); SPD, 35.9 percent (+3.9); KPD, 7.8
percent (−6.2); FDP, 6.9 percent (+1.0).

42. Brockmann to "Hubert," December 10, 1948, ZD-32; Brockmann to
Hamacher, November 10 and December 11, WH-35; *Kurier der Mitte*,
no. 7, December 1948; *RRZ*, nos. 120 and 121, December 3 and 7;
Kampf oder Verständigung?, pp. 8–10; *Das Zentrum im Lande
Niedersachsen*, 2 no. 31–32, December 11 (HW-411); Executive Board
minutes, December 19, RM-11; compare Ute Schmidt, *Zentrum oder
CDU* (Opladen, 1987), p. 280.

43. Executive Board minutes, RM-11.

44. Interviewed December 6, 1982.

45. *Kampf oder Verständigung?*, p. 12, and *Kurier der Mitte*, no. 8/9/10,
March 1949 (CDU-LVR-137). Contrast Schmidt, *Zentrum oder CDU*,
pp. 279–280, who sees Adenauer as having "suddenly turned around."

46. *Kampf oder Verständigung?*, pp. 13–14; Spiecker, RM-3. A later compromise in the Parliamentary Council over Kulturpolitik (Chapter 12)
allowed Adenauer to return to his opposition to referendums.

47. *RRZ*, nos. 96, 97, 98, 100, October 4, 6, 8, 13, 1948 (France); *RRZ*, no.
117, November 23 (Romania, quotation); *RRZ*, no. 120, December 3
(Berlin); *RRZ*, nos. 129, December 28, and 16, February 4, 1949 (Hungary).

48. See *RRZ*, nos. 123, 125, 127, December 10, 15, 21, 1948.

49. RM-11, December 19, 1948; *Kurier der Mitte*, no. 7, December 1948.

50. CDU circles put a different spin on the matter: the "debates over basic

rights in Bonn" had "answered in the affirmative" the question of "whether Weltanschauung and politics have anything at all to do with each other" (*RP*, January 29, 1949); by illustrating the need for Christian solidarity, they had facilitated fusion (*Deutschland-Union-Dienst,* no. 13, January 19).

51. HW-63, January 17, 1949.

52. *Der Spiegel,* no. 4, January 22, 1949. On January 21, Spiecker called for the "de-Weltanschauunging of all parties": RM-11.

53. *Die Welt,* no. 8, January 20, 1949 (on Bremen); *Frankfurter Rundschau,* January 27; additional clippings in KA-08.70.

54. Oberhausen minutes, RM-49, pp. 4–13, 33–36.

55. Ibid., pp. 9–13.

56. Ibid., pp. 20–25.

57. Ibid., pp. 26–28. Spiecker later charged that Stricker himself had prepared a manifesto for fusion in 1948. Stricker replied that his goal had been a new party composed of the Center and the left wing of the CDU, not the CDU swallowing the Center. He added that the case for fusion with the SPD was just as good as with the CDU, since the former would advance tolerance regarding Weltanschauung within the SPD; but since fusion with either party would split the Center and dilute its influence, the existing party had to be maintained. *Kurier der Mitte,* no. 8/9/10, March 1949; *NWK,* no. 14, February 2, 1949 (HW-4); *Das Zentrum,* 3, no. 2, February 1949 (WH-10).

58. Oberhausen minutes, RM-49, pp. 29–33.

59. Ibid., pp. 49–57; *Kampf oder Verständigung?,* pp. 17–19.

60. RM-2. Anti-Oberhausen polemics from the *RRZ* were distributed as flyers bearing similar instructions: CDU-LVR-137.

61. *RRZ,* no. 24, February 16, 1949; CDU-LVR-137; KA-08.70; RM-3; RM-5. Spiecker and Muckermann officially joined the CDU on March 16: *Kampf oder Verständigung?,* p. 32.

62. *RRZ,* no. 24, February 16, 1949; Recklinghausen minutes, February 23, CDU-LVR-137. Compare Spiecker, "Meine Antwort": the "sentimentalist" Center had proven insufficiently aware of the true breadth of the "idea of the political middle."

63. Spiecker, "Meine Antwort"; Muckermann, undated speech, RM-3 ("essentially"); Muckermann to Max Schäfer, March 1, 1949, RM-2 ("CDU," Bundestag).

64. CDU-LVR-137, February 23, 1949.

65. "Konferenz politischer Gesinnungsfreunde," April 10, 1949, RM-49, pp. 204–205; also *Reicht Euch die Hände!,* p. 13.

66. *Reicht Euch die Hände!,* pp. 7–8 (emphasis added), 18–19 (Arnold query); RM-5 ("compliment").

67. Spiecker, "Meine Antwort."

12. Helene Wessel and the Christian Opposition

1. Josef Rösing, who was Centrist General Secretary in 1952–1953 and a Brockmann man, later asserted that Wessel became chair largely because the party was fascinated with the idea of having a woman in that post: interview, December 6, 1982. On gender matters, see also Elisabeth Friese, "Helene Wessel und die Deutsche Zentrumspartei in der Nachkriegszeit" (M.A. thesis, University of Cologne, 1983).
2. "Was geschah im Zentrum?" (Siegburg, March 1949), CDU-LVR-137. Meanwhile Muckermann, who had regularly cited Windthorst in his anti-CDU polemics, now invoked Windthorst for fusion: *RRZ*, no. 16, February 4.
3. Printed in his hometown of Siegburg, it contains phrases that recur in his contemporaneous letter to readers of the *RRZ*, whose license, by order of the military government, temporarily reverted exclusively to him on March 15, 1949.
4. *NWK*, October 14, 1947 (HW-3); HW-411, February 22, 1949; Wessel, "Ist das Zentrum überflüssig?" *Das Zentrum im Lande Niedersachsen*, 3, no. 2, February 1949 (WH-10); CDU-LVR-137, March 4 (CDU notes on Wessel's speech).
5. Wessel, "Zentrum überflüssig?"
6. CDU-LVR-137, March 4, 1949.
7. Wessel, "Zentrum überflüssig?"
8. *NWK*, no. 45, February 2, 1949 (HW-3).
9. Wessel, "Zentrum überflüssig?"
10. RM-2, February 15, 1949; *Deutscher Pressedienst*, March 11 (RM-4).
11. "Die Abstimmung über die Bremer Klausel" (March 1949), CDU-LVR-137 (Centrist leaflet).
12. CDU-LVR-137, March 4, 1949; statement of Center party's Executive Board, reprinted in "Die Niederlage von Bonn!" (Münster, March 12), CDU-LVR-137.
13. "Niederlage," CDU-LVR-137. An alarming report (March 17) that high clerics had been affected by the leaflet prompted Lambert Lensing (March 19) to bring it to Adenauer's attention.
14. Parliamentary Council, Drucksache 857 (referendum), 860 (parents' rights), May 6, 1949, HW-410.
15. *NWK*, no. 67, June 10, 1949 (HW-278).
16. "Erklärung der Zentrumsfraktion zum Grundgesetz," May 8, 1949, HW-411.
17. "Zur Information: Das Zentrum und der 'verkürzte' Verfassungsentwurf der SPD," April 26, 1949, CDU-LVR-137.
18. ZD-32, June 27, 1949. The Center had little incentive to seek an election accord. Since both parties were sure to pass the state-based 5 percent

hurdle in North Rhine–Westphalia, linking the lists would have had a minor effect only in Lower Saxony.

19. Ibid.
20. Böhler, KA-08.68.
21. Stricker to Böhler, KA-08.68.
22. Böhler-Adenauer exchange, July 9 and 13, 1949, KA-08.68.
23. KA-08.68. Since the end of proportional representation would have meant the death of small parties, the election law was a serious bone of contention between CDU and Center.
24. Adenauer to Böhler, July 13, 1949, KA-08.68. Adenauer and Wessel subsequently did meet, but reached no agreement. Adenauer had earlier tried to open a second front with Hamacher, who, though coy and given to recrimination, wanted a meeting; but (a sign of Hamacher's diminished importance) Adenauer never found the time: Adenauer to Hamacher, June 22; reply and telephone message, June 26 and 29; Böhler to Adenauer, July 15, KA-08.68; Adenauer to Hamacher, July 23, WH-29. In the last letter as in some others, Adenauer misspelled Hamacher's name. This repeated error by a man with whom he had once worked closely could only have further aggravated the touchy Centrist leader.
25. For a sampling of Center-CDU campaign rhetoric, see: *Heute* (Munich), no. 90, August 3, 1949, p. 5 (HW-281-I) (Wessel: the Center had opposed the Basic Law because "the issue of parents' rights stands above every right of the state and cannot be subordinated to any compromise among the parties"); *NWK*, no. 81B, July 13 (HW-288) (Wessel: the "social and Christian" Center "acts Christian instead of talking about it"); Centrist candidates' statement, August, HW-3; and "Plumper Wahlschwindel!", CDU leaflet, August, HW-288 (the Bremen clause applied only to Bremen, a city whose Center party had gone over "wholesale" to the anti–parents' rights SPD).
26. "Auswirkungen der Zentrumsstimmen bei der Bundestagwahl am 14. August 1949," JK-249. For the election law and the trizonal seat totals, see Chapter 9. The mixed system produced the following percentages of seats in the Bundestag: CDU/CSU 34.6 percent, SPD 32.6 percent, FDP 12.9 percent, BP 4.2 percent, DP 4.2 percent, KPD 3.7 percent, Center 2.5 percent, others 5.2 percent. Had the system been based exclusively on direct mandates, the results would have been: CDU/CSU 47.1 percent, SPD 40.1 percent, FDP 5.0 percent, BP 4.5 percent, DP 2.1 percent, KPD and Center 0 percent, others 1.2 percent. These numbers show why Adenauer favored and the Center opposed the latter system.
27. Adenauer to Wessel, August 27, 1949, and reply, September 3, WH-29.
28. To illustrate the point: although Wessel claimed that her party was having to prod the federal government on Kulturpolitik because of the internal opposition of the FDP and the DP (*Das Zentrum*, 5, no. 12, July

1951, HW-280), such prodding would doubtless have been more effective had the Center lent its weight to the CDU *within* the coalition government.

29. *NWK*, no. 123, October 17, 1949 (HW-281-II); see also *Das Zentrum*, 3, no. 16, October 1949 (HW-280).

30. *Das Zentrum*, 4, no. 20, October 1950.

31. Otto Pannenbecker of the Center party described Adenauer's aim as "coordination [*Gleichschaltung*] of North Rhine–Westphalia with the federal government": "Gefährdet das Zentrum den christlichen Wahlsieg?" (Centrist leaflet, Oberhausen, 1950), CDU-LVR-145. Brockmann seems also to have used the loaded word "Gleichschaltung": CDU-LVR-145, July 16. Adenauer had meanwhile set up a "coordinating committee" *(Koordinierungsausschuss)* between the Rhenish and Westphalian party organizations in order to combat a Grand Coalition.

32. *Das Zentrum*, 4, no. 20, October 1950. For Brockmann's view that the FDP was controlled by reactionary "Harzburg" elements and his support for Arnold's Bundesrat plans, see "Zur Information! Die Zentrumspartei und die Wahlen in Nordrhein-Westfalen," *CDP-Pressedienst*, February 22, 1950, CT-30; on the North Rhine–Westphalian events see also Detlev Hüwel, *Karl Arnold* (Wuppertal, 1980), pp. 159–165, 224–235, 300; Ute Schmidt, *Zentrum oder CDU* (Opladen, 1987), pp. 329–330; *Vertrauliche Information der Zentrumspartei (VIZ)*, no. 65, September 25, 1950, CDU-LVR-145. As early as May 6, Brockmann publicly assured Arnold that he could count on the Center to keep from being forced into a Bonn coalition: CDU-LVR-145, May 8.

33. For example, Wessel described a visit in 1945 by Kurt Schumacher to the Walberberg Dominican champions of Christian socialism and regretted that the "great possibilities" therein contained had not borne fruit: *Das Zentrum*, 4, no. 20, October 1950.

34. Friese, "Wessel," pp. 123–124 (Wessel quotation); Gordon Drummond, *The German Social Democrats in Opposition, 1949–1960: The Case against Rearmament* (Norman, 1982), chapters 1–3 ("marionettes": p. 80). Pankow was the government district in East Berlin. Wessel's quoted words came perilously close to putting into question the Federal Republic's claim to be the sole legitimate representative of all of Germany *(Alleinvertretungsanspruch)*, a claim Wessel (like Schumacher) elsewhere explicitly affirmed: see her Council of Europe speech, June 1950, HW-5.

35. Drummond, *Social Democrats*, pp. 34–65; *Fuldaer Volkszeitung*, June 21, 1950 (HW-5).

36. See Drummond, *Social Democrats*, pp. 51–65, and Friese, "Wessel," pp. 123–124, 132–133.

37. Drummond, *Social Democrats*, pp. 48–53; *Das Zentrum*, 4, no. 20, Oc-

tober 1950. For the role of Adenauer's foreign policy in bonding his party and defining its Christian Weltanschauung, see Anneliese Poppinga, *Konrad Adenauer: Geschichtsverständnis, Weltanschauung und politische Praxis* (Stuttgart, 1975), and Geoffrey Pridham, *Christian Democracy in Western Germany: The CDU/CSU in Government and Opposition 1945–1976* (London, 1977). For intelligent affirmative assessments of Adenauer's contested seriousness about reunification, see Wolfram Hanrieder, *Germany, America, Europe: Forty Years of German Foreign Policy* (New Haven, 1989), Chapter 5; Hans-Peter Schwarz, *Adenauer: Der Aufstieg: 1876–1952* (Stuttgart, 1986), especially pp. 690–710, 854, 887; and Schwarz, *Adenauer: Der Staatsmann: 1952–1967* (Stuttgart, 1991). On Catholics and rearmament, see Anselm Doering-Manteufel, *Katholizismus und Wiederbewaffnung: Die Haltung der Deutschen Katholiken gegenüber der Wehrfrage 1948–1955* (Mainz, 1981); on Confessing Christians and rearmament, see extracts of interviews in Victoria Barnett, *For the Soul of the People: Protestant Protest against Hitler* (New York, 1992), Chapter 13.

38. CDU memorandum citing *Westdeutsche Nachrichten,* November 30, 1950, CDU-LVR-145.
39. *VIZ,* no. 70, December 11, 1950; *VIZ,* no. 72, January 25, 1951. A confidential Center party newsletter, the *VIZ* was somehow collected by the CDU's Rhenish organization: CDU-LVR-145.
40. According to a CDU report, the Center's regional conferences of September 9 and 10, 1950, were dominated by Brockmann, while Wessel, no longer so influential, had to defend her foreign policy: CDU-LVR-145. Josef Rösing reports that Wessel had poor relations with Hamacher and others; due to defense issues, she completely went her own way: interview, December 6, 1982. See also Quirin Blümlein (Siegburg) to Helmut Bertram, June 23, 1950, WH-8. For Brockmann's growing tendency to subordinate everything to the perceived need to please the clergy, see Schmidt, *Zentrum oder CDU,* pp. 328–343. On April 30, 1951, the Bishop of Trier complained to Brockmann that Wessel's party was not Windthorst's; another correspondent regaled Brockmann with rumors of Wessel's ties with East Berlin: Schmidt, pp. 332–334.
41. ZD-263, September 21, 1951 (Centrist caucus).
42. ZD-98 (and CDU-LVR-145), August 21 and December 8, 1950, June 17 and 27, 1951. Brockmann's Landtag caucus continued to insist that its goal was to expand the coalition to include the SPD, if that party would only cooperate on school legislation: ZD-263, September 11, 1951, and January 12, 1952.
43. Federal Party Congress (Münster), November 24–25, 1951, ZD-15.
44. Federal Party Committee, January 26, 1952, ZD-11; press release, January 31, ZD-115. For Wessel's lasting bitterness toward Brockmann, see Wessel to Krapp, June 26, 1957, HW-143.

45. State Party Committee, August 8, 1953, ZD-98; Schmidt, *Zentrum oder CDU,* pp. 335–341. The previous fall, unity lists had run in some local elections: ZD-115; HW-3. This time, the Center had to accept draconian terms: it withdrew from all but one direct constituency, ran a state list only in North Rhine–Westphalia, placed a CDU member second on that list, and agreed to a joint parliamentary delegation during the Chancellor's election.

46. Federal and State Party Committee, October 11, 1953, ZD-11.

47. See Hüwel, *Arnold,* pp. 261–267.

48. Ironically, Adenauer's federal government withstood the crisis of 1956 (largely caused by the federal CDU) much better than did Arnold's state government. Adenauer had earlier warned his party that the moment was impropitious for election-law reform, which in principle he favored. After the events in Düsseldorf, the FDP split on the federal level, with enough members staying with Adenauer, who meanwhile had secured the withdrawal of the CDU's bill, to safeguard his government. Ibid., pp. 285–326; HW-114 and Wessel to Krapp, June 26, 1957, HW-143 (1957 Centrist overture to SPD); LS-549.2 (Centrist vote in 1957); see also Schmidt, *Zentrum oder CDU,* pp. 355–356, 361 (the "Federal Union" of Center and Bavarian Party garnered 254,000 mostly Bavarian votes and no seats).

49. LS-549.2, April 1958; *Rheinische Monatsblatt,* November 1961 (LS-545).

50. ZD-115.

51. On Centrist views, see *Frankfurter Allgemeine Zeitung,* no. 265, November 14, 1952.

52. The General Treaty was attacked from both left and right. The chairman of the German Party called it a "second Versailles"; Schumacher stated that whoever signed it "ceases to be a German." Drummond, *Social Democrats,* pp. 68–69. On the controversial Soviet notes, see Schwarz, *Adenauer Aufstieg,* pp. 906–924, and Andreas Hillgruber, "Adenauer und die Stalin-Note vom 10. März 1952," in Dieter Blumenwitz et al., eds., *Konrad Adenauer und seine Zeit,* vol. 2 (Stuttgart, 1976), pp. 111–130.

53. Karl Arndt, "Erfahrungsbericht," HW-94.

54. "Manifest der Christlich-Europäischen Union," HW-66 ("worldwide"); Adolf Scheu, "Gedanken für eine Gesamtdeutsche Wirtschaftpolitik," HW-67 ("slap"). A list of twenty-seven possible party names included Concentration of the Independent Middle, Social Conservative Party of Germany, Independent National Opposition, and Reconciliation Party. HW-94.

55. "Aufruf! der GVP gegründet in Frankfurt a.M. am 30. November 1952," with drafts and correspondence, HW-94; Heinemann, "GVP," HW-95 ("resistance").

56. See Stephen Fisher, *Minor Parties of the Federal Republic of Germany* (The Hague, 1974), pp. 94–107, and Franz Neumann, *Der Block der Heimatvertriebenen und Entrechteten 1950–1960* (Meisenheim am Glan, 1968).

57. *Deutsche Volkszeitung* (Wirth's newspaper), no. 95, September 2, 1953 (DS); Wirth, *Die Reise hinter den Eisernen Vorhang* (Freiburg, 1952) ("pilgrims") (DS); Interior Ministry documents, May and July 1952 (DS); also *Gesamtdeutsche Rundschau, Organ der GVP*, no. 31, August 28, 1953 (HW-110); for more issues of Wirth's newspaper and clippings linking the GVP through the BdD to Communism, see HW-97. See also Albert Esser, *Wilhelm Elfes 1884–1969: Arbeiterführer und Politiker* (Mainz, 1990), especially section 6.6. Immediately after the war, Elfes had been Christian Democratic chairman in Mönchengladbach, where he had used stationery headed "Christlich-Demokratische Union—Partei der Arbeit."

58. See HW-114 and HW-143.

Epilogue

1. RM-1.

2. RM-5, April 29, 1949.

3. Karl Forster, "Deutscher Katholizismus in der Adenauer-Ära," in Dieter Blumenwitz et al., eds., *Konrad Adenauer und seine Zeit*, vol. 2 (Stuttgart, 1976). In December 1956, the SPD-led government in North Rhine–Westphalia even completed a treaty with Rome creating a bishopric in Essen: Detlev Hüwel, *Karl Arnold* (Wuppertal, 1980), p. 324.

4. RM-49, April 10, 1949; HW-114, April 5, 1956; HW-143, 1957.

5. Wessel to Mother Maria Victoria, June 17, 1957, HW-143, with other similar letters.

6. HW-143, July 10, 1957. To overcome Wessel's hesitations, Adolf Scheu (GVP) asked the SPD for two assurances: that her concerns about Weltanschauung would be respected; and that the SPD would not join Adenauer in a Grand Coalition. Scheu's notes on a meeting with Wilhelm Mellies (SPD), February 27, and Scheu to Mellies, March 25, HW-114. In a party system with a "clear political physiognomy," then, Wessel embraced a bipolar system of government and opposition.

7. Konrad Repgen, "Finis Germaniae: Untergang Deutschlands durch einen SPD-Wahlsieg 1957?" in Blumenwitz et al., eds., *Adenauer*, vol. 2, pp. 294–315. Percentages (seats): CDU/CSU, 50.2 (270); SPD, 31.8 (169); FDP, 7.7 (41); DP, 3.4 (17); BHE, 4.6 (0); others, 2.3 (0). With the CDU's help, the DP qualified to retain its proportion of seats through the direct-election clause of the election law. In 1960, the party's ministers joined the CDU.

8. Recall Spiecker's demand (Chapter 11) for the "de-Weltanschauunging of all parties": RM-11, January 21, 1949.

9. Rudolf Uertz, *Christentum und Sozialismus in der frühen CDU* (Stuttgart, 1981), refers to the CDU's "Godesberg" in the narrow sense of its early turn away from Christian socialism, not in the sense of general de-Weltanschauunging and subcultural integration asserted here.

10. Speech of February 7, 1962, in Adenauer, *Reden 1917–1967, eine Auswahl,* ed. Hans-Peter Schwarz (Stuttgart, 1975), p. 439. Earlier, Adenauer had used the SPD's apparent indecision on Marxism against it: speeches of August 28, 1948, and January 31, 1951, ibid., pp. 123, 203.

11. Zonenauschuss der CDU in der britischen Zone, ed., *Was ist—was will die CDU? Gedanken zur politischen Arbeit der Christlich-Democratischen Union* (Köln-Marienburg, n.d.), KBr-4.

12. Partisan tenure in the U.S. White House, 1896–1992, averaged eleven years; in the French Elysée, 1958–1995, twelve years; in the German Chancellery, 1949–1982, sixteen years.

13. While some new FDP voters may have come from the dying DP and the BHE, most DP voters probably followed their ministers into the CDU, while many refugees supported the SPD.

14. See Erich Mende, "Die schwierige Regierungsbildung 1961," in Blumenwitz et al., eds., *Adenauer,* vol. 1, pp. 302–325; and Klaus Gotto, "Der Versuch einer Grossen Koalition 1962," in Blumenwitz et al., eds., *Adenauer,* vol. 2, pp. 316–338.

15. Kaltefleiter, "Die Entwicklung des deutschen Parteiensystems in der Ära Adenauer," in Blumenwitz et al., eds., *Adenauer,* vol. 2, p. 286; contrast Chapters 8 and 9 in this volume.

16. For example, Adenauer, *Reden,* pp. 139 (July 21, 1949), 416 (August 14, 1961).

17. Gotto, "Versuch," p. 331 ("crown"); memorandum by Reinhold Mercker, Ministerial Director in the Chancellery, December 5, 1962, quoted by Gotto, pp. 328–329.

18. Adenauer, speech to party congress, British zonal CDU, Recklinghausen, August 14, 1947, *KA-CDU-BBZ,* pp. 330–351; see also the settlement on Kulturpolitik in the Parliamentary Council (Chapter 11 in this volume); also speech of July 21, 1949, in Adenauer, *Reden,* p. 143. The same principle can be said to have applied to the East German Grand Coalition of 1990 following the first free elections.

19. Guido Goldman, *The German Political System* (New York, 1974), p. 115.

20. The so-called second founding of 1878–1879 (Chapter 1) offers a milder, though still overly illiberal and (in terms of the career of the protagonist) less strikingly timed analogy.

21. See Anneliese Poppinga, *Konrad Adenauer: Geschichtsverständnis,*

Weltanschauung, und politische Praxis (Stuttgart, 1975), p. 103. In 1945, Adenauer remarked that the Kulturkampf had prevented a three-party system (an agrarian-conservative eastern party, an industrial-liberal western party, and the SPD): Josef Hofmann (1962), based on notes from 1945, LS-342.3. On February 17, 1966, recalling his youth, Adenauer stated: "We were conquered territory; the Rhineland became Prussian only in 1815; we were Catholic and consequently objects of suspicion. For example, I could never have had the bright idea of some-day coming into a government position, because I was Catholic and a Rhinelander—completely hopeless!" Quoted by Poppinga, p. 285.

22. Moreover, it was the CDU that now went through a taming process in foreign affairs, moving away from Adenauer's "policy of strength" and closer to the SPD's perceived need for a flexible eastern policy. See Clay Clemens, *Reluctant Realists: The CDU/CSU and West German Ostpolitik* (Durham, 1989).

Index

competing postwar visions of the new party system, this book moves Catholic Germany from the periphery to the heart of the continuity issue in modern German history.

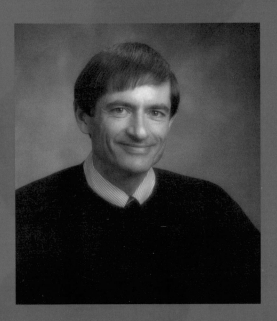

NOEL D. CARY is Associate Professor of History, College of the Holy Cross.